Hiking Montana

Help Us Keep This Guide Up to Date

Every effort has been made by the author and editors to make this guide as accurate and useful as possible. However, many things can change after a guide is published—trails are rerouted, regulations change, techniques evolve, facilities come under new management, etc.

We would love to hear from you concerning your experiences with this guide and how you feel it could be improved and kept up-to-date. While we may not be able to respond to all comments and suggestions, we'll take them to heart, and we'll also make certain to share them with the authors. Please send your comments and suggestions to the following address:

The Globe Pequot Press
Reader Response/Editorial Department
P.O. Box 480
Guilford, CT   06437

Or you may e-mail us at:

editorial@GlobePequot.com

Thanks for your input, and happy travels!

A FALCON GUIDE®

Hiking
Montana

Twenty-fifth Anniversary Edition

Bill Schneider and Russ Schneider

FALCON GUIDE®

GUILFORD, CONNECTICUT
HELENA, MONTANA
AN IMPRINT OF THE GLOBE PEQUOT PRESS

A FALCONGUIDE®

Text design: Nancy Freeborn
Photos: All photos by Bill Schneider unless otherwise
noted.
Profiles by Trailhead Graphics © Morris Book Publishing,
LLC.
Maps redesigned by Josh Comen © Morris Book Publish-
ing, LLC

ISSN: 1547-8947
ISBN-13: 978-0-7627-2564-9
ISBN-10: 0-7627-2564-8

Manufactured in the United States of America
Fourth Edition/Second Printing

To buy books in quantity for corporate use
or incentives, call **(800) 962–0973, ext. 4551,**
or e-mail **premiums@GlobePequot.com.**

The authors and The Globe Pequot Press assume no liability for accidents happening to,
or injuries sustained by, readers who engage in the activities described in this book.

Contents

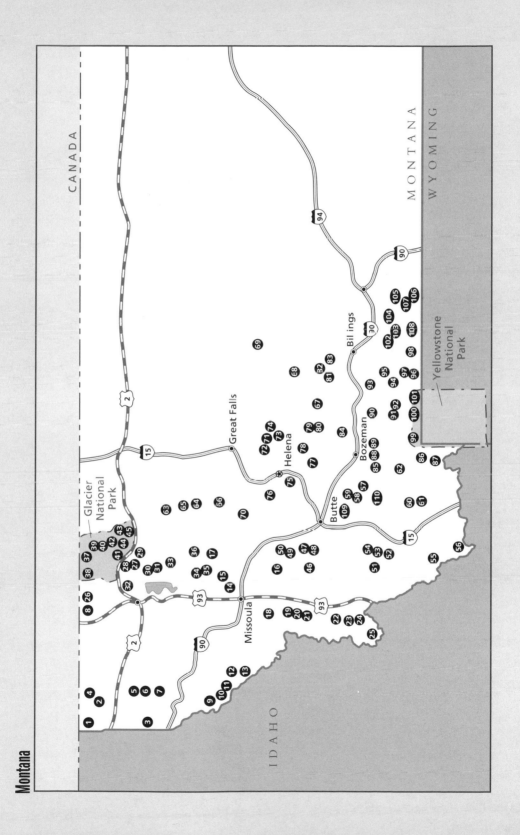

Montana

Yellowstone National Park

Custer National Forest

BLM Areas

Acknowledgments

We would like to thank the following people for helping make this book possible: Wayne Avants, Don Berg, Bill Brown, Pat Caffrey, Bruce Chesler, Mike Comola, Frank Culver, Bill Cunningham, Art Foran, John Gatchall, Herb Gloege, Linda and Tom Hurlock, Jack Johns, Kirk Koepsel, Loren Kreck, Ed Madej, Joe Mussulman, Dave Orndoff, Bob Oset, Don Reed, Karen Renne, Mike Sample, Greg Schneider, Elaine and Art Sedlack, Ann Seifert, Elaine Snyder, Fred Swanson, Larry Thompson, Bob Wagenknecht, Ted Anderson, Susan Bryan, Tom Elpel, Harry Engels, Doug O'looney, Rosemary Rowe, Richard Terra, Mark Tokarski, Fay Valois, John Westenberg, Kim Wilson, and Gary Wolf. If you bump into any of these good folks on a trail, please thank them for helping make *Hiking Montana* possible.

In addition, we want to thank the following agency personnel who were particularly helpful in checking facts and reviewing hike descriptions during the revision process: Marty Almquistt, Jaine Arnold, Babete Anderson, Crystal Avey, Elizabeth Brann, Ken Britton, Beth Burren, Marcy Butts, Allen Byrd, Jodie Canfield, Dave Cary, Marc Childress, Frank Cifala, Bob Coats, Nancy Denning, John Ericson, William Fortune, Errol Hammond, Bruce Hoflich, Eric Heyn, Daniel Hogan, Jon Jeresek, Carole Johnson, Jonathan Klein, Kraig Lang, Ernie Lundberg, Charlie Mabbot, Mark Mason, Kay McCoy, Steven Penner, Mark Petroni, Remy Pochelon, Ron Roginske, Bill Sansler, Mary Skordinsky, Bill Sprauer, Diane Teliaferro, Eric Tolf, Dan Tyers, Mike Wilson, and Ron Wiseman.

And, of course, we would like to thank the many thousands of hikers who have purchased and used earlier editions of this book over the past twenty-five years.

Collectively, all of the above have helped make this book a Montana tradition.

Preface: This Book Has a History

In 1979 Mike Sample and I started a publishing company called Falcon Press. This book, originally called *The Hiker's Guide to Montana,* was one of our first two books published that year. Twenty-five years later, this book is thriving, which in the world of publishing is somewhat amazing. Most books have a much shorter life, starting strong and tailing off in sales until they go out of print a few years later. *Hiking Montana* has reversed that trend. Sales have steadily increased through the years so that a quarter century later, this book is more popular than ever. Now there are more than 700 FalconGuides in print, and these guides are the most recognizable brand in the outdoor recreation guidebook marketplace. I can safely say that it all started with this book. Who would have guessed?

Coauthor Russ Schneider on Sawtooth Peak.

Coauthor Bill Schneider taking a break on Illinois Peak. MARNIE SCHNEIDER PHOTO

Constantly changing. The first edition had 80 hikes; with each edition we add new hikes (and remove some), and the selection has grown to 110 hikes. For example, this edition contains 24 hikes that weren't in the previous edition.

More than hiking. Since 1998 we have rehiked almost all of the routes in the book to check for accuracy and changing conditions. During this process, it became clear that the book offers more than a wilderness experience. Part of the experience is seeing all the Montana back roads, hidden valleys, and little communities far away from the freeway—places like Pony, where they like ranchers more than wolves but still have Fat Tire on tap (and a sculpture of a woolly mammoth across the street); or Sula, where they sell handguns at the gas station; or Roscoe, home of the Grizzly Burger; or York, the Cribbage Capital of the World. We enjoyed this aspect as much as the hiking, and you might, too.

The soft sell. Through the years this book has helped me prove something to myself. I believe the most effective way to convince people to support the protection of our last wilderness is to introduce them to it. This book has helped introduce many thousands of people to the wildest places in Montana, and I have no doubt that most of these people will vote for more wilderness areas when they get a chance. The soft sell can be better than advocacy.

Ahead of its time. Nowadays hikers diligently accept and practice zero-impact ethics. Today it's hard to find even a gum wrapper along a wilderness trail. But such was not the case twenty-five years ago, not hardly. In the early years I personally carried the equivalent of many backpacks full of trash out of the wilderness, but no more. This is one battle that has been won, and *Hiking Montana* played a small, early part in winning it. In the first edition of this book, we included a section called Touch the Land Lightly. Later this title was changed to Zero Impact, but the message didn't change much.

A family affair. *Hiking Montana* has always been a family affair. Our family has enjoyed many wonderful days hiking Montana's trails. Of special note is the little guy leading the pack on the front cover—my son Russ on his first backpacking trip at age six. Now Russ is thirty something and the coauthor of the last three revisions of this book—although in reality the byline should read "Marnie, Bill, Heidi, Greg, and Russ Schneider." Normally the publisher likes to change the photo on the cover of guidebooks with each new edition, but I appealed successfully to keep this photo for personal reasons and to emphasize the classic nature of this book.

The reward. I remember clearly the day a few years back when I hiked into a remote lake in the Beartooths and came across another group of backpackers camped there. One of them was sitting on a stump reading *Hiking Montana*. I didn't introduce myself, but I asked him what he thought of the book, and he went on and on about how he had made it his lifelong vacation planner and was in the process of hiking every hike in the book. Through the years other people have told me the same thing—all enjoying a lifetime of adventure because of this book. From a guidebook author's perspective, that is my ultimate reward.

Something else happened. I believe some trails became overused because they were featured in the original book. Through the years we have removed a few of them from revised editions to lessen exposure. But something else happened, and it was a big surprise to me. While rehiking most of the trails in the book, we noticed a trend. During the past twenty-five years, timber cutting and road building have claimed many thousands of acres of roadless Montana, but the routes described in the original book have been spared. I could speculate that because the book helped bring more and more hikers into these areas, their presence prompted the land-managing agencies to avoid developing the area. We found a few examples where development surrounded the area covered in the hike, but the immediate area remained an untouched island. On second thought, this is my ultimate reward.

—Bill Schneider

Introduction

Although we still hear claims that only the young and the rich use wilderness, quite the reverse is true. Anybody who believes such claims hasn't been out on the trails very much where everybody enjoys hiking and backpacking—all ages, sizes, with no restriction on net worth. All they need is a small amount of physical conditioning and a small amount of equipment—a minimal investment compared to almost any other form of outdoor recreation.

Like any other sport, hiking can be expensive if you choose to make it so, but it doesn't have to be. Day hiking requires little more than a pair of hiking shoes and minimal safety gear. You can even use spent running shoes and clothes you have in the closet. How many sports can you take up without at least one trip to the store to buy gear?

Overnight trips cost more, but even this expense would qualify as a small investment. The price of a two-week vacation with motel stays and restaurant meals would be sufficient to outfit an entire family for backpacking, and the equipment can be used year after year. After that initial investment, you could see millions of acres of spectacular, roadless country without spending another penny on equipment. You would only need to spend a few dollars for food and for transportation to the trailheads.

Not only is hiking almost free in the economic sense, but it is also almost free of the stress of modern America. Once on the trail, you can forget the tension of your work, the Internal Revenue Service, the unpaid bills, the noise, and the pollution. It's all behind you for a few hours or days. You can't even hear the bad news on the radio. Hiking gives you an escape—a chance to smell the fragrance of wildflowers, to hear the wind whistling through mature pines, to see the sunset reflected in a mountain lake, to taste the waters of a clear mountain stream, to feel the tug of a native trout at the end of your fly line.

All this and more is there for the taking, and in Montana it is there in abundance. After using *Hiking Montana* to get an introduction to a hiking area, you can find nearby trails on your own or you can go from hike to hike in this book and get a taste of all major hiking areas in Montana. But be forewarned; it could mean a lifetime of backcountry adventure.

In this book we have included hikes from almost every roadless portion of Montana. We describe trails through well-known areas, such as Glacier and Yellowstone National Parks and Absaroka-Beartooth and Bob Marshall Wilderness Areas. Yet we have been careful not to forget the many splendid areas that aren't as well known

◀ *Hiking the Lee Metcalf Wilderness with the Helmet in the background.*

but are just as beautiful. We have included hikes for all kinds of hikers—beginners, families, and the elderly, as well as experienced backpackers. There is bound to be a hike just right for you and a trailhead nearby to begin your adventure.

Hikes Near Your Town

Libby: Northwest Peak, Fish Lakes Canyon, Baree and Bear Lakes, Cedar Lakes, Leigh Lake
Eureka: Boulder Lakes, Ten Lakes, Thoma Lookout
Thompson Falls: Ross Creek Cascade
Whitefish/Kalispell/Columbia Falls/Bigfork: Jewel Basin, Crater Lake, Stanton Lake, Marion Lake, Great Northern, Granite Park, The Nyack Loop, Alpine Trail, Akokala Lake
Seeley/Swan: Palisade Lake, Sapphire Lake, Crescent Lake, Cold Lakes
Missoula: Stuart Peak, Welcome Creek, Peterson Lake, Boulder Lake
Superior: Bonanza Lakes, Hub Lake, Heart Lake, Illinois Peak, The Great Burn
Hamilton: Stony Lake, Canyon Lake, Blodgett Canyon, Blodgett Canyon Overlook
Darby/Sula: Tin Cup Lake, Trapper Peak, Overwhich Falls, Blue Joint
Deer Lodge: Trask Lakes, Dolus Lakes, Little Blackfoot Meadows
Phillipsburg: Rainbow Lake, The Pintler Loop
Anaconda/Butte: Humbug Spires, Hollow Top Lake, Curly Lake, Louise Lake
Dillon: Snowcrest, Antone Peak, Grayling Lake, Torrey Lake, Sawtooth Lake, Bobcat Lakes, Selway Mountain, Deadman and Nicholas Creeks
Ennis: Helmet and Sphinx
White Sulphur Springs: Castle Mountains
West Yellowstone: Hilgard Basin, Coffin Lakes, Sky Rim
Bozeman/Belgrade: Hyalite Lake, Emerald and Heather Lakes, Spanish Peaks, Sacajawea Peak
Livingston: Pine Creek Lake, Cottonwood Lake
Gardiner: Passage Falls, Elbow Lake, Black Canyon
Cooke City: Lady of the Lake, Aero Lakes, Rock Island Lake, Pebble Creek
Big Timber: Blue Lake, Crazy Mountain Crossing, West Boulder Meadows, Lake Plateau, Bridge Lake
Townsend: Edith-Baldy Basin, Boulder Basin, Crow Creek Falls
Three Forks: Bear Trap Canyon
Lewistown: Big Snowies Crest, Sand Point
Great Falls/Choteau/Augusta: Mount Wright, Our Lake, Devils Glen, Gateway Gorge
Browning: Dawson and Pitamaken Passes, Lake Isabel, Upper Two Medicine Lake, Triple Divide Peak, Iceberg Lake, Boulder Pass
Lincoln: Heart Lake

Helena: Mann Gulch, Hanging Valley, Trout Creek Canyon, Mount Helena Ridge, Bear Prairie

Boulder: Elkhorn and Crow Peaks

Billings/Red Lodge/Columbus: Sylvan Lake, Silver Run Plateau, Island Lake, Sundance Pass, Glacier Lake, Granite Peak, Martin Lake Basin

Trail Finder

The following section attempts to help hikers find special types of trips, but please keep in mind that no hike automatically falls into any category. A long backpacking trip could be a moderate day hike or an overnighter for some hikers, just as a moderate day hike could be an extended backpacking trip. Nonetheless, the following trail finder should help you choose your next adventure.

Best Easy Day Hikes: Bonanza Lakes, Heart Lake, Trout Creek Canyon, Blodgett Canyon Overlook, Upper Two Medicine Lake, Passage Falls, Devils Glen, Crow Creek Falls, Lady of the Lake

Long, Hard Day Hikes for the Fit and Experienced: Tin Cup Lake, Torrey Lake, Palisade Lake, Dawson and Pitamakan Passes, Bear Prairie, Stuart Peak, Edith-Baldy Basin (loop option), Great Northern, Mount Wright, Silver Run Plateau, Sky Rim, Helmet and Sphinx, Snowcrest (thru option), Bridge Lake, Overwhich Falls

For That First Backpacking Trip: Fish Creek Canyon, Ten Lakes, Hub Lake, Bonanza Lakes, Jewel Basin, Upper Two Medicine Lake, Devils Glen, Lady of the Lake

Moderate Overnighters: Cedar Lakes, Baree and Bear Lakes, Hub Lake, Peterson Lake, Bobcat Lakes, Grayling Lake, Louise Lake, Curly Lake, Hollow Top Lake, Bear Trap Canyon, Little Blackfoot Meadows, Our Lake, Granite Park, Crater Lake, Blue Lake, Pebble Creek, Sylvan Lake, Rock Island Lake, West Boulder Meadows

Extended Backpacking Trips: Boulder Pass, The Great Burn, The Pintlar Loop, The Nyack Loop, Spanish Peaks, Hilgard Basin, Black Canyon, Lake Plateau, Aero Lakes, Martin Lake Basin, Crazy Crossing, Blue Joint

Good Base Camp Hikes: Island Lake, Martin Lake Basin, Hilgard Basin, Blue Lake, Stuart Peak, Sapphire Lake, Jewel Basin, Edith-Baldy Basin

For Trail Runners: Illinois Peak, Stuart Peak, Blodgett Canyon Overlook, Curly Lake, Trout Creek Canyon, Hanging Valley, Mount Helena Ridge, Pine Creek Lake, Sacajawea Peak, Castle Mountains, Sylvan Lake, Sundance Pass, Blue Joint (Divide Trail section only)

For Peak Baggers: Northwest Peak, Illinois Peak, Trapper Peak, Hollow Top Lake, Antone Peak, Snowcrest, Elkhorn and Crow Peaks, Mount Wright, Great Northern, Thoma Lookout, Sacajawea Peak, Sky Rim, Granite Peak

For Hikers Who Want a Real Adventure: Ross Creek Cascade (Sawtooth Mountain option), Boulder Pass, Lake Isabel, Snowcrest, Aero Lakes, Granite Peak, The Nyack Loop, Blue Joint

Razoredge Mountain and Medicine Grizzly Lake from the Triple Divide Pass Trail.

Hikes to Waterfalls: Fish Lakes, Crow Creek Falls, Overwhich Falls, Our Lake, Hyalite Lake, Passage Falls, Iceberg Lake, Upper Two Medicine Lake, Blue Lake, Crazy Mountains Crossing

Hikes You Can Do in May or June: Ross Creek Cascade, Black Canyon, Bear Trap Canyon, Crow Creek Falls, Trout Creek Canyon, Bear Prairie, Beartrap Peak, Mann Gulch

Hikes Where You're Most Likely to See a Grizzly Bear: Boulder Pass, Iceberg Lake, Granite Park, Lake Isabel, The Nyack Loop, Triple Divide Pass, Dawson and Pitamaken Passes, Sky Rim, Black Canyon, Pebble Creek

Using This Guidebook

This guidebook won't answer every question you have concerning your planned hiking route, but then most people don't want to know everything before they go, lest they remove the thrill of making their own discoveries while exploring Montana's wild country. This book does provide the basic information needed to plan a successful trip, and here are some tips on better using this book to help you have a more pleasant trip.

Types of Trips

Suggested hikes have been split into the following categories:

Loop: Starts and finishes at the same trailhead, with no (or very little) retracing of your steps. Sometimes the definition of *loop* is stretched to include "lollipops" and trips that involve a short walk on a road at the end of the hike to get back to your vehicle.

Shuttle: A point-to-point trip that requires two vehicles (one left at the other end of the trail) or a prearranged pickup at a designated time and place. One good way to manage the logistical problems of shuttles is to arrange for another party to start at the other end of the trail. The two parties meet at a predetermined point and then trade keys. When finished, they drive each other's vehicles home.

Out-and-back: Traveling to a specific destination, then retracing your steps back to the trailhead.

Base camp: A point-to-point hike where you spend several nights at the same campsite, using the extra days for fishing, relaxing, or day hiking.

Difficulty Ratings

The original edition of this book listed a vast difference in the difficulty ratings from hike to hike. The good folks who helped put this book together had different levels of physical fitness and tolerance for hill climbing. We tried to standardize these ratings as much as possible for this edition, as follows:

Easy trails are suitable for any hiker, including children and elderly persons. They feature little or no elevation gain, no serious trail hazards, and no off-trail or faint trail route finding.

Moderate trails are suitable for most hikers who have some experience and at least an average fitness level. These hikes may be suitable for children or elderly persons with above-average fitness levels. The hikes may have some short sections where the trail is difficult to follow and may include up to 1,500 feet in elevation gain.

Strenuous trails are suitable for experienced hikers with above-average fitness levels. These trails may be difficult to follow or feature off-trail routes requiring serious map and compass skills. These hikes almost all have serious elevation gain and possibly hazardous river fords or other hazards.

Distances

It's almost impossible to get precisely accurate distances for most trails. The distances used in this guidebook are based on a combination of actual experience hiking the trails, distances stated on Forest Service signs, and estimates from topographic maps. In some cases, distances may be slightly off, so consider that when planning a trip. Keep in mind that distance is often less important than difficulty—a rough, 2-mile cross-country trek can take longer than 5 or 6 miles on a good trail. Also, keep mileage estimates in perspective because they are all at least slightly off. Almost all trail signs use estimates in whole miles. You've probably seen a sign saying it's 5 miles to a lake, but what's the chance that it's exactly 5 miles? Should we really worry about it?

Trail Running

Many hikes are rated according to suitability for trail running. In reality there is no real difference between a trail-running guidebook and a hiking guidebook, but the two criteria the authors used to recommend some routes for trail running were trail surface and bear awareness. If a trail was not rocky and rough and went through country where the likelihood of surprising a bear was minimal, it was recommended for trail running—keeping in mind, of course, that you could run into a bear on any route in this book and that all trails have some rough sections.

Special Regulations and Permits

Land managing agencies have special regulations for hikers and backcountry trail riders on many trails. In some cases the regulations apply throughout a large area, but in other cases they apply to specific trails or ranger districts. Check with the appropriate agency before you leave on your trip, and be sure to read and follow any special regulations posted on the information board at the trailhead. Agencies don't come up with regulations to inconvenience backcountry visitors. Instead, the regs are designed to promote sharing and preservation of the wilderness and make your trip as safe as possible.

In Montana we're lucky enough to not need permits in most areas. In this book, only hikes in Glacier and Yellowstone National Parks require you to get a permit, and then only for overnight trips. You can take a day hike in the parks without a permit.

Best Time to Hike

The best months to hike in Montana are usually July, August, and September. Snow lingers in the high country in most places until at least June and often into mid-July. The snow gives up some routes earlier in the year, however. Check the Trail Finder for these routes. Montana weather being what it is, however, you should be prepared for winter weather at any time of the year and especially when hiking before and after the traditional July/August/September season.

Maps

USGS topographic quadrangles have contour lines of the landscape and identify landmarks and landscape features such as lakes, streams, and peaks. Most quadrangles usually have contour intervals of 40 feet, cover an area of approximately 9 miles by 7 miles, and are on a scale of 1:24,000—that is, 1 inch on the map is equivalent to 24,000 inches on the ground. Topographic maps are available at most sporting goods stores or can be ordered directly from the USGS.

U.S. Geological Survey
Denver Federal Center
Box 25286
Denver, CO 80225
(303) 202–4700

Forest Service Maps have no contour lines but focus on roads, lakes, peaks, rivers, trails, and other major landmarks. They do have trail and road numbers for all current Forest Service roads and trailheads, which are especially helpful in reaching the trailhead. (Beyond finding the trailhead, however, a USGS quad map is necessary.) Forest Service maps are also the most up-to-date maps for hiking in Montana. They are available at district offices, ranger stations, and most regional sporting goods stores.

Also, check your local library for a collection of topographic and Forest Service maps. Photocopies of these maps are just as good as the originals if kept dry. They are also easier on your budget.

The maps in this guidebook were designed to assist in your overall preparation for hiking in Montana. They aren't intended to be used in place of topographic or other detailed maps, which are a critical part of any backcountry adventure.

Getting to the Trailhead

Some trailheads are located along major state highways, and others are found in remote backcountry locations. Make sure your vehicle is in good condition and appropriate for the roads to the trailhead. Have a full tank of gas and carry basic emergency equipment, such as a shovel, an ax, a saw, extra water, emergency food, and warm clothing. If you're unsure about road conditions, check ahead with the appropriate agency. In this book we've made a point to alert hikers when to expect a rough road on the way to the trailhead and if you'll need a high-clearance vehicle to get there.

Elevation Profiles

The hike descriptions in this book include elevation profiles. These charts represent the changes in elevation over the distance of the hike. The vertical axis shows the elevation in feet; the horizontal axis shows the distance in miles. Because these scales vary from hike to hike, some profiles may show gradual hills to be steep and steep hills to be gradual. Instead of simply glancing at the profile and forming an opinion on how strenuous a hike might be, pay close attention to the vertical and horizontal scales. This will give you a better understanding of the difficulty of the hike. You can also compare the grade and distance to routes you've already hiked. Hikes without elevation charts have little or no elevation gain.

Rating the Hills

In the process of publishing dozens of hiking guides, Falcon Publishing has been trying to come up with a consistent rating system to help hikers determine how difficult those "big hills" really are. Such a system would help hikers decide how far they wanted to hike that day or even whether they wanted to take that trail at all. In the past, guidebook authors have described hills to the best of their ability, but subjectively. What is a big hill to one hiker might be a slight upgrade to the next.

Also, it isn't only going up that matters. Some hikers hate going down steep hills and the knee problems that go along with descending with a big pack. These "weak-kneed" hikers might want to avoid Category 1 and Category H hills.

This new system combines the elevation gain and the length of that section of trail with a complicated mathematical formula to come up with a numerical hill rating similar to the system used by cyclists. The system only works for climbs of half a mile or longer, not short, steep hills.

Here is a rough description of the categories, listed from easiest to hardest.

Category 5: A slight upgrade.

Category 4: Usually within the capabilities of any hiker.

Category 3: A well-conditioned hiker might describe a Category 3 climb as "gradual," but a poorly conditioned hiker might complain about the steepness. It's definitely not steep enough to deter you from hiking the trail, but these climbs will slow you down.

Category 2: Most hikers would consider these "big hills," steep enough, in some cases, to make hikers choose an alternative trail, but not the real lung-busting, calf-stretching hills.

Category 1: These are among the steepest hills in the park. If you have heart or breathing problems, or you simply dislike climbing big hills, you might look for an alternative trail.

Category H: These are hills that make you wonder if the person who laid out the trail was on drugs. Any trail with a Category H hill is steeper than any trail should be. (Incidentally, *H* stands for "Horrible.")

The hills in this book are rated according to the following chart. Some climbs are rated in the hike descriptions of this book, but if not included (or to use this formula in other hiking areas), get the mileage and elevation gain off the topo map and look them up on this chart.

Following Faint Trails

Trails that receive infrequent use often fade away in grassy meadows, on ridges, or through rocky sections. If the trail fades away before you, don't panic. These sections are usually short, and you can often look ahead to see where the trail goes. If so, focus on the trail ahead and don't worry about being off the trail for a short distance. Also watch for other indicators that you are indeed on the right route, even if the trail isn't clearly visible. Watch for cairns, blazes, downfall cut with saws, paths cleared through thick timber, and trees with the branches whacked off on one side.

FALCON HILL RATING CHART

ELEVATION GAIN (in feet)	DISTANCE (in miles)											
	0.5	**1.0**	**1.5**	**2.0**	**2.5**	**3.0**	**3.5**	**4.0**	**4.5**	**5.0**	**5.5**	**6.0**
200	4.2	5.0	5.4	5.5	5.6	5.6	5.7	5.7	5.7	5.7	5.7	5.7
300	3.3	4.5	4.9	5.2	5.3	5.4	5.5	5.5	5.5	5.5	5.6	5.6
400	1.8	4.0	4.5	4.8	5.1	5.2	5.3	5.3	5.4	5.4	5.4	5.4
500	1.0	3.5	4.2	4.5	4.7	5.0	5.1	5.2	5.2	5.2	5.3	5.3
600	H	3.0	3.8	4.2	4.4	4.6	4.9	4.9	5.0	5.1	5.1	5.1
700	H	2.5	3.4	3.9	4.2	4.3	4.5	4.8	4.9	4.9	4.9	5.0
800	H	1.4	3.1	3.6	3.9	4.1	4.2	4.3	4.7	4.7	4.8	4.9
900	H	H	2.7	3.3	3.6	3.9	4.0	4.1	4.2	4.6	4.7	4.7
1,000	H	H	2.3	2.9	3.4	3.6	3.8	3.9	4.0	4.1	4.5	4.6
1,100	H	H	1.9	2.7	3.1	3.4	3.6	3.7	3.8	3.9	3.9	4.5
1,200	H	H	H	2.4	2.8	3.1	3.4	3.5	3.6	3.7	3.8	3.9
1,300	H	H	H	2.1	2.6	2.9	3.2	3.3	3.5	3.5	3.6	3.7
1,400	H	H	H	1.8	2.3	2.7	2.9	3.1	3.3	3.4	3.5	3.5
1,500	H	H	H	1.6	2.1	2.4	2.7	2.9	3.1	3.2	3.3	3.3
1,600	H	H	H	H	1.9	2.2	2.3	2.7	2.9	2.9	3.1	3.2
1,700	H	H	H	H	1.7	1.9	2.3	2.5	2.7	2.8	2.9	3.0
1,800	H	H	H	H	1.5	1.8	2.0	2.3	2.5	2.6	2.7	2.8
1,900	H	H	H	H	1.3	1.7	1.9	2.1	2.3	2.4	2.6	2.6
2,000	H	H	H	H	H	1.5	1.7	1.9	2.1	2.2	2.4	2.5
2,100	H	H	H	H	H	1.3	1.6	1.8	1.9	2.0	2.2	2.3
2,200	H	H	H	H	H	1.2	1.4	1.6	1.8	1.9	1.9	2.1
2,300	H	H	H	H	H	1.0	1.3	1.5	1.7	1.8	1.9	1.9
2,400	H	H	H	H	H	H	1.2	1.4	1.5	1.6	1.8	1.8
2,500	H	H	H	H	H	H	1.0	1.2	1.4	1.5	1.6	1.7
2,600	H	H	H	H	H	H	H	1.1	1.3	1.4	1.5	1.6
2,700	H	H	H	H	H	H	H	H	1.1	1.3	1.4	1.5
2,800	H	H	H	H	H	H	H	H	H	1.1	1.3	1.4
2,900	H	H	H	H	H	H	H	H	H	1.0	1.2	1.3
3,000	H	H	H	H	H	H	H	H	H	H	1.0	1.1

On the Park Trail loop option coming back from Hollow Top Lake with the backbone of the Tobacco Roots in the background.

Nowadays land managers discourage the use of blazes, and rangers use small metal reflective markers instead. However, you can still see old blazes along many trails in Montana. If you rely on blazes to follow a faint trail, make sure you follow only official blazes, which are shaped like an upside-down exclamation point, instead of blazes made by hunters, outfitters, or other hikers.

Sharing

We all want our own wilderness area all to ourselves, but that happens only in our dreams. Lots of people use the trails of Montana, and to make everyone's experience better, we all must work at politely sharing the wilderness. For example, hikers must share trails with trail riders. Both groups have every right to be on the trail, so please do not let it become a confrontation. Keep in mind that horses and mules are much less maneuverable than hikers, so it becomes the hiker's responsibility to yield the right-of-way. All hikers should stand on the downhill side of the trail, well off-trail for safety's sake, and let the stock quietly pass.

Another example of politely sharing the wilderness is choosing your campsite. If you get to a popular lake late in the day and all the good campsites are taken, don't crowd in on another camper. Doing so is most aggravating, as these sites rightfully go on a first-come, first-served basis. If you're late, you have the responsibility to move on or take a less desirable site a respectable distance away from other campers.

Zero Impact

Going into a national park or wilderness area is like visiting a famous museum. You wouldn't leave your mark on an art treasure in the museum. If everybody going through the museum left one little mark, the piece of art would be quickly destroyed—and of what value is a big building full of trashed art? The same goes for a pristine wilderness, which is as magnificent as any masterpiece. If we all left just one little mark on the landscape, the wilderness would soon be despoiled.

A wilderness can accommodate human use as long as everybody behaves. But a few thoughtless or uninformed visitors can ruin it for everybody who follows. All wilderness users have a responsibility to know and follow the rules of zero-impact camping. An important source of these guidelines, including the most updated research, can be found in the book *Leave No Trace*. Visit your favorite bookseller or outdoor retailer to purchase this book.

Nowadays most wilderness users want to walk softly, but some aren't aware that they have poor manners. Often their actions are dictated by the outdated habits of a past generation of campers who cut green boughs for evening shelters, built campfires with fire rings, and dug trenches around tents. In the 1950s these "camping rules" may have been acceptable. But they leave long-lasting scars, and today such behavior is absolutely unacceptable. The wilderness is shrinking, and the number of users is mushrooming. More and more camping areas show unsightly signs of heavy use.

Consequently, a new code of ethics is growing out of the necessity of coping with the unending waves of people who want a perfect wilderness experience. Today we all must leave no clues that we have gone before. Canoeists can look behind the canoe and see no sign of their passing. Hikers, mountain bikers, and four-wheelers should have the same goal. Enjoy the wildness, but make it a zero-impact visit.

Falcon Guide's Zero-Impact Principles
- Leave with everything you brought in.
- Leave no sign of your visit.
- Leave the landscape as you found it.

Most of us know better than to litter—in or out of the wilderness. Be sure you leave nothing, regardless of how small it is, along the trail or at the campsite. This means you should pack out everything, including orange peels, flip tops, cigarette butts, and gum wrappers. Also pick up any trash that others leave behind. In addition please follow this zero-impact advice.

- Follow the main trail. Avoid cutting switchbacks and walking on vegetation beside the trail.
- Don't pick up "souvenirs," such as rocks, antlers, or wildflowers. The next person wants to see them, too, and collecting such souvenirs violates national park regulations.
- Avoid making loud noises that may disturb others. Remember, sound travels easily to the other side of a lake. Be courteous.
- Carry a lightweight trowel to bury human waste 6 to 8 inches deep and pack out used toilet paper. Keep human waste at least 300 feet from any water source.
- Finally, and perhaps most important, strictly follow the pack-in/pack-out rule. If you carry something into the backcountry, consume it or carry it out.

Leave zero impact of your passing—and put your ear to the ground in the wilderness and listen carefully. Thousands of people coming behind you are thanking you for your courtesy and good sense.

Make It a Safe Trip

Perhaps the best single piece of safety advice I can offer you is this: Be prepared! For starters, that means carrying survival and first-aid materials, proper clothing, a compass, and topographic maps—and knowing how to use them.

Perhaps the second-best piece of safety advice is to tell somebody where you're going and when you plan to return. Pilots file flight plans before every trip, and anybody venturing into a blank spot on a map should do the same. File your "flight plan" with a friend or relative before taking off.

Close behind your flight plan and being prepared with proper equipment is physical conditioning. Being fit not only makes wilderness travel more fun, it makes it safer. To whet your appetite for more knowledge of wilderness safety and preparedness, here are a few more tips.

- Check the weather forecast. Be careful not to get caught at high altitude by a bad storm or along a stream in a flash flood. Watch cloud formations closely so that you don't get stranded on a ridgeline during a lightning storm. Avoid traveling during prolonged periods of cold weather.
- Avoid traveling alone in the wilderness.
- Keep your party together.
- Study basic survival and first-aid skills before leaving home.
- Don't eat wild plants unless you have positively identified them and know they are safe to consume.
- Before you leave for the trailhead, find out as much as you can about the route, especially any potential hazards.

- Don't exhaust yourself or other members of your party by traveling too far or too fast. Let the slowest person set the pace.
- Don't wait until you're confused to look at your maps. Follow them as you go along, from the moment you start moving up the trail, so you have a continual fix on your location.
- If you get lost, don't panic. Sit down and relax for a few minutes while you carefully check your topo map and take a reading with your compass. Confidently plan your next move. It's often smart to retrace your steps until you find familiar ground, even if you think it might lengthen your trip. Lots of people get temporarily lost in the wilderness and survive—usually by calmly and rationally dealing with the situation.
- Stay clear of all wild animals.
- Take a first-aid kit.
- Take a survival kit.

Last but not least, don't forget that the best defense against unexpected hazards is knowledge. Read up on the latest in wilderness safety information.

Lightning: You Might Never Know What Hit You

The high-altitude topography of the northern Rockies is prone to sudden thunderstorms, especially in July and August. If you get caught by a lightning storm, take special precautions. Remember:

- Lightning can travel far ahead of a storm, so be sure to take cover before the storm hits.
- Don't try to make it back to your vehicle ahead of the storm. It isn't worth the risk. Instead seek shelter even if there is only a short distance back to the trailhead. Lightning storms usually don't last long, and from a safe vantage point, you might enjoy the sights and sounds.
- Be especially careful not to get caught on a mountaintop or exposed ridge, under large solitary trees, in the open, or near standing water.
- Seek shelter in a low-lying area, ideally in a dense stand of small, uniformly sized trees.
- Stay away from anything that might attract lightning, such as metal tent poles, graphite fishing rods, or pack frames.
- Get in a crouch position and place both feet firmly on the ground.
- If you have a pack (without a metal frame) or a sleeping pad with you, put your feet on it for extra insulation against shock.
- Don't walk or huddle together. Instead, stay 50 feet or more from each other, so if somebody gets hit by lightning, others in your party can give first aid.
- If you're in a tent, stay there, in your sleeping bag with your feet on your sleeping pad.

Hypothermia: The Silent Killer

Be aware of the danger of hypothermia—a condition in which the body's internal temperature drops below normal. It can lead to mental and physical collapse and death.

Hypothermia is caused by exposure to cold and is aggravated by wetness, wind, and exhaustion. The moment you begin to lose heat faster than your body produces it, you're suffering from exposure. Your body starts involuntary exercise, such as shivering, to stay warm and makes involuntary adjustments to preserve normal temperature in vital organs, restricting blood flow in the extremities. Both responses drain your energy reserves. The only way to stop the drain is to reduce the degree of exposure.

Be wary of trendy "ultra-light" backpacking ideas and equipment. To guard against hypothermia, you need a good tent, rain gear, a sleeping bag, and a set of always-dry clothes.

With full-blown hypothermia, as energy reserves are exhausted, cold reaches the brain, depriving you of good judgment and reasoning power. You aren't aware that it is happening, however. You lose control of your hands. Your internal temperature slides downward. Without treatment, this slide leads to stupor, collapse, and death.

To defend against hypothermia, stay dry. When clothes get wet, they lose about 90 percent of their insulating value. Wool loses relatively less heat; cotton, down, and some synthetics lose more. Choose rain clothes that cover the head, neck, body, and legs and provide good protection against wind-driven rain. Most hypothermia cases develop in air temperatures between thirty and fifty degrees Fahrenheit, but hypothermia can also develop in warmer temperatures.

If your party is exposed to wind, cold, and wet, think hypothermia. Watch yourself and others for these symptoms: uncontrollable fits of shivering; vague, slow, slurred speech; memory lapses; incoherence; immobile, fumbling hands; frequent stumbling or a lurching gait; drowsiness (to sleep is to die); apparent exhaustion; and inability to get up after a rest. When a member of your party has hypothermia, he or she may deny any problem. Believe the symptoms, not the victim. Even mild symptoms demand treatment, as follows:

- Get the victim out of the wind and rain.
- If the victim is only mildly impaired, give him or her warm drinks. Get the victim into warm clothes and a warm sleeping bag. Place well-wrapped water bottles filled with heated water close to the victim.
- If the victim is badly impaired, attempt to keep him or her awake. Put the victim in a sleeping bag with another person—both naked. If you have a double bag, put two warm people in with the victim.

Fording Large Streams

When done correctly and carefully, crossing a big stream or river can be safe, but you must know your limits. So, be smart and cautious. There are cases where you simply should turn back. Even if only one member of your party (such as a child) might not be able to follow taller, stronger members, you might not want to try a risky ford. Never be embarrassed to be overly cautious.

One key to fording rivers safely is confidence. If you aren't a strong swimmer, you should become one. Not only does being a strong swimmer allow you to safely get across a river that is a little deeper and stronger than you thought, but it also gives you the confidence to avoid panic. Just as in the case of getting lost, panic can easily make a bad situation worse.

Another way to build confidence is to practice. Find a river near your home and carefully practice crossing it both with a pack and without one. You can also start with a smaller stream and work up to a major river. After you've become a strong swimmer, get used to swimming in the current.

Here is some sound advice for safely fording rivers in the northern Rockies:

- When you get to the ford, carefully assess the situation. Don't automatically cross at the point where the trail comes to the stream and head on a straight line for the marker on the other side. A mountain river can reform itself every spring during high runoff, so a ford that was safe last year might be too deep this year. Study upstream and downstream and look for a place where the stream widens and the water is not more than waist deep on the shortest member of your party. The tail end of an island is usually a good place, as is a long riffle. The inside of a meander sometimes makes a safe ford, but in other cases a long shallow section can be followed by a short, deep section next to the outside of the bend where the current picks up speed and carves out a deep channel.

- Before starting any serious ford, make sure your matches, camera, billfold, clothes, sleeping bag, and other items you must keep dry are in watertight bags.

- In the northern Rockies most streams are cold, so have dry clothes ready for when you get to the other side to minimize the risk of hypothermia, especially on a cold, rainy day.

- Minimize the amount of time you spend in the water, but don't rush across. Instead go slowly and deliberately, taking one step at a time, being careful to get each foot securely planted before lifting the other foot. Take a forty-five-degree angle instead of going straight across, following a riffle line if possible.

- Don't try a ford with bare feet. Wear hiking boots without socks, sneakers, or tightly strapped sandals.

- Stay sideways with the current. Turning upstream or downstream greatly increases the force of the current.

- In some cases two or three people can cross together, locking forearms, with the strongest person on the upstream side.

- If you have a choice, ford in the early morning when the stream isn't as deep. In the mountains, cool evening temperatures slow snow melt and reduce the water flow into the rivers.

- On small streams a sturdy walking stick used on the upstream side for balance helps prevent a fall, but in a major river with a fast current, a walking stick offers little help.
- Loosen the belt and straps on your pack. If you fall or get washed downstream, a waterlogged pack can lead to drowning by anchoring you to the bottom, so you must be able to easily get out of your pack. For a short period your pack might actually help you become buoyant and float across a deep channel, but in a minute or two, it could become an anchor.
- If you're 6 feet 4 inches tall and a strong swimmer, you might feel secure crossing a big river, but you might have children or vertically challenged hikers in your party. In this case the strongest person can cross first and string a line across the river to aid those who follow. This line (with the help of a carabiner) can also be used to float packs across instead of taking a chance of a waterlogged pack dragging you under. (If you know about the ford in advance, you can pack along a lightweight rubber raft or inner tube for this purpose.) Depending on the size and strength, you might also want to carry children.
- Be prepared for the worst. Sometimes circumstances can arise where you simply must cross instead of going back, even though the ford looks dangerous. Also, you can underestimate the depth of the channel or the strength of the current, especially after a thunderstorm when a muddy river hides its true depth. In these cases, whether you like it or not, you might be swimming. It's certainly recommended to avoid these situations, but if it happens, be prepared. Don't panic. Try not to swim directly across. Instead, pick a long angle and gradually cross or swim to the other side, taking as much as 100 yards or more to finally get across. If your pack starts to drag you down, get out of it immediately, even if you have to abandon it. If you lose control and get washed downstream, go feetfirst so that you don't hit your head on rocks or logs.
- And finally, be sure to report any dangerous ford as soon as you finish your trip.

Be Bear Aware

The first step of any hike in bear country is an attitude adjustment. Nothing guarantees total safety. Hiking in bear country adds a small additional risk to your trip. However, that risk can be greatly minimized by adhering to this age-old piece of advice: Be prepared. And being prepared doesn't only mean having the right equipment. It also means having the right information. Knowledge is your best defense.

You can—and should—thoroughly enjoy your trip to bear country. Don't let the fear of bears ruin your vacation. This fear can accompany you every step of the way. It can be constantly lurking in the back of your mind, preventing you from enjoying the wildest and most beautiful places left on the earth. And even worse, some bear experts think bears might actually be able to sense your fear.

Being prepared and being knowledgeable give you confidence. And this confidence allows you to fight back the fear that can burden you throughout your stay in bear country. You won't—nor should you—forget about bears and the basic rules of safety, but proper preparation allows you to keep the fear of bears at bay and let enjoyment rule the day.

And on top of that, do we really want to be totally safe? If we did, we probably would never go hiking in the wilderness—bears or no bears. We certainly wouldn't, at much greater risk, drive hundreds of miles to get to the trailhead. Perhaps a tinge of danger adds a desired element to our wilderness trip.

Hiking in Bear Country

Nobody likes surprises, and bears dislike them, too. The majority of bear maulings occur when a hiker surprises a bear. Therefore, it's vital to do everything possible to avoid these surprise meetings. Perhaps the best way is to know the six-part system. If you follow these six rules, the chance of encountering a bear on the trail sinks to the slimmest possible margin.

- Be alert at all times.
- Watch the wind.
- Go with a group and stay together.
- Stay on the trail.
- Hike in the middle of the day.
- Make noise.

No substitute for alertness

As you hike, watch ahead and to the sides. Don't fall into the all-too-common and particularly nasty habit of fixating on the trail 10 feet ahead. It's especially easy to do so when dragging a heavy pack up a long hill or when carefully watching your step on a heavily eroded trail.

Using your knowledge of bear habitat and habits, be especially alert in areas most likely to be frequented by bears, such as avalanche chutes, berry patches, streambeds, and stands of whitebark pine.

Watch carefully for bear signs and be especially watchful (and noisy) if you see any. If you see a track or a scat but it doesn't look fresh, pretend it's fresh. Such an area is obviously frequented by bears.

Watch the wind

The wind can be a friend or a foe. The strength and direction of the wind can make a significant difference in your chances of an encounter with a bear. When the wind is blowing at your back, your smell travels ahead of you, alerting any bear that might be on or near the trail ahead. Conversely, when the wind blows in your face, your chances of a surprise meeting with a bear increase, so make more noise and be more alert.

A strong wind can also be noisy and limit a bear's ability to hear you coming. If a bear can't smell or hear you, the chances of an encounter greatly increase, so watch the wind.

Safety in numbers

There have been very few instances where a large group has had an encounter with a bear. On the other hand, a large percentage of hikers mauled by bears were hiking alone. Large groups naturally make more noise and put out more smell and probably appear more threatening to bears. In addition, if you're hiking alone and get injured, there is nobody to go for help. For these reasons rangers often recommend parties of four or more hikers when going into bear country.

If the large party splits up, the advantage is lost, so stay together. If you're on a family hike, keep the kids from running ahead. If you're in a large group, keep the stronger members from going ahead or weaker members from lagging behind. The best way to prevent this natural separation is to ask one of the slowest members of the group to lead. This tactic keeps everybody together.

Stay on the trail

Although bears use trails, they don't often travel on them during midday when hikers commonly use them. Through generations of associating trails with people, bears probably expect to find hikers on trails, especially during midday.

Contrarily, bears probably don't expect to find hikers off trails. Bears rarely settle down in a day bed right along a heavily used trail. However, if you wander around in thickets off the trail, you are more likely to stumble into an occupied day bed or cross paths with a traveling bear.

Sleeping late

Bears—and most other wildlife—usually aren't active during the middle of the day, especially on a hot summer day. Wild animals are most active around dawn and dusk. Therefore, hiking early in the morning or late in the afternoon increases your chances of seeing wildlife, including bears. Likewise, hiking during the middle of a hot August day greatly reduces the chance of an encounter.

Be noisy

Perhaps the best way to avoid a surprise meeting with a bear is to make sure the bear knows you're coming, so make lots of noise. Some experts think metallic noise is superior to human voices, which can be muffled by natural conditions, but the important issue is making lots of noise, regardless of what kind.

In addition to the aforementioned six rules, there are other precautions you can take to avoid an encounter.

Running. Many avid runners like to get off paved roads and running tracks and onto backcountry trails. But running on trails in bear country can be seriously hazardous to your health. Bears can't hear you coming and you approach them faster than expected, and of course it's nearly impossible to be fully alert when you have to watch the trail closely to keep from falling.

Leave the night to the bears. Like running on trails, hiking at night can be very risky. Bears are more active after dark, and you can't see them until it's too late. If you get caught out at night, be sure to make lots of noise, and remember that bears commonly travel on hiking trails at night.

You can be dead meat, too. If you see or smell a carcass of a dead animal when hiking, immediately vacate the area. Don't let your curiosity keep you near the carcass a second longer than necessary. Bears commonly hang around a carcass, guarding it and feeding on it for days until it's completely consumed. Your presence could easily be interpreted as a threat to the bear's food supply, and a vicious attack could be imminent.

If you see a carcass ahead of you on the trail, don't go any closer. Instead, abandon your hike and return to the trailhead. If the carcass is between you and the trailhead, take a very long detour around it, upwind from the carcass, making lots of noise along the way. Be sure to report the carcass to the local ranger. Doing so might prompt a temporary trail closure or special warnings and prevent injury to other hikers. Rangers will, in some cases, go in and drag the carcass away from the trail.

Cute, cuddly, and lethal. If you see a bear cub, don't go even 1 inch closer to it. It might seem abandoned, but it most likely is not. Mother bear is probably close by, and female bears fiercely defend their young.

It doesn't do you any good in your pack. If you brought a repellent such as pepper spray, don't bury it in your pack. Keep it as accessible as possible. Most pepper spray comes in a holster or somehow conveniently attaches to your belt or pack. Such protection won't do you any good if you can't have it ready to fire in one or two seconds. Before hitting the trail, read the directions carefully and test fire the spray.

Regulations. Nobody likes rules and regulations. However, national parks have a few related to hiking and camping in bear country that you must follow. These rules aren't meant to take the freedom out of your trip. They are meant to help bring you back safely.

"But I didn't see any bears." You know how to be safe: Walk up the trail constantly clanging two metal pans together. It works every time. You won't see a bear, but you'll hate your "wilderness experience." Didn't you leave the city to get away from loud noise? Yes, you can be very safe, but how safe do you want to be and still be able to enjoy your trip? It's a balancing act. First, be knowledgeable and then decide how far you want to go. Everybody has to make his or her own personal choice.

Here's another conflict. If you do everything listed here, you most likely will not see any bears—or any deer, moose, eagles, or any other wildlife. Again, you make the choice. If you want to be as safe as possible, follow these rules religiously. If you want to see wildlife, including bears, take all of this advice in reverse, but then you are increasing your chances of an encounter instead of decreasing it.

Camping in Bear Country

Staying overnight in bear country is not dangerous, but it adds a slight additional risk to your trip. The main difference is the presence of more food, cooking, and garbage. Plus, you are in bear country at night when bears are usually most active. Once again, however, following a few basic rules greatly minimizes this risk.

Storing food and garbage.

If the campsite doesn't have a bearproof storage box or bear pole, be sure to set one up or at least locate one before it gets dark. It's not only difficult to store food after darkness falls, but it's also easier to overlook a juicy morsel on the ground. Also, be sure to store food in airtight, waterproof bags to prevent food odors from circulating throughout the forest. For double protection, put food and garbage in securely closed zip-locked bags and then seal tightly in a larger plastic bag.

The illustrations in this chapter depict three popular methods for hanging food bags. In any case try to get food and garbage at least 10 feet off the ground.

Special equipment.

It's not really that special, but one piece of equipment you definitely need is a good supply of zip-locked bags. This handy invention is perfect for keeping food smell to a minimum and helps keep food from spilling on your pack, clothing, or other gear.

Take a special bag for storing food.

The bag must be sturdy and waterproof. You can get "dry" bags at most outdoor specialty stores, but you can get by with a trash compactor bag. Regular garbage bags can break and leave your food spread on the ground.

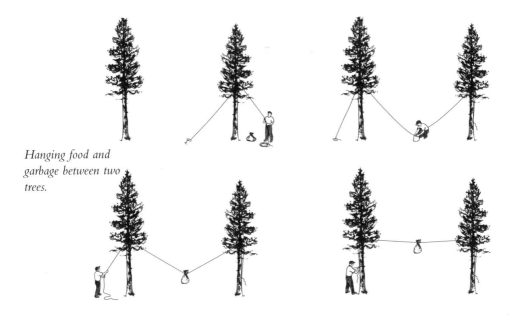

Hanging food and garbage between two trees.

Hanging food and garbage over a tree branch.

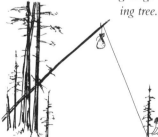

Hanging food and garbage over a leaning tree.

You also need 50 feet of nylon cord. You don't need a heavy climbing rope to store food. Go light instead. Parachute cord will usually suffice unless you plan to hang large quantities of food and gear (which might be the case on a long back-packing excursion with a large group).

You can also buy a small pulley system to make hoisting a heavy load easier. Again, you can usually get by without this extra weight in your pack unless you have a massive load to hang.

What to hang.

To be as safe as possible, store everything that has any food smell. This includes cooking gear, eating utensils, bags used to keep food in your pack, all garbage, toiletries, and even clothes with food smells on them. If you spilled something on your clothes, change into other clothes for sleeping and hang clothes with food smells with the food and garbage. If you take these items into the tent, you aren't separating your sleeping area from food smells. Try to keep food odors off your pack, but if you can't, put the food bag inside and hang the pack.

What to keep in your tent.

You can't be too careful in keeping food smells out of the tent. Just in case a bear has become accustomed to coming into that campsite looking for food, it's vital to keep all food smells out of the tent. This often includes your pack, which is hard to keep odor-free. Usually only take valuables (like cameras and binoculars), clothing, and sleeping gear into the tent.

If you brought a bear repellent, such as pepper spray, sleep with it. Also, keep a flashlight in the tent. If an animal comes into camp and wakes you up, you need the flashlight to identify it.

The campfire.

In many areas, regulations prohibit campfires, but if you're in an area where fires are allowed, treat yourself. Besides adding the nightly entertainment, the fire might make your camp safer from bears.

The campfire provides the best possible way to get rid of food smells. Build a small but hot fire and thoroughly burn everything that smells of food—garbage, left-overs, fish entrails, everything. If you brought food in cans or other incombustible containers, burn those, too. You can even dump extra water from cooking or dish-water on the edge of the fire to erase the smell.

Be very sure you have the fire hot enough to completely burn everything. If you leave partially burned food scraps in the fire, you are setting up a dangerous situation for the next camper who uses this site.

Before leaving camp the next morning, dig out the fire pit and pack out anything that has not completely burned, even if you believe it no longer carries food smells. For example, many foods like dried soup or hot chocolate come in foil packages that might seem like they burn, but they really don't. Pack out the scorched foil and cans (now with very minor food smells). Also pack out foil and cans left by other campers.

Types of food.

Perhaps the safest option is freeze-dried food. It carries very little smell, and it comes in convenient envelopes that allow you to "cook it" by merely adding boiling water. This means you don't have cooking pans to wash or store. Freeze-dried food is expensive, however. Many backpackers don't use it, but they still safely enjoy bear country.

Dry, prepacked meals (often pasta- or rice-based) offer an affordable compromise to freeze-dried foods. Also take your favorite high-energy snack. Avoid fresh fruit and canned meats and fish.

The key point is this: What food you have along is much less critical than how you handle it, cook it, and store it. An open can of tuna fish has a strong smell, but if you eat all of it in one meal, don't spill it on the ground or on your clothes, and burn the can later, it can be quite safe.

Hanging food at night is not the only storage issue. Make sure you place food correctly in your pack. Use airtight packages as much as possible. Store food in the containers it came in or, when opened, in zip-locked bags. Doing so keeps food smells out of your pack and off your camping gear and clothes.

How to cook.

The overriding philosophy of cooking in bear country is to create as little odor as possible. Keep it simple. Use as few pans and dishes as you can.

Unless it's a weather emergency, don't cook in the tent. If you like winter backpacking, you probably cook in the tent, but you should have a different tent for summer backpacking.

If you can have a campfire and decide to cook fish, try cooking in aluminum foil envelopes instead of frying them. Then, after removing the cooked fish, quickly and completely burn the fish scraps off the foil. Using foil also means you don't have to wash the pan you used to cook the fish.

Be careful not to spill on yourself while cooking. If you do, change clothes and hang the clothes with food odor with the food and garbage. Wash your hands thoroughly before retiring to the tent.

Don't cook too much food, so then you don't have to deal with leftovers. If you do end up with extra food, however, you have only two choices: carry it out or burn it. Don't bury it or throw it in a lake or leave it anywhere in bear country. A bear will most likely find and dig up any buried food or garbage.

Taking out the garbage.

In bear country, you have only two choices: burn garbage or carry it out. Prepare for garbage problems before you leave home. Bring along airtight zip-locked bags to store garbage. Be sure to hang your garbage at night along with your food. Also, carry in as little garbage as possible by discarding excess packaging while packing.

Washing dishes.

This can be a problem, but there is one easy solution. If you don't dirty dishes, you don't have to wash them. So try to minimize food smells by using as few dishes and pans as possible. If you use the principles of zero-impact camping, you are probably doing as much as you can to reduce food smells from dishes.

If you brought paper towels, use one to carefully remove food scraps from pans and dishes before washing them. Then, when you wash dishes, you have much less food smell. Burn the dirty towels or store them in zip-locked bags with other garbage. Put pans and dishes in zip-locked bags before putting them back in your pack.

If you end up with lots of food scraps in the dishwater, drain out the scraps and store them in zip-locked bags with other garbage or burn them. You can bring a lightweight screen to filter out food scraps from dishwater, but be sure to store the screen with the food and garbage. If you have a campfire, pour the dishwater around the edge of the fire. If you don't have a fire, take the dishwater at least 200 feet downwind and downhill from camp and pour it on the ground or in a small hole. Don't put dishwater or food scraps in a lake or stream.

Although possibly counter to accepted rules of cleanliness for many people, you can skip washing dishes altogether on the last night of your trip. Instead, simply use the paper towels to clean the dirty dishes as much as possible. You can wash them when you get home. Pack dirty dishes in zip-locked bags before putting them back in your pack.

Finally, don't put it off. Do dishes immediately after eating so that a minimum of food smell lingers in the area.

Selecting a campsite.

Bears and people often like the same places, which makes selecting a campsite an important decision. Sometimes you have little choice about where you camp. If you're backpacking in a national park, regulations probably require that you stay in a designated campsite reserved in advance.

When you get to your campsite, immediately think about bears. Look around for bear sign. If you see fresh sign, move on to another site with no signs of bear activity. If you see a bear in or near the campsite, don't camp there—even if you're in a national park and you have reserved this campsite. If you have time before nightfall, return to the trailhead and report the incident to a ranger. If it's getting late, you have little choice but to camp at an undesignated site and report it to the ranger after you finish the hike. Safety always prevails over regulations. Don't get yourself in a situation where you have to hike or set up camp in the dark.

Plan your hike so you aren't setting up camp a half-hour before nightfall, because this won't leave enough time to move to another campsite if necessary. If you set up camp in the dark, you have little chance to check around for bear sign or signs of previous campers.

Key features of a good campsite.

One key feature of a good campsite in bear country is a place to store food. Most designated sites in national parks and in some national forests have a food-storage device or "bear pole." However, in most national forests and in some national parks, you're on your own, so scout the campsite for trees that can serve as a food-storage device. You need a tree at least 100 yards from your tent with a large branch or two trees close enough to suspend your food between them on a rope. You can also use a tree that has partially fallen but is still leaning securely on other trees. In any case, however, the trees must be tall enough to get the food at least 10 feet off the ground and 4 feet from the tree trunk.

Avoid camping along trails, streams, or lakeshores, which often serve as travel corridors for bears. Camping above timberline or north of the treeline make food storage difficult, so avoid this when possible.

Choosing a tent site.

Try to keep your tent site at least 100 yards from your cooking area. Store food at least 100 yards from the tent. You can store it near the cooking area to concentrate food smells.

Not under the stars.

Some people prefer to sleep out under the stars instead of using a tent. This might be okay in areas not frequented by bears, but it's not a good idea in bear country. The thin fabric of a tent certainly isn't any real physical protection from a bear, but it does present a psychological barrier to a bear that wants to come closer.

Do somebody a big favor.

Report all bear sightings to the ranger after your trip. It might not help you, but it could save another camper's life. If rangers get enough reports to spot a pattern, they will manage the area to prevent potentially hazardous situations.

The Bear Essentials of Hiking and Camping in Bear Country

- Knowledge is the best defense.
- There is no substitute for alertness.
- Hike with a large group and stay together.
- Don't hike alone.
- Stay on the trail.
- Hike in the middle of the day.
- Make lots of noise while hiking.
- Never approach a beer.
- Females with cubs are very dangerous.
- Stay away from carcasses.
- Defensive hiking works. Try it.

- Choose a safe campsite.
- Camp below timberline.
- Separate sleeping and cooking areas.
- Sleep in a tent.
- Cook just the right amount of food and eat it all.
- Store food and garbage out of reach of bears.
- Never feed bears.
- Keep food odor out of the tent.
- Leave the campsite cleaner than you found it.
- Leave no food rewards for bears.

Be Aware of Mountain Lions, Too

The most important safety element for recreation in mountain lion country is simply recognizing their habitat. Mountain lions feed primarily on deer, so these common ungulates are a key element in cougar habitat. Basically, where you have a high deer population, you can expect to find mountain lions. Fish and wildlife agencies usually have good information about deer distribution from population surveys and hunting results.

If you are not familiar with identifying deer tracks, seek the advice of someone knowledgeable, or refer to a book on animal tracks such as FalconGuide's Scats and Tracks series.

Safety Guidelines for Traveling in Mountain Lion Country

To stay as safe as possible when hiking in mountain lion country, follow this advice.

- Travel with a friend or group. There's safety in numbers, so stay together.
- Don't let small children wander away by themselves.
- Don't let pets run unleashed.
- Avoid hiking at dawn or dusk—the times mountain lions are most active.
- Know how to behave if you encounter a mountain lion.

What to Do If You Encounter a Mountain Lion

In the vast majority of mountain lion encounters, these animals exhibit avoidance, indifference, or curiosity that never results in human injury. But it is natural to be alarmed if you have an encounter of any kind. Try to keep your cool and consider the following:

Recognize threatening mountain lion behavior. There are a few cues that may help you gauge the risk of attack. If a mountain lion is more than 50 yards away and it directs its attention to you, it may be only curious. This situation represents only a slight risk for adults but a more serious risk to unaccompanied children. At this point you should move away, while keeping the animal in your peripheral vision. Also look for rocks, sticks, or something to use as a weapon, just in case.

If a mountain lion is crouched and staring intensely at you from less than 50 yards away, it may be assessing the chances of a successful attack. If this behavior continues, the risk of attack may be high.

Do not approach a mountain lion. Instead give the animal the opportunity to move on. Slowly back away, but maintain eye contact if close. Mountain lions are not known to attack humans to defend young or a kill, but they have been reported to "charge" in rare instances and may want to stay in the area. It's best to choose another route or time to hike through the area.

Do not run from a mountain lion. Running may stimulate a predatory response from the mountain lion.

Make noise. If you encounter a mountain lion, be vocal and talk or yell loudly and regularly. Try not to panic. Shout in a way that makes others in the area aware of the situation.

Maintain eye contact. Eye contact presents a challenge to the mountain lion, showing you are aware of its presence. Eye contact also helps you know where the animal is. However, if the behavior of the mountain lion is not threatening (if it is, for example, grooming or periodically looking away), maintain visual contact through your peripheral vision and move away.

Appear larger than you are. Raise your arms above your head and make steady waving motions. Raise your jacket or another object above your head. Do not bend over, as that will make you appear smaller and more "preylike."

If you are with small children, pick them up. First bring children close to you, maintaining eye contact with the mountain lion, and pull the children up without bending over. If you are with other adults or children, band together.

Defend yourself and others. If attacked, fight back. Try to remain standing. Do not feign death. Pick up a branch or rock; pull out a knife, pepper spray, or other deterrent device. Remember that everything is a potential weapon, and individuals have fended off mountain lions with blows from rocks, tree limbs, and even cameras. In past attacks on children, adults have successfully stopped attacks. Physically defending a pet is not recommended.

Respect any warning signs posted by agencies. Before leaving on your hike, discuss lions and teach others in your group how to behave in case of a mountain lion encounter. For example, anyone who starts running could bring on an attack.

Report encounters. If you have an encounter with a mountain lion, record your location and the details of the encounter, and notify the nearest land owner or land management agency. The land management agency (federal, state, or county) may want to visit the site and, if appropriate, post education or warning signs. Fish and wildlife agencies should also be notified because they record and track such encounters. If physical injury occurs, it is important to leave the area and not disturb the site of attack. Mountain lions that have attacked people must be killed, and an undisturbed site is critical for effectively locating the dangerous mountain lion.

How to Get Really Bear and Mountain Lion Aware

Most of the information in this and the previous chapter come from *Bear Aware* and *Mountain Lion Alert,* handy, inexpensive FalconGuides. These small, "packable" books contain the essential tips you need to reduce the risk of being injured by a bear or mountain lion to the slimmest possible margin, and they are written for both beginner and expert:

- Day Hikers
- Backpackers
- Tent Campers
- Backcountry Horseback Riders
- Hunters
- Mountain Bikers
- Anglers
- Trail Runners
- Outfitters
- Photographers

In addition to covering the all-important subject of how to prevent an encounter, these books include advice on what to do if you are involved in an encounter.

Legend

Interstate	00	Picnic Area	
U.S. Highway	00 000	Campground	
State or County Road	00 000	Backcountry Camp	
Interstate Highway	→	Bridge	
Paved Road	→	Cabins/Buildings	
Gravel Road	→	Ranger Station	
Unimproved Road	======>	Peak/Elevation	9,782 ft.
Trailhead/Parking	START P	Falls	
Main Trail		Pass/Saddle	)(
Secondary Trail		Overlook/Point of Interest	
River/Creek		Trail Number	35
Lake		Continental Divide	
Spring			
Geyser/Hot Spring		Scale	N
Forest/Wilderness Boundary			
State Boundary	MONTANA WYOMING		0 1 2 Miles

Kootenai National Forest

1 Northwest Peak

Description: An old lookout cabin, vast views of the Northwest Peak Scenic Area and on a clear day, the Canadian Rockies.
Start: 40 miles northwest of Libby.
Type of hike: Day hike; out-and-back.
Total distance: 4.6-mile round trip.
Difficulty: Moderate.

Maps: Northwest Peak USGS Quad and Kootenai National Forest Map.
Trail contacts: Three Rivers Ranger District, Kootenai National Forest, 1437 North Highway 2, Troy, MT 59935; (406) 295-4693; www.fs.fed.us/r1/kootenai.

Finding the trailhead: Drive west of Libby on U.S. Highway 2 for 29 miles (through Troy) and turn right, heading north on Yaak River Road. After a beautiful 27-mile drive up the Yaak River Valley, turn left, heading northwest on Pete Creek Road (Forest Road 338). If you reach the tiny town of Yaak, you have gone too far. Drive 13 miles north on the narrow, mostly paved Pete Creek Road (Forest Road 338) and then turn left (west) onto West Fork Road, continuing to follow FR 338. Finally, turn right onto Winkum Creek Road (still FR 338) for the last several miles to the trailhead. After 19 miles from Yaak River Road, at 6,100 feet, you will find the trailhead on the left (south) side of the road. There is limited parking at the trailhead.

The Hike

Northwest Peak (elevation 7,705 feet) is the central attraction of a high mountain ridge, the most striking portions of which are included in the Northwest Peak Scenic Area, an official designation of the Forest Service. Under this designation the unique qualities of the area are recognized and protected. The peak is a long drive from almost everywhere except Yaak. It receives only moderate numbers of visitors, but it's a great trip if you're car camping or fishing up in the Yaak River Valley. Tank up on water before hiking, because there isn't any along the trail. This area usually gets more than its share of snow, however, so wait until July to conquer Northwest Peak.

Trail 169 follows an old logging road through a clear-cut for 0.3 mile and then enters thick stands of timber. The trail is well marked and easy to follow. It climbs

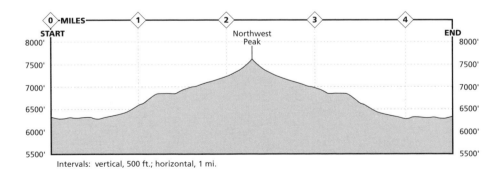

Intervals: vertical, 500 ft.; horizontal, 1 mi.

Northwest Peak

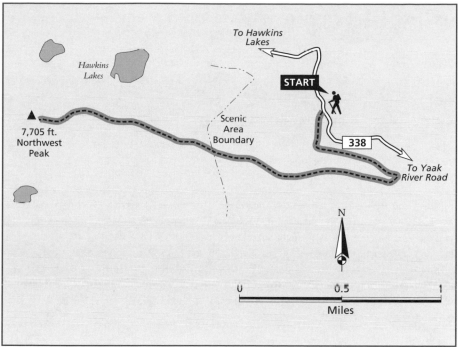

steadily for 2 miles to the top of the peak, the last quarter of a mile across open talus (rock debris). At the top is an old, abandoned lookout cabin, complete with rusty pans and other nostalgic artifacts. The terrain drops down to alpine lakes on three sides of the peak. The views are extensive, with the Cabinet Mountains to the south and the Canadian Rockies far to the north. Northwest Peak is an easy place to pass the time if you aren't in a hurry to do something or go somewhere.

Options

If you didn't get enough exercise on the way up and if you have time, consider continuing south along the ridge toward 7,583-foot Davis Mountain. (Originally contributed by Pat Caffrey)

Key Points

0.0 Trailhead
0.3 End of old logging road/trail
2.3 Northwest Peak
4.6 Trailhead

2 Fish Lakes Canyon

Description: A 50-foot waterfall and a chain of five lakes in a rugged, low-elevation canyon.
Start: 30 air miles north of Libby on the east side of the Yaak River.
Type of hike: Day hike or overnighter; out-and-back.
Total distance: 12-mile round trip.
Difficulty: Moderate.

Maps: Lost Horse Mountain, Mount Henry, and Yaak USGS Quads; and Kootenai National Forest Map.
Trail contacts: Three Rivers Ranger District, Kootenai National Forest, 1437 North Highway 2, Troy, MT 59935; (406) 295–4693; www.fs.fed.us/r1/kootenai.

Finding the trailhead: Drive west of Libby on U.S. Highway 2 for 29 miles (through Troy) and turn right, heading north on Yaak River Road. After a 29.5-mile drive up Yaak River Road to the town of Yaak, turn right, heading south on South Fork of the Yaak River Road 68 for 4.2 miles, then turn left, heading north on Vinal Lake Road 746. You can also reach Vinal Lake Road by driving north of Libby on South Fork of the Yaak River Road, but it is a dirt road drive in contrast to the paved route to Yaak described earlier. Drive 6.1 miles north on Vinal Lake Road past the Vinal Lake turnoff and look for Vinal Creek/Fish Lakes Trailhead on your right. Limited parking is available at the trailhead.

The Hike

To some people Fish Lakes is an overnight trip. To others it's a full day's hike. For every hiker, however, it's one of the most scenic and diverse trips he or she will ever take. The trail is well maintained and gets rocky only along a few talus slopes, and there's plenty of drinking water along the way. Elevation gain is a mere 600 feet to the northernmost lake. Fish Lakes Canyon and its chain of five lakes are suitable for almost any hiker, including families with children and veteran backpackers.

The area feels remote if you start at the Vinal Lake Road trailhead, but logging roads to the north and to the south parallel the trail, and when I visited the area in 1998, I was able to drive to within a mile of Lower Fish Lake. Much of the

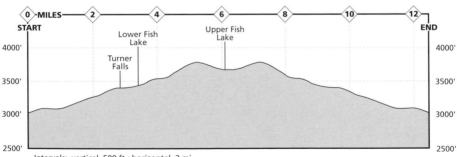

Fish Lakes Canyon

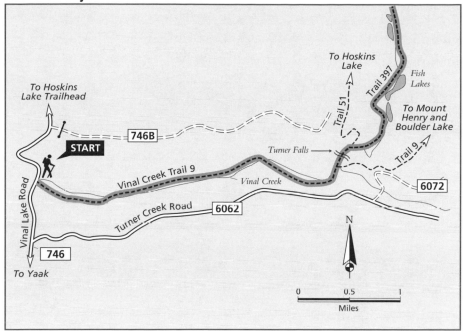

surrounding area has been logged, but you don't really know that when hiking down in the canyon.

Wildlife and wildflowers abound and are characteristic of northwestern Montana—moose, deer, black bear, wake-robin, Canada dogwood, and clematis, to name a few. Wild roses line Vinal Creek in great abundance. Bear danger is low, but mosquitoes can be vicious in June and July. Try this hike anytime during the late summer or fall.

From the trailhead follow Vinal Creek Trail 9 along Vinal Creek for the first 3 miles to Turner Falls, where it splits. You turn left (north) on Trail 397 where the Vinal Creek Trail 9 goes right (west) toward Mount Henry. After the junction, you head into Fish Lakes Canyon and its string of lakes. After enjoying them, turn around at the last lake and retrace your steps back to the trailhead.

Perhaps the most outstanding feature of the hike is Turner Falls. Even without the falls, however, this would be one of the most beautiful hikes in Montana. Here are five mountain lakes strung through a narrow, rugged canyon lined with a quiet forest of large cedar and larch trees. The Fish Lakes/Vinal Creek Trail has been designated a National Recreation Trail and has been given semiprimitive, nonmotorized recreation status in the Kootenai National Forest Plan. In 2000 a forest fire burned a few areas along this trail. (Originally contributed by Linda and Tom Hurlock, rehiked by authors in 1998)

Key Points

0.0 Trailhead

3.0 Turner Falls and junction with Mount Henry Trail; turn left

3.5 Lower Fish Lake

6.0 Upper Fish Lake

12.0 Trailhead

3 Ross Creek Cascade

Description: Old-growth western red cedar forest and an optional trip up Sawtooth Peak or across Pillick Ridge, where views of the Cabinet Mountains and the Bull and Clark Fork Valleys are superb.
Start: 35 miles southwest of Libby in the West Cabinet Mountains.
Type of hike: Day hike or backpacking trip; out-and-back.
Total distance: 9-mile round trip.

Difficulty: Moderate.
Maps: Sawtooth Mountain, Smeads Bench, and Heron USGS Quads; and Kootenai National Forest Map (Smeads Bench and Heron needed only for optional Pillick Ridge adventure).
Trail contacts: Three Rivers Ranger District, Kootenai National Forest, 1437 North Highway 2, Troy, MT 59935; (406) 295-4693; www.fs.fed.us/r1/kootenai.

Finding the trailhead: Drive 15 miles west of Libby on U.S. Highway 2 to the junction with Montana Highway 56 and then turn left, heading south for 17.7 miles. Here turn right, heading west on Ross Creek Road 398 for 4 miles to Ross Creek Cedar Grove Scenic Area. After 0.9 mile stay left at a junction. The road is paved and dead-ends at Ross Creek Trailhead at the far end of the picnic area loop. Facilities include a 0.9-mile self-guided nature trail, a picnic area across the creek, toilet, and ample parking.

The Hike

The trail leaves the parking lot on the west side and follows the Ross Creek Cedars Interpretive Trail, passing through some of the most beautiful forest in the state. The very wild Ross Creek drainage offers a firsthand look at western red cedar trees hundreds of years old, some 8 feet in diameter and 175 feet in height. Stay right along the interpretive trail loop, and after about 0.4 mile leave the loop, continuing on Ross Creek Trail 142.

The grade is gentle as you climb up the valley. You'll notice the burned cores of gargantuan ancient stumps. Wildfire burned up this valley around the turn of the last century and killed some of the ancient trees. You'll also notice several changes in the makeup of the forest as you walk up the trail.

In 2 miles, the trail reaches a ford of Ross Creek. It may look like a trail continues up the northwestern bank, but both trails cross the creek. This ford would be a serious task in spring. If you visit in May or June (and don't want to risk the ford) or just want a flat, easy walk, you should turn back now.

After fording Ross Creek, you also cross the South Fork of Ross Creek. At 2.4 miles, there's an unmarked trail junction. A maintained trail goes left (south) past a large (12 feet across) twin cedar tree, and the right (west) trail continues up the North Fork of Ross Creek. Although I did not hike up the North Fork, the trail looks similarly maintained to the South Fork trail.

Once in the South Fork, the trail goes steeply uphill on a soft bedding of western hemlock cones. At 4.8 miles the good trail ends beside a beautiful cascade along the South Fork of Ross Creek.

A partially flagged elk trail continues to climb through dense forest until breaking out into what is best described as overgrazed meadows. As the trail peters out, you can turn back, continue up to Sawtooth Mountain via a steep scramble, or bushwhack your way up to the ridge for a trip to Pillick Ridge.

Options

To climb Sawtooth Mountain from Ross Creek Cascade (adding 8 difficult miles to your hike), continue up on a faint trail through devil's club, alder, and snowbrush. The faint trail crosses the creek, and if you find yourself looking up the right slope, you're off course. Cross the creek or follow the creek until you pick up the trail again. When we hiked this, someone had flagged the route.

This faint trail dead-ends in some large elk meadows. Here you should look around the valley and look at your watch to make sure you have enough time to climb Sawtooth Mountain. You'll need another six hours to climb the mountain and get back to the trailhead.

You can climb Sawtooth Mountain via two routes. The best way is to hike up the creek another 0.3 mile and find a dry creek bed to follow up the north slope, directly toward Sawtooth Mountain. If you choose carefully, this path should take you to the avalanche bowl below the summit and a small melt pond. From that point, you can take either ridge of talus slope and intermediate rock scrambling to the top. However, remember that you gain almost 2,500 feet from the valley floor to the top in a little over 2 miles.

Once on top, angle down toward the most down valley talus slope on the opposite side of the South Fork of Ross Creek drainage. This bushwhack can be nasty, but this place is packed with elk, and we found many good elk trails to follow on the way back to the trail. Once back on the trail, it's another two hours to the trailhead and (if you planned well) the cold beer waiting in your vehicle, which you may need after this mammoth hike.

Another route up Sawtooth Mountain is to continue all the way up the valley to the divide between the South Fork of Ross Creek and Blue Creek. There was a pond on top in late September 1998 (a dry year). From there you can walk the ridge up and over Middle Mountain to the summit. Again, both routes involve serious bushwhacking and heart attack elevation gain, so use caution. This option is for well-conditioned and experienced hikers only.

◀ *Coauthor Russ Schneider in the Ross Creek Cedars.*

Ross Creek Cascade

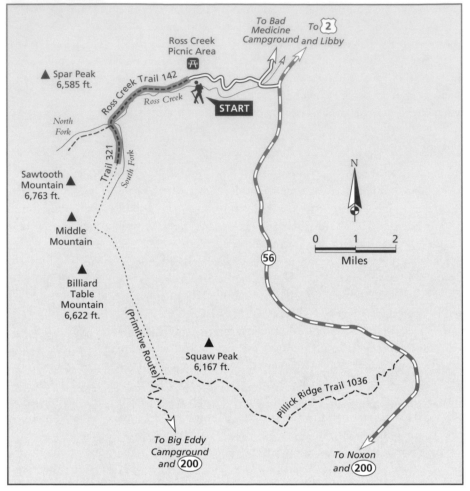

Sawtooth Mountain offers a panorama of the glacially carved upper North Fork of Ross Creek drainage and excellent views of Billiard Table Mountain toward Pillick Ridge and Spar Peak in the opposite direction. I also thought this view of the Cabinets was the best I've seen. In addition, this peak is a crucial part of what will, we hope, be designated the Scotchman Peak Wilderness Area.

The Pillick Ridge option requires a vehicle left at Pillick Ridge Trailhead. It has little water and a trail for only the last 11 miles of this hike.

To get to Pillick Ridge Trailhead, continue south on MT 56 for another 15 miles and watch for a possibly marked logging road to the right (west) 6.5 miles before the junction with MT 200. The trailhead may or may not be signed. Unfortunately, trailhead signs are often stolen or vandalized.

South Fork of Ross Creek.

This hike is strictly for woods-wise hikers with topographic maps and compass. I think this trip is best described as a true Montana wilderness experience and cruel to the unprepared. Hikers who don't mind rugged country with little water and who appreciate wild scenery and solitude should like this trip. Pillick Ridge is the pristine, southeastern spur of the Scotchman Peaks and forms the scenic western backdrop to the Bull River Valley.

From the divide ridge between the Blue Creek and South Fork of Ross Creek drainages, follow the rugged, trailless ridge for 6 miles to the top of Squaw Peak. You stand a good chance of seeing deer and possibly a few mountain goats. In addition, the southern slopes of the ridge have an abundance of dry site wildflowers. Take plenty of water, especially if you're camping. Subalpine basins below the northeast side of the ridge have water and possible campsites (there was water on the divide between Blue and South Fork of Ross Creeks in September of a dry year). Once off the ridge, however, the terrain becomes very steep and brushy. So don't expect easy going or an abundance of level camping spots.

From Squaw Peak, maintained Pillick Ridge Trail 1036 follows the crest for 11 miles to Pillick Ridge Trailhead. Although the going is very rugged, the view is excellent and solitude assured. Be on the alert for elk and mountain goats or possibly one of the few grizzlies still in this area. (Originally contributed by John Westenberg, rehiked by authors in 1998)

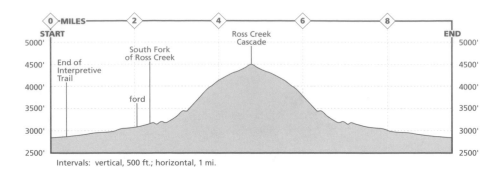

Intervals: vertical, 500 ft.; horizontal, 1 mi.

Key Points

0.0   Ross Creek Trailhead

0.4   End of Ross Creek Cedars Interpretive Trail

2.0+ Ross Creek

2.4   Junction with South Fork of Ross Creek Trail 321; turn left

4.8   Ross Creek Cascade and end of maintained trail

7.0   Sawtooth Mountain or Blue Creek Divide

9.0   Ross Creek Trailhead

4 Boulder Lakes

Description: The Boulder Lakes area provides habitat for black bears and features a variety of wildflowers including bear grass and glacier lilies.

Start: 30 miles north of Libby or 7 miles west of Lake Koocanusa Bridge.

Type of hike: Day hike or easy overnighter; out-and-back.

Total distance: 5.6-mile round trip for Lower Boulder Lake and 10.6-mile round trip for Purcell Marsh.

Difficulty: Easy to Lower Boulder Lake and moderate to Purcell Marsh.

Maps: Boulder Lakes USGS Quad and Kootenai National Forest Map.

Trail contacts: Rexford Ranger District, Kootenai National Forest, 1299 Highway 93 North, Eureka, MT 59917; (406) 296-2536; www.fs.fed.us/r1/kootenai.

Finding the trailhead: Drive southwest from Eureka for about 14 miles on Montana Highway 37, and then turn west across the Lake Koocanusa Bridge. (Koocanusa is not an Indian name. It combines the first three letters of the words *Kootenai, Canada,* and *USA,* hence the name *Koo-can-usa.*) Once across the bridge, turn north on Forest Road 92 for 2.7 miles and then turn left, heading west on Boulder Creek Road. Follow Boulder Creek Road 337 for about 9 miles, then follow the left fork on FR 7183, go about 2 miles past this junction to the junction of FR 7183 and FR 7229, and park here. Limited parking at the trailhead; be careful not to block the road. You used to be able to drive 1.5 miles up FR 7229 to the trailhead, but in recent years this section has been closed to vehicles to protect grizzly bear habitat. It is about 13.5 miles from FR 92 to Boulder Lakes Trailhead. (If you find yourself driving on the level for miles, you missed the last road junction, as the road levels off after the turnoff to Boulder Lakes.)

The Hike

If you want to see a subalpine lake without vehicle access, this may be the easiest hike you could take. It's only 1.5 miles to the Lower Boulder Lake along a slight incline—about 440 feet of elevation gain.

The trail is well maintained, and it stays in the woods most of the way. At 2.6 miles, just before the lake, the trail forks. Go left (south) about a quarter mile farther to the lake. The right-hand trail continues to Purcell Marsh. Bring drinking water; it can be dry until you reach the lower lake.

You can get a feeling of remoteness on this hike, but not until after the first quarter of a mile, which goes through a logged area. The rest of the trail has been designated a National Recreation Trail with motorized vehicles prohibited. The threat of bear trouble is minimal, but this area is within a grizzly bear recovery unit, so use normal bear country precautions.

Boulder Lakes

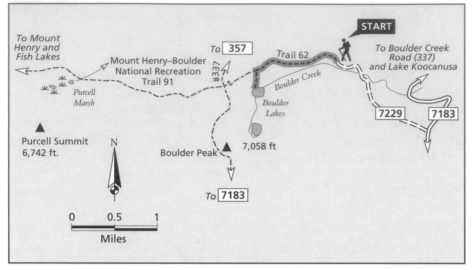

Lower Boulder Lake has fair fishing for pan-size cutthroat trout. Boulder Lakes country hosts the same diversity of wildlife found throughout northwestern Montana—deer, black bear, moose, elk, and the like. Around the lakes you will find bear grass, glacier lilies, and a variety of other wildflowers.

Side Trips

If you're an experienced hiker, you may want to add on 5 more miles and take an interesting side trip to Purcell Marsh. From Lower Boulder Lake, backtrack about a quarter of a mile and take Trail 62 west to Boulder Ridge at the head of Basin Creek, which is about a 500-foot climb. (From the top of the ridge, you can also make a side trip to the top of Boulder Peak by heading south along the ridge for less than a mile.) To continue on to Purcell Marsh (or Fish Lakes and beyond), from the junction with Trail 337 on top of Boulder Ridge, drop 900 feet to Purcell Marsh. Here you find few signs of human presence, and you have an excellent chance to see moose. It's an extra 5-mile round trip to Purcell Marsh from Boulder Lakes. At Purcell Marsh you might find the uncommon alpine bog kalmia.

You can continue on the Mount Henry–Boulder National Recreation Trail past Purcell Marsh all the way to Fish Lakes Canyon, but the area around Mount Henry crosses several logging roads and harvest areas before dropping into pristine Fish Lakes Canyon. It's another 10 miles to Fish Lakes from Boulder Lakes and another 6 miles to Vinal Lake Road. See Hike 2, Fish Lakes Canyon. (Originally contributed by Linda and Tom Hurlock)

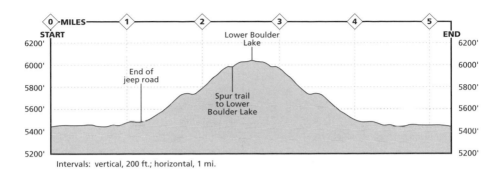

Intervals: vertical, 200 ft.; horizontal, 1 mi.

Key Points

0.0 Trailhead

1.3 End of closed jeep road

2.6 Spur trail to Boulder Lakes; turn left

2.8 Lower Boulder Lake

5.6 Trailhead

5 Cedar Lakes

Description: Two fish-filled mountain lakes, good camping.
Start: 9 miles south of Libby in the Cabinet Mountains Wilderness.
Type of hike: Day hike or overnighter; out-and-back.
Total distance: 11-mile round trip.
Difficulty: Moderate.

Maps: Scenery Mountain USGS Quad, Cabinet Mountains Wilderness Map, and Kootenai National Forest Map.
Trail contacts: Libby Ranger District, Kootenai National Forest, 12557 Highway 37 North, Libby, MT 59923; (406) 293-7773; www.fs.fed.us/r1/kootenai.

Finding the trailhead: From the junction of U.S. Highway 2 and Montana Highway 37 in Libby, drive west on US 2 for 4.4 miles. Turn left, heading southwest on Cedar Creek Road 402 for 2.4 miles to the junction with Parmenter Creek Road 4727, where you turn left. The trailhead is on your right just before crossing Cedar Creek. There's a small parking lot.

The Hike

Cedar Creek Trail 141 climbs steadily on stream grade up Cedar Creek Valley. As you might guess, many young cedar trees surround the trail, creating a shady walk, perfect for a hot summer day. The trail was once lined with stately old cedars, but now you see only the stumps.

The trail is in excellent condition and sometimes used by stock parties. It stays on the north side of Cedar Creek all the way. If you go in August, plan on taking an extra hour to gorge yourself in the abundant huckleberry patches.

Soon after leaving the trailhead (0.7 mile), turn left (west) at junction with the Scenery Mountain trail. At 4.4 miles, turn left (west) again at the new trail up Grambauer Ridge.

After 5 miles, you'll see a spur trail going left to the lower lake. You can follow this trail down to Lower Cedar Lake and continue up a steep, half-mile climb to Upper Cedar Lake. The trail climbs above the lower lake, and you get a great view from it.

Both lakes have a few well-used campsites. To reduce resource damage, use existing campsites rather than create new ones. The Cabinets still supports a few grizzly bears, but this remnant population is severely endangered. Black bears are common, however, so be sure to keep a zero-impact camp.

Both lakes have a few small rainbow trout, but you might need some patience to catch them.

Lower Cedar Lake in the Cabinet Mountains. ▶

Cedar Lakes

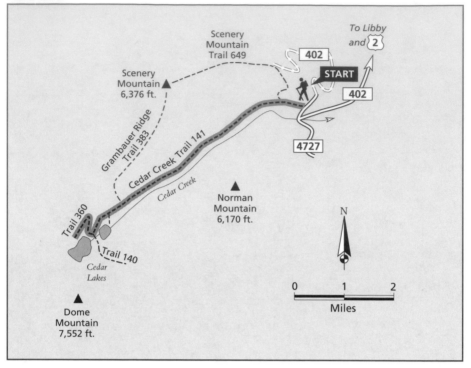

Options

You can make a loop of this hike by taking the new trail along Grambauer Ridge (not shown on the Cabinet Mountains Wilderness Map) to Scenery Mountain and back to the trailhead on Scenery Mountain Trail 649 instead of retracing your steps down Cedar Creek. Make sure you have enough time, though. This option makes your trek a long day hike, about 13 miles total with more elevation gain. (Originally contributed by John Westenberg, rehiked by authors in 2002)

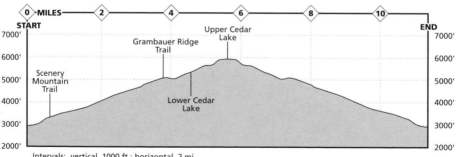

Key Points

0.0 Trailhead

0.7 Junction with Scenery Mountain Trail 649; turn left

4.4 Grambauer Ridge Trail 383; turn left

5.0 Spur trail to Lower Cedar Lake

5.5 Upper Cedar Lake and Trail 140 to Parmenter Creek

11.0 Trailhead

6 Leigh Lake

Description: The largest lake in the Cabinet Wilderness (nearly a mile across) with views of Snowshoe Peak, the highest peak in Montana west of Glacier National Park.
Start: 12 miles south of Libby.
Type of hike: Day hike; out-and-back.
Total distance: 2.6-mile round trip.

Difficulty: Moderate.
Maps: Snowshoe Peak USGS Quad and Kootenai National Forest Map.
Trail contacts: Libby Ranger District, Kootenai National Forest, 12557 Highway 37 North, Libby, MT 59923; (406) 293-7773; www.fs.fed.us/r1/kootenai.

Finding the trailhead: Drive 8 miles south on U.S. Highway 2 from its junction with Montana Highway 37 in Libby and turn right (west) on the paved Bear Creek Road 278 (which is 80 miles from Kalispell). After 5.2 miles, turn right on Leigh Lake Trail 132 (Forest Road 4876 on the map). From here it's 2.1 miles to the end of the road where the trail starts. You can make it to the trailhead in any vehicle, but the last 2 miles are rough. Because of the heavy logging activity, the numerous roads in this area can change periodically, and sometimes (such as the day I hiked this route) some of the signs are nowhere to be found. Make sure you have a current Forest Service map or, better yet, check with the Forest Service before leaving for the trailhead. No signs at the trailhead when I was there in 2002. There is limited parking along the road and no room for horse trailers.

The Hike

Leigh Lake Trail 132 climbs steeply uphill through thick forest with breaks providing views of Leigh Creek Valley. It's only 1.5 miles to the lake, but the steep grade and rocky trail make it an hour-long trip, and longer with an overnight pack. Along the trail you'll see some massive western hemlocks, a beautiful tree you don't see often in Montana. The vegetation is wonderfully lush all along the route.

Less than a half mile before the lake, you get a great view of a gorgeous waterfall. Just before the falls, the trail turns right and goes straight up. This short section is very steep and requires handholds in a few places—it wouldn't be fun with a heavy pack.

After climbing about 1,000 feet in 1.5 miles (a tough Category 2 hill), the trail ends at the 5,144-foot-elevation lake. Leigh Lake offers marginal fishing. If you're a hardy soul, you can pack in a small rubber raft to improve your chances.

This area gets phenomenal amounts of snow—as much as 20 to 30 feet. In July the lake is still full of ice floes. The waves lap them into strange shapes, and paddling around them, looking down, and seeing the odd shapes down in the deep blue water gives one an eerie feeling.

This area also receives heavy use. The Forest Service reports hiker visits as high as 2,400 people per year. Because of this volume, observing zero-impact ethics is

Leigh Lake in the Cabinet Mountains. ▶

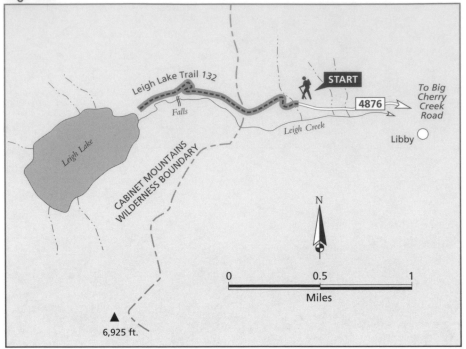

especially important. Camping and fires are prohibited within 300 feet of the lake. The lake is in the Cabinet Mountains Wilderness. This makes it popular locally, so try to hit this one on a weekday.

This route is more suited for day hiking, but you can camp at the lake. Good campsites are hard to find, and local regulations prohibit camping within 300 feet of the lake.

Side Trips

At the west end of the lake is a massive, 3,000-foot wall, the high point being 8,712-foot Snowshoe Peak, the highest peak in the Cabinet Range and the highest peak between Glacier National Park and the Cascades.

You can climb this peak from the lake, but it takes most of a day and would be classified as strenuous. From the outlet of the lake, head northwest straight up the face of a large eastern ridge. Once on the ridge, follow it southwest to the main ridge, being careful to notice Blackwell Glacier to the right and also being careful not to fall in that direction. After intersecting the main ridge, work your way up along the western side of this ridge until it levels out at the peak. Do not venture out onto the snowfields on the eastern side of the main ridge unless you are prop-

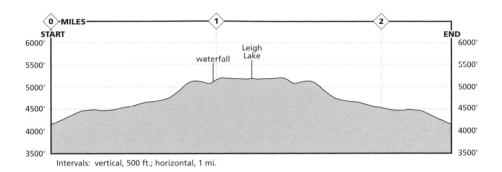

Intervals: vertical, 500 ft.; horizontal, 1 mi.

erly trained and equipped for ice climbing. (Originally contributed by Pat Caffrey, rehiked by authors in 2002)

Key Points

0.0 Trailhead

1.1 Waterfall

1.3 Leigh Lake

2.6 Trailhead

7 Baree and Bear Lakes

Description: Several mountain lakes with fish, high alpine ridge walks, and a possible climb up Baree Peak.
Start: 30 miles south of Libby at the southern tip of the Cabinet Mountains Wilderness.
Type of hike: A moderate day hike or overnighter that can be stretched into a leisurely three-day backpacking trip; loop.
Total distance: 10 miles.

Difficulty: Moderate.
Maps: Goat Peak and Silver Butte Pass USGS Quads, Cabinet Mountains Wilderness Map, and Kootenai National Forest Map.
Trail contacts: Libby Ranger District, Kootenai National Forest, 12557 Highway 37 North, Libby, MT 59923; (406) 293-7773; www.fs.fed.us/r1/kootenai.

Finding the trailhead: Drive west of Kalispell on U.S. Highway 2 for 59 miles and turn left, heading southwest on Silver Butte Road, Forest Road 148. After 3.4 miles stay right past a private drive to the left and continue on FR 148. After 9.2 miles, pass the turnoff for Bear Lakes Trailhead and continue straight on FR 148 for another mile. At 10 miles, turn right and drive 0.2 mile to Baree Lake Trailhead underneath the power lines. There's ample parking.

The Hike

If you don't like to retrace your steps and you dislike the difficult two-car logistics that most one-way hikes involve, you should like this hike. The trailheads to the two lakes are only a mile apart, and the lakes are connected by a trail along the top of the Cabinet Divide.

Baree Creek Trail 489 reaches Baree Lake in 3 miles and gains 1,700 feet. A spur trail heads left down to the lake where there is a survey cabin and a snow gauging station. The lake is very pretty and offers views up to the Cabinet Divide along slopes covered with beargrass and huckleberry.

After Baree Lake, the trail makes a steady climb to the Cabinet Divide. At 3.5 miles—half a mile beyond the lake—turn right (north) on the Cabinet Crest Trail 360 and follow it along the divide. The view from the ridge is terrific, particularly to the west and the northwest into Swamp Creek, Wanless and Buck Lakes, and the

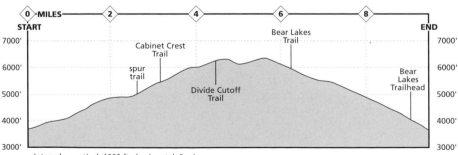

Intervals: vertical, 1000 ft.; horizontal, 2 mi.

Baree Lake.

peaks surrounding them. Although grizzlies are uncommon along the Cabinet Divide, huckleberries (prime grizzly food) are, and you may want to make noise along the trail as an extra precaution.

After a mile of ridgeline hiking, turn right (east) at an unmarked junction on the Divide Cutoff Trail 63 to Bear Lakes. The trail that continues left along the ridge appears to be more heavily used than this route down. This trail runs just below the top of a spur ridge off the Cabinet Divide.

Without continuing along the ridge, you can follow Divide Cutoff Trail 63 for another 1.5 miles on a gentle downward traverse to the junction with Bear Lakes Trail 178. Follow Bear Lakes Trail for 3 miles back to Silver Butte Road. The trail descends past a spur trail to the outlet of the southernmost Bear Lake, then generally southeast through forested country. After reaching the power line corridor that runs parallel to Silver Butte Road, follow it southwest for a mile to Baree Lake Trailhead and your vehicle.

Options

The Trail Creek and Iron Meadows areas to the north and east of Bear Lakes offer interesting variations on the Baree/Bear Lakes hike. One variation requires leaving a car at Silver Dollar Trailhead, 9 miles up West Fisher River Road (4 miles north on US 2). Rather than returning to Silver Butte Road from Bear Lake, take the Iron

Baree and Bear Lakes

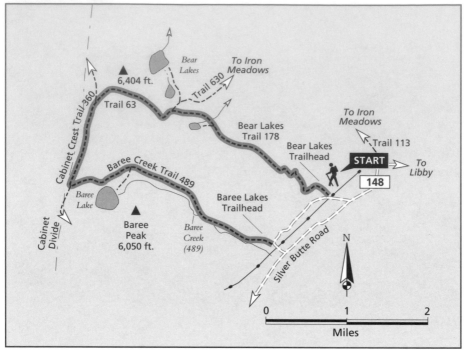

Meadows Trail 630. You will walk through some of the best elk country in the Kootenai National Forest. From Iron Meadows, take Silver Dollar Trail 113 to your vehicle. (Originally contributed by John Westenberg)

Key Points

0.0 Baree Lake Trailhead

3.0 Spur trail to Baree Lake

3.5 Cabinet Crest Trail 360; turn right

4.5 Junction with Divide Cutoff Trail 63 to Bear Lakes; turn right

6.0 Junction with trail to Big Bear Lake and Bear Lakes Trail 178; turn right

9.0 Bear Lakes Trailhead

10.0 Baree Lake Trailhead

8 Ten Lakes

Description: Lake-filled alpine scenery in one of the last roadless areas in the Whitefish Range.
Start: 50 miles north of Whitefish.
Type of hike: Day hike or overnighter that could be stretched into a three-day backpacking trip; shuttle.
Total distance: 12 miles.

Difficulty: Moderate.
Maps: Ksanka Peak and Stahl Peak USGS Quads, and Kootenai National Forest Map.
Trail contacts: Fortine Ranger District, Kootenai National Forest, P.O. Box 116, Fortine, MT 59918; (406) 882-4451; www.fs.fed.us/r1/kootenai.

Finding the trailhead: Drive north of Whitefish on U.S. Highway 93 for 41.5 miles (8 miles south of Eureka) and turn northeast onto paved Grave Creek Road (Forest Road 114). After 10 miles the pavement ends; stay right past the Stahl Creek Road turnoff, continuing on FR 114. After 13.8 miles, continue straight on FR 319 after FR 114 takes a sharp right. After 24.7 miles from US 93, FR 319 reaches the junction with FR 7086.

To reach Wolverine Lakes Trailhead, turn right and follow FR 7086, a less-improved dirt road, for 2 miles to the junction with FR 7091. Stay left (right takes you to Rainbow Trailhead) on FR 7086 for another 0.3 mile to the trailhead on your right. This is also the trailhead for a 3-mile cutoff trail (Tie Thru Trail 82) between Bluebird and Wolverine Trailheads.

Leave a vehicle at Big Therriault Lake. From the junction of FR 7086 and FR 319, go left instead of right and follow FR 319 for 2.5 miles to the junction with FR 7116 and FR 7085. Stay left on FR 7116 for 0.5 mile to Big Therriault Lake Campground and Trailhead. Trailhead registers, parking, rest rooms and campgrounds at Big Therriault Lake and Little Therriault Lake both have trailheads for Highline Trail access. Wolverine Lakes Trailhead has ample parking.

The Hike

The Ten Lakes Scenic Area gets buried with snow, so don't attempt this hike before July. Some of the lakes in this area receive heavy summer use, so if you're staying overnight, be sure to set up a zero-impact camp. The area still has a few resident grizzlies, so be bear aware.

From the Wolverine Lakes Trailhead, Wolverine Lakes Trail 84 starts on the right side of the road, and Tie Thru Trail 82 (Clarence Ness Trail) to Bluebird Trailhead starts on the left. The Wolverine Lakes Trail to Wolverine Lakes climbs steeply at first. At 2.5 miles, the trail flattens out past Wolverine Lakes Basin. Then the trail continues past the lakes and up to the Highline Trail 339 on the ridge between the Ten Lakes Basin on the north and the Wolverine Flats on the south. The views are expansive in all directions with glimpses of the ice-clad Bugaboos far into Canada.

At 4.5 miles, turn left (south) on the Highline Trail 339 and follow this trail across the slopes of Green Mountain into the Bluebird Lake Basin and, at 6 miles, Bluebird Lake, which you can reach via a short spur trail to the right.

Bluebird Lake.

About a quarter mile past Bluebird Lake, you can turn left (east) and head down to Paradise Camp and Little Therriault Lake on Bluebird Trail 83 for a shorter trip, but to stay on this route, turn right (south) at this junction. Continue on Highline Trail to the southeast across the northern shoulder of St. Clair Peak, turning right (south) at the junction with Trail 341 to Little Therriault Lake (another way you can make this a shorter loop hike). From here it's another 3 miles to Therriault Pass. From the pass take Trail 86 another 2.7 miles down to the Big Therriault Lake Campground and your waiting vehicle.

Options

You can come back via Bluebird Trail 83 and Tie Thru Trail 82 to make a loop, but you miss the Stahl Peak area beyond Bluebird Lake.

Side Trips

At Therriault Pass you can hike up to Stahl Peak to visit the lookout and get a panoramic view of the southern portions of the Ten Lakes region, but this route contains one section of exposed dirt road. Keep your eyes open for bighorn sheep, which wander the crags during the summer months. Ernest Thompson Seton, the famous naturalist, wrote of the wild sheep in this area in several of his short stories

Ten Lakes

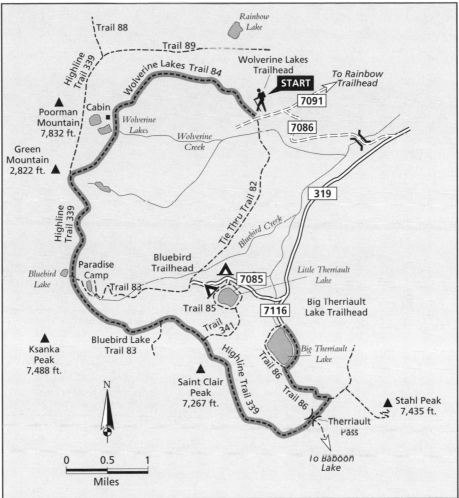

published around the turn of the twentieth century. In fact, his namesake mountain, Mount Thompson Seton, lies 7 miles to the southeast of Stahl Peak. (Originally contributed by Bill Cunningham)

Key Points

0.0 Wolverine Lakes Trailhead

2.5 Wolverine Lakes

4.5 Junction with Highline Trail 339; turn left

6.0 Bluebird Lake

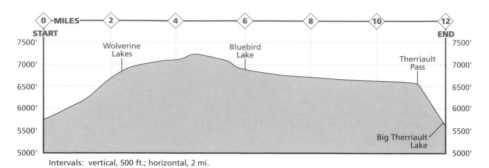

Intervals: vertical, 500 ft.; horizontal, 2 mi.

6.3 Bluebird Lake Trail 83; turn right

10.2 Therriault Pass; Trail 339 continues to Stahl Peak Trail

12.0 Big Therriault Lake Trailhead

Lolo
National Forest

9 Hub Lake

Description: Beautiful subalpine country on a scale small enough to be easily enjoyed by families with small children.
Start: 90 miles northwest of Missoula in the Bitterroot Mountains.
Type of hike: Day hike or overnighter; out-and-back.
Total distance: 5-mile round trip.

Difficulty: Moderate.
Maps: McGee Peak and Deborgia South USGS Quads, and Lolo National Forest Map (West Half).
Trail contacts: Superior Ranger Station, Lolo National Forest, 209 West Riverside, Superior, MT 59872; (406) 822-4233; www.fs.fed.us/r1/lolo.

Finding the trailhead: From Missoula take Interstate 90 west for 80 miles to exit 25 (11 miles west of St. Regis) and then get in the eastbound lane, go back toward Missoula, and take exit 26 onto the Ward Creek Road 889. There is no exit 26 from the westbound lane. Follow Ward Creek Road for about 6.5 miles. The trailhead is on the right (west) side of the road just before Forest Road 889 crosses Ward Creek. Parking is limited; there's only room for three or four vehicles, so don't take two spots. You can filter water in Ward Creek.

The Hike

The Ward–Eagle Peaks area offers small doses of the medicine that gives Montana's mountains their healing power—beautiful forests, waterfalls, wildlife, berries, interesting history, and fishing. Moreover, they are accessible to all hikers. This area is a "pocket wilderness" that, in spite of its small size, holds many scenic and recreational attractions. Despite all of these attractions, this trail receives little use.

Most of western Montana's big game species are found in this area, and if you're alert, you'll have a chance of seeing them. Although grizzlies are gone from the Bitterroots, a good population of black bears remains.

From the trailhead follow Ward Creek Trail 262 along Ward Creek as it enters a beautiful, fern-bottomed cedar grove with some cedars over 6 feet across at the base—and a few monarchs close to 10 feet in diameter. This stretch of trail is like

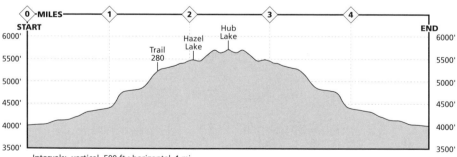

Intervals: vertical, 500 ft.; horizontal, 1 mi.

Giant western red cedars along the trail to Hub Lake.

walking among the "old wise ones" and a glimpse of what much of western Montana used to be like before the logging age.

Soon after leaving the grove, the trail overlooks Dipper Falls, a pleasant spot for a break. The first part of the trail is mostly flat, but the grade kicks up slightly as you approach the lakes. Allow an extra half hour for grazing the abundant fields of huckleberries.

At 1.5 miles turn right (west) at the junction with Hub-Hazel Trail 280. The next mile of walking is steep, consuming most of the 1,500 feet of altitude gained in the hike to Hub Lake. Here the main diversion is picking huckleberries. About 2 miles from the trailhead, the trail passes Hazel Lake, which has pan-size cutthroat trout, but its shores are too steep and brushy for camping.

Hub Lake is only half a mile beyond Hazel Lake. The remains of an old prospector's cabin, now almost hidden in brush, lie between the trail and an abandoned mine that overlooks the upper end of the lake.

Hub Lake offers good fishing for easy-to-catch but small west slope cutthroat. The small lake sits in a picturesque subalpine setting.

Hub Lake

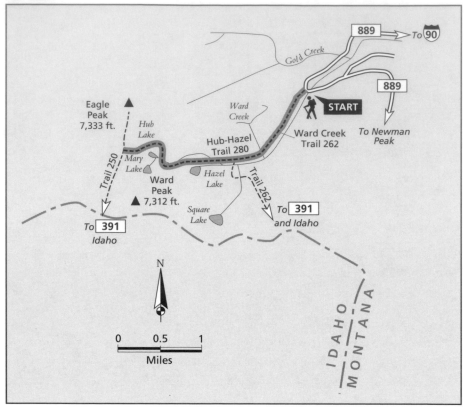

Side Trips

Hub Lake is also a good jumping-off place for day hikes to Ward or Eagle Peaks or fishing trips to Clear (small brook trout), Gold (rainbow trout), Square (brook trout), and Hazel (cutthroat trout) Lakes. You won't catch anything large, but you can definitely have fish for dinner. You'll want a USGS quad for the cross-country hiking needed to reach some of these lakes. Mary Lake, in the cirque below Ward Peak, has no fish, but it is a pleasant stop en route to Ward Peak. (Originally contributed by John Westenberg, rehiked by authors in 2001)

Key Points

- **0.0** Trailhead
- **1.5** Junction with Hub-Hazel Trail 280; turn right
- **2.0** Hazel Lake
- **2.5** Hub Lake
- **5.0** Trailhead

10 Bonanza Lakes

Description: An abundance of easily accessible subalpine country.

Start: 50 miles west of Missoula in the Bitterroot Mountains.

Type of hike: Day hike or overnighter; out-and-back.

Total distance: 5.6-mile round trip.

Difficulty: Easy.

Maps: Illinois Peak USGS Quad and Lolo National Forest Map (West Half).

Trail contacts: Superior Ranger Station, Lolo National Forest, 209 West Riverside, Superior, MT 59872; (406) 822-4233; www.fs.fed.us/r1/lolo.

Finding the trailhead: From Missoula take Interstate 90 west to Superior. Take exit 47 and turn left (south) under the freeway. Take another left (east) just beyond the underpass onto a paved county road. After 1.2 miles, turn right (south) onto Cedar Creek Road (Forest Road 320). Follow FR 320 for 24 miles of winding dirt road to the Bitterroot Divide (pavement ends after 2.4 miles) and the trailhead for Stateline National Scenic Trail, shortly after passing the Missoula Lake Campsite turnoff. The Stateline National Recreation Trail runs northwest and southeast from where Cedar Creek Road crosses the divide into Idaho. The parking area for this hike is on your left as you crest the divide. The trail starts on your right. This is the same parking area used for the Illinois Peak hike. It has ample parking. You'll find toilet and water at the nearby Missoula Lake Campground.

The Hike

Most Montanans think of the spectacular eastern front of the Selway-Bitterroot Wilderness when the Bitterroot Mountains are mentioned. However, from Lolo Pass north to Lookout Pass lies a section of the Bitterroots with a slightly different but equally appealing character. Although the northern Bitterroots are less craggy than their southern counterparts, they are heavily dotted with lakes. There are more than forty fishable lakes on the Montana side of the Bitterroot Divide, most within an easy walk from a trailhead.

From the trailhead take Stateline Trail 738 to the northwest, which takes off just to the Idaho side of the divide. Just after leaving the trailhead, Stateline Trail forks;

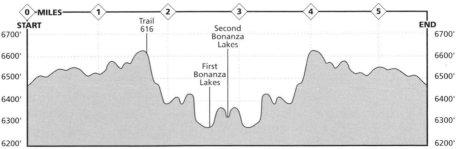

Fishing Bonanza Lakes.

stay right, continuing along the contour to the northwest (the Idaho side of the ridge). Stateline Trail forks again 1.5 miles beyond the trailhead. Take the right (northeast) fork and follow the Bonanza Gulch Trail 616 (no sign at this junction when I hiked this, but there was a large cairn) back across the divide into Montana and through a grassy basin for 1 mile to the first Bonanza Lake. The meadow before the lakes is awash with paintbrush and many other wildflowers. The second Bonanza Lake is about a quarter mile beyond the first. Both lakes have small brookies and several good camping spots.

Options

Back on the divide, Stateline Trail, which was designated a National Recreation Trail in 1981, continues northwest beyond Bonanza Lakes along the divide past Eagle Cliff. This makes an excellent shuttle hike if you leave another vehicle on Dry Creek Road 342 where it crosses the Bitterroot Divide. However, that involves a long dirt road shuttle and you may want to do an out-and-back instead. (Originally contributed by John Westenberg, rehiked by authors in 2001)

Bonanza Lakes

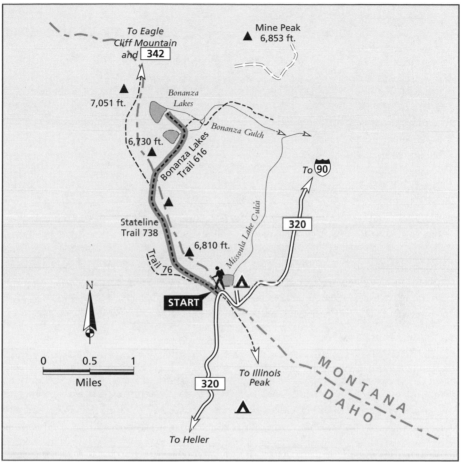

Key Points

0.0 Trailhead

1.5 Junction with Bonanza Gulch Trail 616; turn right

2.5 First Bonanza Lake

2.8 Second Bonanza Lake

5.6 Trailhead

11 Illinois Peak

Description: Spectacular—and seldom seen—mountain scenery.
Start: 45 miles west of Missoula in the Bitterroot Mountains.
Type of hike: Day hike; out-and-back.
Total distance: 10-mile round trip.
Difficulty: Moderate.

Maps: Illinois Peak and Hoodoo USGS Quads, and Lolo National Forest Map (West Half).
Trail contacts: Superior Ranger Station, Lolo National Forest, 209 West Riverside, Superior, MT 59872; (406) 822–4233; www.fs.fed.us/r1/lolo.

Finding the trailhead: From Missoula, take Interstate 90 west to Superior. Take exit 47 and turn left (south) under the freeway. Take another left (east) just beyond the underpass onto a paved county road. After 1.2 miles turn right (south) onto Cedar Creek Road (Forest Road 320). Follow FR 320 for 24 miles of winding dirt road to the Bitterroot Divide (pavement ends after 2.4 miles) and the trailhead for Stateline National Scenic Trail, shortly after passing the Missoula Lake Campsite turnoff. The Stateline National Recreation Trail runs northwest and southeast from where Cedar Creek Road crosses the divide into Idaho. This is the same trailhead used for the Bonanza Lakes hike. The ample parking area and the trailhead for this hike are on your left as you crest the divide. Toilet and water can be found at the nearby Missoula Lake Campground.

The Hike

Perhaps because the higher portions of the Bitterroot Mountains north of Lolo Pass aren't visible from a major highway, they remain relatively unknown. On a map they are easily overlooked and underrated. None of the peaks exceeds 8,000 feet, but because they are among the westernmost of Montana's mountain ranges, the Bitterroots receive an abundance of rain and snow. The result is an abundance of alpine scenery at lower elevations than in most mountain ranges. Many ridgeline trails are dry and parched, but this hike goes through a lush, green landscape.

At 7,690 feet, Illinois Peak is one of the highest peaks in the northern Bitterroots. The fairly easy walk to the top goes through subalpine country and offers many scenic views, as does the peak itself.

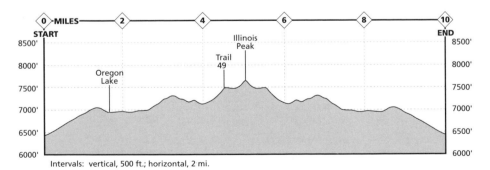

Intervals: vertical, 500 ft.; horizontal, 2 mi.

The Bitterroot Divide Trail (and Montana/Idaho border) on the way to Illinois Peak.

From the trailhead at the divide, take Stateline Trail 738, which heads southeast from the parking area on the south side of the road. The trail and the pass are dry, so bring plenty of water. The trail stays close to the divide all the way.

At 4.5 miles, watch carefully for the junction with St. Joe Trail 49. The sign is on your right and could be missed. Shortly after the junction with Trail 49, watch for Trail 169 going off to your left (east). There was no sign when we hiked this route. You don't want to miss it and end up on Hoodoo Pass.

Try to do this hike early in the morning. The first light of the day adds beauty to an already scenic landscape, and it will be cooler. Also, you can avoid afternoon thunderstorms, and you definitely don't want to be up here when the lightning starts flashing.

Illinois Peak, 1,200 feet higher than the trailhead, offers a good view of much of the proposed Great Burn Wilderness to the southeast. Illinois Peak's grassy top is a good place to sit back and enjoy lunch and soak in the scenery, especially the Mission Mountains, southern Bitterroot Mountains, and vast roadless areas in Idaho. You

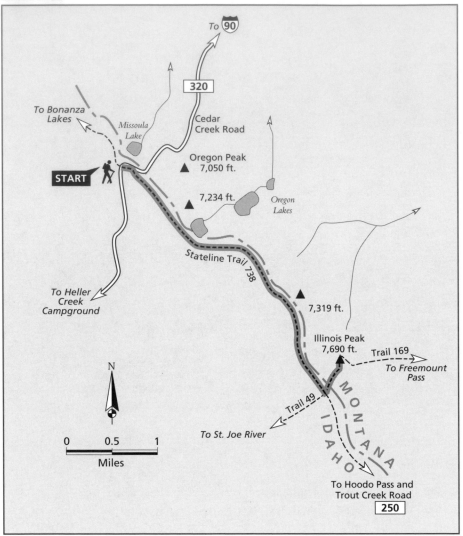

To ⑨0

320

To Bonanza
Lakes

*Missoula
Lake*

Cedar
Creek Road

Oregon Peak
▲ 7,050 ft.

START

7,234 ft.
▲

*Oregon
Lakes*

Stateline Trail 738

To Heller
Creek
Campground

7,319 ft.
▲

Illinois Peak
7,690 ft.

Trail 169
To Freemount
Pass

N

Trail 49

To St. Joe River

M O N T A N A
I D A H O

0   0.5   1

Miles

To Hoodo Pass and
Trout Creek Road
250

can also spend an hour or more reading all the messages left in the mountaintop registers.

Options

You can continue south on Stateline Trail 738 all the way to Hoodoo Pass, but it
requires a long shuttle on Trout Creek Road 250. In 1981 this trail was designated
a National Recreation Trail in recognition of its outstanding recreational qualities.
Therefore, no motorized vehicles are allowed on it. The route along the divide has

been used since aboriginal times, and the National Recreation Trail portion stretches 18.3 miles from near Eagle Cliff on the north to Hoodoo Pass on the south. (Originally contributed by John Westenberg, rehiked by authors in 2001)

Key Points

0.0 Trailhead
1.5 Oregon Lake overlook
4.5 Junction with St. Joe Trail 49; turn left
4.7 Junction with Trail 169; turn left
5.0 Illinois Peak
10.0 Trailhead

12 Heart Lake

Description: A subalpine lake basin with lots of trout in the lakes and huckleberries along the trail.
Start: 70 miles west of Missoula in the proposed Great Burn Wilderness.
Type of hike: Day hike; out-and-back.
Total distance: 4-mile round trip.

Difficulty: Easy.
Maps: Straight Peak USGS Quad and Lolo National Forest Map (West Half).
Trail contacts: Superior Ranger Station, Lolo National Forest, 209 West Riverside, Superior, MT 59872; (406) 822-4233; www.fs.fed.us/r1/lolo.

Finding the trailhead: Drive west from Missoula on Interstate 90 and turn south on Trout Creek Road 250 from Superior exit 47. The first 6 miles are a paved frontage road. After 20 miles the road makes a sharp switchback to the right. At this switchback Heart Lake Trail 171 leads off to your left (south). Parking is limited.

The Hike

The proposed Great Burn Wilderness sprawls for almost 40 miles along the Bitterroot Divide west of Missoula. This short hike is sure to tantalize you with the hiking possibilities in this 200,000-acre area, one of the wildest roadless areas in Montana.

From the trailhead Heart Lake Trail 171 climbs some 1,200 feet in 2 miles to the shore of Heart Lake, crossing the South Fork of Trout Creek several times—all on bridges except the last crossing just before the lake. This is a beautiful trail that goes through a lush, green forest all the way to the lake and climbs so gradually that it seems flat—with the exception of a little hill as you get close to the lake.

When you get to the stream crossing just before the lake, be careful you don't miss the trail sign pointing to the lake. It's immediately after crossing the stream. If you miss it, you'll head up toward the Bitterroot Divide and have to backtrack to find the lake. A hundred yards after you turn left (south) at this junction, you're at the lake.

In late August and early September, ripe huckleberries line the trail and make this trek memorable for its incredible edibles. Heart Lake has a good population of

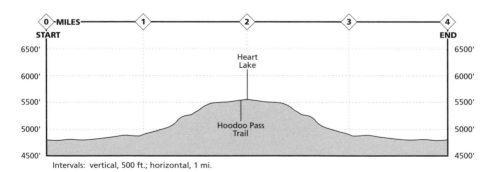

Intervals: vertical, 500 ft.; horizontal, 1 mi.

Heart Lake in the Bitterroot Mountains.

cutthroat and brook trout, and it makes a good turnaround point for day hikers. Late summer is the best time to take this hike—when the bugs are gone, the berries are ripe, and hunting season hasn't started.

Options

If you wish to explore farther, you have three options. Your first option is to follow Pearl Lake Trail 175 as it climbs higher up the lake basin (only 1 mile to the lake but on a very brushy trail), past Pearl Lake, and over a low pass to Dalton Lake. Pearl and Dalton Lakes support small cutthroat trout and have the advantage of being more remote (and less fished) than Heart Lake.

A second option is a steep trail that leads westward from Heart Lake to the Bitterroot Divide and the Idaho border, providing astounding views of vast roadless country in the forested mountains of Idaho. You can connect with either Illinois Peak (Hike 11) to the northwest or the Great Burn (Hike 13) to the southeast along

Heart Lake

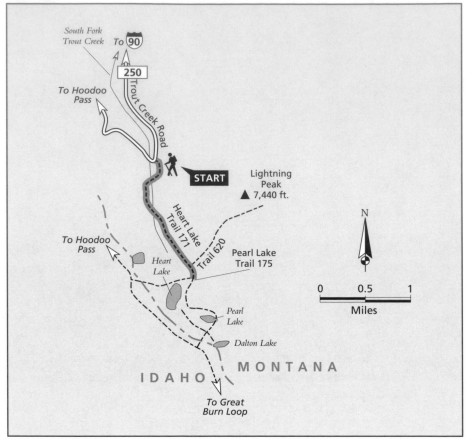

the divide. You can also come down off the divide to Pearl Lake and then back to Heart Lake to make a small loop.

A third option is Trail 620, unmarked and primitive, which leads to the 7,440-foot summit of Lightning Peak, just east of Heart Lake, and eventually drops down into Cement Gulch and returns to Trout Creek Road. However, most hikers will want to return to their vehicles by way of Heart Lake and skip this 8-mile-long side trip. (Originally contributed by Bill Cunningham, rehiked by authors in 2001)

Key Points

0.0 Trailhead

1.9 Junction with Hoodoo Pass Trail; turn left

2.0 Heart Lake

4.0 Trailhead

13 The Great Burn

Description: Beautiful subalpine country along the Bitterroot Divide through the heart of the proposed Great Burn Wilderness, including rare groves of giant cedars.
Start: 30 miles west of Missoula.
Type of trip: Extended backpacking trip; loop.
Total distance: 31.4 miles.

Difficulty: Strenuous.
Maps: Straight Peak USGS Quad and Lolo National Forest Map (West Half).
Trail contacts: Ninemile Ranger Station, Lolo National Forest, 20325 Remount Road, Huson, MT 59846; (406) 626-5201; www.fs.fed.us/r1/lolo.

Finding the trailhead: Drive west from Missoula on Interstate 90, turn south at Fish Creek exit 60 (before Tarkio), and get on the Fish Creek Road (Forest Road 343), which passes the largest ponderosa pine tree in the state. Turn left (south) after half a mile and then left (south) again at 1.9 miles where the pavement ends. Follow FR 343 a total of 10.1 miles from the interstate before going right (south) on FR 7750 and continuing for another 5.6 miles to Hole in the Wall Lodge. Go straight through the lodge (driving slowly) for another 1.2 miles to Clearwater Crossing Campground and the trailhead at the end of the road. The trail starts on your right just before the large parking area, which is set up for horse trailers. Toilet and water are available in the campground.

Recommended itinerary: For four nights out, consider this itinerary:
First night: Along the North Fork, 6–8 miles from trailhead
Second night: Goose Lake
Third night: Fish Lake
Fourth night: Halfway down the West Fork

The Hike

The Great Burn is a huge roadless area of almost 200,000 acres straddling the Idaho-Montana border due west of Missoula. This superb loop hike takes you through long, timbered valleys and along open subalpine country on the Bitterroot Divide. However, even this 31-mile hike touches only a small portion of the backcountry hiking in the Great Burn. This description goes counterclockwise up the North Fork of Fish Creek (Trail 103) and along the Bitterroot Divide (Stateline Trail 738), then returns to the trailhead via the West Fork of Fish Creek (Trail 101).

With all the forest fires of recent years, especially in the Bitterroots, it's hard to find a trail that doesn't go through a burned forest. Ironically, the Great Burn loop, named for the famous 1910 fire, has remained unburned.

From the trailhead take Trail 103 for the first 10 miles of the hike along the North Fork of Fish Creek as it curves north and then west up to the Bitterroot Divide. Go right after 1 mile at the first junction with the trail up Straight Creek. Continue about 4 more miles and then turn left at the next two junctions up St.

Hiking the Bitterroot Divide, sometimes called the Stateline Trail because it follows the Montana/Idaho border.

Pats and French Creeks. From the 5- to 7-mile mark, the trail passes through formerly private land next to the Greenwood Cabin. The area included patented mining claims dating back to early 1900. Prepare for wet crossings up Greenwood and French Creeks. Also prepare to see a few stands of mature western red cedars, always a rare treat, especially a big grove around French Creek. Seeing these great cedars exploding out of a lush carpet of ferns is worth the trip.

It's a steep and brushy 1,000-foot ascent out of the upper North Fork basin to a low pass on the state line. At 10.7 miles you reach Stateline Trail 738, where you turn left (south). Continuing south on Stateline Trail for half a mile, you descend into Idaho and Goose Lake. Fill with water here, since the trail stays high and dry for the next 9 miles. Goose Lake is in a big meadow and has lots of campsites, but like the rest of this loop, it's heavily used by stock parties.

From the low point on the pass near Goose Lake (5,840 feet in elevation), Stateline Trail rolls up and down over the minor summits of the northern Bitterroot Range, eventually reaching a high point of 7,334 feet. Some of the short pitches on the divide can really stretch out your calves and get your heart rate up. The trail crosses broad meadows and knife-edged ridges as it follows the crest of the divide

The Great Burn

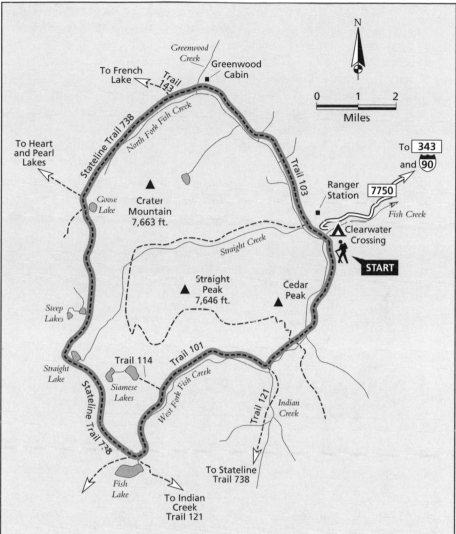

To French Lake

Greenwood Creek

Greenwood Cabin

Trail 143

Stateline Trail 738

North Fork Fish Creek

To Heart and Pearl Lakes

Goose Lake

Crater Mountain 7,663 ft.

Ranger Station

To 343 and 90

7750

Fish Creek

Trail 103

Clearwater Crossing

START

Straight Creek

Straight Peak 7,646 ft.

Cedar Peak

Steep Lakes

Straight Lake

Trail 114

Trail 101

Siamese Lakes

West Fork Fish Creek

Stateline Trail 738

Trail 121

Indian Creek

To Stateline Trail 738

Fish Lake

To Indian Creek Trail 121

N

0   1   2
Miles

south to Fish Lake. Above Straight Lake the trail goes through two small burns, both fairly old, that give the landscape an aura of mystery as you pass through groves of ghost trees.

Here you're in the center of the proposed Great Burn Wilderness with great views in every direction. On clear days the tops of the Mission Mountains appear far to the east; the crumpled ranges of the huge Bighorn–Weitas roadless country stretch off to the west in Idaho. Wildflowers are spectacular early in the summer, and ghostly snags remind the hiker of the Great Burn that swept through this country in August 1910.

At 17.5 miles, you'll see a spur trail heading steeply down to Upper Siamese Lake. Continue on Stateline Trail unless you're camping here or have time for a side trip to catch a few cutthroats.

After about 20 miles of hiking, you reach the junction with Trail 101, which heads northward up the West Fork of Fish Creek.

From the junction of Stateline Trail 738 and Trail 101, it's about 11 miles down to Clearwater Crossing and your vehicle. The central portion of this stretch is quite boggy and might slow your progress. Trail 101 also passes through groves of old western red cedar, western larch, and big lodgepole pine, which make this valley hiking more pleasant.

The Bitterroot Divide gets more snow than most parts of Montana, so do not attempt this loop before early July. It might be worth your while to check on snow conditions with the Forest Service before you try an early July hike in a heavy snow year. Being wet country, bugs can be a problem, so bring something to keep them at bay. When we did this trip, several of the junctions were unsigned, so be alert not to miss them. The signs that are there don't have mileages, which add to the special wildness of the Great Burn.

Options

This route could be done in reverse with about the same level of difficulty. Also, you can skip Fish Lake and take the unmaintained social trail down and around Siamese Lakes and then take Trail 114 down to Trail 101. (Originally contributed by Ed Madej, rehiked by authors in 2002)

Key Points

0.0 Trailhead

1.0 Junction with Straight Creek Trail; turn right

4.0 Greenwood Cabin and junction with St. Pats Trail 176; turn left

5.0 Junction with French Creek Trail 143; turn left

10.7 Bitterroot Divide and junction with Stateline Trail 738; turn left

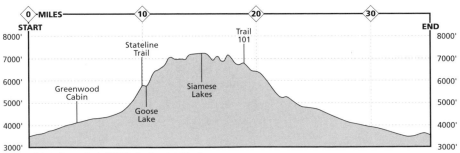

Intervals: vertical, 1000 ft.; horizontal, 10 mi.

Upper Siamese Lake along the Bitterroot Divide.

11.2 Goose Lake and junction with Gooco Creek Trail 414; turn left

17.5 Spur trail to Siamese Lakes

20.2 Junction with Trail 101; turn left

21.7 Junction with Siamese Lakes Trail 114; turn right

26.2 Junction with Indian Creek Trail 121; turn left

26.3 Junction with Trail 104; turn left

28.0 Bridge over West Fork and junction with Trail 110; turn left

31.4 Trailhead

14 Stuart Peak

Description: Vistas of at least four mountain ranges from the summit of Stuart Peak.
Start: Just north of Missoula in the Rattlesnake National Recreation Area and Wilderness.
Type of hike: Two- or three-night backpacking trip; out-and-back; well suited for a base camp.
Total distance: 18-mile round trip.

Difficulty: Strenuous.
Maps: Northeast Missoula and Stuart Peak USGS Quads, and Rattlesnake National Recreation Area and Wilderness Map.
Trail contacts: Missoula Ranger Station, Lolo National Forest, Fort Missoula Building. 24-A, Missoula, MT 59804; (406) 329-3814; www.fs.fed.us/r1/lolo.

Finding the trailhead: Drive north on Van Buren Street from the Van Buren Interstate 90 interchange, bearing to the right until you find yourself on Rattlesnake Drive. Turn left onto the Sawmill Gulch Road (about a half mile beyond Wildcat Road and 4 miles total from the interchange). The parking area and entrance to the upper Rattlesnake area are located at the mouth of Sawmill Gulch, just a few yards beyond the bridge over Rattlesnake Creek. The parking lot has a toilet and an information board with a map of the area but no water unless you want to filter out of Rattlesnake Creek.

The Hike

Probably no other city has such a spectacular yet accessible wild area as Missoula with its backyard paradise, the 61,000-acre Rattlesnake National Recreation Area and Wilderness. This hike will take you into some of the alpine lake country around Stuart Peak.

The recreation area is open to mountain biking, so hikers can see how non-problematic it can be to share the trails with these recreationists. Multiuse trails can work well as long as all recreation is nonmotorized, and here is a great example of it. Local mountain bikers in cooperation with the Forest Service have developed a code of riding ethics and posted it at the trailhead and put up several RIDE FRIENDLY signs at key trail junctions.

The heavy use of this giant urban playground has made some special regulations necessary. Depending on the time of year, dogs are either prohibited or must be on a leash for the first part of the trail, and shooting, camping, and campfires are prohibited. No motor vehicles are allowed. At the end of the "three-mile zone," these restrictions are lifted. You can pick up a brochure at the information board, which has a map of part of the trail system and summarizes the regulations.

Beginning backpackers like the Rattlesnake because they feel comfortingly close to civilization throughout the trip. And indeed, from time to time en route, one is within sight—and sometimes even the sound—of Missoula. The route is physically challenging for first-timers, however. It's a long, uphill grind (9 miles total) to the lake basin beyond Stuart Peak, which is really the only good place to camp on this route.

Twin Lakes from the Stuart Peak overlook.

Start the hike on the old road (FR 99) heading up Rattlesnake Creek at the far end of the parking area by the information board. Stay on the road for a half mile before turning left (northwest) on Stuart Peak Trail 517. You can continue up the road for another half mile and take the Spring Gulch Trail, which stays on the east side of Spring Gulch, but it might be better to save this for the return trip.

The first 2 miles up the bottom of Spring Gulch are quite easy. The route goes past the sites of homesteads established a century or more ago, though all that remain are traces of foundations and hearths, a few persistent lilac bushes and apple trees, and two alien Lombardy poplars. Spring Gulch is a popular descent for mountain bikers, so keep your head up and yield for safety. At 2 miles, the trail from the east side of the creek crosses a bridge and joins the Stuart Peak Trail. There's a toilet just across the bridge, but that's about the last sign that you're in a heavily used, semideveloped area. From this point on, the trail steadily climbs up to the shoulder of Stuart Peak. You'll see two or three unmarked junctions, but stay on the main trail as it continues north. At 3 miles you reach the top of Sawmill Gulch, where the "three-mile zone" restrictions end. At 3.5 miles turn right (north) where the Curry Gulch Trail rejoins.

After the gradual climb to the top of Spring Gulch, the Stuart Peak Trail winds relentlessly upward for another 5 miles to an overlook on the flanks of Stuart Peak.

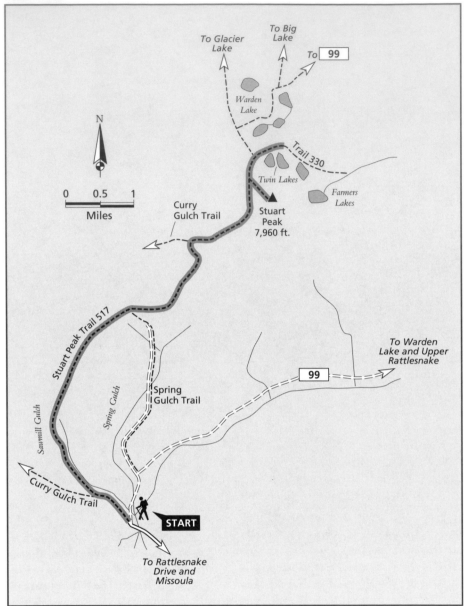

Take lots of water because on a dry year you won't find any along the trail. At about 5.5 miles, the trail goes through a series of long, annoyingly flat switchbacks, which probably adds a mile to the length of the trip. At 7 miles, you leave the National Recreation Area and enter the Rattlesnake Wilderness. All this means is no more mountain bikes; otherwise, you won't notice the difference. The trail is in as good a shape as a trail can be and is nicely suited for trail running.

When you get to the overlook into Twin Lakes at 8.3 miles, you can take a half-mile spur trail to your right to the top of 7,960-foot Stuart Peak. Stuart Peak may not get you too far from the sights and sounds of the city, but it's not easy to get there, and you find solitude despite the urban proximity.

After passing the overlook, go about another quarter mile and then you reach the junction with Trail 330, where you turn right (north) and descend for about a half mile to Twin Lakes. Much of the Rattlesnake high country remains without trails or served by only the faintest tracks. Despite the Rattlesnake's popularity, secluded, almost undiscovered basins and lakes dot its far reaches. Set up a base camp at Twin Lakes or one of the nearby lakes and enjoy this site for a day or two.

Twin Lakes are fishless, but Farmers Lakes support populations of cutthroat trout, as do most nearby lakes (McKinley, Warden, Carter, Big, and Sheridan). You might also pick up a few rainbows in some of them. The lake basin, beyond the Trail 517/330 junction, is closed to stock parties.

Proximity to Missoula results in high use of much of the area. This location—plus the fragile nature of the high country itself and the area's status as Missoula's municipal watershed—demands that you take every precaution to leave zero impact of your visit. Evidence of high-country campsites is proliferating. Make every effort to pass lightly over this fragile terrain; don't add to the blight of fire rings; and take a few minutes to help repair the damage made by others.

Options

On the way back, cross Spring Gulch and take the eastside trail back to the trailhead. It will probably be late afternoon, and you'll find a bit more shade here.

You also have the option of making a big loop out of this trip by taking either Trail 534 or 502 down to the trail down Rattlesnake Creek, which merges with FR 99 and goes back to the trailhead. Most of this route is still open to mountain bikers, and if you take it, expect to see more people, because this is the main thoroughfare of the Rattlesnake National Recreation Area.

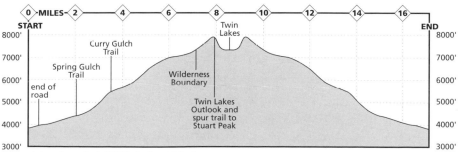

Intervals: vertical, 1000 ft.; horizontal, 2 mi.

Side Trips

The must-do side trip is the top of Stuart Peak, where you get a fantastic vista of the entire area. After that's done, take your choice from the many lakes and mountaintops to explore. (Originally contributed by Joseph A. Mussulman and Bill Brown, rehiked by authors in 2003)

Key Points

- **0.0** Trailhead
- **0.5** Spring Gulch Trail 517; turn left
- **1.1** Junction with Curry Gulch Trail; turn right
- **2.0** Junction with Spring Gulch Trail from east side of stream; turn left
- **3.0** Top of Sawmill Gulch and end of special restrictions
- **3.5** Junction with Curry Gulch Trail; turn right
- **7.0** Wilderness boundary
- **8.3** Overlook into Twin Lakes and spur trail to Stuart Peak
- **8.6** Junction with Trail 330; turn right
- **9.0** Twin Lakes
- **18.0** Trailhead

THE VIEW FROM HERE: SWITCHBACKING GONE AMOK

Who doesn't like switchbacks, those zigs and zags that make the hills easier? Nobody. Everybody likes them, including yours truly. But as often happens, we sometimes carry a good thing too far.

Lately, during trail reconstruction, land managers have started to put in what I'll call "mall walk" switchbacks, the nearly level and looonnnng variety that can not only transform a 2-mile Category 1 hill into an easy walk but also turn it into a 4-mile hike. I much prefer to turn it into a 2.5-mile or even a 3-mile hill and get to camp sooner so I can spend more time fishing, day hiking, or taking a nap.

People who go hiking expect to have hills, so it's not necessary to make these switchbacks so easy. A few good examples of this are Upsidedown Creek coming out of the Lake Plateau, Stuart Peak, Louise Lake, and the Hidden Lake Trail coming out of the Edith-Baldy Basin.

These mall walk switchbacks are not only unnecessary, but they actually create environmental damage by disturbing a much bigger area during construction and by seducing some hikers into switchback cutting because they can save so much time, probably causing as many or more erosion problems than the original trail did.

Let's get back to sensible zigs and zags with water bars that get us up a hill without a heart attack but don't deface the entire mountainside—and get us to our destination an hour sooner.

15 Boulder Lake

Description: A nice hike to a high mountain lake away from the heavily used lower Rattlesnake.
Start: North of Missoula in the upper Rattlesnake National Recreation Area.
Type of hike: Day hike or overnighter; out-and-back.
Total distance: 10-mile round trip.

Difficulty: Moderate.
Maps: Gold Creek Peak and Wapiti Lake USGS Quad and Rattlesnake National Recreation Area and Wilderness Map.
Trail contacts: Missoula Ranger Station, Lolo National Forest, Fort Missoula Building 24-A, Missoula, MT 59804; (406) 329-3814; www.fs.fed.us/r1/lolo.

Finding the trailhead: Drive north of Bonner (east of Missoula) on Montana Highway 200 along the Blackfoot River. Turn left (northwest) and continue on the Gold Creek Road (Forest Road 126) for 6 miles. (This is private land, so be courteous of commercial logging operations.) Then turn left (west) on FR 2103. Follow FR 2103 for 5 miles until it forks. Take the left (west) fork on FR 4323 as it switchbacks up the left side of the valley before dropping to the valley floor and ascending the north side of the valley to the West Fork of Gold Creek Trailhead, 16 miles total from the highway. Limited parking is available along the road; be careful not to block it.

The Hike

In 1980 Congress established the Rattlesnake National Recreation Area and Wilderness to provide a place where water, wilderness, wildlife, and recreational and educational values are preserved. Boulder Lake offers all. This hike presents a stark contrast between land preserved as wilderness and land open to timber cutting. All along the 16-mile gravel road to the trailhead and along the first 1.5 miles of the hike, you go through an endless ocean of clear-cuts before escaping into the solitude of the Rattlesnake Wilderness.

From the trailhead Trail 333 heads north for 2.5 miles on relatively flat terrain with two creek crossings. This area is partially private land, so be respectful. Watch for trail markers and cairns while crossing a logged area. The trail follows a logging road for about 100 yards before turning right. A cairn marks the turnoff.

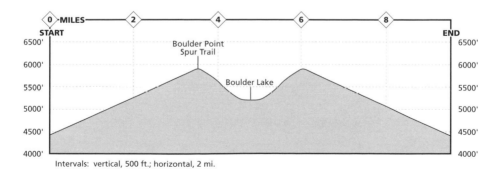

Intervals: vertical, 500 ft.; horizontal, 2 mi.

The old Boulder Point Lookout above Boulder Lake, claimed by a forest fire in 2002.

At 1.5 miles is the junction with Trail 518 from Gold Creek; take a sharp left, heading west. At the junction there is a small creek, and filtering water at this point is a good idea. Past the junction the trail climbs gradually for 2.5 miles before you get to the junction with Trail 533. Turn right (northwest) and descend another mile on steep trail into Boulder Lake. At 3.5 miles, turn left (west) at junction with spur trail to Boulder Point. Save this side trip for your return.

Boulder Lake is the largest lake with fish in the Rattlesnake Wilderness. Some of the campsites are showing serious signs of overuse, so leave zero impact of your visit.

Side Trips

Before descending to the lake, a spur trail veers right to Boulder Point. An old fire lookout was still standing at the top when we were there in 2002. The panoramic view of the lake and Mission Mountains to the north is well worth the short walk to the point. Regrettably, a forest fire claimed the lookout in 2003, but the view is still there. (Hiked by authors in 1993 and 2002)

Boulder Lake

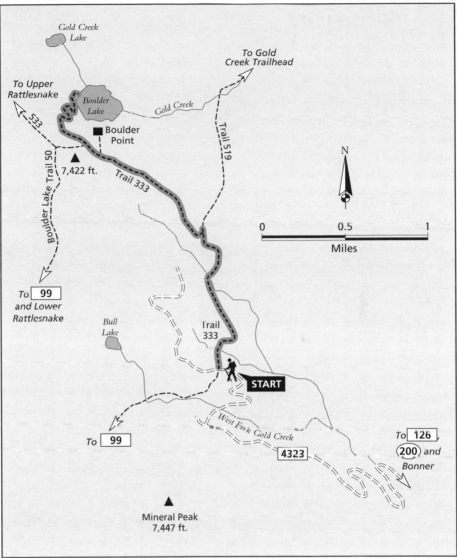

Key Points

0.0 Trailhead

1.5 Junction with Trail 518 from Gold Creek; turn left

3.3 Junction with spur trail to Boulder Point; turn left

4.0 Junction with Trail 533; turn right

5.0 Boulder Lake

10.0 Trailhead

16 Welcome Creek

Description: An accessible, pleasant hike in one of Montana's smallest wilderness areas, the Welcome Creek Wilderness.
Start: 25 miles southeast of Missoula in the Sapphire Mountains.
Type of hike: Day hike or overnighter; out-and-back.
Total distance: Up to 10-mile round trip.

Difficulty: Moderate.
Maps: Cleveland Mountain and Grizzly Point USGS Quads, and Lolo National Forest Map.
Trail contacts: Missoula Ranger Station, Lolo National Forest, Fort Missoula Building 24-A, Missoula, MT 59804; (406) 329-3814; www.fs.fed.us/r1/lolo.

Finding the trailhead: Drive east from Missoula for 25 miles on Interstate 90 and turn right (south) at Rock Creek exit 126. Go south on the Rock Creek Road 102 for 14 miles (11.5 paved) and watch for a sign on your right (west) marking Welcome Creek Trail 225. You'll find famous fishing in Rock Creek and ample parking. Vehicle camping and water are available at nearby Welcome Creek and Dalles campgrounds. There's a toilet at the trailhead.

The Hike

Besides offering scenic, timbered hiking trails, the Welcome Creek Wilderness has a rich history. Mined extensively around the turn of the twentieth century, the area has many haunting reminders, now abandoned and decaying into the landscape, to greet you.

From the trailhead, Welcome Creek Trail 225 crosses Rock Creek on a suspension bridge. Then veer right, following the creek downstream for about a quarter mile before turning, crossing Welcome Creek on a bridge and turning west. From here follow the stream until you feel like camping or turning around. Trail 225 continues 5 miles to the low summit of Cleveland Mountain. The trail is rocky (not for trail running), and the grade is so gradual that you don't realize you're climbing.

This valley is steep and narrow. It has a mystery and loneliness of its own as you walk by old mining sites and note how the forest is gradually reclaiming them.

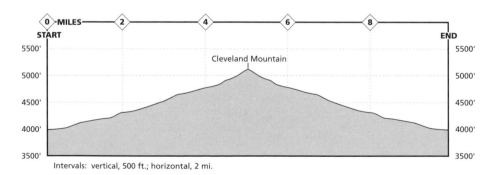

Intervals: vertical, 500 ft.; horizontal, 2 mi.

The classic suspension bridge over Rock Creek at the beginning of the Welcome Creek hike.

This is a wet area with a beautiful old-growth forest and a lush understory (including, regrettably, a good crop of nettles), so wait until July for hiking. If you go earlier, expect a boggy trail and mosquitoes out in force. Drinking water poses no problem, however, as water is everywhere. Although Welcome Creek has small brook trout, the fishing there takes a backseat to the famous Rock Creek running past the trailhead.

Although some people who oppose wilderness designation for Welcome Creek claimed the area had too many signs of civilization to qualify for wilderness, the reverse is true. Man's hold on the area has long faded into history. Now, the ghosts of old-timers (such as outlaw Frank Brady, who was shot in 1904 in Welcome Creek) only enrich the wilderness experience. The area also provides an excellent example of how quickly nature heals the wounds of past carelessness. (Originally contributed by Don Berg, rehiked by authors in 2003)

Welcome Creek

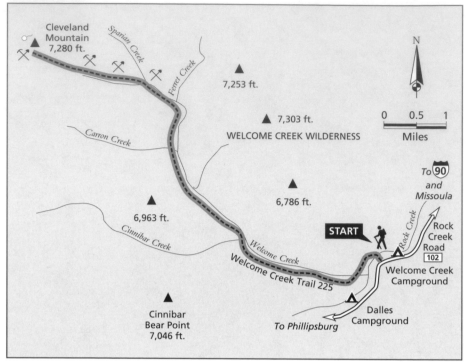

Key Points

0.0 Trailhead

5.0 Cleveland Mountain

10.0 Trailhead

17 Pyramid Lake

Description: A way to explore several high mountain lakes and the surrounding peaks.
Start: 10 miles northeast of Seeley Lake.
Type of hike: Day hike or overnighter, out-and-back.
Total distance: 12-mile round trip.
Difficulty: Moderate.

Maps: Morrell Lake and Crimson Peak USGS Quads, and Lolo National Forest Map.
Trail contacts: Seeley Lake Ranger District, Lolo National Forest, 3583 Highway 83, Seeley Lake, MT 59868; (406) 677-2233; www.fs.fed.us/r1/lolo.

Finding the trailhead: From Seeley Lake turn east on Cottonwood Creek Road 477 on the north edge of town. After 1.2 miles turn left (northeast) on the Morrell Creek Road 4353. After driving 7.1 miles from Seeley Lake, turn right (east) on Pyramid Pass Road 4381 and follow it to the large trailhead where it ends. The sign in Seeley Lake says it's 9 miles to the trailhead, but it was 10.4 on our odometer. The large trailhead is set up for horse trailers, and it has ample parking and toilet.

The Hike

This trail, Trail 416, is one of the major entry points to the Bob Marshall Wilderness, so it gets heavy horse traffic. There are no boggy areas, though, so the trail is in great shape all the way. For the first mile, you're on an old logging road converted to a trail. After that it's mostly a gradual climb, broken up by a few switchbacks, that doesn't seem as steep as it actually is.

About a quarter mile below the Pyramid Pass, at mile 4.7, you'll see an unnamed lake on your left. After you go over the low-profile pass, turn left (northeast) at the junction with Trail 278. Shortly thereafter, turn left on the spur trail to Pyramid Lake. If you aren't alert you can miss this spur trail and keep heading into the depths of the Bob. This isn't an official Forest Service trail, and it wasn't marked when I hiked this route. Watch for it directly after crossing the first stream after coming over the pass. You can't see the lake from here even though it's only about a quarter mile farther.

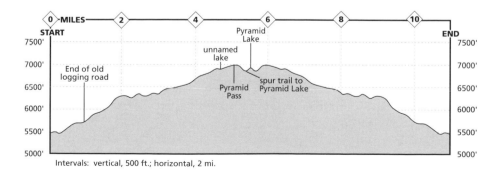

Intervals: vertical, 500 ft.; horizontal, 2 mi.

Pyramid Lake on the edge of the Bob Marshall Wilderness.

Pyramid Lake is big, round, and filled with cutthroats. Mighty Pyramid Peak looms over the lake to the west to provide a scenic backdrop.

Side Trips

If you're energetic, try the scramble up to Pyramid Peak. It's not dangerous and mostly through open country, but it's quite strenuous. (Hiked by authors in 2002)

Key Points

0.0 Trailhead

1.0 End of old logging road

4.7 Unnamed lake

5.0 Pyramid Pass and wilderness boundary

5.5 Junction with Trail 278; turn left

Pyramid Lake

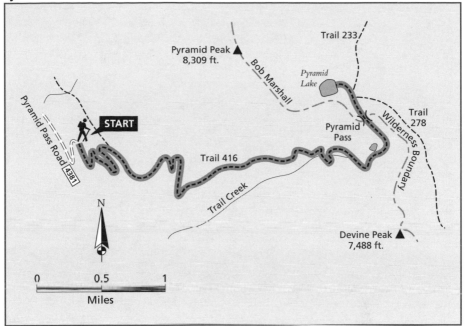

5.6 Junction with spur trail to Pyramid Lake; turn left

6.0 Pyramid Lake

12.0 Trailhead

Bitterroot National Forest

18 Peterson Lake

Description: A way to explore several high mountain lakes with views of Sweeney Canyon and the surrounding peaks.
Start: 8 miles west of Florence in the Bitter-root Mountains.
Type of hike: Day hike or overnighter; out-and-back.
Total distance: 10-mile round trip.

Difficulty: Moderate.
Maps: Carlton Lakes, Dick Creek, and St. Mary's Peak USGS Quads; and Selway-Bitterroot Wilderness Map.
Trail contacts: Stevensville Ranger Station, Bitterroot National Forest, 88 Main, Stevensville, MT 59870; (406) 777-5461; www.fs.fed.us/r1/bitterroot.

Finding the trailhead: Drive south of Missoula on U.S. Highway 93, 1.5 miles south of Florence. Turn right, heading west on Sweeney Creek Road (Forest Road 14), a paved road, which veers to the left 0.9 miles later. Stay right on unpaved FR 1315, turn right 0.4 miles (1.3 miles from US 93) later, and drive for 6.4 miles to the trailhead (7.7 miles from US 93). The Sweeney Creek Road climbs steeply from the valley floor, and the last section of switchbacks on FR 1315 might stretch the limits of a low-clearance two-wheel-drive vehicle. Parking is limited, so squeeze in to avoid taking two spaces. There's no room for horse trailers to turn around.

The Hike

This hike is close to the Missoula area, so you might see a few other hikers on busy summer weekends. However, the hike is pleasant and an excellent overnight trip to absorb the joys of ancient trees and mountain lakes. Duffy, Holloway, and Peterson Lakes all have fish. At Peterson Lake, however, there isn't much room for a back cast except at the inlet.

From the trailhead Trail 393 climbs steadily west along Sweeny Ridge for 2 miles before reaching a natural spring. Be sure to carry enough water for the climb. Along the way you may want to note the girth of some of the remaining Douglas fir and ponderosa pine trees; some are 4 feet in diameter. In addition, midway to the spring, there is a large rock overlook perfect for pictures. If you use the right angle, it will look as if you were atop a mountain above the Bitterroots. From this overlook and a few more along the way, you get a great view of the upper Sweeny Creek Valley and Pyramid Butte.

From the spring the trail levels off and then over the next 2 miles gradually descends before it drops steeply for the last mile into the lake. The trail is in great shape all the way but rocky enough to make it marginal for trail running. A spur trail takes you to the inlet of the lake where you'll find a few heavily used campsites. Avoid creating new impacts by using existing campsites. Bring the bug dope and head net; Peterson Lake has more than its share of mosquitoes.

Peterson Lake and Pyramid Butte in the Bitterroot Mountains. ▶

Peterson Lake

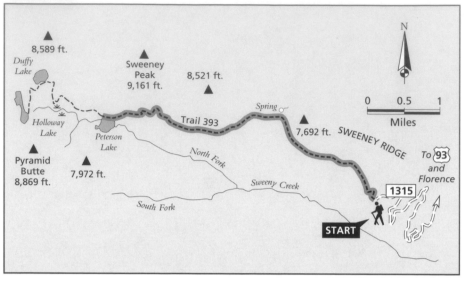

Side Trips

If you feel ambitious, continue on to Duffy and Holloway Lakes. Duffy is another 2 miles of climbing on a much rougher and less maintained trail. The farther from civilization you travel, the less wary fish get. (Hiked by authors in 2003)

Key Points

0.0 Trailhead

2.0 Spring

2.5 Wilderness boundary

5.0 Peterson Lake

10.0 Trailhead

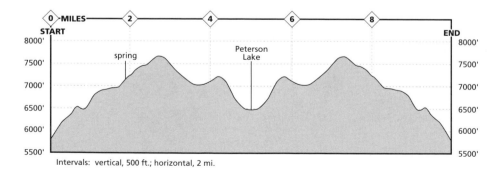

19 Blodgett Canyon

Description: Spectacular scenery and good rock climbing.
Start: 5 miles northwest of Hamilton in the Bitterroot Mountains.
Type of hike: Day hike or backpacking trip; out-and-back.
Total distance: Up to 25-mile round trip.

Difficulty: Easy (short day hikes) to moderate (long day hikes or backpacking trips).
Maps: Printz Ridge USGS Quad and Selway-Bitterroot Wilderness Map.
Trail contacts: Stevensville Ranger Station, Bitterroot National Forest, 88 Main, Stevensville, MT 59870; (406) 777-5461; www.fs.fed.us/r1/bitterroot.

Finding the trailhead: Take U.S. Highway 93 south from Missoula through the Bitterroot Valley for 41 miles and turn right (west) onto Bowman Road (2 miles north of Hamilton just before US 93 crosses the Bitterroot River). Follow this road west for 0.6 mile and then turn left (south) onto Richetts Road and continue for 2 miles. At a stop sign at Geer Road, go straight (west) on Forest Road 736 for 2.4 miles (pavement ends after 0.6 miles) to the intersection of the Blodgett Canyon Road. Turn right (north) here and drive 1.5 miles until the road dead-ends at the trailhead. You'll find vehicle camping, ample parking, and a toilet at Blodgett Campground at the trailhead.

The Hike

There's a tendency to think that hiking is something you do to get somewhere. In Blodgett Canyon no object is necessary beyond the hike itself. Just a hundred yards from the vehicle, you will be walking along a beautiful stream and looking up at spectacular canyon walls.

These basic scenic ingredients continue throughout the hike. Because there is no need to get to any particular point, a hike up Blodgett Canyon is ideal for families and anyone who enjoys unhurried walking with lots of pleasant stops.

Blodgett Canyon is the most spectacular of the many canyons penetrating the eastern front of the Selway–Bitterroot Wilderness. The vertical relief from canyon

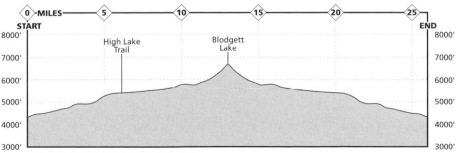

Intervals: vertical, 1000 ft.; horizontal, 5 mi.

Blodgett Canyon in the Bitterroot National Forest. FOREST SERVICE PHOTO

bottom to ridgetop is nearly 4,000 feet. Blodgett Creek itself, like all the streams in the Bitterroots, is clear and cold. It also has good fishing for pan-size rainbow trout. However, consider catch-and-release practices for the lower, heavily fished section of Blodgett Creek. The trail, which is never steep for extended periods, generally goes through pleasant forest environment, sometimes crosses talus slopes, and is always close to Blodgett Creek. Sheer granite faces of 500 to 600 feet are common on the north side of the canyon, and there are several waterfalls between 3 and 6 miles into the hike.

Because the trail stays low, it is passable earlier than many hikes. Chances of seeing wildlife increase farther up the canyon. Moose, elk, and deer are found in Blodgett Canyon, and mountain goats range the ridgetop. If you are willing to tackle the steep 1,400-foot climb up to High Lake on the south rim of the canyon, you have a good chance of seeing mountain goats. At 6 miles turn left (west) onto High Lake Trail 303 to make that trek. The trail to High Lake is not maintained and can be hard to follow.

Blodgett Canyon

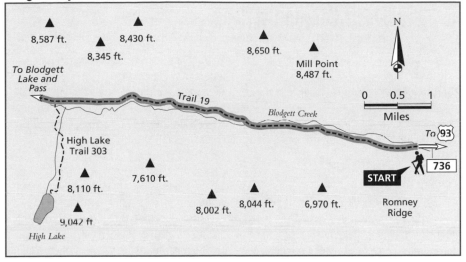

Although you can hike a full 12.5 miles up the canyon to Blodgett Lake, most hikers take shorter day or overnight hikes into the area. Go until you feel like stopping and either pick a campsite (use zero-impact methods if you have a fire) or turn back to the trailhead.

Although Blodgett Canyon is surrounded by the Selway-Bitterroot Wilderness, only the upper portion (7 miles from the trailhead) is part of it. When the Selway-Bitterroot Wilderness was set aside in 1939, most of Blodgett Canyon was excluded because it was considered a possible site for a dam and reservoir for Bitterroot Valley water users. Lower Blodgett Canyon was included in the proposed 1988 wilderness bill vetoed by President Reagan. (Originally contributed by John Westenberg, rehiked by authors in 1998)

Key Points

0.0 Trailhead

3.6 Waterfall

6.0 High Lake Trail 303; turn left

12.5 Blodgett Lake

25.0 Trailhead

20 Blodgett Canyon Overlook

Description: New trail with interpretive stations.
Start: 5 miles northwest of Hamilton in the Bitterroot Mountains.
Type of hike: Day hike; out-and-back.
Total distance: 3-mile round trip.
Difficulty: Easy.

Maps: Printz Ridge USGS Quad and Selway-Bitterroot Wilderness Map.
Trail contacts: Darby Ranger Station, Bitterroot National Forest, 7612 North Main, Darby, MT 59870; (406) 821–3913; www.fs.fed.us/r1/bitterroot.

Finding the trailhead: Take U.S. Highway 93 south from Missoula through the Bitterroot Valley for 41 miles and turn right (west) onto Bowman Road (2 miles north of Hamilton just before US 93 crosses the Bitterroot River). Follow this road west for 0.6 mile, turn left (south) onto Richetts Road, and continue for 2 miles. At a stop sign at Geer Road, go straight (west) on Forest Road 736 for 2.4 miles (pavement ends after 0.6 mile) to the intersection of the Blodgett Canyon Road. Turn left (west) here on FR 735 and drive 3 miles until the road dead-ends at the trailhead. You'll find vehicle camping, ample parking, and a toilet at Blodgett Campground at the trailhead.

The Hike

This trail was constructed after the dramatic Bitterroot fires of 2000. In addition to offering up the best possible view of fabulous Blodgett Canyon, it also gives you a good education on the dynamics of forest fires. The Forest Service has put up six interpretive stations keyed to a free brochure you can pick up at the trailhead. The brochure tells about the different types of forest fires, the impacts on plants and wildlife, and how people can help reduce the impact of fires. Along the trail you can clearly see how nature is reclaiming the landscape after the fire came through.

The Blodgett Canyon Overlook trail gradually switchbacks up from the Canyon Lake Trailhead to the ridge overlooking Blodgett Canyon, the next valley to the north. On top be sure to watch children and pets carefully, because the overlook is on the edge of a steep cliff.

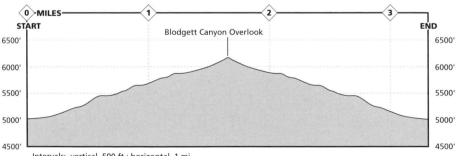

Intervals: vertical, 500 ft.; horizontal, 1 mi.

Blodgett Canyon Overlook

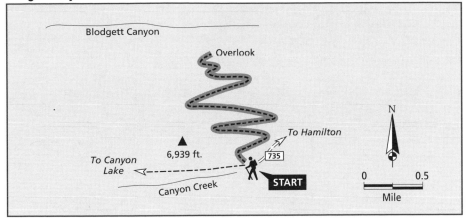

This could be a half-mile steep climb, but the switchbacks make it an easy, 1.5-mile ascent suitable for any hiker. If you get tired along the way, the Forest Service has installed benches where you can rest, enjoy the view, and think about the ecology of forest fires. (Hiked by authors in 2003)

Key Points

0.0   Trailhead
1.5   Blodgett Canyon Overlook
3.0   Trailhead

21 Canyon Lake

Description: One of the most scenic mountain lakes in the Bitterroot Range.
Start: 7 miles west of Hamilton in the Selway-Bitterroot Wilderness.
Type of hike: Day hike or overnighter; out-and-back.
Total distance: 11-mile round trip.

Difficulty: Strenuous.
Maps: Printz Ridge and Ward Mountain USGS Quads, and Selway-Bitterroot Wilderness Map.
Trail contacts: Darby Ranger Station, Bitterroot National Forest, 7612 North Main, Darby, MT 59870; (406) 821-3913; www.fs.fed.us/r1/bitterroot.

Finding the trailhead: Take U.S. Highway 93 south from Missoula through the Bitterroot Valley for 41 miles and turn right (west) onto Bowman Road (2 miles north of Hamilton just before US 93 crosses the Bitterroot River). Follow this road west for 0.6 mile, turn left (south) onto Richetts Road, and continue for 2 miles. At a stop sign at Geer Road, go straight (west) on Forest Road 736 for 2.4 miles (pavement ends after 0.6 mile) to the intersection of the Blodgett Canyon Road. Turn left (west) on FR 735 here and drive 3 miles until the road dead-ends at the trailhead. Parking is available for about a dozen vehicles.

The Hike

Canyon Creek drains one of the smaller canyons penetrating the east side of the Bitterroots, but what it lacks in size, it makes up for in scenic beauty. This is one of the smaller gems in the vast Selway-Bitterroot Wilderness. The 2000 fires spared this valley with the exception of a short stretch of burned forest about a mile from the trailhead.

From the trailhead Trail 525 stays to the northern side of the creek, avoiding stream crossings, and ascends gradually through a mature, unburned forest for about 4 miles. Along the trail on the first two-thirds of the hike, you might want to harvest some huckleberries, because you'll need the energy for the last one-third of the trip. At 4 miles the trail turns steeply uphill, climbing about 1,200 feet over the next mile, a Category 1 hill—and on a very rough trail. About a half mile before the lake,

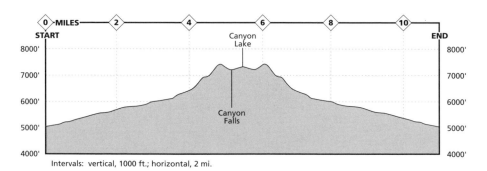

Intervals: vertical, 1000 ft.; horizontal, 2 mi.

Canyon Lake in the Bitterroot Mountains.

you crest the ridge and go down into the lake. Just before the lake, you can see Canyon Falls, which is actually a series of cataracts with a total drop of 200 feet, off to your left.

If you're out for more than a strenuous day hike, you can camp at Canyon Lake, which has been made larger by an artificially created rock-and-wood dam. You'll find a few campsites at the lower end of the lake. The lake supports enough cutthroat trout to keep anglers happy.

Side Trips

From Canyon Lake it's a short climb up the canyon to Wyant Lake. If you're interested in a little mountaineering, you can go beyond Wyant Lake and climb Canyon Peak (9,153 feet) via its rocky southern ridge. (Originally contributed by Don Reed, rehiked by authors in 2003)

Canyon Lake

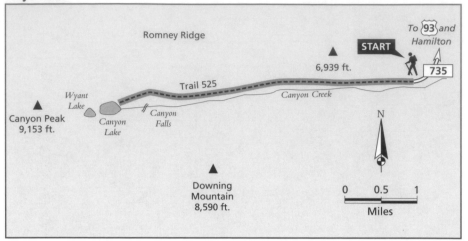

Key Points

0.0 Trailhead

5.0 Canyon Falls

5.5 Canyon Lake

11.0 Trailhead

22 Trapper Peak

Description: At 10,157 feet, the highest peak in the Selway-Bitterroot Wilderness.
Start: South of Darby in the Bitterroot Range.
Type of hike: Day hike; out-and-back.
Total distance: 12-mile round trip.
Difficulty: Strenuous.

Maps: Trapper Peak and Boulder Peak USGS Quads, and Selway-Bitterroot Wilderness Map.
Trail contacts: Darby Ranger Station, Bitterroot National Forest, 7612 North Main, Darby, MT 59870; (406) 821–3913; www.fs.fed.us/r1/bitterroot.

Finding the trailhead: Drive south of Darby on U.S. Highway 93 for 5 miles. Just before crossing the Bitterroot River, turn right onto the West Fork of the Bitterroot Road (Forest Road 473). Head southwest on FR 473 for 9 miles, and then turn west on FR 5630A. Follow FR 5630A for 7 miles of dirt road switchbacks to the trailhead. Parking is limited; be careful not to block the road.

The Hike

Until July, snow covers much of the trail. The almost 4,000 feet of elevation gain in 6 miles makes this hike hard but exciting because of the destination. From the top of Trapper Peak, the world falls away into endless cascades of rocky ridges.

Trail 133 climbs abruptly from the parking lot, along the ridge above Boulder Creek to the south. The first part of the hike involves two steep climbs with a flat spot in between. The break is enough to lower your heartbeat a little. At early rest stops, take the extra time to walk the 20 feet to the edge of the ridge for a taste of the view from the top. The Boulder Creek Valley was formed by glaciation, creating a long, narrow, ice-gouged trough common to the eastern slope of the Bitterroots.

After the steep ascent in the first 2 miles, the trail climbs gradually. A little less than halfway up is a small spring to the right of the trail. The gurgling water is audible from the trail, and a small path veers off to the right. This is a good spot to replenish water bottles.

After the spring, the trail climbs steadily up and out of the trees. The view opens up to a world of ice-sculptured granite peaks and high-altitude weather patterns.

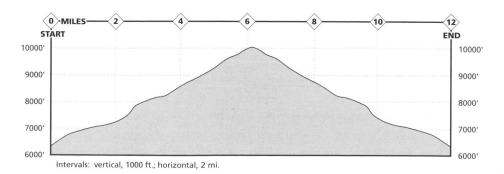

Intervals: vertical, 1000 ft.; horizontal, 2 mi.

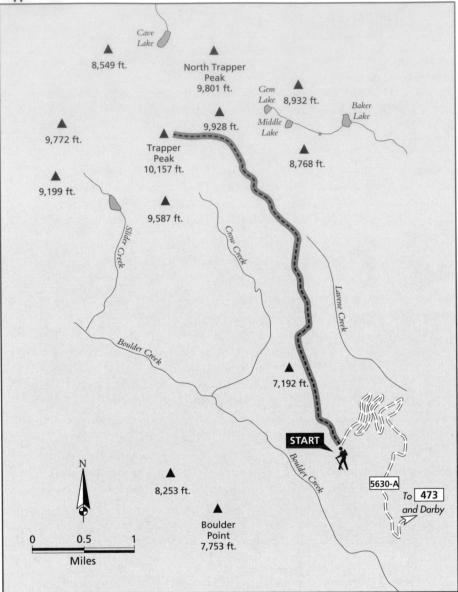

Cave
Lake

▲
8,549 ft.

▲
North Trapper
Peak
9,801 ft.

Gem
Lake ▲
8,932 ft.

Baker
Lake

▲
9,772 ft.

▲
9,928 ft.

Middle
Lake

Trapper
Peak
10,157 ft.

▲
8,768 ft.

▲
9,199 ft.

▲
9,587 ft.

Slider Creek

Crow Creek

Lavene Creek

Boulder Creek

▲
7,192 ft.

START

Boulder Creek

5630-A

To 473
and Darby

N

▲
8,253 ft.

▲
Boulder
Point
7,753 ft.

0   0.5   1

Miles

Montana is known for unpredictable weather, and at 10,000 feet, it can snow in July.

Once out in the open, it is necessary to follow the cairns that mark the trail. Often the trail is hard to follow on the exposed rock. The route traverses the south face of Trapper Peak, angling toward the summit.

From the top, look for the sharp glaciated ridgelines and peaks of the Selway-Bitterroot Wilderness. More than 500,000 acres of this 1.3 million–acre wilderness are located in the Bitterroot National Forest. Unprotected areas such as parts of Trapper Creek to the north warrant future Wilderness designation. The hike out can be hard on the knees. (Hiked by authors in 1998)

Key Points

0.0 Trailhead
6.0 Trapper Peak
12.0 Trailhead

23 Tin Cup Lake

Description: A large, trout-filled subalpine lake deep in the Selway-Bitterroot Wilderness.
Start: 7 miles west of Hamilton in the high peaks of the southern Bitterroot Range.
Type of hike: A two- or three-day backpacking trip; out-and-back.
Total distance: 20-mile round trip.
Difficulty: Strenuous.

Maps: Como Peaks, Trapper Peak, and Tin Cup Lake USGS Quads; and Selway-Bitterroot Wilderness Map.
Trail contacts: Darby Ranger Station, Bitterroot National Forest, 7612 North Main, Darby, MT 59870; (406) 821-3913; www.fs.fed.us/r1/bitterroot.

Finding the trailhead: On the south edge of Darby, turn west on the Tin Cup Road (Forest Road 639). After about 3.4 miles (pavement ends at 2.4 miles), turn left (south) on FR 639A as FR 639B continues straight. The trailhead is on the right (west) just after crossing Tin Cup Creek, 0.1 mile after turning on FR 639A. Park in the large parking area on your left across from the trailhead.

The Hike

The jagged peaks of this portion of the Bitterroots are the highest mountains in the entire range, which stretches more than 300 miles along Montana's western border. This hike will take you in to see some of the more interesting peaks of the Selway–Bitterroot Wilderness, such as El Capitan, the Lonesome Bachelor, and the Como Peaks.

From the trailhead, follow Tin Cup Trail 96 as it travels through dense timber in the lower reaches of the canyon, crossing Tin Cup Creek three times. Sorry, no bridges. These crossings can be tricky early in the summer and after heavy rains, so it is best to wait and attempt this trek after the middle of July. At the first crossing a log across the stream might tempt you, and if you can't resist, crawl or sit on it instead of trying to walk it. Keeping your feet dry isn't worth a dangerous straddle over such a log.

The trail follows beautiful Tin Cup Creek, a large mountain stream, all the way to the lake. The grade kicks up a bit in the last 2 miles, but most of the route is a very gradual ascent. There are no steep sections, and you hardly notice the elevation gain. It's a long day with an overnight pack, though, so start early. The trail is in great shape and stays in the shady, unburned forest for the entire 10 miles.

You can choose from several campsites at the lower end of this large lake, which is filled with hungry cutthroat trout.

Side Trips

About 6 miles from the trailhead and just before reaching the Kerlee drainage, you can leave the main trail and bushwhack up to Kerlee and Goat Lakes. You might be

Tin Cup Lake, worth the long hike.

able to find a primitive social trail, but don't bank on it. For this side trip, you'll need a topo map, compass, and route-finding skills. Kerlee Lake has great scenery, with views of the high, rocky peaks to the north of the lake.

If you're ambitious, you can attempt to scramble to the summit of massive El Capitan, 2 miles to the northwest. Climb the hillsides to the northwest of Kerlee Lake, making sure to stay low enough to avoid the vertical rock walls on the southern slopes of the Lonesome Bachelor. After reaching a low pass between the Bachelor and El Capitan, cautiously follow the eastern ridge to the windswept summit, 9,983 feet high. Here are stupendous views of the Como Peaks, the Lonesome Bachelor, and the lakes in the Little Rock Creek drainage below. To the west lie the forested ridges of the vast Selway-Bitterroot Wilderness and the canyons of the wild Selway River. To the south is a sawtooth ridge with granite towers separating the valley of Tin Cup Creek from the North Fork of Trapper Creek. Few views of the Bitterroots are better than from the summit of El Capitan.

Technical rock climbers will find challenging routes on the many faces of El Capitan, the Lonesome Bachelor, and Como Peaks. If you are not trained in rock climbing, you should avoid the more difficult mountains in the area and limit yourself to the eastern slope of El Capitan. This trip makes a superb three-day or longer

Tin Cup Lake

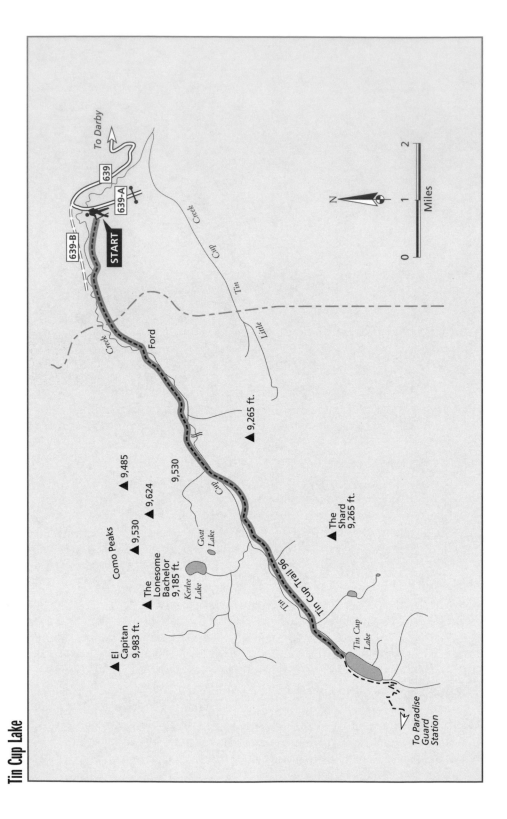

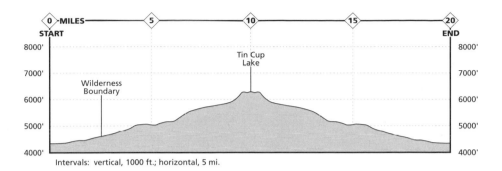

Intervals: vertical, 1000 ft.; horizontal, 5 mi.

introduction to the high country of the Selway-Bitterroot. (Originally contributed by Don Reed, rehiked by authors in 2003)

Key Points

0.0 Trailhead

2.5 Wilderness boundary

3.0 First stream crossing

5.5 Second stream crossing

8.0 Third stream crossing

10.0 Tin Cup Lake

20.0 Trailhead

24 Overwhich Falls

Description: 200-foot Overwhich Falls.
Start: 8 miles southwest of Sula or about 80 miles south of Missoula.
Type of hike: Long day hike or overnighter; shuttle.
Total distance: 17 miles.
Difficulty: Moderate.

Maps: Medicine Hot Springs and Piquett Mountains USGS Quads, and Bitterroot National Forest Map.
Trail contacts: Sula Ranger Station, Bitterroot National Forest, 7338 Highway 93 South, Sula, MT 59871; (406) 821-3201; www.fs.fed.us/r1/bitterroot.

Finding the trailhead: Drive south of Missoula on U.S. Highway 93 for about 80 miles to the Indian Trees Campground (4 miles south of the Sula Ranger Station). As you enter the campground area, turn left onto Forest Road 729 and follow it about 0.8 mile to the junction with FR 8112. Take FR 8112 to the spur road signed Porcupine Saddle Trail and follow it to the trailhead parking lot. Roads may be bumpy. (You can also start this hike from FR 5734 near Saddle Mountain, reached via Lost Trail Pass.)

Leave a vehicle or have somebody pick you up at the Crazy Creek Campground. To find this campground drive 2.8 miles north of Sula on US 93 (or 15 miles south of Darby) to Medicine Springs Road 5728, which turns directly across from Spring Gulch Campground. Turn left, heading southwest, and follow FR 370 past Warm Springs Campground for 4.1 miles to Crazy Creek Campground (first mile paved). You'll find ample parking and nearby vehicle campgrounds with toilet and water at both trailheads.

The Hike

Since there isn't a steep climb—as is the case with most long hikes—the Overwhich Falls trip is suitable for all hikers. Most hikers are interested in a leisurely hike and take at least two days, but ambitious hikers could hike this in one day and enjoy a scenic trek that's downhill most of the way.

From the trailhead take Porcupine Saddle Trail 196, which leads through lodgepole pine forest for 0.8 mile, to the junction with Warm Springs Ridge Trail 177. Turn left, heading south on Warm Springs Ridge Trail, which merges with Shields Creek Trail 673 at mile 2.8. Then, after descending into the Shields Creek Valley, the trail joins Coulter Creek Trail 606 from the southeast. Stay right on Shields Creek Trail for another 2.5 miles downstream to Overwhich Falls.

All of these trails are generally well maintained, and most junctions are well marked. Although not abundant, drinking water is usually available.

The highlight of the trip is of course 200-foot Overwhich Falls, which can be viewed from the trail. For a closer look, drop your pack and bushwhack a short way to the creek below the falls.

Shortly after passing the falls, reach the junction with Trails 103 and 248/400. You can take a short side trip up Trail 400 to Pass and Capri Lakes. Although both lakes have a few cutthroat trout, fishing is considered marginal, as it is in the streams

Overwhich Falls

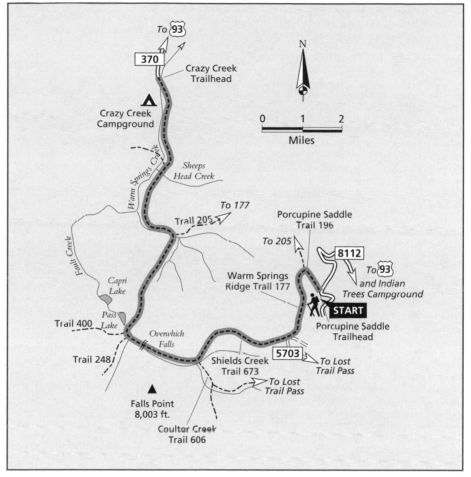

along the way, with the possible exception of Warm Springs Creek, which can be good. The area is noted for its large, productive huckleberry patches, so consider substituting berry picking for fishing.

From the junction of Shields Creek Trail and Trails 103 and 248/400, turn north on Trail 103 and stay on it all the way to Crazy Creek Campground (about 9 miles). Trail 103 follows streams most of the way, but since the lower portions are grazed by domestic cattle, you should be sure to treat water before drinking. (Originally contributed by Wayne Avants)

Key Points

0.0 Porcupine Saddle Trail trailhead

0.8 Junction with Warm Springs Ridge Trail 177; turn left

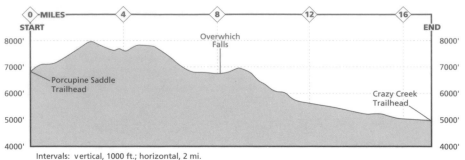

Intervals: vertical, 1000 ft.; horizontal, 2 mi.

2.8 Junction with Shields Creek Trail 673; turn right

5.25 Junction with Coulter Creek Trail 606; turn right

8.0 Overwhich Falls, junction with Trail 103; turn right

11.5 Three Forks Junction Trail 205; turn left

17.0 Crazy Creek Campground trailhead

25 Blue Joint

Description: Remote wilderness meadows, mountains, and wild country seldom seen.
Location: 35 miles southwest of Hamilton on the Idaho-Montana border.
Type of hike: Three- or four-day backpacking trip; loop.
Total distance: 36-mile round trip.
Difficulty: Strenuous.

Maps: Blue Joint, Painted Rocks Lake NW, and Nez Perce Peak USGS Quads; and Bitterroot National Forest Map. Also useful is the Forest Service's River of No Return Wilderness Map.
Trail contacts: West Fork Ranger Station, Bitterroot National Forest, 6735 West Fork Road, Darby, MT 59829; (406) 821-3269.

Finding the trailhead: Drive south from Darby on U.S. Highway 93 for 5 miles. Just before you cross the Bitterroot River, turn right onto the West Fork of the Bitterroot Road (Forest Road 473). Follow FR 473 southwest for 18 miles until you see the Forest Service's West Fork Ranger Station. Go past the ranger station, and after half a mile, turn right, heading west on Nez Perce Road (FR 468); drive 16 miles to Nez Perce Pass. At the pass, turn left and park in the ample parking lot, where the trail starts. There's also a toilet.

The Hike

This is a 36-mile loop starting and ending at Nez Perce Pass Trailhead. It can be taken in either direction, but it's easier to take the Stateline Trail 16 first and then come back to the trailhead by hiking down Blue Joint Creek Trail 614 and back up to the pass via Jack the Ripper Trail 137.

From the trailhead, start hiking on Stateline Trail 16 to the south. After 0.3 mile, stay right (south), continuing south past Castle Rock Trail 627. Jack the Ripper Trail 137 down Jack the Ripper Creek takes off to the left about a mile from the trailhead. This trail will bring you back to your vehicle three days later.

Except for a small creek at about 5 miles and Two Buck Springs at about 11 miles from the trailhead, there is no water until you reach Reynolds Lake. So carry full water bottles and fill them again at Two Buck Springs (farther from the ridge than shown on map), a good place to spend the first night. The entire Stateline (or Divide) Trail is in great shape, either flat or with a few short hills. It goes through the mature forests of the Frank Church River of No Return Wilderness but doesn't offer many vistas along the way. This is subalpine country, featuring whitebark pine and lots of standing snags.

Unless you stop at the stream at about 5 miles or can make it to Two Buck Springs, the first night out could be a dry campsite, so be prepared for this possibility. It's about 9 miles from Two Buck Springs to Reynolds Lake, a good choice for the second night out. At 9 miles turn left (south) at the junction with Trail 8 to Hell's Half Acre. Don't miss the trail 167 junction just before Reynolds Lake. It occurs in a small, grassy valley with water. Take the left-hand trail to the lake. Reynolds Lake has fishing for cutthroat trout to add to the evening's entertainment.

After leaving Reynolds Lake, continue on Trail 158 for about 2 miles to the junction with Blue Joint Creek Trail 614. A primitive road (FR 044) leads to this trail junction, and it's possible to leave a vehicle here to make this a point-to-point hike. However, it would be a loss to miss Blue Joint Creek. The Blue Joint Creek Trail winds through a wide valley with grassy meadows and a meandering Blue Joint Creek. The stream has good fishing for small cutthroat. Blue Joint Meadows, a good choice for the third night out, is about 7 miles from Reynolds Lake.

Jack the Ripper Trail 137 takes off about 4 miles from Blue Joint Meadows. Watch carefully for this junction. It juts off to the left just after a creek crossing. It's easy to see, and it might not have a sign. Jack the Ripper Trail gradually climbs along troutless Jack the Ripper Creek for about 3 miles through small but gorgeous meadows. The last half mile is steep as you approach the ridgeline. Then, retrace your footsteps from three days earlier for about a mile, turning right onto Stateline Trail 16 and then right onto Castle Rock Trail 627, to reach the trailhead and your vehicle, leaving some of Montana's most spectacular, yet gentle backcountry behind you.

Although you won't see grizzly bears (unfortunately) on this hike, black bears are common. Be careful with your food and keep a clean camp. The area also has most other wildlife associated with western Montana, including mountain lions, mountain goats, elk, deer, and moose. Mosquitoes usually are not a big problem after June. You will want to wait until at least July anyway to let the snow melt.

The 61,400-acre Blue Joint Wilderness Study Area is actually a portion of the immense Frank Church River of No Return Wilderness country that extends across the Idaho border into Montana. The 2.2 million-acre area is the largest designated Wilderness in the lower forty-eight states, and Blue Joint would make a fine addition to this spectacular area. (Originally contributed by Bob Oset, partially rehiked by authors in 2003)

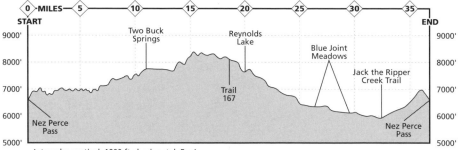

Intervals: vertical, 1000 ft.; horizontal, 5 mi.

Blue Joint

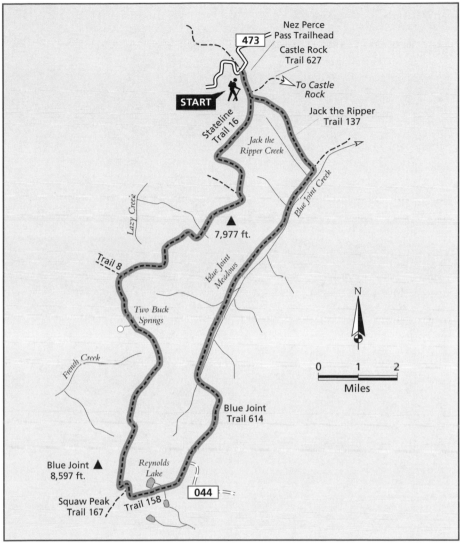

Key Points

0.0 Nez Perce Pass Trailhead

0.3 Junction with Castle Rock Trail 627; stay right

1.0 Junction with Jack the Ripper Trail 137; stay right

5.0 Creek

9.0 Junction with Trail 8 to Hell's Half Acre Spring; turn left

11.0 Two Buck Springs

18.0 Squaw Peak Trail 167; turn left

20.0 Reynolds Lake

22.0 Forest Road 044 and Blue Joint Creek Trail 614; turn left

27.0 Blue Joint Meadows

32.0 Junction with Jack the Ripper Trail 137; turn left

35.0 Junction with Stateline Trail 16; turn right

35.7 Junction with Castle Rock Trail 627; turn right

36.0 Nez Perce Pass Trailhead

Flathead
National Forest

26 Thoma Lookout

Description: A climb in the North Fork of the Flathead River wildlands, with panoramic views of the Kintla Massif in Glacier National Park.
Start: 40 miles north of Columbia Falls.
Type of Hike: Day hike; out-and-back with shuttle option.
Total distance: 6-mile round trip.

Difficulty: Moderate.
Maps: Mount Hefty USGS Quad and Flathead National Forest Map (north half).
Trail contacts: Glacier View Ranger District, Flathead National Forest, P.O. Box 190340, 8975 Highway 2 East, Hungry Horse, MT 59919; (406) 387-3800; www.fs.fed.us/r1/flathead.

Finding the trailhead: Drive north of the Nucleus Avenue/U.S. Highway 2 junction in Columbia Falls on Outside North Fork Road for 49.5 miles (paved to the Glacier Rim access and partially paved before the Polebridge turnoff) past the Ford River access and turn left, heading west on Trail Creek Road 114. Follow this dirt road for 3.3 miles past the old Mount Hefty Trailhead (shuttle option). After another 1.5 miles, the road forks. Follow FR 114A to the right (may not be passable with a two-wheel-drive vehicle) for another 3 miles to where the road dead-ends past an unmaintained jeep trail and a sharp curve. Parking is minimal, and there's no toilet or water.

The Hike

The hardest part of this hike is the long, long dirt road drive to the trailhead, which likely makes this a lesser-used trail. Thoma Lookout lies in an area between Trail Creek Road and the Canadian border, west of the North Fork Flathead Road and east of the Whitefish Range. The period of time this trail is passable is determined by the amount of last winter's snowfall, but hikers should wait at least until July. The trail is not heavily used at any time, although hunters use it in the fall. Grizzly bears frequent the area but have not been a problem to day hikers. This part of the North Fork of the Flathead is reported to have one of the densest grizzly concentrations in the state, so you would be wise to keep alert along the trail. Deer and elk are also present, but probably not as conspicuous as the wilderness traveler would like.

Thoma–Colts Creek Trail 18 begins as an old logging road past the trailhead gate and winds gradually uphill past an old harvest area. The road may have some downfall on it and is slightly clogged with alder growth, but it's easy to follow. After about half a mile, a cairn indicates a trail junction, and a well-maintained trail is visible descending down and to the right. Take this trail as it climbs gently up Colts Creek, which should have water even in September of a dry year.

The route up Colts Creek passes through a cool spruce forest and steepens as you get closer to the top of the ridge. At about 2 miles, turn right (south) at the

Thoma Lookout.

junction with Mount Hefty Trail 15. Past the junction, the trail switchbacks a couple times and then summits the ridge for incredible views of Glacier National Park and beyond. A forest of limber pine and subalpine larch highlights this huckleberry-covered ridge.

After about a mile from the junction and a slight descent is the Thoma Lookout. The sweep and magnitude of the view is magnificent. East are the mountains of Glacier; west is the Whitefish Range; but to the north, the view is blocked by the bulk of Mount Hefty. The view is both grandly aesthetic and educational.

Options

After visiting the lookout, you have several options. If you left a vehicle at the old Thoma Lookout–Hefty Trailhead, you can continue down to it on Trail 15. However, most people would not want to drive two vehicles this far on dirt roads for a day hike, so I suggest you instead climb Mount Hefty. Retrace your steps back to the junction with the Thoma–Colts Creek Trail, but instead of heading back down, follow a primitive trail north up Mount Hefty. The "trail" up Mount Hefty is more of an off-trail route at times, but as long as you keep going up and are careful about your return, you should not get off track. Nonetheless, frequently and carefully check your map. (Originally contributed by Jack Johns, rehiked by authors in 1998)

Thoma Lookout

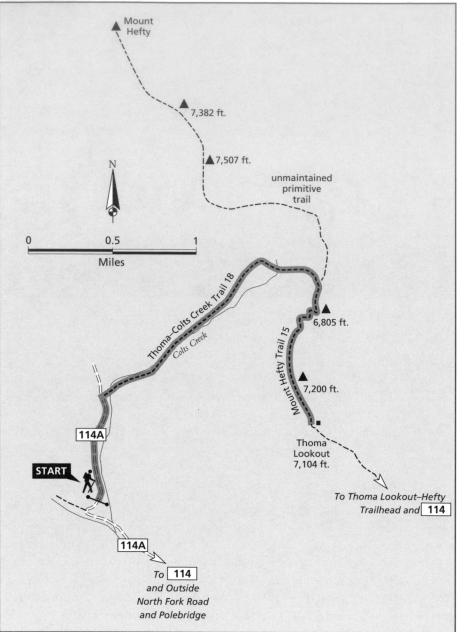

Mount
Hefty

▲ 7,382 ft.

▲ 7,507 ft.

unmaintained
primitive
trail

N

0   0.5   1
Miles

Thoma–Colts Creek Trail 18

Colts Creek

Mount Hefty Trail 15

▲ 6,805 ft.

▲ 7,200 ft.

Thoma
Lookout
7,104 ft.

To Thoma Lookout–Hefty
Trailhead and 114

114A

START

114A

To 114
and Outside
North Fork Road
and Polebridge

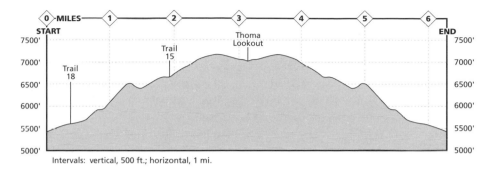

Intervals: vertical, 500 ft.; horizontal, 1 mi.

Key Points

0.0   Trailhead

0.5   Thoma–Colts Creek Trail 18 leaves logging road

2.0   Junction with Mount Hefty Trail 15; turn right

3.0   Thoma Lookout

6.0   Trailhead

27 Great Northern

Description: A mountain ascent through timbered undergrowth and up scree slopes for scramblers with good stamina, with goat trails, fine scenery, Stanton Glacier, and spectacular views of southern Glacier National Park.

Start: 30 miles east of Kalispell in the Great Bear Wilderness.

Type of hike: Off-trail day hike; out-and-back.

Total distance: Roughly 8-mile round trip.

Difficulty: Very strenuous. For experienced and well-conditioned hikers only.

Maps: Mount Grant USGS Quad, Flathead National Forest Map, and Bob Marshall, Great Bear, and Scapegoat Wilderness Complex Map.

Trail contacts: Hungry Horse Ranger District, Flathead National Forest, P.O. Box 190340, 8975 Highway 2 East, Hungry Horse, MT 59919; (406) 387-3800; www.fs.fed.us/ r1/flathead.

Finding the trailhead: From Columbia Falls, drive east on U.S. Highway 2 through Hungry Horse. Turn right 0.9 mile past Hungry Horse, heading south on East Side Hungry Horse Reservoir Road. Drive south through Martin City until 8.7 miles past the Emery Bay turnoff, then turn left, heading east on Forest Road 1048 for half a mile to a parking area before the bridge over Hungry Horse Creek. You'll find ample parking, and there's filterable water in Hungry Horse Creek, but no toilet.

The Hike

Although named for a former railroad, the name of the mountain suggests exactly what it is. Its graceful curves and broad faces are irresistible to the individual who has acquired a taste for high places. Even with the incomparable peaks of Glacier Park nearby, this mountain attracts many individuals solely on the merits of its own beauty. This is a difficult off-trail route suitable only for well-conditioned and experienced hikers.

Remember to stock up on water before the climb. You may find water in Dudley Creek Basin before the last climb, but don't count on it.

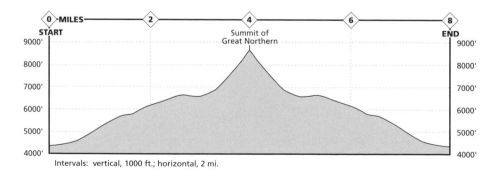

Great Northern.

Look south of the bridge over Hungry Horse Creek and notice the impenetrable thickets of brush and small trees. After briefly considering whether the whole idea is worthwhile, charge into these thickets. They don't last long and are the hardest part of the climb. Climb the ascending ridge on the southern side of Hungry Horse Creek. Pick your way straight up the hill, following game trails to help escape this jungle. Initially, work to the south, climbing and contouring to get out of the brush and windfalls on the northern side of the ridge. In early August try not to delay too long in the massive huckleberry patches.

After a very steep mile, top out on the ridge, where a faint trail develops. Follow this ridge for another mile to where it peaks out at timberline. From a knob, just before dropping into Dudley Bowl, you get a view of marshy meadows, a small timbered saddle, and Great Northern.

From here you have a choice of two routes. Note the rocky, open spur ascending to the right of the bowl along a ridgeline directly to the peak. Save this route for the descent. It's loose scree, and with great care and concentration, you can make a fast descent. Now note another ascending spur to the left (north) of the main peak, with clumps of gnarled trees reaching almost to the summit ridge.

After deciding to follow the left route up, you may want to consider a trip down into the bowl to filter water. When we did this hike in September of a dry year, there was still water in the creek.

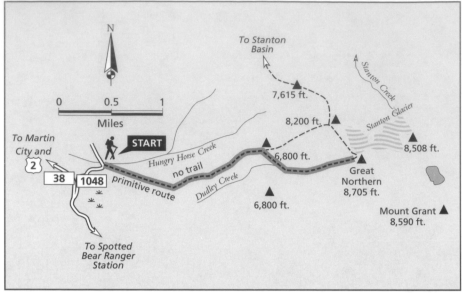

After getting water, head up and into the trees along the left (northern ridge) to the top of the ridge. The going is steep and involves some nontechnical rock climbing. Once on top of the ridge, pick up a trail from the Stanton Lake basin and follow cairns south along the face toward the summit. Remember, if you have a choice, stay high rather than low; the final rock face is easiest at the top of the ridge and gets steeper down the face.

By now you have noticed 120-acre Stanton Glacier, which reaches all the way to the summit ridge on the eastern side. Although much receded in recent years, Stanton Glacier still has hard, slippery ice and deep crevasses, so stay off it unless you're properly equipped.

To the east is the Middle Fork of the Flathead River and across it the usually unseen array of peaks of southern Glacier Park. One unusually monstrous-looking peak sticks up above the others. The southern portion of this peak is pyramid shaped, with a chopped-off ridge to the north. This is Mount Stimson, at 10,142 feet the second highest peak and the most exhausting (but not the most technically challenging) climb in the park. It's just north of Church Butte, a flat-topped rectangle. St. Nicholas, a few miles south of Mount Stimson, is easy to spot because, quite literally, it sticks out like a sore thumb. Moreover, it appears impossible to climb. Despite all these impressive peaks, Great Northern maintains its own magical lure.

After summiting, head down the southern ridge toward Dudley Bowl. The scree is uneven, so rapid travel may be difficult, but it's surely faster than the way you came. Once back down in the bowl, climb the knob back on the ridge and follow the ridge down. One note on the return bushwhack: Err to the north (your

Final traverse up Great Northern, obviously for experienced hikers only.

right) as you head down, and remember your baselines, Hungry Horse Creek and Forest Road 1048. If you find yourself on flat ground, even though you didn't cross flat ground on the way up, you have drifted too far south and should head north to the road and your vehicle. (Originally contributed by Pat Caffrey, rehiked by authors in 1998)

Key Points

0.0 Trailhead

1.0 Summit south side of Hungry Horse Creek ridge

2.0 Reach knob above Dudley Bowl

3.0 Summit ridge junction

4.0 Great Northern summit

8.0 Trailhead

28 Stanton Lake

Description: An easily accessible lake with fishing opportunities in the Great Bear Wilderness south of Glacier National Park.
Start: 13 miles southeast of West Glacier.
Type of hike: Day hike; out-and-back.
Total distance: 4-mile round trip.
Difficulty: Easy.

Maps: Stanton Lake USGS Quad, Great Bear Wilderness Complex Map, and Flathead National Forest Map.
Trail contacts: Hungry Horse Ranger District, Flathead National Forest, P.O. Box 190340, 8975 Highway 2 East, Hungry Horse, MT 59919; (406) 387-3800; www.fs.fed.us/r1/flathead.

Finding the trailhead: From West Glacier, take U.S. Highway 2 east for 15 miles until just past Stanton Lake Lodge, where Stanton Lake Trail 146 begins right next to US 2. There is ample parking. No camping, but cabin rentals are available at Stanton Lake Lodge.

The Hike

The Stanton Lake Trail 146 is well maintained and gently climbs through larch-fir forest to the lake. At 0.9 mile is a junction with Grant Ridge Trail 339. The Grant Ridge Trail to the left is a popular horse and outfitter trail, which climbs steeply up Grant Ridge for views of Great Northern and Mount Grant. Stay right (southwest), and after a little hump, you reach the foot of Stanton Lake, which has a small log-jam at the outlet. A strong hiker can make it to the lake in twenty to thirty minutes, but you may wish to take longer to enjoy the preserved forest of the Great Bear Wilderness. Stanton Lake Trail continues to the head of the lake around the west shore to your right.

There is not any drinking water until you reach the lake, and the trail receives heavy use. Remember to bring your insect repellent in June and July. The likelihood for bear trouble is minimal, but normal bear country precautions apply.

Hikers often get a glimpse of a moose at the head of the lake or a beaver in the beaver ponds where the stream leaves the lake. Wildflowers are common—bear grass, wild hollyhocks, cow parsnip, and others.

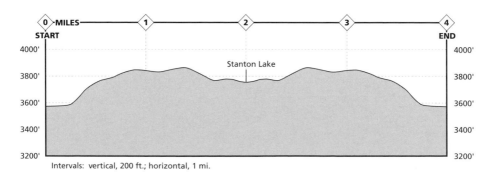

Intervals: vertical, 200 ft.; horizontal, 1 mi.

Stanton Lake

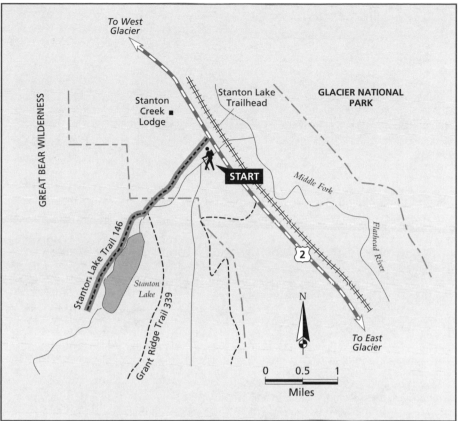

Some hikers carry in small rubber rafts to fish. Usually this is worth the effort, making it possible to catch larger rainbow and cutthroat trout. You might be able to catch some smaller cutthroat from shore. (Originally contributed by Elaine and Art Sedlack, rehiked by authors in 1994 and 1999)

Key Points

0.0 Trailhead

0.9 Junction with Grant Ridge Trail 339; turn right

1.2 Stanton Lake

2.0 Head of Stanton Lake

4.0 Trailhead

29 Marion Lake

Description: A high-altitude lake deep in the Great Bear Wilderness.
Start: On the south edge of Glacier National Park near the Izaak Walton Inn.
Type of hike: Day hike; out-and-back.
Total distance: 3.4-mile round trip.
Difficulty: Moderate.

Maps: Pinnacle USGS Quad, Great Bear Wilderness Complex Map, and Flathead National Forest Map (north half).
Trail contacts: Hungry Horse Ranger District, Flathead National Forest, P.O. Box 190340, 8975 Highway 2 East, Hungry Horse, MT 59919; (406) 387–3800; www.fs.fed.us/r1/flathead.

Finding the trailhead: Drive east of West Glacier on U.S. Highway 2 for about 28 miles to the turnoff for Dickey Creek Road 1639. Head south as the road crosses the railroad tracks and forks. Take the left (east) fork and follow Essex Creek Road 1640 for 1.5 miles to the trailhead on the right, just before crossing Marion Creek. You'll find limited parking and filterable water, but there's no toilet.

The Hike

Marion Lake is easily accessible and has good fishing. Consequently, it probably receives more use than other mountain lakes in designated wilderness areas.

The way to Marion Lake is a steady, uphill pull along Marion Lake Trail 150. The trail gains about 1,800 feet in less than 2 miles, a Category 1 climb. The trail is well maintained, there's plenty of drinking water, and usually the number of mosquitoes is tolerable. Since this lake lies within the Great Bear Wilderness, the hike has a remote feeling, and of course, motorized vehicles are banned. Bear problems are minimal, although black bears are numerous, and an occasional grizzly frequents this area. Skip this hike in June unless you want to risk hiking through snowbanks.

At the head of the lake lies a gorgeous, grassy slope blanketed with wildflowers—bear grass, fireweed, wild hollyhocks, dogwood, bunchberry, and others. The main trail comes to the foot of the lake, but a faint trail circles about half a mile around to the head of the lake.

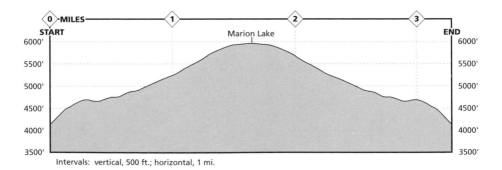

Intervals: vertical, 500 ft.; horizontal, 1 mi.

Marion Lake

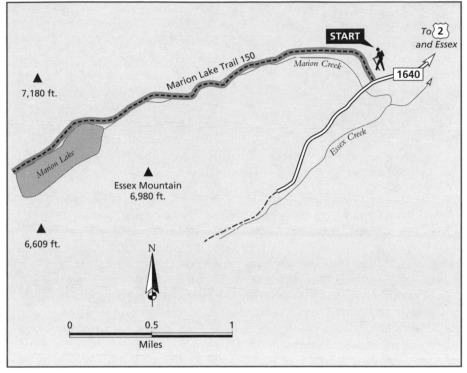

Fishing at the lake is good, particularly in June when the ice breaks up. The lake has a healthy population of cutthroat and rainbow trout. Each winter, a few avid anglers ski or snowshoe to the lake to fish through the ice, and they usually have good success.

Side Trips

For an excellent side trip, work your way through the meadowy slope to the pass on the horizon. It is only about half a mile from where the trail hits the lake. At the top you can look down over 1,000-foot cliffs into the headwaters of Essex Creek. (Originally contributed by Elaine and Art Sedlack, rehiked by authors in 1998)

30 Jewel Basin

Description: An easy trip into a popular hiking and fishing area in the Swan range in the northwestern corner of the Bob Marshall Wilderness.
Start: 10 miles northeast of Bigfork.
Type of trip: Day hike or base camp back-packing trip; out-and-back with loop option.
Total distance: 8.6-mile round trip.
Difficulty: Moderate.

Maps: Jewel Basin, Big Hawk Mountain, and Crater Lake USGS Quads; and Forest Service's Jewel Basin Hiking Area map/brochure.
Trail contacts: Hungry Horse Ranger District, Flathead National Forest, P.O. Box 190340, 8975 Highway 2 East, Hungry Horse, MT 59919; (406) 387-3800; www.fs.fed.us/r1/flathead.

Finding the trailhead: From Bigfork drive north for 3 miles on Montana Highway 35 and turn right (east) onto Montana Highway 83 for 2.3 miles. Turn left (north) at the Echo Lake Cafe on Foothills Road, also called the Echo Lake Road. Follow this road past Echo Lake for 3 miles, turn right (east) onto Forest Road 5392, and follow this dirt switchback road 7 miles to the Jewel Basin Hiking Area parking lot. The route is well marked, but the final stretch is bumpy, featuring whoop-dee-dos (abrupt mounds of dirt), and not recommended for RVs or trailers. The road extends beyond the Camp Misery Trailhead and parking lot, but it is closed to motorized use at the trailhead. The trailhead has a large parking lot, but it fills up on summer weekends. There is a toilet. No camping or drinking water. The site has a ranger cabin with a volunteer interpretive ranger usually on duty.

The Hike

Jewel Basin is ideal for an easy base camp, so the itinerary is simple. The only decisions are where to set up the base camp, how long to stay, and which day hikes to take from your base camp.

Jewel Basin isn't a designated Wilderness, but the Forest Service manages it like one—no logging, motor vehicles, or development. Because of the easy access from the Flathead Valley, this area can get crowded, but mainly on weekends. If you hike here during the week, the human population won't seem too large. There is a maze of trails, so you definitely need a map, and the special hiking map/brochure published by Glacier National History Association is by far the best.

The first order of business on this hike is to pick your base camp. Two excellent options are Black Lake, 8 miles out-and-back, or any one of the four Jewel Lakes, a 9-mile round-trip. An even easier choice would be Twin Lakes, a stunningly beautiful pair of "jewels" in a small basin only a 5-mile round-trip from the trailhead.

Two trails leave the trailhead. You can get to Black Lake and Jewel Lakes on either one with no extra distance. If you prefer to hike on a trail instead of a road, take Trail 8 by the ranger cabin. After 0.6 mile, turn right (south) onto Trail 68 unless you have decided to base camp at Twin Lakes, in which case go left.

When Trail 68 junctures with Mount Aeneas Trail, turn left (east) and climb up to the rim of Jewel Basin. Two trails depart this point. You can get to Black Lake and

Twin Lakes, typical scenery in Jewel Basin.

Jewel Lakes on either one, but I prefer to go right (south), which seems to be a more scenic route through Picnic Lakes, where you turn left (north) onto Trail 392. Follow this trail to a junction with Trail 1 at Black Lake. Turn right (east) onto Trail 1 and drop down to Black Lake (if you like this one for your base camp) or follow it just back from Black Lake to a junction with Trail 719 where you turn left (north). When you reach the Jewel Lakes, find a suitable base camp on one of the four lakes.

After you find your way through the labyrinth of trail junctions and get your base camp set up, start checking the map for suitable day trips. You could spend a week hiking in this area, all on excellent trails with the exception of the long loop around Clayton Lake, a rough and brushy trail you might want to avoid. The Forest Service brochure calls Clayton Lake an easy hike, but rest assured it is not.

Jewel Basin is bear country, including the possibility of seeing a grizzly, so be bear aware and be especially careful with food and garbage. Campsites are not officially designated, but they are well established. To leave less impact, use one of the established camps instead of camping in a virgin site—and practice zero-impact camping principles.

Most lakes in the basin are filled with cutthroat and a few rainbow trout, but they have seen lots of artificial flies and lures and might not be cooperative. To lower the impact, you might want to release your fish so they can be caught again.

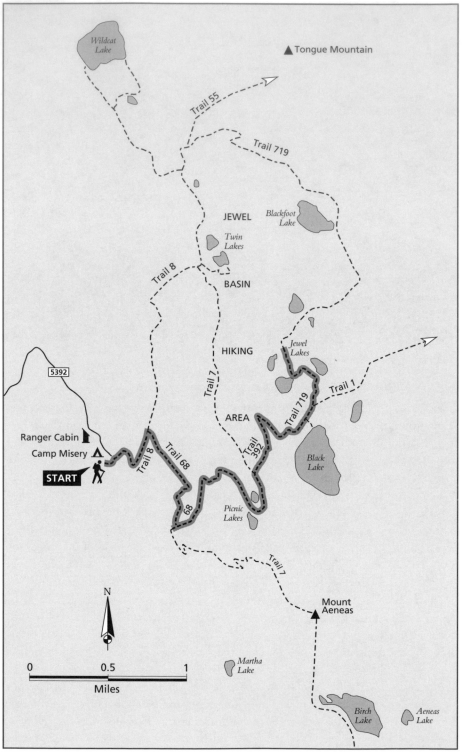

Wildcat
Lake

▲ Tongue Mountain

Trail 55

Trail 719

JEWEL

Blackfoot
Lake

Twin
Lakes

Trail 8

BASIN

HIKING

5392

Jewel
Lakes

Trail 7

Trail 1

Trail 719

AREA

Ranger Cabin

Camp Misery

Trail 392

Black
Lake

START

Trail 8

Trail 68

68

Picnic
Lakes

Trail 7

N

Mount
Aeneas

0   0.5   1

Miles

Martha
Lake

Birch
Lake

Aeneas
Lake

Note the special regs at the trailhead information board: Dogs must be on leashes; no campfires at Birch, Crater, Picnic, and Twin Lakes; and no more than twelve people in a party.

Options

This does not have to be a base camp trip. You could move your camp from lake to lake, but since the distances are so small, a base camp provides a less strenuous option. You can also make this a loop trip. Instead of retracing your steps to the trailhead, take the small loop through the basin via Black Lake, Jewel Lakes, Blackfoot Lake, and Twin Lakes, departing the basin on either Trail 7 or Trail 68.

Side Trips

Numerous side trips are possible throughout the basin. Check the map and find one that matches your interest and ability. If you need a long trip, you can head over to Crater Lake or Wildcat Lake, but there are also choice short trips to Blackfoot Lake, Twin Lakes, and Birch Lake. A 2003 forest fire burned a section of the trail around Blackfoot Lake. (Originally contributed by the authors, rehiked in 2001)

Key Points

0.0 Trailhead

0.6 Junction with Trail 68; turn right

1.4 Junction with Mount Aeneas Trail; turn left

2.3 Junction with Alpine Trail 7; turn right

2.7 Picnic Lakes and junction with Trail 392; turn left

3.4 Junction with Trail 1, turn right

3.7 Black Lake

4.0 Junction with Trail 719; turn left

4.3 Jewel Lakes

8.6 Trailhead

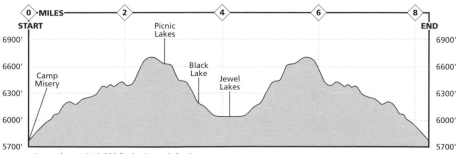

Intervals: vertical, 300 ft.; horizontal, 2 mi.

31 Crater Lake

Description: A popular Jewel Basin hike through subalpine terrain to a good fishing lake.
Start: 10 miles northeast of Bigfork.
Type of hike: Day hike or short backpacking trip; out-and-back.
Total distance: 12-mile round trip.
Difficulty: Moderate.

Maps: Jewel Basin and Crater Lake USGS Quads, Jewel Basin Hiking Area Map, and Flathead National Forest Map.
Trail contacts: Hungry Horse Ranger District, Flathead National Forest, P.O. Box 190340, 8975 Highway 2 East, Hungry Horse, MT 59919; (406) 387–3800; www.fs.fed.us/r1/flathead.

Finding the trailhead: From Bigfork drive north for 3 miles on Montana Highway 35 and turn right (east) onto Montana Highway 83 for 2.3 miles. Turn left (north) at the Echo Lake Cafe on Foothills Road, also called the Echo Lake Road. Follow this road past Echo Lake for 3 miles, turn right (east) onto Forest Road 5392, and follow this dirt switchback road 7 miles to the Jewel Basin Hiking Area parking lot. The route is well marked, but the final stretch is bumpy, featuring whoop-dee-dos (abrupt mounds of dirt), and not recommended for RVs or trailers. The road extends beyond the Camp Misery Trailhead and parking lot, but it is closed to motorized use at the trailhead. The trailhead has a large parking lot, but it fills up on summer weekends. There is a toilet. No camping or drinking water. The site has a ranger cabin with a volunteer interpretive ranger usually on duty.

The Hike

To reach high-elevation lakes, you usually have to make a healthy climb. Crater Lake is an exception. The trail starts high, so it's 6 easy miles to this scenic fishing lake. The Forest Service adequately maintains this trail all summer. The trail is very popular, so expect to see other hikers. Note the special regs at the trailhead information board: Dogs must be on leashes; no campfires at Birch, Crater, Picnic, and Twin Lakes; and no more than twelve people in a party.

Two trails leave the parking lot. Take the major trail (actually an old road) near the big information board on the east side of the lot, not the single-track trail leaving the north end near the interpreter's cabin. Follow the road (closed to vehicles) for about a mile before it turns into a trail. About a quarter mile later you reach "malfunction junction," where six trails (three official, three social) all come together in the same spot. Take the sharpest right onto Alpine Trail 7, where you enjoy a terrific view of the Flathead Valley off to your right.

At 2.2 miles you see little Martha Lake on the right and a tough social trail leading to it, a side trip you might want to skip unless you have energy to burn. At 3 miles you reach Birch Lake, which is right along the trail. It has several great campsites (all heavily impacted) and a good population of little cutthroats that have seen a lot of artificial flies. Before reaching Squaw Lake, Trail 187 veers off to the right.

Crater Lake

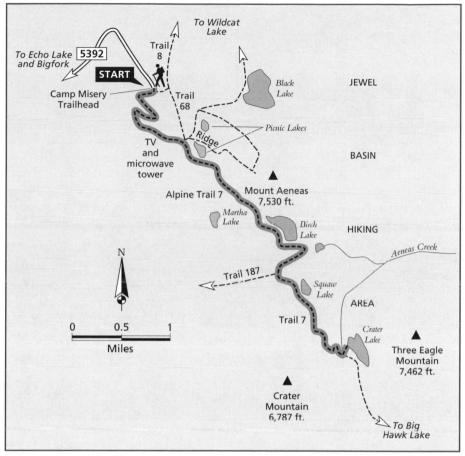

You turn left (southeast) and go by Squaw Lake, which can be seen a few hundred yards east of the trail.

Continue on Alpine Trail 7 as it cuts through a lush forest sprinkled with wet meadows before making a slight drop into Crater Lake. Crater Lake can be nearly perfect for a family overnighter. The hike is moderately easy, about the right distance, and cool, and it can be taken anytime from July through October. Be sure to bring mosquito repellent, however, as Crater Lake seems to have more than its share of these annoying insects.

Perhaps the highlight of this trip is the rocky, glacier-scoured basin around Crater Lake. There seems to be more rock than vegetation in this basin. Except for the Crater Lake basin, the entire trail goes through a series of moist, mountain glades similar to those of Glacier Park.

If you're sharp-eyed, you might spot a mountain goat on the crags above the trail or a deer or elk in one of the many open parks. Wildflowers abound, especially at the

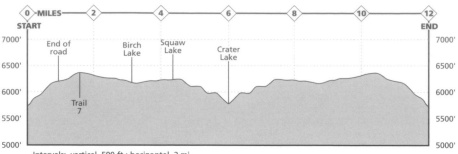

Intervals: vertical, 500 ft.; horizontal, 2 mi.

beginning of the hike along the face of Mount Aeneas. An occasional grizzly is reported in this area, and black bears are common. Reports of bear trouble are almost nonexistent, but don't forget to be bear aware. Also, take great care to set up a zero-impact camp. The entire Jewel Basin area is heavily used and starting to show it.

Side Trips

The Crater Lake hike has a wide selection of possible side trips. Perhaps the most popular is to continue south on the same trail for 2 more miles to Big Hawk Lake, which is slightly larger than Crater Lake but not quite as scenic. You can also take short trips to Martha and Squaw Lakes. (Originally contributed by Larry Thompson, rehiked by authors in 2002)

Key Points

0.0 Trailhead

1.0 End of road

1.5 Junction with Alpine Trail 7; turn right

2.2 Martha Lake

3.0 Birch Lake

4.2 Junction with Trail 187; turn left

4.5 Squaw Lake

6.0 Crater Lake

12.0 Trailhead

32 Alpine Trail

Description: Outstanding panoramic views of northwestern Montana and Flathead Lake from a delightful ridgeline trail.
Start: 5 miles southeast of Columbia Falls.
Type of trip: A backpacking trip with several side trips; shuttle.
Total distance: 20.5 miles.
Difficulty: Strenuous.

Maps: Doris Mountain, Jewel Basin, and Hash Mountain USGS Quads; and Flathead National Forest Map.
Trail contacts: Hungry Horse Ranger District, Flathead National Forest, P.O. Box 190340, 8975 Highway 2 East, Hungry Horse, MT 59919; (406) 387-3800; www.fs.fed.us/r1/flathead.

Finding the trailheads: To reach the Columbia Mountain Trailhead, drive east of Columbia Falls on U.S. Highway 2 and turn east at the junction with Highway 206 (from Bigfork). Shortly after the junction and 3.5 miles from Columbia Falls, turn right off US 2 on an unmarked dirt road just past the House of Mystery. Follow this road south for 0.2 mile until you see the Columbia Mountain Trailhead on your left. (This is a fairly newer trailhead that became necessary to avoid crossing private land.) Columbia Mountain Trail 51 starts to the southeast of the parking area.

To reach Strawberry Lake Trailhead (for leaving a vehicle, having someone pick you up, or doing the Strawberry Lake day hike), drive east of Kalispell on Montana Highway 35 (or south back on Highway 206 from Columbia Mountain Trailhead). Just after the junction with Highway 206, turn left, heading east as the highway turns south, on Lake Blaine Road. Two miles farther the road splits; stay straight on Foothills Road (Lake Blaine Road heads north) for another 7 miles (9 miles from MT 35) and turn left (east) on Krause Creek Road (Forest Road 5390). Drive 3.2 miles on FR 5390 until it dead-ends at Strawberry Lake Trail 5 Trailhead. There is ample parking at both trailheads, but there are no toilets.

The Hike

This backpacking route is not for beginners or small children. (You may, however, consider an easier and popular option of hiking only to Strawberry Lake.) You can cover this route (and 3,500-foot elevation gain) in two days, but to really enjoy the scenery on this high-altitude hike, allow three days. Although the trail is remote and primitive, it's well maintained and easy to follow. There is a fair chance of spotting elk or deer, and a great variety of wildflowers will greet you in summer, particularly in mid-July. Snow may block this trail until early July. The main attraction is the views. There is water at many places along the trail, but there are also some dry stretches on the northern half of this hike. Mosquitoes can be a problem early in the season, but they seem less severe than in many areas. Drinking water and shelter from the wind can often be found by dropping over the ridge to the east into the high meadows.

Starting on the Columbia Mountain Trail 51, you climb steadily up the slopes of Columbia Mountain for about 8 miles to the intersection with Alpine Trail 7. Turn right (south) and follow Trail 7 as it follows the top of the ridge, with views in all

Strawberry Lake and Strawberry Mountain.

directions, including Hungry Horse Reservoir, the peaks of Glacier National Park, and the Flathead Valley. There are several places to camp along the trail, including Doris, Jenny, and Lamoose Lakes. Although there is some fishing in Strawberry and Lamoose Lakes, this hike isn't known for its fishing. Once you descend another 9.5 miles to Strawberry Lake, turn right (west) on Strawberry Lake Trail 5 for a 3-mile descent to the Strawberry Lake Trailhead and the end of your three-day excursion.

Black bears and grizzlies inhabit this area, so there is a chance of a confrontation. The likelihood of such an encounter might be higher here than on many trails in Montana's national forests, but the probability of bear trouble is still much lower than in nearby Glacier National Park. Proper bear country manners will further lower the chance of bear trouble.

Options

You could easily be lured into extending your trip beyond Strawberry Lake on Alpine Trail to nearby Jewel Basin or even farther south. Alpine Trail follows the crest of the Swan Range all the way to just south of Broken Leg Mountain. Then, about 6 trail-less miles later along the crest, the trail begins again and continues to Inspiration Pass

Alpine Trail

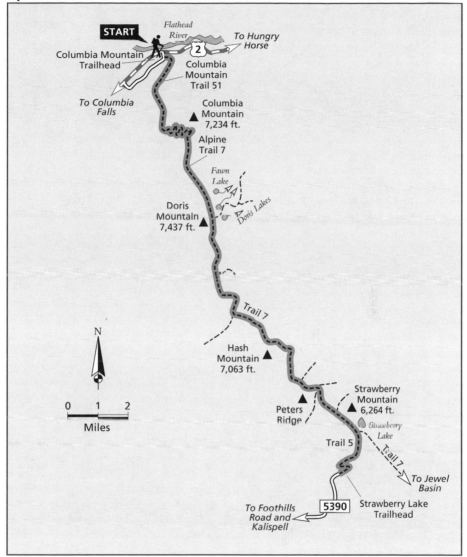

near Swan Lake. You could spend anywhere from a week to two weeks hiking and camping along the Alpine Trail, but the off-trail section between Broken Leg and Sixmile Mountains makes this a trek for experienced and physically fit hikers only. You can also reach Inspiration Pass via Trail 484 from Soup Creek Road (FR 10510).

Strawberry Lake is a very popular day hike for locals and tourists, so plan on seeing a few hikers, mountain bikers, and horses along the trail. (Originally contributed by Loren Kreck)

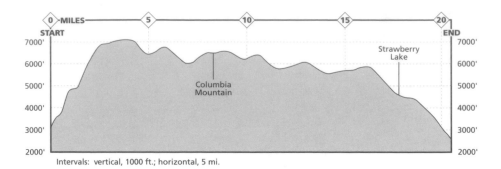

Intervals: vertical, 1000 ft.; horizontal, 5 mi.

Key Points

0.0 Columbia Mountain Trailhead

8.0 Columbia Mountain and Junction with Alpine Trail 7; turn right

17.5 Strawberry Lake/Junction with Strawberry Lake Trail 5; turn right

20.5 Strawberry Lake Trailhead

33 Palisade Lake

Description: A mixed old-growth forest and scenic views of the Swan and South Fork of the Flathead River Valleys.
Start: 40 miles southeast of Kalispell, just northeast of Condon in the wild Swan Range.
Type of hike: Backpacking trip; out-and-back.
Total distance: 22-mile round trip.
Difficulty: Strenuous.

Maps: Swan Peak and Sunburst Lake USGS Quads, and Flathead National Forest Map (south half).
Trail contacts: Swan Lake Ranger District, Flathead National Forest, 200 Ranger Station Road, Bigfork, MT 59911; (406) 837–7500; www.fs.fed.us/r1/flathead.

Finding the trailhead: Drive south of the junction of Montana Highways 35 and 83 on MT 83 for 39.4 miles (about 20 miles past "downtown" Swan Lake). Turn east off MT 83 onto Lion Creek Road 9769. Follow this road for 3 miles to the trailhead on the left. The road continues as an access to private land adjacent to the creek, but there is no public access farther in. There is ample parking at the trailhead.

The Hike

In contrast with most hiking in the rugged Swan Range, the trail up Lion Creek climbs gradually from the Swan Valley to the large basin beneath the Swan Divide. From the trailhead Trail 25 descends and crosses the creek on a bridge and then ascends gently through an open forest of old ponderosa pine and larch trees. At 0.8 mile a trail enters from the left, an extension to the Van Lake Road; stay right (east) on the main trail. The trail leaves the main Swan Valley, climbing rocky benches sprinkled with a few old ponderosa pines. After a short drop an outfitter trail enters from the right; stay left, continuing east on Trail 25.

The trail is heavily used by horses and becomes wide and muddy, even during dry periods, as it enters the narrow canyon of Lion Creek. At about 5 miles is the first of the several waterfalls on Lion Creek, which cascades down from the glaciers and snowfields of Swan and Union peaks.

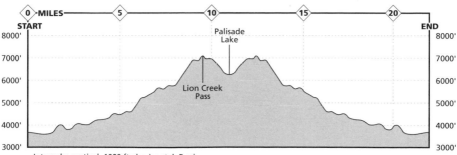

Intervals: vertical, 1000 ft.; horizontal, 5 mi.

Ponderosa pines along Lion Creek.

Continuing on, the trail passes through a majestic grove of old western red cedars. After the grove, another series of falls appears on the creek just after the South Fork of Lion Creek joins the main stream.

It's 9.5 miles from the trailhead to Lion Creek Pass and the Bob Marshall boundary. Palisade Lake, 1.5 miles farther on in the Bob Marshall Wilderness, is also a popular and beautiful destination. The trail is not maintained past Palisade Lake, making trip extensions difficult. Remember that when you enter Lion Creek Canyon, you enter the grizzly's domain. Please respect the great bear and be cautious.

A small portion of the lower trail crosses private land, but access is currently granted by an operating agreement between the landowner and the Forest Service. Please show your respect when on this private property. (Originally contributed by John Gatchall)

Key Points

0.0 Trailhead
0.8 Trail enters from Van Lake Road; stay right on main trail
1.5 Outfitter trail joins main trail
5.0 Waterfall

Palisade Lake

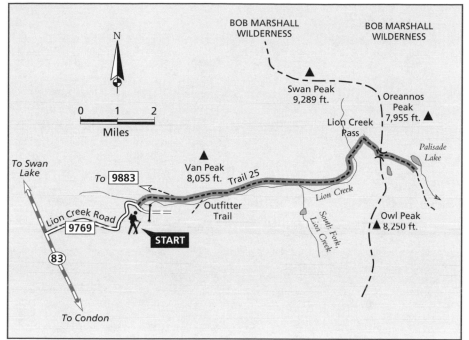

9.5 Lion Creek Pass

10.0 Small ponds

11.0 Palisade Lake (end of maintained trail)

22.0 Trailhead

34 Cold Lakes

Description: An easy hike to experience Mission Mountain beauty and fish in high mountain lakes.
Start: South of Swan Lake, near Condon in the Mission Mountains Wilderness.
Type of hike: Day hike; out-and-back.
Total distance: 4.6-mile round trip.

Difficulty: Easy to lower lake and moderate to upper lake.
Maps: Piper-Crow Pass and Peck Lake USGS Quads and Flathead National Forest Map.
Trail contacts: Swan Lake Ranger District, Flathead National Forest, 200 Ranger Station Road, Bigfork, MT 59911; (406) 837-7500; www.fs.fed.us/r1/flathead.

Finding the trailhead: Drive south of Swan Lake on Montana Highway 83 for 23 miles and turn right on Cold Creek Road (Forest Road 903A). Drive southwest on FR 903A for 3 miles and turn right on FR 9568 and then left on FR 9599. It's 7 miles to the trailhead from MT 83. The trailhead has parking, filterable water, and primitive camping.

The Hike

This hike is an example of the positive changes taking place in the wilderness even with increased use. Lower Cold Lake had been severely damaged by years of high-impact camping. With the Mission Mountains Wilderness designation, the Forest Service has made an effort to help areas like Cold Lakes recover from past abuses. This Wilderness Restoration Project has been a success so far. Native vegetation has regrown over old campsites. Camping is not allowed within 0.3 mile of either lake. However, it's a nightmare to find a suitable campsite that distance away. The brush is too thick, and there are few flat spots to put up a tent. This makes this a great day hike but a marginal overnighter. This is grizzly country, so make plenty of noise.

Trail 121 climbs along the stream (and sometimes in the stream) to the lake. About half a mile up the trail on the right is a cascading waterfall. A small path veers off to the right for a closer look. After 2.0 miles on the trail, you reach Lower Cold Lake. There is a roped-off vegetation recovery area here and a nice log to sit on and

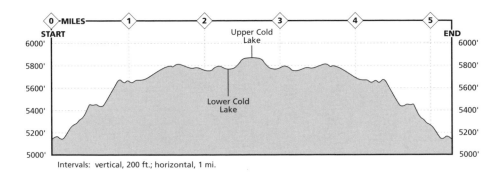

Intervals: vertical, 200 ft.; horizontal, 1 mi.

Cold Lakes in Mission Mountains.

rest. The fishing is good, but good fly casting spots are scarce. The shore of the lake is covered with dense foliage. The easy hike ends here if you choose to turn around and hike out.

There is a faint path to Upper Cold Lake. It circles the north side of Lower Cold Lake and follows the stream up to the upper lake. The hard part is getting around the lake. Thick brush and deadfall cover the trail. Some of the fallen Engelmann spruce are 4 feet thick, and crawling over, around, and under fallen trees is exhausting. Some have suggested that this trail should be maintained, but having a bushwhacking barrier minimizes the impact of hikers on the upper lake. Not as many people get there as would if the trail were maintained.

Once you make it around the lower lake to the inlet, it gets easier. The stretch between the lakes is gentle. The outlet of the upper lake is a logjam. If you choose to cross it or fish from it, be careful of unstable logs. The fishing is better at the upper lake. Twelve-inch cutthroat trout are common, and more casting spots are available. The view from the upper lake is breathtaking. The glaciated peaks of the Missions are sharp and rugged, carved from uplifted sedimentary rock. The surrounding cliffs offer a home to mountain goats. Bring your binoculars and see if you can spot any.

The return hike retraces your original path. This is a relaxing day hike if you take your time. (Originally contributed by the authors)

Cold Lakes

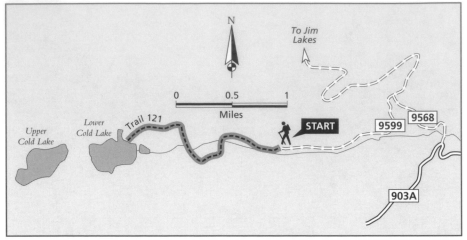

Key Points

0.0 Trailhead

0.5 Waterfall

2.0 Lower Cold Lake

2.3 Upper Cold Lake

4.6 Trailhead

35 Crescent Lake

Description: A forested lake basin in the Mission Mountains Wilderness.
Start: 25 miles northwest of Seeley Lake.
Type of hike: A day hike or overnighter; out-and-back.
Total distance: 7 miles.
Difficulty: Moderate.

Maps: Gray Wolf Lake and Hemlock Lake USGS Quads and Mission Mountains Wilderness Map published by the Forest Service.
Trail contacts: Swan Lake Ranger District, Flathead National Forest, 200 Ranger Station Road, Bigfork, MT 59911; (406) 837-7500; www.fs.fed.us/r1/flathead.

Finding the trailhead: Drive 22 miles north of Seeley Lake or 32 miles south of Swan Lake on U.S. Highway 83, and then turn west on FR 561 (between mile markers 37 and 38). From here it's 11.5 unpaved miles to the large trailhead. Several roads turn off, but stay on well-signed FR 561, the main road. The trailhead has ample parking and a toilet.

The Hike

This is a heavily used area, so be sure to check the information board at the trailhead to review current regulations. For example, the shoreline of Glacier Lake is open to day use only, no camping.

For the first mile you go gradually uphill on a stream grade through mature forest on Trail 690, crossing Glacier Creek twice, both on bridges. Go right (west) at the junction with spur trail to Glacier Lake, unless you want to take a short side trip on the way in. After the junction, the trail climbs above Glacier Lake and gives you a great view of the lake.

At the junction with Turquoise Lake Trail 708 at mile 2.5, go right (west) again. From here Trail 690 goes up long, forested switchbacks, most lined with huckleberry bushes, so plan on extra time for some grazing. The last mile of trail to Crescent Lake gets fairly brushy. The trail continues along the south side of Crescent Lake to Heart Lake.

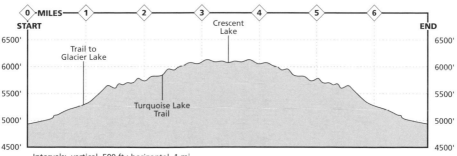

Intervals: vertical, 500 ft.; horizontal, 1 mi.

Crescent Lake

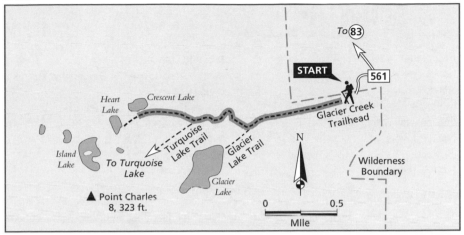

Crescent Lake has a few heavily impacted campsites, but it is still better camping than Heart Lake. Both lakes have a few hungry cutthroats to keep you busy fishing after supper.

Side Trips

Try the short (half-mile) side trip to Glacier Lake. If you're experienced and ambitious, you can bushwhack up to Island Lake, the next lake up the drainage above Heart Lake. (Hiked by authors in 2001)

Key Points

0.0 Trailhead

1.0 Junction with Glacier Lake Trail; turn right

2.5 Junction with Turquoise Lake Trail; turn right

3.5 Crescent Lake

7.0 Trailhead

◀ *Crescent Lake in the Mission Mountains.*

36 Sapphire Lake

Description: A high alpine lake with scenic views of the Swan Range and the Mission Mountains.

Start: 20 miles north of Seeley Lake near the Bob Marshall Wilderness.

Type of hike: Day hike or short backpacking trip; loop.

Total distance: 12 miles.

Difficulty: Strenuous.

Maps: Holland Lake USGS Quad and Flathead National Forest Map.

Trail contacts: Swan Lake Ranger District, Flathead National Forest, 200 Ranger Station Road, Bigfork, MT 59911; (406) 837-7500; www.fs.fed.us/r1/flathead.

Finding the trailhead: Drive north from Seeley Lake for about 20 miles on Montana Highway 83 and turn east onto Holland Lake Road 44. Follow this road for about 4 miles, staying left around the north shore of the lake, until it dead-ends at the large trailhead, which has ample parking. Full visitor services are available at Holland Lake Lodge and nearby campgrounds.

The Hike

This hike describes the second busiest access route into the Bob Marshall Wilderness (Benchmark in the Rocky Mountain Front is the busiest), so the main trail can get crowded at times. To avoid the hordes try this loop hike as early in the season as snow conditions will allow. Once off the main drag and onto the Sapphire Trail, the crowds drop off dramatically.

Start up the main East Holland Connector Trail 415, which leads through dense forest for a mile and begins to climb into the Swan Range. Just after you start hiking, you reach the junction with Trail 416, which leads off to the right along Holland Lake to Holland Falls; stay left (east), climbing on the East Holland Connector Trail.

At 1 mile, stay right (east) opposite your return trail (Trail 42), which leads to the old Holland Lookout, Necklace Lakes, and Sapphire Lake. Along the main trail, the route cuts across steep side hills, which offer beautiful views of lower Holland Lake, the Swan Valley, and the Mission Mountains.

The roar of waterfalls becomes overwhelming as the path passes above Holland Falls. (A spur trail to the right leads to the base of the falls and takes off from the main trail near the trailhead.) After passing above the falls, East Holland Connector Trail crosses Holland Creek and climbs to the junction with Holland Gordon Trail 35 on the south side of the canyon.

Stay left (east) on Holland Gordon Trail as it climbs parallel to Holland Creek. Several other falls and cascades greet you, as the stream rushes down the abrupt western slope of the Swan Range. In late June the thunder of the stream will be almost deafening and will almost drown out the buzzing of early-season mosquitoes. Take care crossing the narrow footlogs over Holland Creek during high water.

Sapphire Lake

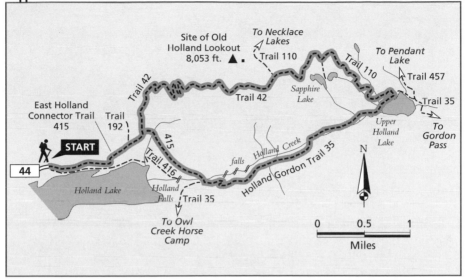

At 6 miles you reach Upper Holland Lake, situated in a gorgeous subalpine basin beneath the crest of the Swan Range. Hike around the north shore to the junction with Trail 110 to Sapphire Lake.

Turn left (north) on Trail 110, which leads upward from the north shore of the lake, passing through sparse stands of spruce and fir and meadows filled with glacier lilies. For the next 3 miles, the trail is a hiker's delight, with views opening up to the south along the Swan Range and distant vistas of huge mountains appearing to the east, deep within the Bob Marshall Wilderness. About a mile from Upper Holland Lake, the trail reaches the rumpled plateau on which several ponds and Sapphire Lake are located.

Just before Sapphire Lake you'll see a spur trail veering off to your left to the lakes. This is an out-and-back spur trail. Trail 110 doesn't skirt the north shore of the lake, as shown on some maps. Instead it stays north of the lakes.

After leaving the upper basin above Sapphire Lake, the trail ascends a steep slope to a notch in a high ridge. Once through the notch, the trail continues along a south-facing slope, with the great pyramid of Carmine Peak rising over the deep canyon of Holland Creek below you. This spectacular skywalk through the alpine meadows on the western slope of the Swan Range brings you almost to eyeball level with the Mission Mountain peaks across the valley.

Stay left (west) at the junction where Trail 110 meets Trail 42, continuing down endless switchbacks on Trail 42. Three miles on the trail from Sapphire Lake and another mile on the main trail will bring you back to the trailhead and the completion of the loop.

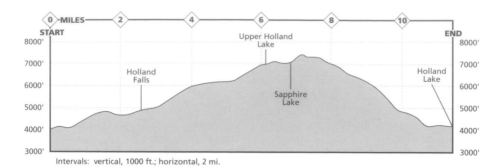

Intervals: vertical, 1000 ft.; horizontal, 2 mi.

The hike can be done as a loop day hike, or you can camp overnight at Sapphire Lake. If you want to avoid the traffic on the Holland Gordon Trail and you enjoy climbing steep switchbacks, the trip can be done as an out-and-back trip on Trail 42.

The mosquitoes in the Swan are well known for their voraciousness. Bring lots of bug dope to keep them under control. This entire hike is outside the western boundary of the Bob Marshall Wilderness, but it has been proposed as an addition to the Wilderness.

Options

You can make this an extended backpacking trip by spending a night at Necklace Lakes, which have fish but not a lot of big ones, and you get skunked in some lakes. You can also take this loop in reverse, but it might seem more difficult.

Side Trips

After 8 miles (1 mile past Sapphire Lake), a sign indicates the old Holland Lookout as Trail 110 turns right (north), climbing the ridge to the north. If you have time and energy, this is a very worthwhile side trip. (Originally contributed by Ed Madej and Rosemary Rowe, rehiked by authors in 1998)

Key Points

0.0 Trailhead

0.2 Junction with Trail 416 to Holland Falls; turn left

1.0 Junction with return Trail 42; turn right

2.7 Holland Falls

3.0 Junction with Holland Gordon Trail 35; turn left

6.0 Upper Holland Lake/Junction with Trail 110; turn left

7.0 Sapphire Lake

8.0 Junction of Trails 110 and 42; turn left

11.0 Junction with Trail 415; turn right

12.0 Trailhead

Glacier
National Park

37 Boulder Pass

Description: A long, scenic route starting in Canada and ending in the United States with incredible alpine scenery and remoteness; a classic backpacking trip.
Start: Along the Canadian border in Glacier National Park.
Type of trip: Extended backpacking trip; shuttle.
Total distance: 30.6 miles.

Difficulty: Strenuous.
Maps: Kintla Lake, Kintla Peak, Porcupine Ridge, and Mount Carter USGS Quads and either the USGS or Trails Illustrated map for the entire park.
Trail contacts: National Park Service, Park Headquarters, West Glacier, MT 59935; (406) 888-7800; www.nps.gov/glac.

Finding the trailhead: To reach the trailhead you cross through customs into Canada at the Chief Mountain station, drive to the Waterton town site in Waterton Lakes National Park, and, for a modest fee, take the tour boat to Goat Haunt, which also has a visitor center and rest rooms. The boat leaves from the marina on Emerald Bay (also called Divers Bay). There is ample parking at the marina. The cruise runs several times during the day and takes two hours and fifteen minutes. Call or e-mail the Waterton Shoreline Cruise Company (403-859-2362; wscruise@cadvision.com) for an updated schedule and fees. You can also check the information at the Web site www.watertoninfo.ab.ca/m/cruise. Alternatively, you can hike from the Waterton town site along the west shore of Waterton Lake, but the cruise is worth the money.

Leave a vehicle or arrange for a pickup at Kintla Lake Campground at the foot of Kintla Lake. To reach this trailhead drive north of Columbia Falls on County Road 486 (known locally as the North Fork Road) for 30 miles until you see the sign for Polebridge. Turn right here, and cross the North Fork of the Flathead River at the Polebridge Ranger Station. After you pass through the NPS facilities, you intersect with the gravel road along the east side of the North Fork within the park. Turn left (north) here and drive 13 miles to the end of the road at the Kintla Lake Campground. Kintla Lake has a vehicle campground and toilets but limited parking, so be careful not to take more than one space.

Recommended itinerary: Take the earliest boat you can get in order to get a good start on your hike and so you have time to reach Lake Francis, which has a nicer campsite than those at Waterton River, Lake Janet, or Hawksbill.

First night: Lake Francis
Second night: Boulder Pass or Hole-in-the-Wall
Third night: Upper Kintla Lake
Fourth night: Lower Kintla Lake

The spacing of the campsites on the west side of Boulder Pass makes deciding between a four- or five-day trip a difficult choice. You could cut back to a four-day trip by hiking from Boulder Pass Camp to Lower Kintla Lake, a distance of 11 miles, but it's almost all downhill. If you can't get Boulder Pass Campsite and you stay at Hole-in-the-Wall, it's best to take five days.

The Boulder Pass Trail is challenging near the top.

Getting a permit: To have the rare opportunity to experience Boulder Pass, you need a backcountry camping permit from the National Park Service. Since the demand is so great and since the NPS rightfully restricts use for environmental reasons, getting a permit isn't easy. You must use designated campsites on this route. All have pit toilets and food/garbage storage devices.

One way to get a backcountry camping permit is to walk into one of the park's ranger stations or visitor centers, apply right there, and pay the backcountry camping fee. However, waiting until the last minute is risky because many popular campsites, such as those on Boulder Pass, are reserved long in advance.

The safest (but by no means the easiest) way to get your permit is by using the National Park Service's advance reservation system. Refer to Glacier's Web site (www.nps.gov/glac/activity.htm) for the details of the reservation system. You can also download an application from the Web site. Reservations are issued on a first-come, first-served basis, so apply early. However, no applications are accepted if they are postmarked earlier than mid-April. Call (406) 888-7857 for the specific date, which varies slightly from year to year. In 2003 the reservation fee was $20.00 per trip, in addition to a $4.00 per person per night backcountry camping fee, but don't send the camping fee with the reservation fee. You pay that part when you pick up the permit. You must pick up the permit by 10:00 A.M. the day your trip starts or the campsites will go back in the pool and be available to the long line of back-packers waiting for a permit at the visitor center, so don't be late. You also can't pick up permits sooner than the day before your trip starts.

If you get a permit for Boulder Pass and can't, heaven forbid, get to Glacier to take the trip, please call the backcountry office (406–888–7857) and cancel your reservation so others might enjoy these campsites. Reservation fees are nonrefund-able unless your application is unsuccessful or the park officially closes the trail you have chosen.

The Hike

Boulder Pass is a truly classic trip and has achieved some widespread popularity because of it. The National Park Service limits use with the number of designated campsites and permits, so if you're lucky enough to get one, you won't feel crowded.

The hike itself is difficult to beat, but the preparation can test your patience. Use the park's backcountry permit reservation system to try for a permit in advance. Showing up at a ranger station looking for a permit to start the hike the next day might be fruitless, and you probably will be using your alternative route. When you do get a permit, you have to arrange a long, problematic shuttle. The best way to manage this logistical challenge is to take this trip with another party, so you can start at opposite ends of the route and meet at Boulder Pass or Hole-in-the-Wall camps to exchange car keys. Then, of course, you both have to get permits, so more patience is required.

Another special planning task is watching the weather forecast. You really don't want to be up on Boulder Pass in a summer snowstorm. Because of the elevation, snow claims the area until at least late July. It can come back any day, so always pre-pare for the worst weather.

And keep in mind that this is prime grizzly country, so study up on bear aware-ness advice (such as that given in the introductory material for this book) before hit-ting the trail.

But take some solace in the fact that this route is worth any amount of frustra-tion in planning and preparation!

The first leg of the Boulder Pass Trail climbs gradually through the lush Olson Creek valley, thick with thimbleberry and false hellebore. If you leave early, before the sun gets a chance to dry the dew, plan on getting as wet as if it had rained. There are plenty of water sources, which is, in general, true for the entire route.

Shortly after leaving the trailhead, turn right (west) at the junction with the spur trail to Rainbow Falls. At 3.1 miles at Lake Janet you get a great view of the Sen-tinel over the lake, but at 5.6 miles you get a poor view of Lake Francis from the trail. Just past Lake Francis, at the foot of an unnamed lake, the trail starts switch-backing out of the forest into the alpine wonderland you'll enjoy until you plunge

Boulder Pass

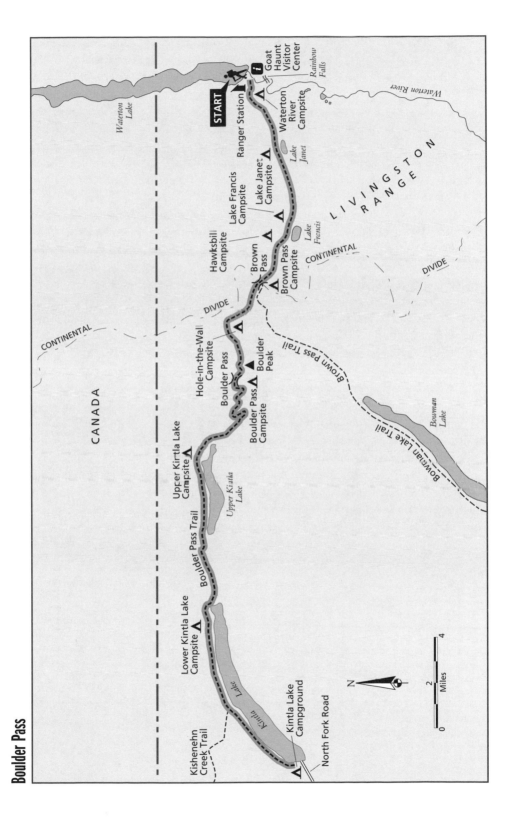

down to the Kintla Valley on the other side of Boulder Pass at about 13 miles. Here you walk out of the thimbleberry forests onto the wildflower carpet. Off to your left (south), Thunderbird Falls cascades down from the mountain and glacier of the same name (originating from several Indian legends about a great bird spirit with lightning flashing from its eyes that creates thunder by flapping its wings) into the unnamed lake. You might think this is scenery at its best, but it gets even better as you proceed uphill. It's a gentle, Category 4 climb to Brown Pass.

When you reach the junction with the Brown Pass Trail at 7.7 miles, which heads down to Bowman Lake, bear right. If you have a permit for the Brown Pass Campsite, you must have bug netting and repellent to survive the infamously vicious Brown Pass mosquitoes—little brown mutants that go right for your eyeballs.

After Brown Pass you are in the high country as you gradually climb for about 5 miles to Boulder Pass, again only a Category 4 climb. About 2 miles from the pass, the wildflowers give way to sheer rock, with a few hardy phlox hanging on to the soilless landscape. Mighty Kintla Peak and its slightly shorter but more austere companion, Kinnerly Peak, dominate the southern horizon most of the way to the top. You can look back and see the park's highest peak, Cleveland, and nearby Stoney Indian Peaks with their thirteen distinct spires.

The trail is in great shape considering the rugged environment. You have to follow cairns in a few places, but the route is easy to find. Earlier in the season (mid-to late July), you may encounter a few dangerous snowbanks.

After enjoying some special time on top of Boulder Pass, start down the giant decline of nearly 9 miles to Upper Kintla Lake. This trail is rougher, rockier, and steeper than the east-side trail, but it isn't as brushy.

Along Upper Kintla Lake you get a constant view of the Matterhorn-like Kinnerly Peak. With the exception of a small hill between the lakes and a few hills along Lower Kintla Lake, it's essentially a gradual downhill the rest of the trip. It's about 5.5 miles between the Upper and Lower Kintla Lake Campsites. Watch for bald eagles around the upper end of Lower Kintla Lake, but be careful not to disturb them.

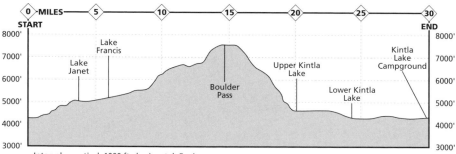

Intervals: vertical, 1000 ft.; horizontal, 5 mi.

At 27 miles you reach the junction with Kishenehn Creek Trail. Turn left (south) and continue another 4 miles to the Kintla Lake Campground Trailhead, the end of your hike.

Normally this route doesn't attract anglers, but Lake Francis has some good fishing for rainbows. They can get large but are difficult to catch. You can also fish Lower Kintla Lake, where you stand a good chance of getting a nice cutthroat from the west shore. Upper Kintla Lake is closed to fishing.

Options

You can do this trip in reverse, of course, but the Category I climb up from Upper Kintla Lake is more strenuous than coming up from the east side. Plus, coming down to the Kintla Valley offers some fantastic scenery that you miss if you're struggling uphill staring at your next foot plant.

Side Trips

If you have time at the beginning of the trip, take the short spur trail over to see Rainbow Falls. Otherwise, there aren't really any logical side trips except some casual exploring amid the scenic grandeur of Boulder Pass. (Originally contributed by the authors, rehiked in 1998)

Key Points

0.0	Goat Haunt Trailhead
0.4	Junction with Rainbow Falls Trail; turn right
0.6	Waterton River Campsite
0.9	Junction with Boulder Pass Trail; turn left
3.1	Lake Janet and Campsite
5.6	Lake Francis and Campsite
6.2	Hawksbill Campsite
7.7	Junction with Brown Pass Trail and campsite 3e; turn right
10.5	Trail to Hole-in-the-Wall Campsite; turn right
13.0	Boulder Pass
13.6	Boulder Pass Campsite
18.8	Upper Kintla Lake and Campsite
21.6	Lower end of Upper Kintla Lake
24.3	Lower Kintla Lake and Campsite
27.0	Junction with Kishenehn Creek Trail; turn left
30.6	Kintla Lake Campground Trailhead

38 Akokala Lake

Description: A remote lake filled with small, native cutthroat trout, with secluded camping opportunities and excellent views of Kintla area peaks.
Start: 35 miles northwest of Columbia Falls in the North Fork region of Glacier National Park.
Type of hike: Day hike or overnighter; out-and-back.
Total distance: 11.6-mile round trip.
Difficulty: Moderate.

Maps: Quartz Ridge and Kintla Peak USGS Quads, and either the USGS map or the Trails Illustrated map for the entire park.
Trail contacts: National Park Service, Glacier National Park, West Glacier, MT 59936; (406) 888–7800; www.nps.gov/glac. A permit is required for overnight camping in the park, so call ahead for information on the advance reservation system. Refer to detailed information in the Boulder Pass (Hike 37) description.

Finding the trailhead: From the junction of U.S. Highway 2 and Nucleus Avenue in Columbia Falls, drive north through town and turn right, heading northeast on Outside North Fork Road. After 35 miles of partially paved but mostly dirt road driving, turn right, heading east for Polebridge. Drive through Polebridge and across the North Fork of the Flathead River for 2 miles to the junction with Inside North Fork Road (also called Glacier Route 7). Turn left, heading north on Inside North Fork Road for 0.1 mile and then turn right, heading east on Bowman Lake Road for 6 miles to Bowman Lake Campground. The last 6 miles are passable by a two-wheel-drive vehicle, but good tires and high clearance are recommended. (You could also take Inside North Fork Road from West Glacier, but it's bumpier, slower, and dustier.) You'll find a wonderful vehicle campground, toilets, and water at Bowman Lake Campground at the trailhead.

The Hike

The North Fork of the Flathead River forms the western boundary of Glacier National Park. Inside the park several lakes drain into the river, with Akokala being one of the smallest. This hike extends through typical North Fork country, with lodgepole pine forests and rolling ridges, but without the snowcapped crags found elsewhere in the park.

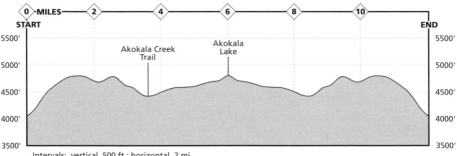

Akokala Lake

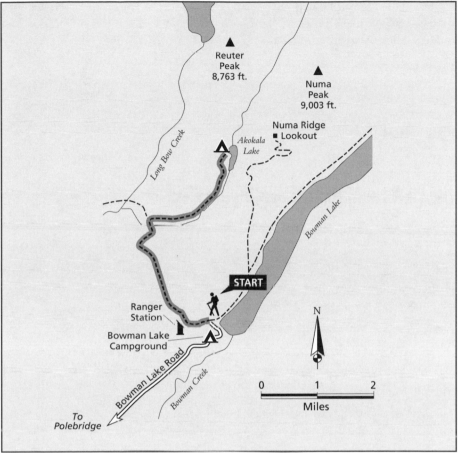

The trail starts from the north edge of Bowman Lake Campground; it's about 5.8 miles to Akokala Lake on an easy-to-follow trail. You have one big hill near the beginning of the hike and a few more small climbs later, but it's an easy grade, only gaining about 600 feet in elevation. When you reach Akokala Creek, you'll see a trail junction with a trail following the creek. Turn right (northeast) and follow Akokala Creek upstream to the lake. The left-hand fork is maintained as a fire-access trail and was used on the Red Bench Fire in 1988. It leads through several burned areas.

The first half of this hike can be dry in late summer or early fall, but there's plenty of drinking water during the last half. Be sure to bring your insect repellent, especially in June, as the Bowman Lake area is infamous for its fierce mosquitoes.

Akokala Lake has a good population of cutthroat trout. The fishing is best halfway around the left-hand (west) side where the water deepens close to shore.

Fires are often prohibited in this area. Don't forget you're deep in Glacier Park grizzly country, so be religious about every possible bear country precaution and sanitary rule. (Originally contributed by the authors, rehiked in 1999)

Key Points

- **0.0** Trailhead
- **3.6** Junction with old Akokala Creek Trail; turn right
- **5.8** Akokala Lake
- **11.6** Trailhead

THE VIEW FROM HERE: FLIPPING ROCKS

When I worked on the trail crew in Glacier long ago, I developed a habit of flipping rocks off trails as I walked down them. I didn't stop or change stride but would just give a loose rock a little flip as I walked by. The trail crew did so to help keep the trails clear without wasting time by breaking stride.

Long after I left that job but continued to hike, I kept on flipping rocks and started wondering what some of these rocky trails would be like if all hikers did it. As a conservative estimate, I flip about three rocks off the trail for every mile I hike, and I probably average about 200 miles of hiking every summer and have since I started in 1965. Well, that's a lot of rocks! About 20,000 of them, in fact.

Think of what we'd have if we multiplied that times the millions of people who go hiking every year. Those rocky trails would be gone forever.

39 Iceberg Lake

Description: A beautiful lake in a spectacular setting with mountain goats, grizzly bears, and lots of humans.
Start: In the Many Glacier area of Glacier National Park.
Type of hike: Day hike; out-and-back.
Total distance: 10-mile round trip.
Difficulty: Moderate.

Maps: Many Glacier USGS Quad maps and either the USGS map or the Trails Illustrated map for the entire park.
Trail contacts: Glacier National Park, West Glacier, MT 59936 (or stop by visitor centers at Apgar or Saint Mary); (406) 888–7800; www.nps.gov/glac.

Finding the trailhead: Drive 8 miles north from St. Mary to Babb on U.S. Highway 89 along the eastern boundary of Glacier National Park, then 12 miles west on Glacier Road 3 into the park to Many Glacier. The trail starts from a parking lot behind Swiftcurrent Motel. Full visitor services are available nearby.

The Hike

More people see grizzly bears along the Iceberg Lake Trail than any other hiking route in this book, partially due to the high concentration of relatively unafraid grizzlies in the Many Glacier Valley. Be extra careful to make noise and stay on the trail. Because of the high bear population, no overnight camping is allowed at Iceberg Lake.

Technically, Iceberg Lake does not have icebergs, but it comes as close as any place in Montana. Chunks of ice float around in the lake, usually until September, but the "icebergs" are larger and more scenic in July and August.

Except for a short section at the very beginning, this trail climbs only 200 feet per mile, a rate most people find comfortable. Wide and relatively smooth, the trail leads through fields of wildflowers. Large flickers with pronounced reddish coloring and swooping flight patterns nest in the ghost trees along the trail. On the last segment of this hike, mountain goats and bighorn sheep are commonly seen on the grassy slopes above and to the right.

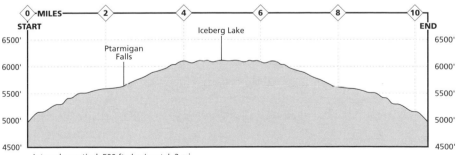

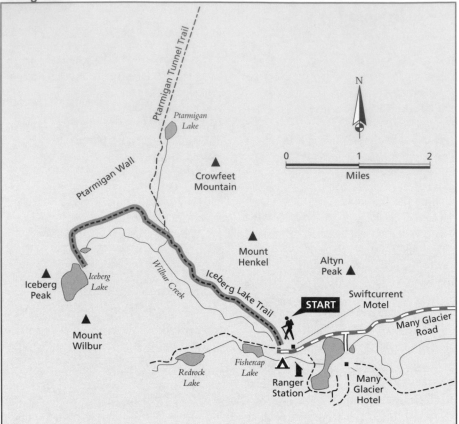

At the 2.5-mile mark, you pass lovely Ptarmigan Falls as it plunges over rocky layers to a deep emerald pool. Shortly thereafter, a clearly marked trail junction indicates a right turn for those wishing to see Ptarmigan Lake and Tunnel and willing to make the stiff, 2.5-mile climb to get there. Iceberg Lake Trail goes straight (west) for another 2.5 miles to the lake.

During the summer the National Park Service installs a bridge over Iceberg Creek just before the lake. This bridge is removed each fall to prevent it from washing out in the spring.

Options

You may sacrifice solitude, but you can take this trip with a group. A National Park Service ranger conducts walks almost every morning in July and August. This is a good option for people who can't quite overcome their fear of bears.

Side Trips

If you have the time and energy, treat yourself by making the steep climb up to Ptarmigan Tunnel and the incredible views you'll find there, including a sweeping vista of the Upper Belly River Valley. (Originally contributed by Mike Sample, rehiked by authors in 1999)

Key Points

0.0 Trailhead

2.5 Ptarmigan Falls and junction with Ptarmigan Tunnel Trail; turn left

5.0 Iceberg Lake

10.0 Trailhead

40 Granite Park

Description: A popular and superscenic route along the Continental Divide in the alpine heart of Glacier National Park, starting at high elevation with no serious hills.
Start: On Logan Pass on the Going-to-the-Sun Road in Glacier Park.
Type of trip: Long day hike or overnighter; out-and-back with a shuttle option.
Total distance: 15.2-mile round trip.

Difficulty: Moderate.
Maps: Ahern Pass, Logan Pass, and many Glacier USGS Quads and either the USGS or Trails Illustrated map for the entire park.
Trail contacts: Glacier National Park, West Glacier, MT 59936 (or stop by visitor centers at Apgar or Saint Mary); (406) 888-7800; www.nps.gov/glac.

Finding the trailhead: The trailhead is across the highway from the Logan Pass Visitor Center. The visitor center has drinking water, toilets, and a large parking lot, which can be full on any summer day.

The Hike

The first 3 miles of the trail go along the Garden Wall directly above Going-to-the-Sun Highway. Some of it is on a ledge, which can be a little nerve-racking but beautifully unique. Then the trail gradually climbs up to Granite Park Chalet across the flanks of Haystack Butte and in the shadow of mighty Mount Gould to the north. (There has never been a haystack on Haystack Butte, but it looks like one.)

To the south Heavens Peak, Longfellow Peak, and others dominate a fantastic horizon. You can also see McDonald Creek tumbling down to the huge lake with the same name. The entire route is on or near the Continental Divide. Don't forget to look behind you on this section for some stunning views.

The hike is mostly flat with a few small upgrades, but nothing serious. It's also extremely popular, so plan on seeing lots of people—and maybe a few mountain goats and bighorn sheep, too, that have become accustomed enough to hikers to freely show themselves. The trail itself is always in great shape. It opens in early July, and if you go soon after the opening, you may have to carefully traverse a few lingering snowbanks.

You can see the wonderfully positioned Granite Park Chalet about 1.5 miles before you get there. Locals appropriately call this stretch of trail Bear Valley because you can often see grizzly bears here from the trail and the chalet. Alpine wildflower enthusiasts will think they're in heaven. Turn left (west) at the junction with the Glacier Overlook Trail, 0.8 mile before the chalet.

If you're out for a long day hike, have lunch at the chalet and then return to Logan Pass. If you plan to stay overnight, make sure to make reservations at the chalet in advance. Rooms are wonderfully rustic and reasonably priced. Get more information at the Web site www.glacierguides.com and make reservations by calling

Granite Park

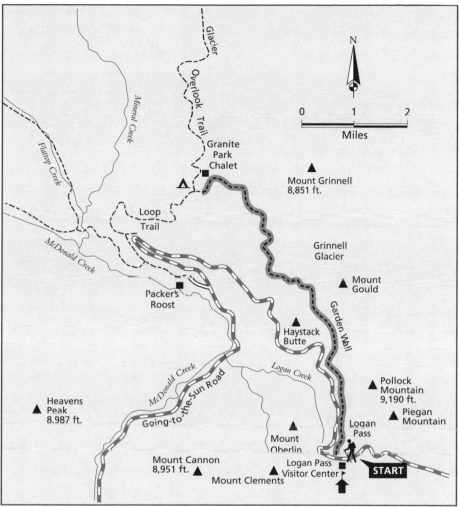

(800) 521–7238. You can also carry your backpack, of course, and stay at the campsite near the chalet, but you'll need a backcountry camping permit to do so.

Options

If you can arrange a shuttle, you can hike 4 miles (all downhill) on the Loop Trail instead of retracing your steps to Logan Pass.

Side Trips

You won't want to miss the terrific view from the Grinnell Glacier Overlook. It's a short (0.6 mile one way) but steep hike, and worth the effort, perhaps something to

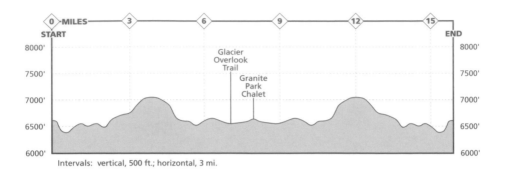

Intervals: vertical, 500 ft.; horizontal, 3 mi.

do after supper at the Granite Park Chalet. From the overlook you can hike on an unofficial trail along the ridge to another saddle and look down into Lake Sherburne, Lake Josephine, and Lake McDonald. (Originally contributed by the authors, rehiked in 1999)

Key Points

0.0 Trailhead

6.8 Junction with Glacier Overlook Trail; turn left

7.6 Granite Park Chalet

15.2 Trailhead

41 The Nyack Loop

Description: One of your best chances for solitude and a true wilderness experience in Glacier National Park.
Start: 15 miles southeast of West Glacier in the Middle Fork region of Glacier National Park.
Type of hike: Extended backpacking trip; shuttle with loop option.
Total distance: 37.3 miles for shuttle and close to 40 miles for loop option.
Difficulty: Strenuous.

Maps: Nyack, Mount Jackson, Mount Stimson, and Mount Saint Nicholas USGS Quads and either the USGS map or the Trails Illustrated map for the entire park.
Trail contacts: Glacier National Park, West Glacier, MT 59936 (or stop by visitor centers at Apgar or Saint Mary); (406) 888-7800; www.nps.gov/glac. A permit is required for overnight camping in the park, so call ahead for information on the advance reservation system. Refer to detailed information in the Boulder Pass (Hike 37) description.

Finding the trailhead: To reach Nyack Trailhead drive east of West Glacier on U.S. Highway 2 for about 10 miles and take the only public, well-maintained road on the left between the Moccasin and Cascadilla River accesses. Follow this gravel road for a short distance and turn right when you reach a dead end just before the railroad tracks. Then drive about another quarter of a mile and park. Walk down the road a hundred yards or so, cross the railroad tracks, follow a trail through a cottonwood stand, and then wade the river, keeping your eyes peeled for trail markers on trees on the opposite riverbank.

To leave a vehicle (or have somebody pick you up) at the Coal Creek crossing, drive another 6 miles east on U.S. Highway 2 until you see a gravel road to your left (north), just before the Stanton Creek Lodge. Follow this road as it takes off from the highway and crosses the tracks before merging into an old logging road. Leave your vehicle at the end of the logging road. If you're doing this trip in reverse, ford the Middle Fork of the Flathead River about 75 yards south of where the old logging road hits the river. You should see an orange marker and trail sign on the opposite shore.

Both of these trailheads are hard to find, and you should obtain a trailhead map at the same time you get your permit. Limited parking is available at both trailheads; there are no facilities. Fording the Middle Fork is possible only in August or perhaps late July in a dry year; however, you can continue this hike by floating to Nyack Creek from the Cascadilla River access and arranging for somebody in a raft to pick you up at the Coal Creek crossing, which is accessed by floating down from the Paola River access.

The easiest way to avoid confusion is to stop at the Walton Ranger Station for detailed and updated directions and a special hand-drawn map of both the Nyack Creek and Coal Creek trailheads. You can also get the map when getting your permit at the Apgar or Saint Mary Visitor Centers.

Recommended itinerary: You can spend more than four nights on this route and not be disappointed, or you could hurry through with a three-night trip, but the following itinerary should be about right.

First night: Lower Nyack designated campsite or undesignated campsite somewhere along Lower Nyack Creek

Second night: Upper Nyack designated campsite or undesignated campsite somewhere along Upper Nyack Creek

Third night: Designated campground at Beaver Woman Lake or undesignated campsite at or near Buffalo Woman Lake or Beaver Woman Lake

Fourth night: Coal Creek designated campsite or undesignated campsite halfway down Coal Creek

The Hike

Many trails in Glacier Park are heavily used. Others receive surprisingly little use, although they host as many backcountry rewards. The Nyack Loop is an excellent example of the latter. Keep in mind, though, that if you plan to ford the river to access the Nyack Creek and Coal Creek Trailheads, you have to wait until August to take this trip.

The trail follows Nyack Creek (named after Nyack Flats on the west side of the river) as it flows over a gorgeous falls and colorful bedrock. Mount Stimson, an incredible hulk of a mountain, dominates the landscape for much of the hike. And you can get a few nice views of mighty Mount St. Nicholas from the Coal Creek Trail. In addition plan on seeing more wildlife, including the grizzly, than you can find in most sections of the park. And unlike most of the park, you can camp almost anywhere instead of in often-trampled designated campsites.

So, what keeps the trail from heavy use? Well, it's a long 37 miles plus side trips— and offers no fishing (the entire drainage closed to protect endangered bull trout habitat). In addition it starts and ends by fording the Middle Fork of the Flathead River, which can be a stressful experience under some circumstances. But if you aren't a fanatic angler, can tolerate getting your feet wet, and do not mind long walks, this could turn out to be the backpacking vacation of your life. Plan to take at least four days, though you could easily spend a week on this hike without regretting it. The Nyack Loop is wild nature at its finest.

After crossing the Middle Fork (the former site of the Nyack Ranger Station), hike northwest on the South Boundary Trail for about three-quarters of a mile until you ford Nyack Creek. A suspension bridge used to straddle Nyack Creek, but it's long gone. Anyway, you will get your feet wet again. And get used to it—there are no footbridges in this, the wildest section of the park.

Nyack Creek is a large stream. This deep ford can be dicey in July but is usually manageable in August. Right after crossing Nyack Creek, you see the Nyack Trail junction. Turn right (east). Expect several boggy sections after Nyack Creek until the trail climbs to higher ground.

The trail gradually climbs (Category 4) in thick forest along Nyack Creek all the way to Surprise Pass at 21.7 miles. When you reach the junction with Cut Bank Pass

The Nyack Loop

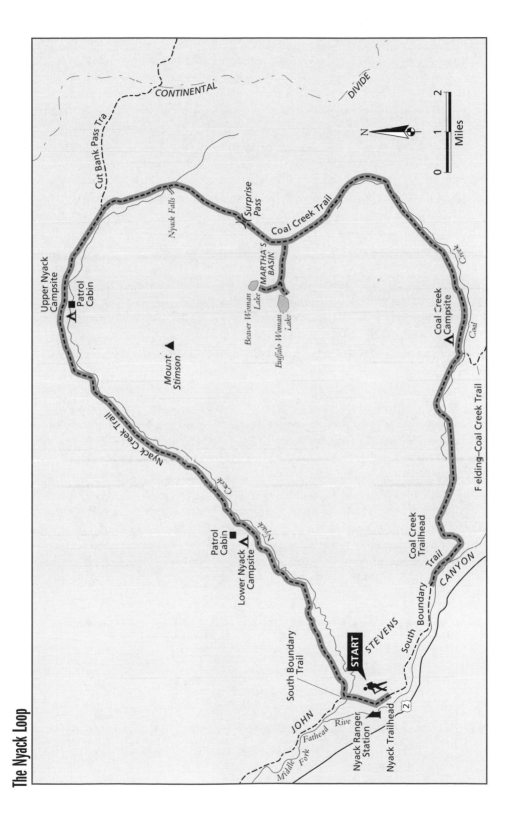

Trail at 17 miles, stay right on Nyack Creek Trail. Along the way to Surprise Pass, you pass through some incredibly large western larch and cottonwood groves. The trail dips down to the stream occasionally but stays high much of the way. The scenery along the trail is superb, but the scenic highlight may be Nyack Falls, with massive Mount Stimson forming the backdrop. At Surprise Pass, the trail becomes the Coal Creek Trail.

Although there are a few dry stretches, you can usually find enough drinking water. In late summer on the way up Surprise Pass, you can gorge yourself on huckleberries. Keep very close watch for grizzlies, however, as this entire hike traverses some of the best grizzly habitat left in the world. As a special precaution, carefully read the earlier section of this book on hiking in bear country to reduce your chances of encountering a grizzly on unpleasant terms. Remember that this is the big bear's home, and you are the visitor. Behave accordingly.

Soon after you drop over Surprise Pass into Coal Creek, at 22.5 miles, a spur trail to Buffalo Woman and Beaver Woman Lakes juts off to the right. Don't miss these "beautiful women" nestled in gorgeous Martha's Basin.

After the lakes, it is a long, forested haul down Coal Creek to the Middle Fork. The last section of this trail burned in 1984 and has been difficult to keep clear of downfall. At 31.2 miles you reach the Coal Creek Campsite. Here the Fielding–Coal Creek Trail veers off to the left. Stay to the right (west) on the main Coal Creek Trail. At the junction with the South Boundary Trail (36.9 miles), continue straight downhill toward the river, which you have to ford again to reach the Coal Creek trailhead. Leave your fishing rod at home. To protect bull trout spawning habitat, the National Park Service prohibits fishing in Nyack Creek, Coal Creek, Buffalo Woman Lake, and Beaver Woman Lake. You'll need the extra room in your pack for food anyway.

Unlike most places in Glacier National Park, you can set up a zero-impact camp anywhere along this route. If you prefer designated sites, however, you can apply for four campgrounds (all nice campsites) along the route. If you use an undesignated site, make sure you don't leave any mark so the next camper can think he or she is the first person ever to use this campsite. You can only stay a maximum of two nights at any campsite, which must be at least 100 feet from any lake or stream and a half mile from any patrol cabin. Also, campsites should be at least 150 feet from the trail

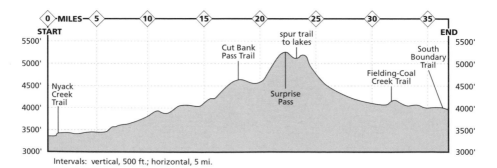

Intervals: vertical, 500 ft.; horizontal, 5 mi.

and out of sight of the trail or other campers. And you must be prepared to hang food 12 feet off the ground and 6 feet from any tree. And as in the rest of Glacier, campfires are prohibited.

Options

If 37 miles isn't enough, once you get to the Coal Creek Trailhead, you could take the Boundary Trail back to Nyack Creek where you started to make this a true loop. Doing so adds 4.5 miles to the trip. This section of the South Boundary Trail is, however, lightly traveled and may be brushy and difficult to follow. This trail takes off to the right (west) about 0.4 mile before reaching the river. The South Boundary Trail heads down to ford Coal Creek shortly after the junction and then closely follows the Middle Fork most of the way to Nyack Creek.

Side Trips

Be sure to take the trip to Beaver Woman and Buffalo Woman Lakes, sometimes referred to as Martha's Basin. You can take Cut Bank Pass Trail for a good view of much of southern Glacier Park. However, the trail up to Cut Bank Pass is one of the toughest climbs in the park. Perhaps the most popular side trip is a climb up Mount Stimson. Plan to take a full day to climb from timberline to the summit of Stimson and back down again. Although one of the most rigorous climbs in the park, it's nontechnical and within reach of most well-conditioned, experienced hikers. (Originally contributed by the authors, rehiked in 2000)

Key Points

0.0 Nyack Trailhead and ford of the Middle Fork of the Flathead River

0.1 South Boundary Trail; turn left

0.7 Ford Nyack Creek

0.8 Junction with Nyack Creek Trail; turn right

5.4 Lower Nyack Campsite

7.4 Lower Nyack Patrol Cabin

14.4 Upper Nyack Campsite

15.4 Upper Nyack Patrol Cabin

16.0 Nyack Falls

17.0 Junction with Cut Bank Pass Trail; turn right

21.7 Surprise Pass

22.5 Spur trail to Buffalo Woman and Beaver Woman Lakes

31.2 Coal Creek Campsite and junction with Fielding–Coal Creek Trail; turn right

33.3 Coal Creek Patrol Cabin

36.9 Junction with South Boundary Trail; turn right

37.3 Coal Creek Trailhead and ford of the Middle Fork of the Flathead River

42 Triple Divide Pass

Description: A difficult day hike to a unique pass.
Start: In the Two Medicine area of Glacier National Park near East Glacier.
Type of hike: Long day hike; out-and-back.
Total distance: 14.4-mile round trip.
Difficulty: Strenuous.
Maps: Cut Bank Pass and Mt. Stimson USGS Quads and either the USGS map or the Trails

Illustrated map for the entire park.
Trail contacts: Glacier National Park, National Park Service, West Glacier, MT 59936; (406) 888-7800; www.nps.gov/glac. A permit is required for overnight camping in the park, so call ahead for information on the advance reservation system. Refer to detailed information in the Boulder Pass (Hike 37) description.

Finding the trailhead: Drive north from East Glacier on Montana Highway 49 for 4 miles to Two Medicine Road. Turn left and follow the road to Two Medicine Lake. The trailhead is west of the boat dock and ample parking lot near the shoreline. You'll also find toilet, water, campground, and ranger station at the trailhead.

The Hike

Triple Divide Peak, which hovers above Triple Divide Pass, is the only place in Montana where water flows into three oceans—Atlantic, Pacific, and Hudson Bay (Arctic Ocean), which are, appropriately, the names of the three streams flowing off the mountain.

From the trailhead the Cut Bank Creek Trail stays gradually uphill all the way to the Pitamakan Pass Junction at 3.9 miles. The southern horizon is dominated by Bad Marriage Mountain, named for a Blackfeet chief, not an old ranger's marital problems. You follow sparkling and slow-moving Cut Bank Creek all the way.

At the junction, turn right (west) toward Medicine Grizzly Lake. About a half mile later, you pass through Atlantic Creek Campground. Shortly after the campground, at 4.6 miles, turn right (north) again onto the Triple Divide Pass Trail at that junction. At this point you leave the thick, unburned forest of the Medicine Grizzly Valley and start the fairly easy but long (2.6-mile) Category 2 grind up to the pass, remarkably without switchbacks.

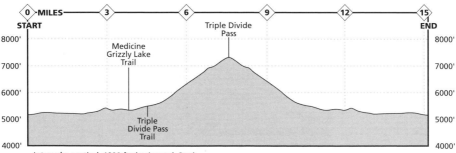

Intervals: vertical, 1000 ft.; horizontal, 3 mi.

Split Mountain and the headwaters of Red Eagle Canyon from Triple Divide Pass.

The trail climbs above Medicine Grizzly Lake, which is a blue jewel in a green ocean in the shadow of the mountain by the same name and Razoredge Mountain hosting the Continental Divide west of the lake. This valley is streaked with avalanche chutes and flush with succulent vegetation, all such great grizzly habitat that the National Park Service had to close the campsite at the lake and consolidate camping at Atlantic Creek. You can also see a small, unnamed lake in a huge gouge out of the side of Medicine Grizzly Lake, a place lots of people probably think about going, but I doubt anybody ever does.

At Triple Divide Pass, you'll probably see some bighorn sheep grazing in the flats on the south side of the pass, and you'll definitely get some great views into the Red Eagle Valley to the north dominated by Split Mountain, on the flanks of which you can see tarns with little icebergs in them.

In summary, you're walking through a moving postcard.

This trail is popular, so don't expect to have it to yourself. On the pass watch your pack because the ground squirrels and marmots have, regrettably, been fed by some hikers and now realize they can always find treats like gorp and granola bars in packs.

Triple Divide Pass

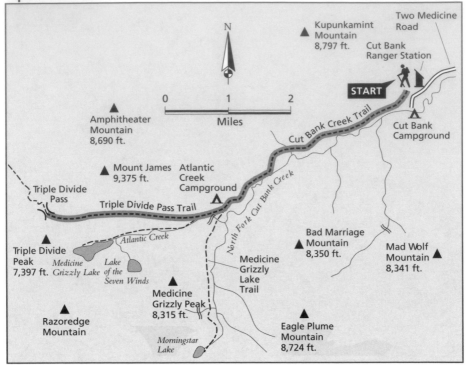

Side Trips

The logical side trip is Triple Divide Peak, but don't try it unless you've left at first light and hurried up to the pass. If you didn't, you probably won't have enough time to make the ascent and get back to the trailhead before darkness. The Cut Bank/Medicine Grizzly area has such a high grizzly population that you definitely don't want to be hiking out at night. You can stay overnight at Atlantic Creek to make it easier, but you should still leave as early as possible in the morning; you should be fit and experienced at off-trail hiking. And, of course, make sure you have good weather.

Another good side trip is Medicine Grizzly Lake, which adds only about 3 miles to the total distance. This trail is, however, frequently closed because of bear problems. (Hiked by authors in 2001)

Key Points

0.0 Trailhead

3.9 Junction with Medicine Grizzly Lake Trail; turn right

4.3 Atlantic Creek Campsite

4.6 Junction with Triple Divide Pass Trail; turn right

7.2 Triple Divide Pass

14.4 Trailhead

43 Upper Two Medicine Lake

Description: An easy hike into a spectacular mountain lake.

Start: In the Two Medicine area of Glacier National Park near East Glacier.

Type of hike: Day hike or overnighter; out-and-back.

Total distance: 3.8-mile round trip with the boat ride option; 10 miles with no boat ride.

Difficulty: Easy.

Maps: Dancing Lady (formerly Squaw Mountain) and Mount Rockwell USGS Quads and either the USGS map or the Trails Illustrated map for the entire park.

Trail contacts: Glacier National Park, National Park Service, West Glacier, MT 59936; (406) 888-7800; www.nps.gov/glac. A permit is required for overnight camping in the park, so call ahead for information on the advance reservation system. Refer to detailed information in the Boulder Pass (Hike 37) description.

Finding the trailhead: Drive north from East Glacier on Montana Highway 49 for 4 miles to Two Medicine Road. Turn left and follow the road to Two Medicine Lake. The trailhead is west of the boat dock and parking lot near the shoreline. The trailhead features the Two Medicine Camp Store, a ranger station, lots of parking, a toilet, a campground, and boat rides with Glacier Park Boat Company.

The Hike

The first part of this hike is as easy as it gets—a boat ride. After 9:00 A.M. you can catch a ride on the Hiker's Express for a small sum. The boat leaves about every hour from the lower end of the lake to a boat ramp and shelter at the upper end. This cuts 3 miles off your hike to Upper Two Medicine Lake.

Perhaps because this is such an easy hike that can be combined with a scenic boat ride, it's extremely popular. On a warm summer day, hundreds of people will take the boat ride and walk as far as Twin Falls, and many of them will extend their day hike to Upper Two Medicine Lake.

From the boat ramp hike west on the well-marked trail. You'll find a pit toilet about a quarter mile along, just past the first junction with the South Shore Trail. A little more than a half mile farther, you'll see a major spur trail veering off to the right to Twin Falls, a magnificent waterfall you won't want to miss.

After enjoying the falls, hike another mile to the lower end of Upper Two Medicine Lake, a blue jewel in the heavy forested mountains of the Two Medicine area. Massive Mount Rockwell rises from the south shore and precipitous Lone Walker Mountain juts up from the upper end of the lake. Late in the season you can walk all or most of the shoreline.

You can also camp at the lake, but most people don't because it's such a short, heavily visited lake. There are three backcountry campsites at the foot of the lake, with the food area strangely close to the trail, preventing much privacy while eating dinner.

Upper Two Medicine Lake

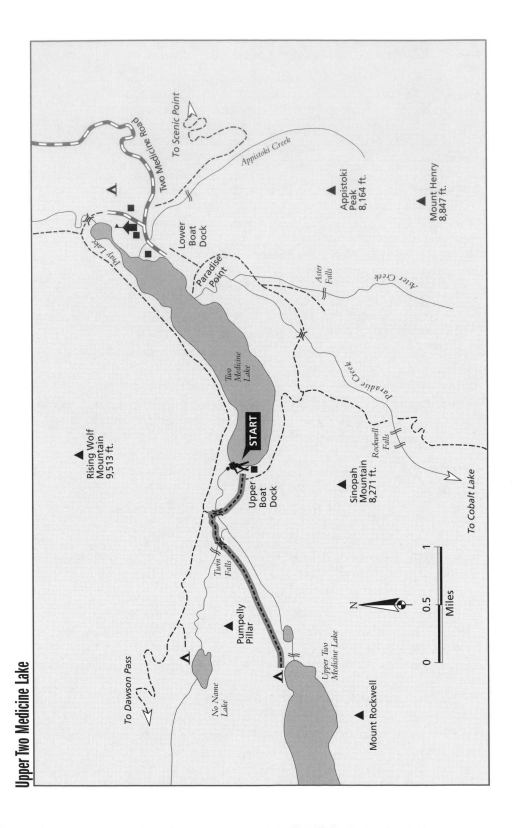

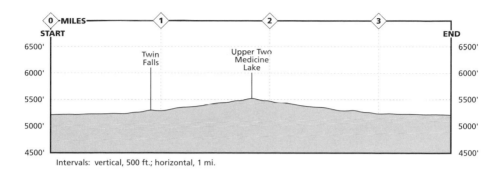

Intervals: vertical, 500 ft.; horizontal, 1 mi.

Options

If this short hike isn't enough exercise, add 3 miles by hiking back along either the north or south shore of Two Medicine Lake. You can also make this a 10-mile hike by hiking both shores. Since both the north and south trails generally follow the shoreline of the lake, they're fairly flat. From the south shore you get a great view of awesome Rising Wolf Mountain, one of the bulkiest mountains in the park.

Side Trips

Take the short spur trail for a good look at Twin Falls. (Hiked by authors in 2001)

Key Points

0.0 Trailhead at Upper Boat Dock of Two Medicine Lake

0.3 Junction with South Shore Trail; turn right

0.9 Spur trail to Twin Falls

1.9 Upper Two Medicine Lake

3.8 Trailhead

44 Lake Isabel

Description: Magnificent Two Medicine Pass and remote Lake Isabel.
Start: In the Two Medicine area of Glacier National Park near East Glacier.
Type of hike: Extended backpacking trip; out-and-back.
Total distance: 30-mile round trip.
Difficulty: Strenuous.
Maps: Dancing Lady Mountain (formerly Squaw Mountain) and Mount Rockwell USGS Quads and either the USGS map or the Trails Illustrated map for the entire park.
Trail contacts: Glacier National Park, National Park Service, West Glacier, MT 59936; (406) 888-7800; www.nps.gov/glac. A permit is required for overnight camping in the park, so call ahead for information on the advance reservation system. Refer to detailed information in the Boulder Pass (Hike 37) description.

Finding the trailhead: Drive north from East Glacier on Montana Highway 49 for 4 miles to Two Medicine Road. Turn left. Follow the road to Two Medicine Lake. The trailhead is west of the boat dock and parking lot near the shoreline. The trailhead features the Two Medicine Camp Store, a ranger station, ample parking, rest rooms, a campground, and boat rides on Two Medicine Lake with Glacier Park Boat Company.

The Hike

The thought of Glacier National Park often conjures up images of bumper-to-bumper traffic on the Going-to-the-Sun Road or people on every trail; Hidden Lake (on Logan Pass) doesn't seem so hidden and wildlife not so wild. Much of the park is truly wild, however, and you only have to get off the beaten path to experience it. There are three ways to get away from the crowds. First, go somewhere no one wants to go. Second, go somewhere few people know about. Third, go somewhere that is too hard for most people to go. The third philosophy works for this hike. There are two routes to Lake Isabel. One is a 16.9-mile flat and in-the-trees hike up Park Creek; the other is the scenic but more difficult 15-mile grunt over Two Medicine Pass. The latter is the one described here.

The difficulty of this route reduces use, of course, but in addition, the National Park Service has only one campsite at the lake, and it's usually reserved. That, too, helps make this trip a true wilderness adventure where you'll have all the solitude you could ever want.

In fact, there's nothing easy about getting to Lake Isabel. The route is really too much for one day with a full pack. The only alternative, however, is staying at Cobalt Lake, but getting a reservation for this campsite is extremely difficult because this destination is so popular. You can also stay the first night at the Upper Park Creek Campsite, which is not particularly scenic, but people who make it this far tend to prefer toughing it out for 2.3 miles more to Lake Isabel.

Lake Isabel

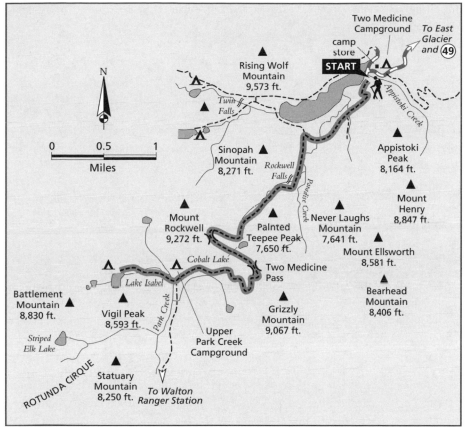

I Iaving said all that, let's be clear on one point. Lake Isabel is worth the effort to get there.

From the Two Medicine Camp Store parking lot, head west along the southern shore of Two Medicine Lake. The South Shore Trail stays in the trees, climbing slightly. Several trails intersect the main trail. Stay left (southwest) at the junction with Paradise Point. Stay right (southwest) at the junction with Aster Falls Trail. After crossing a suspension bridge over Paradise Creek, turn left (southwest) at the junction with the Two Medicine Pass Trail and head for Cobalt Lake.

After 3.4 miles, Rockwell Falls offers a good rest stop. Rockwell Falls is a series of cascades in the shadow of Sinopah Mountain. Be sure to drink lots of filtered water. You'll need to be hydrated for the Category 1 climb up to Two Medicine Pass.

The climb beside Rockwell Falls is fairly steep but short. Then the hike gradually ascends toward Cobalt Lake. The huckleberry bushes along the way offer savory berries if the season is right. Follow the creek through the fir-clad slopes until you are within sight of Cobalt Lake. At the trail junction at the lake, at 5.7 miles, turn right for Two Medicine Pass. The left trail goes to the campground at Cobalt Lake. In July and August Cobalt Lake has a one-night stay limit.

Again, be sure you have enough water for the climb, although snowmelt might provide some relief. The trail gains serious altitude for the next mile. After the climb to the saddle next to Mount Rockwell, the trail remains relatively flat over Chief Lodgepole Peak. From almost anyplace here, notice the view of Paradise Park down and to the left. To the right, Park Creek Valley extends for as far as the eye can see. This evidence of glaciation, along with the cirque containing Lake Isabel across the valley, alludes to a much more harsh and powerful time.

Check your map to name and count the surrounding peaks. Start with Grizzly Mountain above Paradise Park and work to your right: Eagle Ribs Mountain, Mount Despair, across Park Creek to Statuary Mountain, Vigil Peak above Lake Isabel, Caper Peak, Lone Walker Mountain, and Mount Rockwell. The mountains surround you in divine council.

From above Chief Lodgepole Peak, continue along the ridge to Two Medicine Pass at 7.9 miles. Be careful to follow the cairns; they mark the trail that drops down and to the right into Park Creek Valley. Also watch for mountain goats.

The trail descends for almost 4 miles of easy switchbacks to the Upper Park Creek campsite. On the return trip this climb is the hardest part of the hike. The switchbacks last for about a mile, then the trail drops through a thick undergrowth of ferns, bushes, and devil's club. When you reach the Park Creek Trail, turn right (west) and hike the last hill up to Lake Isabel.

Unfortunately, the National Park Service prohibits fishing at Park Creek, but hold your rod, because it's only another 2.3 miles to Lake Isabel. At Lake Isabel the fish bite anything. The water in this lake is clear, and Vigil Peak provides a scenic backdrop.

The 15-mile return hike is tough. Carry and drink plenty of water. Even without a visit to Lake Isabel, the round-trip hike climbs 5,000 feet. (Originally contributed by the authors, rehiked in 1995)

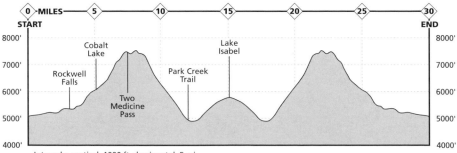

Intervals: vertical, 1000 ft.; horizontal, 5 mi.

Key Points

0.0 Trailhead at Two Medicine Camp Store parking lot

2.3 Junction with Two Medicine Pass Trail; turn left

3.4 Rockwell Falls

5.7 Cobalt Lake

7.9 Two Medicine Pass

12.7 Junction with Park Creek Trail; turn right

15.0 Lake Isabel

30.0 Trailhead

45 Pitamakan and Dawson Passes

Description: An incredible trek through out-standing mountain scenery, mostly above tim-berline, definitely one of the most scenic and popular hikes in Glacier National Park, featur-ing two jewel-like mountain lakes, a traverse along the Continental Divide, and three moun-tain passes. Where else can you hike over three spectacular passes in 4 miles?

Start: In the Two Medicine area of Glacier National Park near East Glacier.

Type of trip: Moderate backpacking trip or long day hike; loop.

Total distance: 18.8 miles.

Difficulty: Strenuous.

Maps: Cut Bank Pass, Mount Rockwell, and Dancing Lady (formerly Squaw Mountain) USGS Quads and either the USGS map or Trails Illustrated map for the entire park.

Trail contacts: Glacier National Park, National Park Service, West Glacier, MT 59936; (406) 888-7800; www.nps.gov/glac. A permit is required for overnight camping in the park, so call ahead for information on the advance reservation system. Refer to detailed informa-tion in the Boulder Pass (Hike 37) description.

Finding the trailhead: From East Glacier drive north on Montana Highway 49 about 4 miles to a well-marked turnoff for Two Medicine Road. Turn right for Two Medicine Campground. Drive through the campground to the bridge over Two Medicine River at the outlet of Pray Lake, a small lake below the outlet of Two Medicine Lake. (Pray Lake is named after Charles N. Pray, one of the congressmen who pushed hard for the establishment of Glacier National Park.) The Pray Lake Trailhead is at the outlet of the two lakes. The trailhead features plenty of parking at the Two Medicine Camp Store, a ranger station, rest rooms, a campground, and Glacier Park Boat Com-pany boat rides on Two Medicine Lake.

Recommended itinerary: Spend the first night at Oldman Lake and the second night at No Name Lake or, if necessary to get permits, in reverse order.

The Hike

The name Two Medicine comes from the Blackfeet history that refers to two med-icine lodges built in the area for performing the sun dance. The exact site of the lodges has not been discovered.

From the Pray Lake Trailhead parking lot, cross the bridge below Pray Lake and turn right toward Oldman Lake, 6.4 miles down the trail. In the first 2.4 miles, you hike around the base of a towering mastiff called Rising Wolf Mountain (shortened version of a Blackfeet term for "the way the wolf rises") and across the bridge over Dry Fork Creek to a marked trail junction with Dry Fork Trail, where you turn left (west). From here you face a steady climb up an open valley. The very wet Dry Fork Creek cascades the length of the valley, and several smaller streams drop out of hidden cirques to add to the volume. Paintbrush and lupine add splashes of color to the scene.

At the head of the valley, you enter a blister rust–plagued whitebark pine forest. The trail splits at 8.2 miles, shortly before Oldman Lake. The right fork heads

Oldman Lake from Pitamakan Pass Trail.

directly for Pitamakan Pass while the left fork leads to the campsites on the lake. Take the left fork. Flinsch Peak dominates the western skyline. At Oldman Lake you might see a family of beavers at the far end of the lake in the twilight hours. Twenty inch Yellowstone cutthroat trout cruise the shoreline. On the northern slopes above the lake, a white cloud of bear grass stands as thick as anywhere in the park in late July. The area around Oldman Lake is prime habitat for grizzlies. Play it safe.

From Oldman Lake to No Name Lake, a stretch of nearly 8 miles, the trail is nearly devoid of water by early August, so fill all your bottles before leaving camp. To reach Pitamakan Pass from Oldman Lake, take the short cutoff trail almost straight north from the outhouse instead of going back to the trail junction. The Category 2 climb to Pitamakan Pass is short and steep—more than 1,000 feet up in 1.8 miles. The pass is actually a saddle in a ridge. Before following the trail up the ridge, pause for a look down at Pitamakan Lake, about 800 feet below. *Pitamakan* is, incidentally, Blackfeet for "running eagle."

Very soon after leaving the saddle, you encounter two well-marked junctions, the first with Cut Bank Creek Trail and the second with Nyack Creek Trail. In each case turn left (west). The first junction is with the trail down to Pitamakan Lake, and the second takes you to the wilds of Upper Nyack Creek. Just after the second junction,

Pitamakan and Dawson Passes

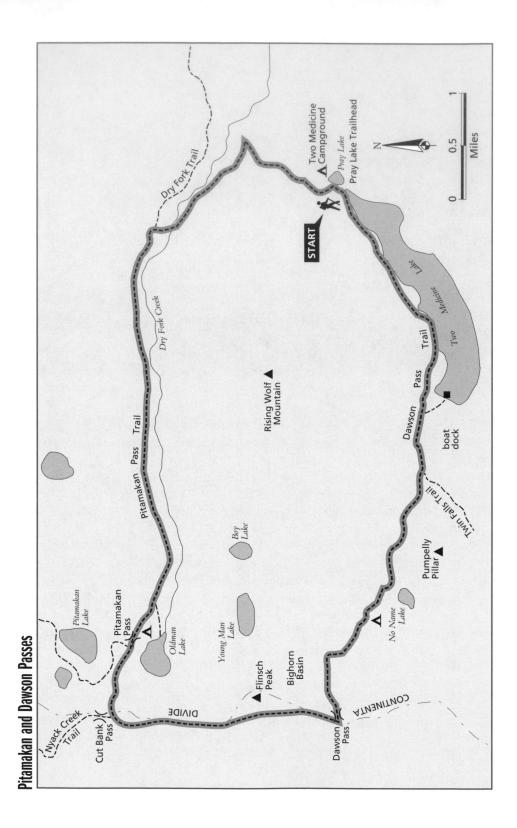

at 8.8 miles, you reach Cut Bank Pass and cross the Continental Divide. Due west stands mighty Mount Stimson, rising 6,000 feet above the Nyack Creek Valley.

From here the trail goes in a southerly direction, paralleling the Continental Divide along the shoulders of Mount Morgan and Flinsch Peak to Dawson Pass (named for an early surveyor of the park), where you cross the divide again. While nearly level through this section, the trail traverses steep slopes of roller-bearing scree, which is dangerous when wet. Some sections of the trail follow ledges with steep drops, so watch your step. Because dangerous snow banks lie across these slopes until late June or early July, the National Park Service opens this trail later than most. Check with the Two Medicine Ranger Station before planning an early trip.

Dawson Pass is a favorite hangout for mountain goats, which are quite tame in this region. Don't feed them and make the situation worse than it already is. You might also see bighorn sheep.

Dawson Pass is a popular cutoff spot for people who wish to make the steep walk up the south face of Flinsch Peak. While you're up high on these passes, watch the weather. You don't want to get caught in a thunderstorm (like we did).

From Dawson Pass the trail drops rapidly through Bighorn Basin to No Name Lake at 14 miles. The lake deserves a more descriptive "no name," for it lies at the base of sheer Pumpelly Pillar, named after an early geologist in the park. It is an evocative pool, especially in the first moments of sunlight on a quiet morning. The No Name Lake Trail veers off to the right (south); stay to the left.

Leaving No Name Lake, you move down the valley about 1.5 miles to the junction with a trail heading up to Upper Two Medicine Lake, Twin Falls, and the South Shore trail. Stay left (east) and keep following the trail along the north side of Two Medicine Lake back to the Pray Lake Trailhead.

Options

You can just as easily hike this loop in reverse, and the availability of campsites might make this option necessary.

From the lower end of Two Medicine Lake, you can take a commercial tour boat to the trailhead—or back to the trailhead at the end of your hike. Doing so cuts about 3 miles off your trip. Check on the arrangements at the boat dock near the trailhead before you leave on the hike or contact Glacier Park Boat Company, (406) 257–2426; gpboats@mountainweb.com.

Oldman Lake and No Name Lake have designated campsites, but they are very popular and frequently reserved, so you might try the park's reservation system to make sure you can get a permit.

As far as fishing goes, Oldman Lake has some nice-size Yellowstone cutthroats. You might also attract a few fish to your fly in the stream below the lake. No Name Lake has small brookies and rainbows and can be fair fishing when conditions are right. You can also stop to fish Two Medicine Lake on the way back—you might catch a

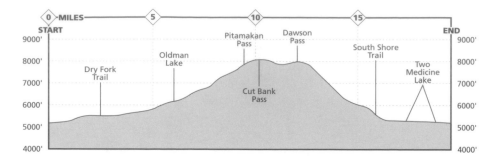

few rainbows or brookies. The brook trout can grow big in Two Medicine Lake, but you need a float tube or canoe to increase your chances of catching a big one.

You can make this an overnighter by camping at either Oldman or No Name Lakes. This option makes for a long day with lots of climbing, but at least it's downhill from Dawson Pass to the trailhead. For fit hikers, this route also makes a fantastic, albeit long, day hike.

Side Trips

On the way back you can take the trail up to Upper Two Medicine Lake as a side trip. From the Dawson Pass Trail it's about 1.3 miles to Upper Two Medicine Lake. Double this figure for the trip back, and you add 2.6 miles to your hike. You might want at least to take a break and take the short hike (about a mile round-trip) to see Twin Falls. You probably will not want to take side trips down the Cut Bank Creek or Nyack Creek Trails unless you like climbing huge hills to get back to this trail. (Originally contributed by Mike Sample, rehiked by authors in 2001)

Key Points

- **0.0** Pray Lake Trailhead
- **2.4** Junction with Dry Fork Trail; turn left
- **6.4** Oldman Lake
- **8.2** Pitamakan Pass and junction with Cut Bank Creek Trail; turn left
- **8.5** Junction with Nyack Creek Trail; turn left
- **8.8** Cut Bank Pass
- **12.4** Dawson Pass
- **14.0** Junction with No Name Lake Trail; turn left
- **15.5** Junction with Twin Falls/Upper Two Medicine Lake/South Shore Trails; turn left
- **18.8** Pray Lake Trailhead and Two Medicine Campground

Beaverhead-Deerlodge National Forest

46 Stony Lake

Description: Dome Shaped Mountain and pristine Stony Lake.
Start: 25 miles northeast of Hamilton near Skalkaho Pass in the Sapphire Mountains.
Type of hike: Day hike or easy overnighter; out-and-back.
Total distance: 8-mile round trip.
Difficulty: Moderate.

Maps: Mount Emerine, Burnt Fork Lakes, Skalkaho Pass, and Stony Creek USGS Quads; and Beaverhead-Deerlodge National Forest Map.
Trail contacts: Pintler Ranger District (Philipsburg office), Beaverhead-Deerlodge National Forest, 88-10A Business Loop, Philipsburg, MT 59858; (406) 859-3211; www.fs.fed.us/r1/bdnf.

Finding the trailhead: Take U.S. Highway 93 south from Missoula to its junction with Skalkaho Road (Montana Highway 38), 3 miles south of Hamilton. Turn left (east) onto this winding mountain road (first 15 miles on pavement), and drive past Skalkaho Falls and over Skalkaho Pass for 28 miles. About 2 miles over the pass is Crystal Creek Campground. The trailhead is across the road and slightly northwest of the campground, where two old logging roads start. Take the one on your left, which is FR 78578. When we were there, there were no signs. Parking is limited, but you can vehicle camp or use the toilet at nearby Crystal Creek Campground.

The Hike

Part of the enjoyment of hiking in the Sapphires is the feeling that you have discovered an area that most hikers would ordinarily drive past without a second glance. The Sapphires (once they have got your attention) prove that there is more to the "wilderness experience" than craggy peaks and snowfields. Stony Lake is one place where this point is well made. It's one of the sapphires of the Sapphire Range.

At the trailhead you'll see Crystal Creek on the right and a logged area on the left. Across from the campground the trail begins as a primitive road (Forest Road 78578) for about half a mile. The road ends and the trail begins, and you turn right on Trail 10, which continues to follow Crystal Creek for about 1.5 miles to its beginning at the Sapphire Divide. The trail goes steadily but gradually uphill, much of the time through meadows.

Upon reaching the divide, Trail 10 heads north for another mile before you reach the junction with Trail 2 down to Stony Lake, where you turn right (east) and drop down to the lake.

Stony Lake offers average fishing for cutthroat trout and has a few good but heavily used campsites.

Options

If you have an extra day or are a strong hiker, it is possible to return to Trail 10 on

Stony Lake

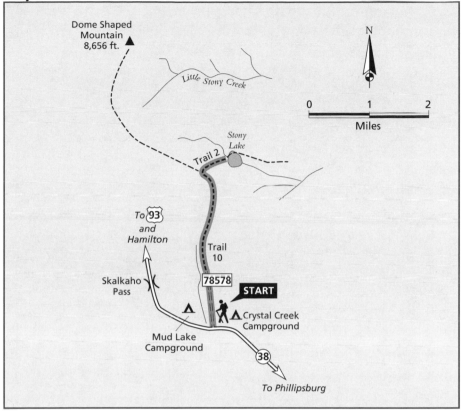

the divide (where it becomes Trail 313 if you go north) and follow it north for approximately 4 miles to Dome Shaped Mountain, which has a broad, grassy summit crisscrossed with snowdrifts that may linger well into July. Also of interest are the thickets of whitebark pine on the summit ridge. The trail to Dome Shaped Mountain is lightly used and may be difficult to follow.

With the Skalkaho Fork Game Preserve on your left (west), you stand a good chance of seeing deer and elk. Although the Sapphires don't appear to be typical mountain goat country, a few hang out around Dome Shaped Mountain. The occasional open spots along the divide provide views of the Pintlers to the southeast, the Flint Creek Range to the northeast, the Bitterroots to the west, and to the south across Skalkaho Pass, the higher peaks of the Sapphire Mountains.

You can also get to Stony Lake by coming up Stony Creek on Trail 2. The distance is about the same, but it's gradually uphill all the way. (Originally contributed by John Westenberg, rehiked by authors in 2002)

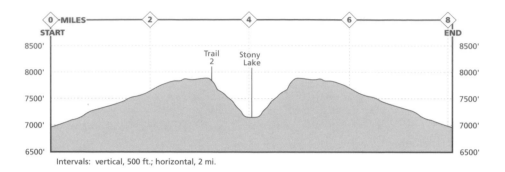

Intervals: vertical, 500 ft.; horizontal, 2 mi.

Key Points

0.0 Trailhead

0.5 Forest Road 78578 changes to Trail 10

3.0 Junction with Trail 2 to Stony Lake; turn right

4.0 Stony Lake

8.0 Trailhead

47 Rainbow Lake

Description: A high lake in the heart of the Anaconda-Pintler Wilderness.
Start: 30 miles southwest of Anaconda in the Anaconda Range.
Type of hike: Moderate backpacking trip or long day hike; out-and-back.
Total distance: 16-mile round trip.
Difficulty: Strenuous.

Maps: Warren Peak, Moose Lake, and Carpp Ridge USGS Quads; Beaverhead-Deerlodge National Forest Map; and Anaconda-Pintler Wilderness Map.
Trail contacts: Pintler Ranger District (Philipsburg office), Beaverhead-Deerlodge National Forest, 88-A Business Loop, P.O. Box H, Philipsburg, MT 59858; (406) 859-3211; www.fs.fed.us/r1/bdnf.

Finding the trailhead: Take Montana Highway 1 south from Philipsburg for 6 miles (or 23 miles north of Anaconda), and then turn west on Montana Highway 38. After 9.2 miles turn left (south) onto Middle Fork Road 5106 and follow the unpaved road until it ends 15.3 miles later at Middle Fork Trailhead, 4 miles past Moose Lake. There is a large parking area with toilet.

The Hike

This spot may not be a secret, but it is still special, especially to those who share its natural gifts. Rainbow Lake, since it was first published in *Hiking Montana,* has increasingly been a popular destination of local hikers and vacationers. Be especially careful to maintain a zero-impact ethic when visiting this lake (and Johnson Lake). Years of use have trampled vegetation and reduced wood supply, so use a stove instead of a campfire to cook. The snow usually clings to Rainbow Pass until at least late June, so mid-July or later is best for this hike. There's plenty of water along the trail except for the stretch between Johnson and Rainbow Lakes.

Start on Falls Fork Trail 29. It's a 5-mile gradual uphill grind to Johnson Lake (elevation 7,720 feet). A forest fire has burned some sections of the trail between the Edith Lake junction and the lake. While hiking along the western shore of the lake, you'll find two trail junctions—Johnson Inlet Trail 96 at 5.2 miles and Continental Divide Trail 9 at 5.4 miles. Turn left at both. After leaving Johnson Lake, it's 2 miles with moderate switchbacks to 9,040-foot Rainbow Pass, about a half mile of it through an old burn. You can see little Martin Lake tucked away below you on your right as you ascend to the pass.

Rainbow Pass is a great place to relax and enjoy the surroundings. To the east is the ominous, broad pyramid of 10,793-foot West Goat Peak, highest in the Pintler Range. To the south are slopes covered with rare alpine larch. Moreover, right below you is your destination—Rainbow Lake. You can see the 1 mile of trail twisting down to the 8,215-foot-long lake. The rainbow trout are especially active in the morning and evening, and trails to explore and peaks to climb are in all directions.

Rainbow Lake

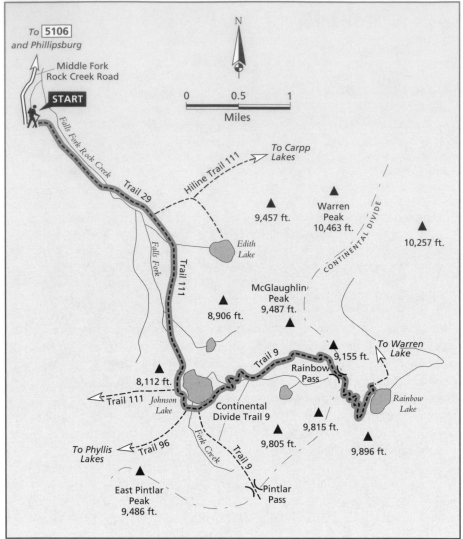

The geology of this area is striking. The range is mainly made up of typical Montana sedimentary rock, but with granite intrusions, which account for all the odd-looking granite boulders strewn about in unexpected places. This phenomenon is especially evident on the trail to Warren Lake.

Rainbow Lake has, appropriately, a nice rainbow trout population. There are a few good campsites along the north shore of the lake.

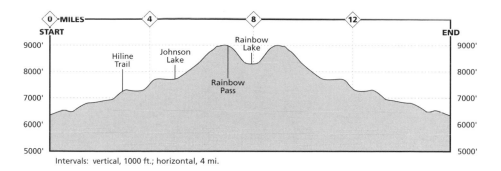

Intervals: vertical, 1000 ft.; horizontal, 4 mi.

Options

You could stay overnight at Johnson Lake and take a day hike into Rainbow Lake.

Side Trips

If you have some extra time on the way back to the trailhead, you can take the short side trip up to Edith Lake. Turn right (north) on the Hiline Trail and then right (east) a half mile later. (Originally contributed by Pat Caffrey, rehiked by authors in 2002)

Key Points

0.0   Trailhead

3.0   Junction with Hiline Trail 111; turn right

5.0   Johnson Lake

5.2   Junction with Trail 111; turn left

5.4   Junction with Continental Divide Trail 9; turn left

7.0   Rainbow Pass

8.0   Rainbow Lake

16.0   Trailhead

48 The Pintler Loop

Description: A scenic circuit through the heart of the Anaconda-Pintler Wilderness.
Start: 30 miles southwest of Anaconda in the Anaconda-Pintler Mountains.
Type of hike: Extended backpacking trip; loop.
Total distance: 23.5 miles.
Difficulty: Strenuous.
Maps: Carpp Ridge, Moose Lake, Kelly Lake, and Warren Peak USGS Quads; Beaverhead-Deerlodge National Forest Map; and Anaconda-Pintler Wilderness Map.
Trail contacts: Pintler Ranger District (Philipsburg office), Beaverhead-Deerlodge National Forest, 88-10A Business Loop, Philipsburg, MT 59858; (406) 859-3211; www.fs.fed.us/r1/bdnf.

Finding the trailhead: Take Montana Highway 1 south from Philipsburg for 6 miles (or 23 miles north of Anaconda) and turn west on Montana Highway 38. After 9.2 miles turn left (south) onto Middle Fork Road 5106 and follow the unpaved road until it ends 15.3 miles later at Middle Fork Trailhead, 4 miles past Moose Lake. There is a large parking lot with toilet.

Recommended itinerary: For a three-night trip, spend the first night at Johnson Lake, the second night at Hidden, Kelly, or Ripple Lake, and the third night at Phyllis or Little Johnson Lake. For a four-night trip, spend the first night at Edith Lake, the second night at Oreamnos Lake or along Pintler Creek, the third night at Hidden, Kelly, or Ripple Lake, and the fourth night at Phyllis or Little Johnson Lake.

The Hike

The Anaconda-Pintler is one of Montana's smaller wilderness areas but also one of the most spectacular. This route makes a convenient circuit through the center of this fairly accessible wild area. It's a great place for hikers from Butte, Missoula, or Helena to spend a three-day weekend.

Start off down Falls Fork Trail 29. The first 5 miles of trail to Johnson Lake gradually ascend through a mature forest with some burned sections between the Edith Lake Trail and the lake. At 3 miles you'll reach the junction with Hiline Trail 111 toward Edith Lake to your left. Stay on Trail 29. Johnson Lake is, perhaps unfortunately, in a logical place to camp for most routes using this trailhead. Consequently, the campsites show signs of heavy use, so please be extra careful to leave zero impact of your visit. The numerous campsites are marked on Forest Service locator maps posted in two places at the lake. Don't camp between the trail and the lake. The lake gets so much use that a few campground deer hang around all day looking for food scraps and licking up urine. Although a fire burned sections along the trail before the lake and the trail to Rainbow Pass, the lake itself escaped the fire. Johnson Lake has a few cutthroats in it, but they've gotten smart after seeing so many artificial flies and lures.

The Pintler Loop

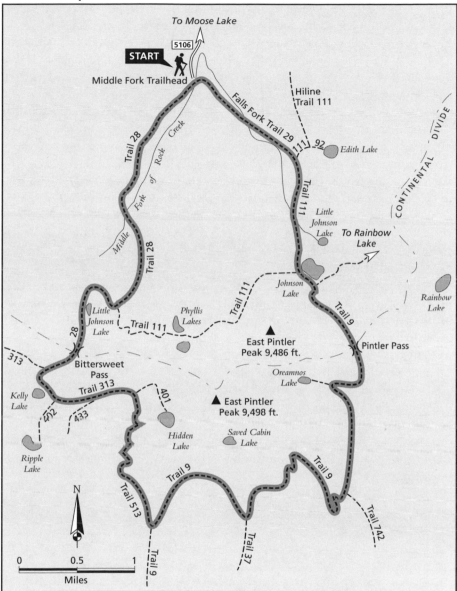

To Moose Lake

5106

START

Middle Fork Trailhead

Falls Fork Trail 29

Hiline Trail 111

Trail 28

Fork of Rock Creek

111

92

Edith Lake

CONTINENTAL DIVIDE

Trail 111

Middle

Trail 28

Little Johnson Lake

To Rainbow Lake

Johnson Lake

Rainbow Lake

Little Johnson Lake

Trail 111

Phyllis Lakes

Trail 111

28

Trail 111

East Pintler Peak 9,486 ft.

Trail 9

Pintler Pass

Bittersweet Pass

313

Oreamnos Lake

Trail 313

401

East Pintler Peak 9,498 ft.

Kelly Lake

402

433

Hidden Lake

Saved Cabin Lake

Trail 9

Ripple Lake

N

Trail 9

Trail 513

Trail 9

Trail 742

Trail 37

0   0.5   1

Miles

As you hike along the western shore of Johnson Lake, you'll reach the Johnson Inlet Trail 96 junction at 5.2 miles. Turn left here. Then turn right at 5.4 miles onto Continental Divide Trail 9. The 2-mile, Category 2, 1,000–foot climb up to the Continental Divide and Pintler Pass isn't difficult, and you'll be distracted by the scenery. From the pass, drop down the other side, and you notice the climb would be more difficult from the south, just in case you decide to do this trip in reverse. At 7.5 miles turn left on the spur trail for a quick visit to Oreamnos Lake.

Back on Trail 9 turn right after 1.5 miles at the junction with the Pintler Creek Trail. Now you face a more difficult 1,300-foot climb over the Continental Divide again and down into the upper reaches of the East Fork of the Bitterroot Drainage. A fairly long stretch of the trail on the Bitterroot side has been burned, including part of the trail up to Hidden Lake, if you decided to take the half-mile, 500-foot climb up there to camp for the night. The lakeshore has also been partially burned.

Several signs are missing at the junctions through this section of the hike, so be alert. It's always safe to assume there won't be signs, lest you become dependent on them to find your way. Turn right (west) on Continental Divide Trail 9 as you pass the junction with Trail 368 at 10.5 miles. Then at 13 miles turn right (west) onto Trail 313 and continue another 2.0 miles to the junction with Hidden Lake Trail 401. Turn right if you're going to the lake. Otherwise keep going on Trail 313. At 15.7 miles you come to the junction with Trail 433, which veers off to your left. Stay right on Trail 313.

After turning right (north) at 16.2 miles on Trail 402 to Kelly and Ripple Lakes (worth the side trip, incidentally), on Trail 28 you have an easy half-mile climb up to Bitterroot Pass, where you'll find some stately whitebark pines and a beautiful, weathered sign that a bear chewed up.

The section of Trail 28 down to Little Johnson Lake is in great shape, as is the 1.2-mile stretch along Trail 111 up to Phyllis Lakes, if you've decided to camp there. Trail 111 goes to Upper Phyllis Lake, which has limited campsites. It's a precipitous, dangerous bushwhack down to the lower lake, but both lakes have good cutthroat populations.

The 5.7 miles down from Little Johnson Lake to the trailhead along Trail 28 is a little boring and muddy in spots because of the heavy horse traffic on this section of trail.

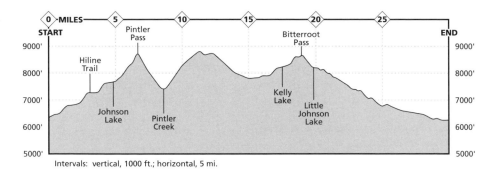

Intervals: vertical, 1000 ft.; horizontal, 5 mi.

Options

I'd say this route would be slightly more difficult in reverse, but you never know for sure.

Side Trips

If you aren't camping at Oreamnos, Hidden, Ripple, Kelly, or Phyllis Lakes, they all make great side trips. Also, if you're staying at Johnson Lake, try Rainbow Pass after supper or Edith Lake on the way in. (Hiked by authors in 2002)

Key Points

0.0   Middle Fork Trailhead

3.0   Junction with Hiline Trail 111; turn right

5.0   Johnson Lake

5.2   Junction with Trail 111; turn left

5.4   Junction with Continental Divide Trail 9; turn right

7.0   Pintler Pass

7.5   Spur trail to Oreamnos Lake; turn left

9.0   Junction with Pintler Creek Trail 47; turn right

10.5   Junction with Trail 368; turn right

13.0   Junction with Trail 313; turn right

15.5   Junction with Hidden Lake Trail 401; turn left

15.7   Junction with Trail 433; turn right

16.2   Junction with Trail 402 to Ripple and Kelly Lakes; turn right

Junction with Trail 28

17.2   Bitterroot Pass

17.8   Little Johnson Lake

19.0   Junction with Hiline Trail 111; turn left

23.5   Middle Fork Trailhead

49 Trask Lakes

Description: Fun family fishing at Trask Lake and a possible climb up Racetrack Peak.
Start: About 15 miles west of Deer Lodge in the Flint Creek Range.
Type of hike: Day hike or short backpacking trip; out-and-back.
Total distance: 12.6-mile round trip.
Difficulty: Moderate.

Maps: Rock Creek Lake, Pike's Peak, and Pozega Lakes USGS Quads; and Beaverhead-Deerlodge National Forest Map.
Trail contacts: Pintler Ranger District (Deer Lodge office), Beaverhead-Deerlodge National Forest, 91 Frontage Road, Deer Lodge, MT 59722; (406) 846–1770; www.fs.fed.us/r1/bdnf.

Finding the trailhead: Drive down the main street of Deer Lodge and turn west on Milwaukee Avenue. Follow this road for 1.7 miles until it splits. Stay right, continuing straight on the Old Stage Road. After 7.2 miles from the bank in Deer Lodge, turn left when the road forks and continue on FR 006. After 9.5 miles, what is now FR 168 splits; stay right for Rock Creek Lake. After half a mile more, reach Rock Creek Lake and drive around the northern shore. (You may need a four-wheel-drive or high-clearance vehicle to make the last mile.) After 13.5 miles, park your vehicle at a turnoff just before three small cabins. There is very limited parking; don't block the road.

The Hike

From the trailhead follow an old jeep road through the Daphne Lode patented mining claims past several cabins. About half a mile up this road at Rock Creek Falls is the closure area boundary. No motorized vehicles are allowed beyond this point except for snowmobiles. From this point, the jeep road is maintained as Rock Creek Trail 53.

At 2.3 miles Rock Creek Trail 53 continues straight, but you must turn left, crossing Rock Creek and then following the South Fork of Rock Creek on Trask Lakes Trail 63. Once you're off the jeep road, the signs of civilization fall behind, and the hike becomes more of a quality backcountry experience. The trail is rocky and

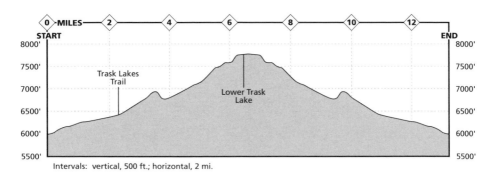

Intervals: vertical, 500 ft.; horizontal, 2 mi.

On the way to Trask Lake Basin.

well defined. Trask Lakes Trail climbs gradually for 4 miles to Lower Trask Lake, one of four lakes (plus several potholes) in this small, gorgeous cirque.

The Forest Service did a great job on the bridges and routing of the Trask Lakes Trail. From its junction with Rock Creek Trail, new bridges and several puncheon walkways have been constructed. Several new puncheon walkways across muddy areas and construction of a short trail from the Trask Lake basin over to Elbow Lake have also been completed.

Trask Lakes, at 7,800 feet, offer excellent fishing for small brook trout. Fish are abundant, and even the youngest angler can expect a good catch. (The fishing is also good in the main Rock Creek along the jeep road in the first 3 miles of the hike.) The good fishing and moderate, 13-mile round-trip (1,900-foot elevation gain) make Trask Lakes perfect for family backpacking. Don't forget the insect repellent, however, or your kids will not want to leave the tent. Drinking water is available all along the trail.

Side Trips

After you are bored with hauling in fish, you might try an interesting side trip to Racetrack Peak. Stay on Trask Lakes Trail for 3 miles past the lakes until it climbs to the top of 8,507-foot Racetrack Pass. Then turn right (west) and make a 1-mile

Trask Lakes

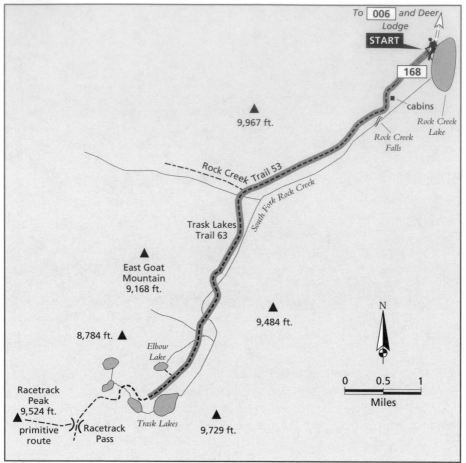

scramble to the summit of 9,524-foot Racetrack Peak for an outstanding view of the entire area. (Originally contributed by Frank Culver, rehiked by authors in 1992 and 1998)

Key Points

- **0.0** Trailhead
- **0.5** Rock Creek Falls; Rock Creek Trail 53 begins
- **2.3** Junction with Trask Lakes Trail 63; turn left
- **6.3** Lower Trask Lake
- **12.6** Trailhead

50 Dolus Lakes

Description: A fairly easy hike to two forested lakes.
Start: About 15 miles west of Deer Lodge in the Flint Creek Range.
Type of hike: A day hike or overnighter; out-and-back.
Total distance: 4.6 miles.
Difficulty: Moderate.

Maps: Rock Creek Lake USGS Quad and Beaverhead-Deerlodge National Forest Map.
Trail contacts: Pintler Ranger District (Deer Lodge office), Beaverhead-Deerlodge National Forest, 91 Frontage Road, Deer Lodge, MT 59722; (406) 846-1770; www.fs.fed.us/r1/bdnf.

Finding the trailhead: Drive down the main street of Deer Lodge and turn west on Milwaukee Avenue. Follow this road for 1.7 miles until it splits. Stay right, continuing straight on the Old Stage Road. After 7.2 miles from the bank in Deer Lodge, turn left when the road forks and continue on FR 006. After 9.5 miles what is now FR 168 splits; stay right for Rock Creek Lake. After half a mile more, reach Rock Creek Lake and drive halfway around the northern shore. (You may need a four-wheel-drive or high-clearance vehicle to make the last mile.) After 13 miles, park your vehicle at a turnoff just before three small cabins. There is very limited parking; don't block the road.

The Hike

Head west on Trail 115. From Rock Creek Lake the trail climbs steeply with a few switchbacks to the junction with Doney Lake Trail 138 half a mile later. This is the toughest part of the hike.

After your turn left (west) at this junction, the trail flattens out and follows an old mining ditch in places as it more gradually climbs to the lower lake. The trail is well defined all the way but gets rocky in places. The trail between the first two lakes is less defined and brushy but still fairly easy to follow.

You can catch pan-size cutthroats in both lakes, but the shoreline is brushy, so watch your back cast. You can find a few campsites at both lakes that aren't heavily used because most people day hike into Dolus Lakes instead of staying overnight. If you camp, you'll probably have the place to yourself that night.

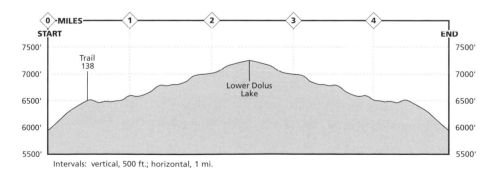

Intervals: vertical, 500 ft.; horizontal, 1 mi.

Dolus Lakes

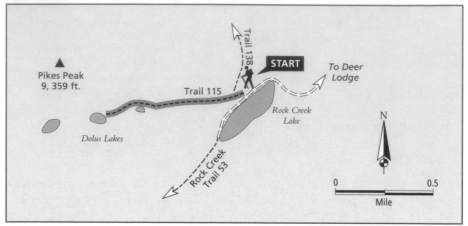

Options

From Upper Dolus Lake an adventuresome hiker can bushwhack another mile up to the third and highest Dolus Lake. (Hiked by the authors in 1998)

Key Points

0.0 Trailhead

0.5 Junction with Doney Lake Trail 138; turn left

2.0 Lower Dolus Lake

2.3 Upper Dolus Lake

4.6 Trailhead

51 Bobcat Lakes

Description: Lower Bobcat Lake is one of several lakes in the West Pioneers that support the rare southern grayling.

Start: 20 miles south of Wise River and 60 miles southwest of Butte in the West Pioneer Mountains.

Type of hike: A day hike or overnighter; out-and-back with two loop options.

Total distance: 8-mile round trip.

Difficulty: Moderate.

Maps: Odell Lake and Shaw Mountain USGS Quads and Southwest Montana Interagency Visitor/Travel Map (West Half).

Trail contacts: Wise River Ranger District, Beaverhead-Deerlodge National Forest, Box 100, Wise River, MT 59762; (406) 832-3178; www.fs.fed.us/r1/bdnf.

Finding the trailhead: Drive south of Wise River on the Pioneer Mountains National Scenic Byway for 17 miles (all paved) or 28 miles from the south end (one 6-mile unpaved section), turn west on Lacy Creek Road 1299, and drive 4 miles to Lacy Creek Trailhead, where the road ends. You'll find ample parking and a toilet, with a campground nearby.

The Hike

From Lacy Creek Trailhead, the main trail into Bobcat Lakes starts up Pioneer Loop Trail 750. Follow this trail for 0.1 mile and turn right (north) onto Bobcat Lakes Trail 50 just after crossing Bobcat Creek. Bobcat Lakes Trail 50 up the Bobcat Creek Canyon passes through stands of lodgepole pine and Douglas fir most of the way, with occasional vistas across the broad slopes of the West Pioneers. It climbs steadily and is steep in places. The trail is quite rocky in places, so progress can be slow. The trail is open to motorcycles but not ATVs.

About 4 miles from Lacy Creek Trailhead, you reach Lower Bobcat Lake. About a half mile up the trail, you'll find smaller Upper Bobcat Lake. If you're staying overnight, you'll probably want to camp at the lower lake, which has better (but heavily impacted) campsites and more fish.

The lakes lie in small glacial cirques in the middle of the gentle West Pioneer Mountains below Bobcat Mountain. At 9,165 feet, this peak is one of the higher

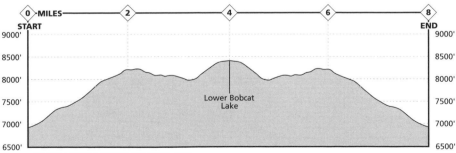

Intervals: vertical, 500 ft.; horizontal, 2 mi.

Fishing for grayling in Bobcat Lakes.

points in the range. From the upper lake, a steep trail leads west to the ridge separating the Bobcat Creek and Pattengail Creek drainages, the latter dissecting the heart of the West Pioneers. Elk often frequent the small meadows that dot this high area. Farther west is a long ridge topped by Odell Peak. Several cirque lakes lie at the base of this ridge.

An interesting feature of Lower Bobcat Lake is its arctic grayling population. These rare native fish survive in limited numbers in the Big Hole River drainage. The grayling have specialized habitat requirements that make it hard for them to compete with other sport fish in lower-elevation waters. The remoteness of the Bobcat Lakes helps them survive. Please take care not to disturb the small stream that drains Lower Bobcat Lake—the grayling depend on the fine gravels in the streambed for spawning. If you decide to catch a few of them (and they are fairly easy to catch), please carefully release them.

Bobcat Lakes

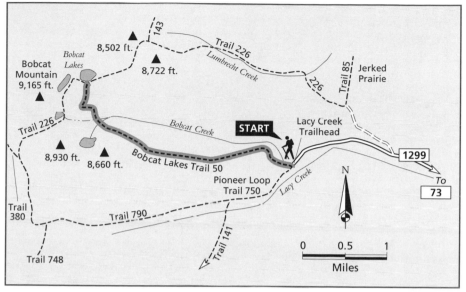

Options

From Bobcat Lakes you have two options in addition to retracing your footsteps back to the Lacy Creek Trailhead. First, you can make an almost a loop trip by taking Trail 226 from the lower lake toward Jerked Prairie. Trail 226 heads east for less than 2 miles to a pretty meadow. Then, at the junction with Trail 143 (to the Kelley Cabin), turn right (southeast) and continue on Trail 226 through thick stands of lodgepole pine, spruce, and Douglas fir. After following a small stream, Trail 226 becomes a jeep road for the last mile to Lacy Creek Road. Where you rejoin Lacy Creek Road, stow your pack and walk a mile or so up the road to retrieve your vehicle. There is drinking water near both trailheads, so fill your water bottles here, as the rest of the hike has little water.

Second, you can make a real loop out of the trip by taking the Pattengail Trail past the upper lake and over some dry switchbacks over the divide and down into Pattengail Creek. Turn left at both the Baldy and Odell Lake junctions. You pass by Grassy Lake (no problem knowing how it got its name) and later, between the two junctions, Schwingar Lake. This makes a nice 13-mile loop, with one exception. After the Odell Lake junction, the trail turns into a heavily used ATV road, which is, like most such roads, covered with loose rocks thrown up by the four-wheelers, making walking difficult. Some of these trails aren't on the topo map, so be sure to take the Forest Service map. (Originally contributed by Fred Swanson, rehiked by authors in 2003)

Key Points

0.0 Lacy Creek Trailhead

0.1 Junction with Bobcat Lakes Trail 50; turn right

4.0 Lower Bobcat Lake and junction with Trail 226

4.5 Upper Bobcat Lake

8.0 Lacy Creek Trailhead

52 Sawtooth Lake

Description: A graceful lake filled with golden trout.
Start: Near Elkhorn Hot Springs northwest of Dillon.
Type of hike: Day hike or overnighter; out-and-back.
Total distance: 8-mile round trip.
Difficulty: Moderate.

Maps: Elkhorn Hot Springs USGS Quad and Southwest Montana Interagency Visitor/Travel Map (West Half).
Trail contacts: Dillon Ranger District, Beaverhead-Deerlodge National Forest, 420 Barrett Street, Dillon, MT 59725; (406) 683–3900; www.fs.fed.us/r1/bdnf.

Finding the trailhead: From Wise River, drive south on the paved Pioneer Mountains National Scenic Byway for 34 miles (one 6-mile section unpaved) or 11 miles from the south. At Elkhorn Hot Springs turn east on well-marked Willman Creek Road (Forest Road 7441), passing through the Taylor subdivision. Follow FR 7441 for 1.8 miles until it forks; stay right for 0.3 mile to the trailhead. There is ample parking and a toilet.

The Hike

From the trailhead Trail 195 follows Clark Creek, crossing the creek on logs twice. The second crossing can be treacherous if the logs are wet. Climbing gently, Trail 195 passes through mature lodgepole pine and Engelmann spruce. After about 3 miles Trail 195 turns southeast toward Goat Mountain and climbs switchbacks to the lake.

Sawtooth Lake rests in a cirque surrounded by Goat, Highboy, and Sawtooth Mountains. Even in summer, light snows often accent the crags and their slopes above the cold lake. The lake has a few campsites, but they're heavily impacted, so please don't make it any worse than it is—and in fact try to remove a fire ring or two to make it better.

This hike is popular because of the unique species of fish that inhabit Sawtooth Lake. Golden trout are rare and colorful, and they grow large. The south shore of the lake is a talus slope that offers an ideal place to throw in a line. The trout are

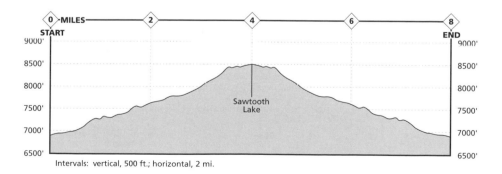

Intervals: vertical, 500 ft.; horizontal, 2 mi.

Sawtooth Lake

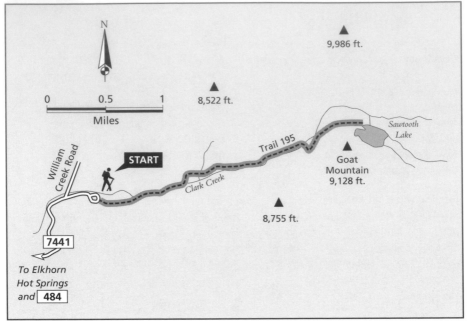

temperamental but catchable. Twelve-inch golden trout are common throughout the lake.

In 2003 a forest fire burned portions of this trail, so be prepared for a few dead trees across the trail. (Hiked by authors in 1993)

Key Points

0.0 Trailhead
4.0 Sawtooth Lake
8.0 Trailhead

THE VIEW FROM HERE: THE LAST FIRE RING

I confess to being the worst enemy a fire ring ever had. I personally have destroyed hundreds, if not thousands, of fire rings while hiking Montana's trails. I'm not only proud of it, but I'm also encouraging other hikers to join me in destroying every last one.

Public-land managers prohibit campfires in some areas, but there are also still places where you can build and enjoy a campfire. If conditions and regulations allow you to have a campfire, however, please make it a zero-impact fire. There is no need to build a new fire ring, and even using an existing one prolongs the age-old problem.

53 Torrey Lake

Description: A nearly 9,000-foot-high lake in the shadows of Torrey and Tweedy Mountains, both over 11,000 feet.
Start: 25 miles northwest of Dillon in the East Pioneer Mountains.
Type of hike: Long, hard day hike or overnighter; out-and-back.
Total distance: 17-mile round trip.
Difficulty: Moderate.

Maps: Torrey Mountain, Maurice Mountain, and Vipond USGS Quads; and Southwest Montana Interagency Visitor/Travel Map (West Half).
Trail contacts: Wise River Ranger District, Beaverhead-Deerlodge National Forest, Box 100, Wise River, MT 59762; (406) 832-3178; www.fs.fed.us/r1/bdnf.

Finding the trailhead: From the north drive south of Wise River on the Pioneer Mountains National Scenic Byway for about 22 miles (or 23 miles north from the south). Turn east on FR 2465 for 0.3 mile to Mono Creek Campground and Jacobson Creek Trail 2 Trailhead on the left. Vehicle camping, toilet, and filterable water are all nearby at Mono Creek Campground.

The Hike

From Mono Creek Campground follow Jacobson Creek Trail 2 as it wanders through some open timber and then skirts Jacobson Meadows. After the meadows, go back into the timber and, just before Jacobson Creek, turn right (southeast) at 2.5 miles at the junction with Torrey Lake Trail 56.

The Torrey Lake Trail immediately drops down to cross Jacobson Creek and then heads up David Creek. You now have 4 miles of gently climbing trail through lodgepole pine stands, intermittent meadows, and spruce bottoms. The last 2 miles ascend 1,000 feet (only a Category 2 climb) as the trail winds its way up through granite boulders to the lake.

The eastern portion of the Pioneer Range is a confusing jumble of formations, and geologists have yet to come up with a complete explanation for what happened here. Torrey Lake, at 8.5 miles, is in the middle of an area where molten rock

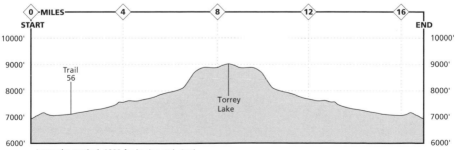

Intervals: vertical, 1000 ft.; horizontal, 4 mi.

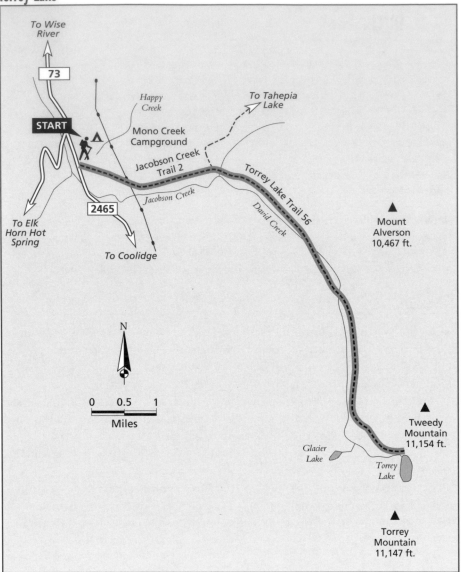

intruded into the older formations from below and cooled there. After time and erosion removed the overburden of older rock, the granite backbone of this range was exposed.

Looking south across the lake, you can see the ragged igneous hump of Torrey Mountain, 11,147 feet high. Behind to the northeast are the shredded granite cliffs and buttresses of Tweedy Mountain, 11,154 feet high. Granite towers stand on the divide between Tweedy and Torrey, west of Torrey. If you decide to climb around on the large rockslide between Torrey Mountain and the lake, note that this slide shifted dramatically in 1981 and may still be unstable. Avoid the steep pitches of rubble, which will start to slide under your weight. (Originally contributed by Pat Caffrey)

Key Points

0.0   Jacobson Creek Trail 2 Trailhead

2.5   Junction with Torrey Lake Trail 56; turn right

8.5   Torrey Lake

17.0   Trailhead

54 Grayling Lake

Description: Three peaceful lakes in the shadow of 10,144-foot-high Sharp Mountain.
Start: West of Melrose at the end of Canyon Creek Road.
Type of hike: Day hike or overnighter; out-and-back.
Total distance: 10-mile round trip.
Difficulty: Moderate.

Maps: Vipond Park and Mount Tahepia USGS Quads and Southwest Montana Interagency Visitor/Travel Map (West Half).
Trail contacts: Wise River Ranger District, Beaverhead-Deerlodge National Forest, Box 100, Wise River, MT 59762; (406) 832-3178; www.fs.fed.us/r1/bdnf.

Finding the trailhead: Drive south of Butte on Interstate 15 and take exit 93 for Melrose. From Melrose follow the fishing access signs west across the Big Hole River, passing by a campground on the left. Continue across a second bridge and straight through a four-way intersection. After 1.5 miles from Melrose, the road forks. The left road goes to Cherry Creek, and the right road continues toward Canyon Creek. Go right. Follow the road straight up Trapper Creek for 5 miles to the old smelter town of Glendale. At the intersection in Glendale, turn right (uphill) on Forest Road 187 for Canyon Creek. After 9 miles from Melrose, cross Canyon Creek. After 3 more miles, pass by the old Canyon Creek charcoal kilns. Then, after 13 miles, turn left on FR 7401 for the last 4 miles to the trailhead. It is 17.5 miles of dirt roads from Melrose to Canyon Creek Campground and Trailhead. You'll find ample parking, a toilet, and vehicle camping.

The Hike

Outfitters from the Canyon Creek Ranch use this area for guided fishing trips. The trail sees regular summer traffic, but this area is still pristine.

Canyon Creek Trail 88 begins by crossing Canyon Creek on a two-log bridge. Canyon Creek supports finger-size brook trout. On the other side of the creek, the trail turns to the right and up the opposite slope. The old trail follows the river, but it was too close to the ranch, so it was relocated. At half a mile Trail 88 crosses through a gate. Be sure to close it behind you. Continue following Canyon Creek Trail 88 for 1.5 miles to its intersection with Lion Creek Trail 28. This section climbs gradually uphill through the trees and along the creek.

At the junction, turn left (south) on Lion Creek Trail 28. It's 3.5 miles from this junction to Grayling Lake. The first 2 miles continue along Canyon Creek at stream grade. Then the trail turns west for the first stream crossing over Lion Creek. In the next 2 miles, the trail crosses Lion Creek four times. Almost all crossings are negotiable without getting wet feet. The next mile is a climb, the only real climb of the hike.

After the ascent, the trail crosses the flatlands below Vera Lake. You can easily reach Vera Lake by navigating off trail south and a little east after the fourth crossing of Lion Creek. Vera Lake used to have fish, but one visit will explain their absence: The lake is not deep enough for fish to survive the winter freeze.

Grayling Lake

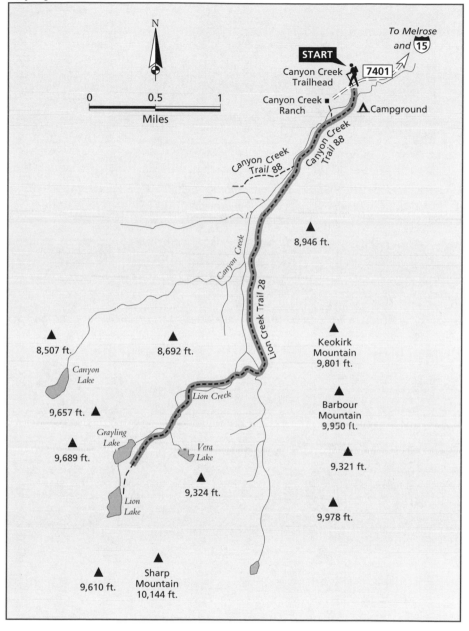

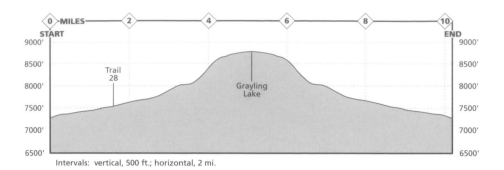

Intervals: vertical, 500 ft.; horizontal, 2 mi.

Grayling Lake is about a half mile farther up the trail. It's listed as having grayling, but according to the Forest Service, the fish died out. However, good fishing for cutthroat-rainbow hybrids lures anglers to this area. Grayling Lake offers a view of the steep ridge separating it from Canyon Lake, which you can get to via Trail 88.

Side Trips

A half mile above Grayling Lake is Lion Lake, which has similar fishing to Grayling and a view of Sharp Mountain. To the south, Sharp Mountain is fairly obvious and definitely sharp. Not too many people hike here, so be sure to do your part to keep the area pristine. (Hiked by authors in 1993)

Key Points

0.0 Trailhead

0.5 Gate along Trail 88

1.5 Junction with Lion Creek Trail 28; turn left

5.0 Grayling Lake

5.5 Lion Lake

10.0 Trailhead

55 Selway Mountain

Description: Impressive views of southwest Montana and the site of an old fire lookout.
Start: 40 miles west of Clark Canyon Reservoir, south of Dillon.
Type of hike: Day hike; out-and-back.
Total distance: 5.4-mile round trip.
Difficulty: Moderate.

Maps: Selway Mountain and Kitty Creek USGS Quads and Southwest Montana Interagency Visitor/Travel Map (West Half).
Trail contacts: Dillon Ranger District, Beaverhead-Deerlodge National Forest, 420 Barrett Street, Dillon, MT 59725; (406) 683-3900; www.fs.fed.us/r1/bdnf.

Finding the trailhead: From Dillon drive 19 miles south on Interstate 15 to Clark Canyon Reservoir exit 44. Turn right onto Highway 324, heading west. After about 20 miles watch for a national forest access sign and then another sign for Reservoir Lake Campground. Turn right onto Forest Road 181 and follow the signs and dirt road 18 miles northwest to Reservoir Lake Campground. Trail 34 starts in the boat trailer parking lot next to the lake. The trailhead features a campground, a toilet, and ample parking.

The Hike

Ascending this nearly 9,000-foot-high peak requires moderate effort for an outstanding view. The trail is easy enough for inexperienced hikers but scenic enough for veterans. The mountain's proximity to Reservoir Lake Campground makes it an appealing day hike while camping on Reservoir Lake. In addition, moose often wander through the marshy Bloody Dick Creek, which runs along the road, and the surrounding Continental Divide area is prime elk habitat.

Trail 34 begins at a gate and runs for about 200 feet along the lake before it forks. Take the right fork to Selway Mountain. (The other fork circles Reservoir Lake.) The trail rises quickly up a hillside meadow. The path is somewhat steep here, switchbacking up the hillside for the next half mile. You can look out onto Bloody Dick Creek and the lake below as you hike up. Soon the trail flattens out and begins a long, steady climb for the next mile.

The woods are almost exclusively lodgepole pine, dotted with patches of blue mountain lupine. This area is a good example of the fire cycle, whereby the overcrowded lodgepole pine and deadfall on the forest floor are due to burn and make way for new vegetation. New generations of lodgepole will slowly accumulate after many years to continue the cycle.

As the trail begins to turn sharply eastward, whitebark pine start taking over from the lodgepole. Then the trail circles Selway Mountain to the northern side of the peak and follows contour along the slope. Through the trees you can see the sides of Bloody Dick Peak to the east. After 0.3 mile, the trail turns north for the top. Some Douglas fir and spruce grow here, but slowly the trees thin out as you reach the top.

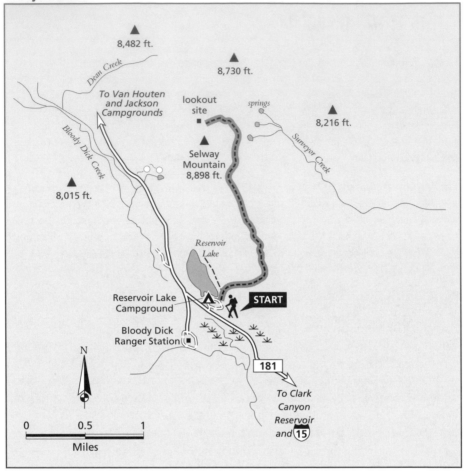

In 1942 the Forest Service built a 30-foot-high lookout tower on top of Selway Mountain. It was staffed for twenty-nine years and supported a heliport but was demolished and burned in 1976. The Forest Service has since abandoned most of its lookouts and now relies on aircraft for spotting fires. There are still some remains of the tower at the summit, and the heliport itself remains intact. The site of the heliport is easy to find and makes a good spot for lunch with a view to the south out across the Continental Divide. The bald south slope of the mountain is talus and extremely steep, dropping quickly into the woods and ridge below.

Once on top of Selway Mountain, it's easy to see why this shaved top made an ideal spot for a lookout tower. Off to the north, you can see past Black Mountain, the timber-covered peak just behind Selway, and across the Big Hole Valley all the way to the snowcapped Anaconda-Pintlers. To the west the view stretches past the Bitterroots and the Continental Divide to the jagged Lemhi Range in Idaho. Far

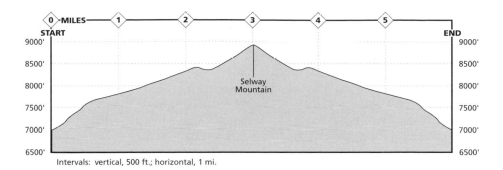

Intervals: vertical, 500 ft.; horizontal, 1 mi.

past Bloody Dick Peak, to the northeast, are the high summits of the Pioneer Range: Torrey, Tweedy, and Baldy Mountains. And to the south Bloody Dick Creek runs past Reservoir Lake toward Lemhi Pass and south to the Montana-Idaho border. (Originally contributed by Douglas Schnitzspahn)

56 Deadman and Nicholia Creeks

Description: A huge glacial cirque of Italian Peak, high on the Continental Divide, in the little-visited Italian Peaks.
Start: 20 miles southwest of Lima.
Type of hike: Extended backpacking trip; loop.
Total distance: 21-mile round trip.
Difficulty: Strenuous.

Maps: Scott Peak, Deadman Lake, and Eighteenmile Peak USGS Quads and Southwest Montana Interagency Visitor/Travel Map (West Half).
Trail contacts: Dillon Ranger District, Beaverhead-Deerlodge National Forest, 420 Barrett Street, Dillon, MT 59725; (406) 683–3900; www.fs.fed.us/r1/bdnf.

Finding the trailhead: The Nicholia Creek Trailhead is remote but relatively easy to find using the Beaverhead-Deerlodge National Forest Map. Turn off Interstate 15 at Dell exit 23, 45 miles south of Dillon. Follow the gravel road that parallels the interstate's western side for 1.5 miles south, where Forest Road 257 turns westward up Big Sheep Canyon. After 18 miles, the road branches; take the left branch toward Nicholia-Deadman. In 2.3 miles FR 3922 branches again. Continue to the left on FR 657 up the broad valley of Nicholia Creek to the trailhead, which is about a half mile inside the national forest boundary. There is a primitive trailhead with limited parking.

The Hike

The following description starts at the Nicholia Creek Trailhead, reached by four-wheel-drive vehicle.

Few hikers visit this remote, isolated mountain range in the far southwestern corner of the state, but its spectacular alpine scenery is sure to make it more popular in years to come.

The trails in this region receive little use and have a tendency to fade away in the many grassy meadows along the track. A few tips are in order. Don't trust the trail as shown on the Scott Peak USGS Quad, which is old and inaccurate. Do trust the blazes on the trees, which look like upside-down exclamation points. The trail stays close to the stream except in places where the trail is built above it to avoid avalanche debris.

For about 2 miles, the trail follows Nicholia Creek before you reach the junction with the Continental Divide Trail. Turn left (south) here and climb over a small divide down into Deadman Creek. The Continental Divide Trail joins Trail 91 about a half mile up the trail from Deadman Lake. From here, Trail 91 follows Deadman Creek, frequently fording the small stream to avoid the little lakes formed by avalanches and mud slides coming off the high, nameless ridge to the west. Even in late July, snow may remain at the base of these avalanche chutes, which can easily be avoided by remaining on the eastern side of the stream.

Deadman and Nicholia Creeks

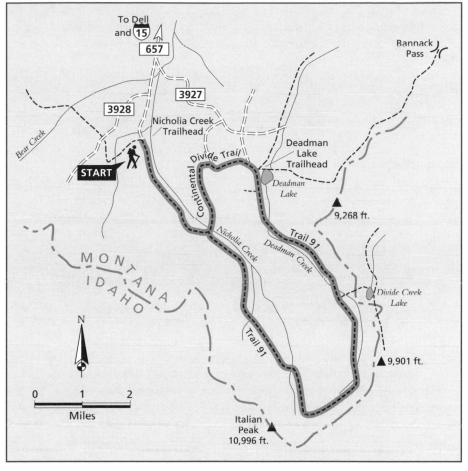

The valley at this point begins to take on a more alpine character, showing signs of the glaciers that once carved the U-shaped upper canyon. If you have the energy, you can hike up to Divide Creek Lake, which lies in a rocky depression just a few yards on the Idaho side of the Continental Divide but is invisible from the Deadman Creek side. The old trail used to climb the grassy slope up to a broad saddle on the divide to the lake, but it's now grown over. Use your topo map, and you shouldn't have any problem.

From here Trail 91 continues to climb gradually through the alpine meadows of the upper Deadman Creek drainage, with the steep rocky ridge of the Continental Divide looming overhead to the left. At one point, a huge geological formation, called a breach anticline, forms a cliff along the divide, resembling a meteor impact crater. About 4 miles from the Divide Creek Lake turnoff, the trail reaches the pass between the Deadman and Nicholia Creek drainages. Here at 9,400 feet, the alpine scenery is spectacular, with the knife-edged ridge of the divide rising up to the 10,998-foot summit of Italian Peak. Keep your eyes peeled for bighorn sheep and goats up on the high slopes.

The trail switchbacks down a steep talus slope into the alpine meadows at the base of the north wall of Italian Peak. A snowfield lingers year-round on Italian Peak's north wall, perhaps aspiring to become a glacier. This alpine basin makes a perfect second night's campsite and may convince you to spend an extra day exploring the meadows and talus slopes of this huge cirque. This is the southernmost point in Montana, and surely, it is one of the prettiest.

Going northward, the trail descends the broad, green valley of Nicholia Creek, staying on the western side of the stream just above the bogs in the creek bottom. Again, the trail tends to disappear in some of the meadows, but it's blazed through the forested parts. At one large meadow, about 3 miles from the cirque basin, the route is marked by a series of 5-foot-high posts.

Past this meadow, Trail 91 enters the lower reaches of Nicholia Creek and becomes well defined, especially after it crosses to the eastern bank of the stream. For 6 miles, the route follows an old, grass-grown jeep track through the sagebrush flats. Be sure to turn around frequently to see the changing views of Italian Peak and Scott Peak over in Idaho. Some 8.5 miles after leaving the cirque at the base of Italian Peak, you reach your waiting vehicle.

Although there are several fresh springs in both the Deadman and Nicholia Valleys, you should be prepared to treat or filter your water, since cows graze the meadows along most of the route. The bugs can be bad as well, so bring lots of insect repellent.

The high pass between Nicholia and Deadman Creeks is usually clear of snow by the Fourth of July, but check local conditions with the Forest Service before you start. The Forest Service has proposed Wilderness status for the Italian Peaks area.

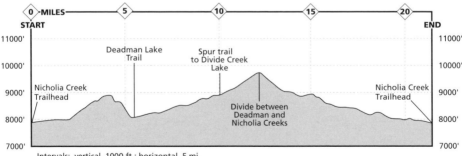

Options

If you have two high-clearance vehicles, you can make a shuttle out of this trip. Check the Forest Service map for a primitive road going to Deadman Lake and leave one vehicle there, but be forewarned that this four-wheel-drive road can get rough and very slick when wet. You can start the shuttle at either trailhead with about the same level of difficulty. (Originally contributed by Ed Madej and Rosemary Rowe)

Key Points

0.0   Nicholia Creek Trailhead

2.0   Continental Divide Trail; turn left

4.5   Deadman Creek Trail 91; turn right

8.0   Spur trail to Divide Creek Lake

12.0   Pass between Deadman and Nicholia Creeks

21.0   Nicholia Creek Trailhead

57 Hollow Top Lake

Description: A mountain lake bordered on three sides by the high peaks of the eastern Tobacco Root Mountains.
Start: 55 miles west of Bozeman.
Type of hike: Day hike or overnighter; loop with out-and-back option.
Total distance: 12.5-mile round trip.
Difficulty: Moderate.

Maps: Pony and Potosie Peak USGS Quads and Southwest Montana Interagency Visitor/Travel Map (East Half).
Trail contacts: Madison Ranger District, Beaverhead-Deerlodge National Forest, 5 Forest Service Road, Ennis, MT 59729; (406) 682–4253; www.fs.fed.us/r1/bdnf.

Finding the trailhead: From the small rural community of Harrison on U.S. Highway 287, drive west 6 miles to Pony, an even smaller rural community. Drive through Pony (where the main street turns into Forest Road 191) for 1 mile until the road forks; stay left until the road dead-ends at a trailhead loop about 2 miles from Pony. North Willow Creek Trail 301 starts to the northwest, and Loop Park Trail 302 returns from the southwest. The trailhead has loop turnaround and ample parking.

The Hike

At the trailhead you get a sense for the local interests. A large Forest Service sign proclaims ATVS AND MOTORCYCLES WELCOME. This is an ominous sign for hikers and backcountry horseman, but it's not quite as bad as it sounds. After 1.5 miles, most ATVs turn off and head up to Albro Lake. A few motorcycles go to Hollow Top Lake, but not many, and if you hike this during the week, you probably won't see any—and you'll have a nice hike to a beautiful lake basin.

From the trailhead North Willow Creek Trail 301 crosses a bridge and then gradually climbs along the north side of the creek. In the spring watch for fuzzy blue pasqueflowers in the grassy meadows

After 1.5 miles, life gets better. Up to this point you've been walking on an ATV road, but here the ATV road turns off to the left as Albro Lake Trail 333 and heads up to Albro Lake. You stay right (west) at this junction and continue to follow North Willow Creek Trail 301, which turns into a single-track (a welcome sight!). The trail

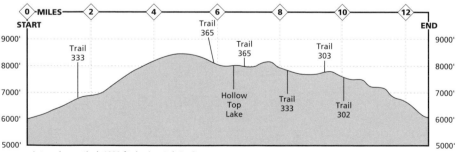

Intervals: vertical, 1000 ft.; horizontal, 4 mi.

On the way to Hollow Top Lake.

continues along the north side of the creek through groves of spruce and fir and back into open meadows. You might see a few cows grazing in these meadows, and you go through a gate. Be sure to securely close it behind you.

About 3.5 miles from the trailhead, the trail again crosses the creek. Pause here to fill water bottles, since the trail heads away from the main creek at this point. This stream crossing can be tricky during early summer runoff. Later in the summer you can cross the stream on jammed logs. Above the crossing the trail climbs more steeply to Hollow Top Lake. You'll pass some beautiful, sloping meadows with great views east into the Gallatin Valley and the Spanish Peaks.

At about 4 miles turn right (west) at the junction with Trail 365. The last mile to the lake gets quite rocky and steep, which makes for rough walking but also makes it difficult for motorcycles to get to the lake.

Hollow Top Lake (which has pan-size rainbow trout) is the source of the stream you've been following. Northwest of the lake is Hollowtop Mountain, at 10,604 feet the highest point in the Tobacco Roots. Mount Jefferson (10,513 feet) lies west of the lake, and to the south is Potosi Peak (10,125 feet), named by miners after a

Hollow Top Lake

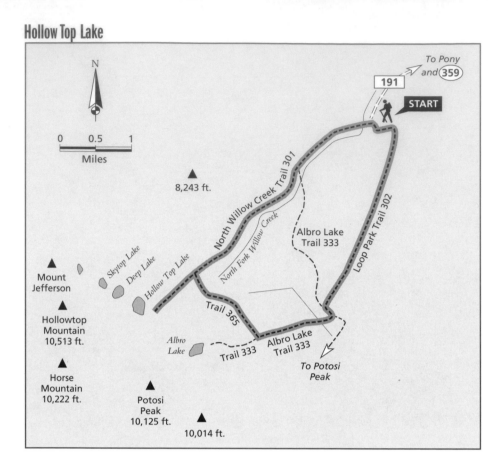

fabulous mine in the Andes. All three mountains are technically easy scrambles, but be prepared for rough weather on the windswept alpine slopes.

After Hollow Top Lake, you may wish to explore Deep Lake, the next lake up the drainage. Simply skirt Hollow Top Lake to the inlet on the northwest end and follow the trail found here a quarter of a mile to Deep Lake. Don't forget your fishing pole.

Hollow Top Lake has lots of good campsites all around the lake. The flow from the outlet has been regulated with a small floodgate, which, regrettably, takes a nick out of the beauty of this mountain lake.

Instead of backtracking on the return trip, you can make a loop out of this trip by dropping a mile down to the junction with Potosi Peak Trail 365 and turning right (south). This trail goes through a lodgepole forest for 1.5 miles until it joins Albro Lake Trail 333. Turn left (east) here, and follow the ATV road for 1.5 miles to the junction with Loop Park Trail 302. Take a left at the junction with North Willow Creek Trail 303, which is about a half mile before Loop Park Trail 302.

This 1.5-mile section is not much to write home about, but once you climb up to the top of a ridge into a huge meadow and see the junction with the Park Trail

302, that changes. This section of trail is closed to all motorized vehicles and is a real beauty. It goes along the open ridgeline for about 2 miles, and the scenery is outstanding. The mountains at the spine of the Tobacco Roots dominate the western horizon, and some fantastic old whitebark pines talk to you up close and personal as you hike by. Even during midday you can usually see elk and deer on this stretch. It's well worth enduring a short walk on the ATV road. It's long and dry, though, so make sure you still have enough water in your bottles.

Trail 302 fades away in several places, but watch for well-placed cairns and fence posts (the lazy man's cairn) to show the way. After a delightful trip along the ridge, the trail switchbacks another 1.5 miles down to the trailhead.

Options

If you're short of time and want to keep as clear of ATV roads as possible, you might want to retrace your steps back to the trailhead instead of taking the loop. (Originally contributed by Fred Swanson, rehiked by authors in 2003)

Key Points

0.0   Trailhead

1.5   Junction with Albro Lake Trail 333; turn right

4.0   Junction with Potosi Peak Trail 365; turn right

5.0   Hollow Top Lake

6.0   Junction with Potosi Peak Trail 365; turn right

7.5   Junction with Trail 333; turn left

8.5   Junction with Trail 303; turn left

9.0   Junction with Trail 302; turn right

12.5 Trailhead

THE VIEW FROM HERE: THE MULTIUSABILITY MYTH

Multiuse routes are a popular idea among public-land managers. Public-land users frequently harangue rangers for more access or more routes for their chosen mode of transportation—snowmobiles, ATVs, motorcycles, mountain bikes, horses, or hiking boots. Taking one route and making it open to all—that is, the so-called multiuse trail—solves the problem, right?

Wrong.

It makes it worse.

Multiuse does work among nonmotorized users. For example, a trail can be open to hikers, trail runners, mountain bikers, and backcountry horsemen. If there are conflicts, they are easily worked out. Two excellent examples of this kind of multiuse are the Stuart Peak and Mount Helena Ridge routes, both heavily used trails near cities.

Likewise, multiuse works well among some motorized users. A route can be open to ATVs, motorcycles, jeeps, and other motorized vehicles with little or no conflict. But if you put packtrains and backpackers on the same route, you have a conflict. One excellent example of this conflict in this book is Hollow Top Lake, a route I left in this book because it's only partially on an ATV road and because it's such a great hike. Another excellent example that I reluctantly removed from the book because the conflict was so great was the Chain of Lakes Trail near Anaconda.

What's the answer to this dilemma? It doesn't seem too far-out to suggest we label routes as nonmotorized or motorized, but never shall the two merge.

58 Curly Lake

Description: A subalpine lake in a little-used section of the Tobacco Root Mountains.
Start: Southeast of Butte.
Type of hike: Day hike or overnighter; out-and-back.
Total distance: 6-mile round trip.
Difficulty: Moderate.

Maps: Manhead Mountain USGS Quad and and Southwest Montana Interagency Visitor/Travel Map (East Half).
Trail contacts: Jefferson Ranger District, Beaverhead-Deerlodge National Forest, 3 Whitehall Road, Whitehall, MT 59759; (406) 287-3368; www.fs.fed.us/r1/bdnf.

Finding the trailhead: From exit 256 in Cardwell (east of Butte on Interstate 90), drive south on Montana Highway 359 for 5 miles. Then turn right, heading south on South Boulder Road (Forest Road 107). The pavement ends after 2.7 miles. Stay on the main road (FR 107), through Mammoth, for 13.6 miles. Curly Creek Trail 151 starts on your right just before crossing Curly Creek, 2.1 miles past the little gathering of cabins called Mammoth. South Boulder Road 107 is rough and rocky in places but passable by a two-wheel-drive vehicle. There is very limited parking, so don't block the road.

The Hike

Curly Creek Trail 151 begins by switchbacking up a steep side hill, quickly gaining elevation with views of the South Boulder Valley to the east. After 1 mile the trail moderates and crosses a series of meadows along Curly Creek. These meadows have a wealth of wildflowers. After 2 miles, Curly Creek Trail climbs again through lodgepole pine forest. Many springs and seeps are found along this stretch. Next, the trail again levels out, crossing another hanging valley before a final climb to the Curly Lake basin.

After 2.5 miles, stay right on Curly Lake Trail 159 to the lake. There is really only one good water source along the way, a small stream at about 2 miles. The trail is in great shape and would be a good candidate for trail runners. It's a long 3 miles to the lake, which is on your right after the junction and past two smaller ponds.

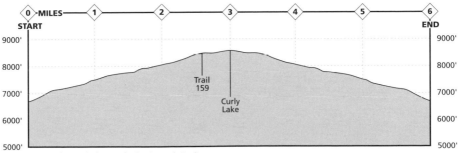

Intervals: vertical, 1000 ft.; horizontal, 1 mi.

Curly Lake in the Tobacco Root Mountains.

Curly Lake sits in a high subalpine basin at 8,800 feet. The lake is tucked in the timber north of the trail. While the fishless lake is not unduly spectacular, the alpine meadows and meandering creek south of the lake are beautiful, offering views of alpine peaks to the south end of the cirque. In addition, chances are great you'll have this serene little sample of wilderness all to yourself for a few hours as you take a nap on the shoreline or, better yet, stay overnight and listen to the sound of silence. As an indication of how little known this area is, none of the 10,000-foot-high peaks surrounding Curly Lake are named.

Options

You could take Trail 159 down to the road and then jog about 2 miles on the road back to your vehicle, a good option for trail runners. (Originally contributed by Kim Wilson, rehiked by authors in 2003)

Curly Lake

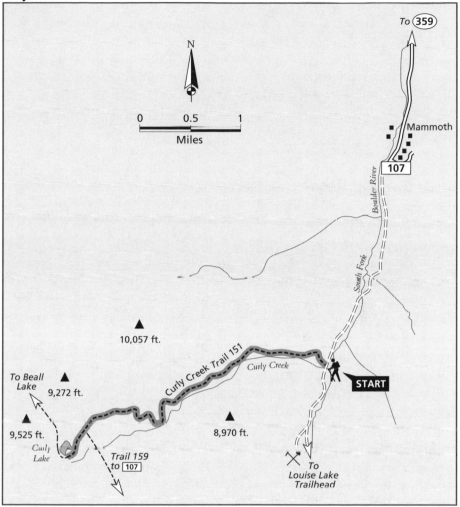

Key Points

0.0 Trailhead

2.5 Junction with Curly Lake Trail 159; turn right

3.0 Curly Lake

6.0 Trailhead

59 Louise Lake

Description: A nice family hike to a high lake deep in the Tobacco Root Mountains.
Start: 40 miles southeast of Butte.
Type of hike: Day hike or overnighter; out-and-back.
Total distance: 7-mile round trip.
Difficulty: Moderate.

Maps: Waterloo USGS Quad and and Southwest Montana Interagency Visitor/Travel Map (East Half).
Trail contacts: Jefferson Ranger District, Beaverhead-Deerlodge National Forest, 3 Whitehall Road, Whitehall, MT 59759; (406) 287-3368; www.fs.fed.us/r1/bdnf.

Finding the trailhead: From exit 256 in Cardwell (east of Butte on Interstate 90), drive south on Montana Highway 359 for 5 miles. Then turn right, heading south on South Boulder Road (Forest Road 107). The pavement ends after 2.7 miles. Stay on the main road (FR 107) through the small community of Mammoth for 14.7 miles. Stay right when the road forks, continuing on FR 107. After 15.7 miles (high-clearance vehicle recommended), you reach the Bismark Reservoir and the trailhead for both Louise Lake and Lost Cabin Lake. The trailhead has ample parking and a toilet. You'll find developed camping at the trailhead and undeveloped camping nearby.

The Hike

The Tobacco Roots offer many short hikes, such as the one to Louise Lake, that are suitable for families. Wait until at least mid-July for the snow to melt, however. We went in early July, and the lake was still partially frozen.

From the Lost Cabin/Louise Lake Trailhead, Trail 168 switchbacks up for 3.5 long miles, mostly on "mall walk" switchbacks, to the lake. You hardly notice the ascent on these nearly level switchbacks. Carry your drinking water, as there are only a few water holes along the way.

Louise Lake sits in a cirque with massive, 10,353-foot Middle Mountain to the south. The lake has a small population of large cutthroat trout that can be very fussy about which fly they might take. If you find the fly that works, catch only enough for supper, leaving the rest for the next angler.

The Forest Service has recognized this route as a National Recreation Trail for its outstanding scenery and exceptional recreational opportunities. It is closed year-round to all motorized vehicles.

Side Trips

Peak baggers in your party will be tempted to scramble up Middle Mountain, a non-technical climb. (Originally contributed by the authors, rehiked in 1995)

Louise Lake in early July, a week too soon to be this ▶
high in the Tobacco Root Mountains.

Louise Lake

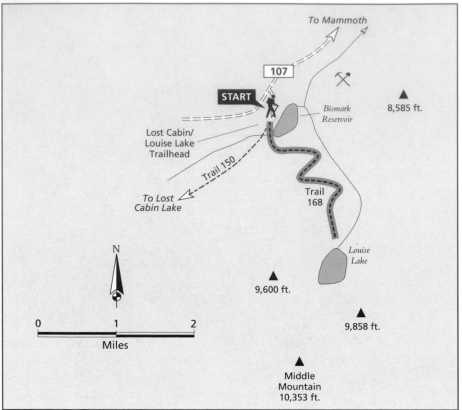

Key Points

0.0 Lost Cabin/Louise Lake Trailhead

3.5 Louise Lake

7.0 Lost Cabin/Louise Lake Trailhead

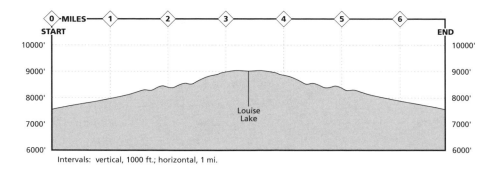

Intervals: vertical, 1000 ft.; horizontal, 1 mi.

60 Snowcrest

Description: A high alpine traverse along the apex of the Snowcrest Range, the nicest place in Montana that nobody knows about.
Start: 40 miles southeast of Dillon.
Type of hike: Extended backpacking trip, with day hike options; loop.
Total distance: 23 miles.
Difficulty: Strenuous.

Maps: Antone Peak and Stonehouse Mountain USGS Quads and Southwest Montana Interagency Visitor/Travel Map (East Half).
Trail contacts: Madison Ranger District, Beaverhead-Deerlodge National Forest, 5 Forest Service Road, Ennis, MT 59729; (406) 682-4253; www.fs.fed.us/r1/bdnf.

Finding the trailhead: Follow the business route of Interstate 15 south through Dillon, past Western Montana College, and then turn left at Barrett Memorial Hospital. After 0.2 mile turn left and head southeast on Blacktail Deer Road for 6.6 miles, where the paved road turns into a wide unpaved roadway. It's easy to drive too fast on this excellent gravel road, so be careful and stay within your abilities. Washboarded sections can throw your vehicle into a spin, as can the loose gravel if you make a sudden correction. Continue straight on FR 1808 for 27 miles, then turn left and head east toward East Fork Blacktail Deer Creek Campground. After another 11.5 miles on a less-improved dirt road (but passable by two-wheel-drive vehicle), the road dead-ends in East Fork Blacktail Deer Creek Campground. The trailhead is at the end of this campground managed by the Bureau of Land Management (BLM). It has a nice campground, and it has a toilet. Because the drive is so long, you may want to spend the night and get an early start the next day.

Recommended itinerary: Although spectacular to see, this route is difficult to backpack. Because of the long, waterless center section, you're left with three less-than-optimal options: (1) putting in a long (13–14-mile) day and two short days (4–5 miles each), (2) spending one night in a dry camp, or (3) dropping down into one of the side drainages off the crest to find water and then carrying your pack up to the divide the next morning—and in the process tacking 3 to 4 miles onto the total distance. Of these three, I prefer the first option, keeping my pack as light as possible, getting up early on my second day, and enjoying a long day on the gorgeous Snowcrest Divide, stopping on the high points to sit and soak in the essence of this special place. Specifically, that means spending the first night along the East Fork below Honeymoon Park and the second night along Lawrence Creek about 5 miles from the trailhead.

The Hike

When you hike hundreds of miles each summer, you sometimes go places that make you say, "I've already been here." While it's certainly true that every piece of wild nature is unique, that doesn't keep some mountains and lakes and streams from looking similar. Then, once in a great while, surprise, the stars are all aligned, and you end

up in a place that blows you away like a 100 mph gust of wind and you say, "This is a truly unique place." Such is the Snowcrest Range.

Snowcrest is probably the nicest hike in Montana that nobody goes on. In fact, when we hiked it in late August 2003, we ran into a trail crew who told us we were the first hikers they'd seen all summer, even though this route had been in this book for twenty-five years. That's incredible, because we were standing on a 9,500-foot ridge amid scenery as amazing as Glacier or Grand Teton or Absaroka-Beartooth, although different in nature—more gentle and peaceful.

The Snowcrest Range stretches for 20 miles north to southwest of the Gravellies in the far southwestern corner of Montana. Because of the high wildlife populations, Snowcrest is now the domain of big game hunters and outfitters, but after experiencing the area, I wonder why it isn't more popular with hikers. The scenery is clearly world-class, and the heavy horse traffic during the hunting season keeps most trails nicely distinct all year.

This route takes you on a delightful circuit that covers most of the southern portion of the range, including 11 miles of the spectacular ridgeline, the area's namesake, mostly at elevations higher than 9,500 feet. Check in with the Forest Service about snow conditions if you're attempting the hike before mid-July.

The only problem with this hike is the confusing maze of trails and junctions (many without signs), and some trails are visible only on the map. Because of this problem, this route is more suited to experienced hikers.

From the trailhead at the BLM campground, it's less than a mile along East Fork Blacktail Deer Creek Trail 69 to a wet crossing of the East Fork. This section of trail that follows the stream is surprisingly lush. After a 40-mile drive through dry, sagebrush country, you might expect more dryness, but you get the opposite. The slow-moving, spring-fed stream winds through a green, lush valley full of moose and other wildlife. A few busy beavers have slowed the flow even more.

After 2 miles on Trail 69, you reach the junction with the Lawrence Creek Trail 669 (incorrectly marked 699), where you go left (north) and Trail 69 turns to Trail 699. Continue on East Fork Blacktail Deer Creek Trail 69 all the way to Honeymoon Park on the Snowcrest Divide. About halfway up turn left (north) at the Two Meadows Trail 74 junction to remain on Trail 69.

In massive Honeymoon Park, turn right (east) onto Snowcrest Trail 4. (The left fork goes down to the Notch Trailhead.) Follow Snowcrest Trail 4 for the next 11 miles, all along the Snowcrest Divide and through some of the most spectacular scenery in Montana. Whitebark pines surround Honeymoon Park and climb up small drainages to the ridgeline. Some of them even make it to the windswept divide, but they suffer the consequences come winter, as witnessed by the absence of west side branches.

◀ *Life is tough on the Snowcrest Divide.*

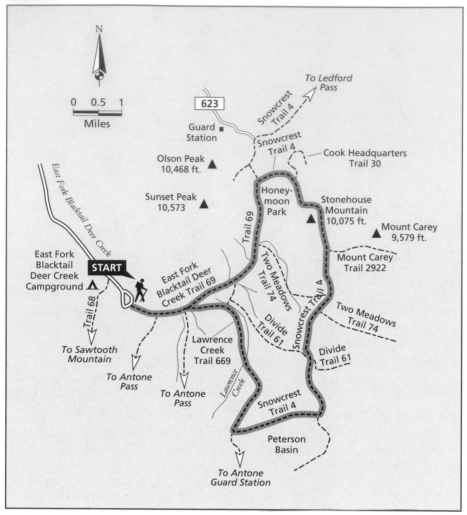

Like most ridgeline trails, you go up and down, up and down, but nothing too long or steep. At 9 miles Stonehouse Mountain is the highest point near the trail at 10,075 feet, and there is actually a "stonehouse" built long ago by shepherds. The trail goes right by it. Olson and Sunset Peaks, both higher than Stonehouse, dominate the western horizon with Hogback Mountain a little farther off joining the celebration.

Before getting too wrapped up in the vistas, make sure you have plenty of water. There isn't any for the next 11 miles unless you drop down for a mile or two into one of the creeks flowing from the ridge. This situation is especially problematic later in the season. If you go early in July, snowbanks may linger, and they can be a source of water. Large cirque basins hug the eastern side of the crest as Trail 4 skirts several minor summits along the divide, always remaining above 9,500 feet. And unlike any other trail I have ever hiked, there are several points along the ridge where you can see the entire 23-mile route covered by the trail description.

As you pass by a series of trail junctions (Mount Carey Trail 2922, Two Meadows Trail 74, Corral Creek Trail 417, Divide Trail 61), you need to do only two things: stay on the top of the ridge and keep your eyes peeled for the magnum cairns marking the way, each its own work of artful resourcefulness. In many places the trail fades away, but no matter. The magnificent cairns, all strategically located, can be seen a mile ahead. Watch for moose, elk, deer, golden eagles, and other wildlife along the way.

Near the end of this 11-mile slice of hiker's heaven, you might have a problem. When we hiked this route, the stretch from the junction where you turn right onto Lawrence Creek Trail 669 (unsigned, basically invisible, and incorrectly marked 699 on the map) at 16.5 miles down to the junction with the East Fork Blacktail Deer Creek Trail 69 at 21 miles, where you turn left, was very confusing. Between those two points are two left turns: at the junction with Lodgepole Trail 73 at 19 miles and at the junction with Divide Creek Trail 61 at 19.5 miles. Keep the map out and be alert. Some trail sections, such as part of the Two Meadows Trail, have been rerouted, making the topo map inaccurate. Fortunately, you're up high and can see where you're heading, so if you temporarily lose the trail, it should only be a minor problem. The terrain is open and easy bushwhacking. When we hiked this route, the Forest Service trail crew we met assured us that all of these trails would be well marked and the junctions signed by end of the 2003 season, so it might not be a problem today.

Options

Although it would be a nightmarish shuttle, you could drive to the Notch Trailhead just north of Honeymoon Park and day hike only the Snowcrest Divide Trail down to the East Fork Blacktail Deer Creek Trailhead, about 16 miles total distance. This would be an amazing day hike but a difficult and time-consuming shuttle. Perhaps

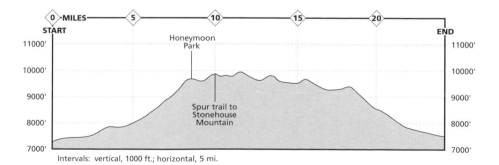

Intervals: vertical, 1000 ft.; horizontal, 5 mi.

the best way to do it would be to have somebody drop you off at the Notch Trailhead and then drive around to pick you up as you hike through the southern section of a hidden treasure called the Snowcrest Range.

You could also do a shorter loop hike from the Notch Trailhead by dropping off the ridge on the Two Meadows or Divide Trails and then climbing back up the East Fork to Honeymoon Park and back down to the Notch Trailhead.

A very experienced, fit hiker could also do this entire route in one long day.

Side Trips

One must-do side trip is a short scramble up to the top of Stonehouse Mountain on a well-marked spur trail. (Originally contributed by Bob Wagenknecht and Ed Madej, rehiked by authors in 2003)

Key Points

0.0 Trailhead at East Fork Blacktail Deer Campground

0.7 Wet crossing of Blacktail Creek

2.0 Junction with Lawrence Creek Trail 669 (incorrectly marked 699); turn left

5.5 Junction with Two Meadows Trail 74; turn left

7.5 Honeymoon Park and junction with Snowcrest Trail 4; turn right

8.0 Junction with Cook Headquarters Trail 30; turn right

9.0 Spur trail to the summit of Stonehouse Mountain; turn left

10.5 Junction with Mount Carey Trail 2922; turn right and stay on ridgetop

11.5 Junction with Two Meadows Trail 74; turn left and stay on ridgetop

12.0 Junction with Corral Creek Trail 417; turn right and stay on ridgetop

13.5 Junction with Divide Trail 61; go straight and stay on ridgetop

16.5 Junction with Lawrence Creek Trail 669 (incorrectly marked 699); turn right

19.0 Junction with Lodgepole Trail 73; turn left

19.5 Junction with Divide Creek Trail 61; turn left

21.0 Junction with East Fork Blacktail Deer Creek Trail 69; turn left

22.5 Cross Blacktail Deer Creek

23.0 East Fork Blacktail Deer Creek Trailhead and Campground

◀ *Coauthor Bill Schneider in Honeymoon Park on the Snowcrest Divide and one of the truly magnificent cairns that show the way.*
GREG SCHNIEDER PHOTO

61 Antone Peak

Description: A short but steep climb to 10,247-foot Antone Peak.
Start: 40 miles southeast of Dillon in the Snowcrest Range.
Type of hike: Day hike; out-and-back.
Total distance: 5-mile round trip.
Difficulty: Strenuous to Antone Peak and easy to Antone Pass.

Maps: Antone Peak USGS Quad and Southwest Montana Interagency Visitor/Travel Map (East Half).
Trail contacts: Madison Ranger District, Beaverhead-Deerlodge National Forest, 5 Forest Service Road, Ennis, MT 59729; (406) 682-4253; www.fs.fed.us/r1/bdnf.

Finding the trailhead: Drive south from Dillon on Interstate 15 for 47 miles to Lima exit 15. Head north through town and turn right, heading east on Forest Road 205 toward Lima Dam. Follow FR 205 for 23.2 miles past Lima Reservoir to the junction with FR 202. Turn left (northwest) for Antone Guard Station. Drive northwest for 5.2 miles and turn right onto FR 325 (0.3 mile past Clover Divide). Drive 5.3 miles on FR 325 to Antone Guard Station. The Forest Service rents this cabin for a reasonable fee. Contact the Madison Ranger District in Ennis at (406) 682-4253 for information on this and other rental cabins. The trailhead has a parking lot and rest rooms but no water.

Sawtooth Mountain from Antone Peak.

Antone Peak

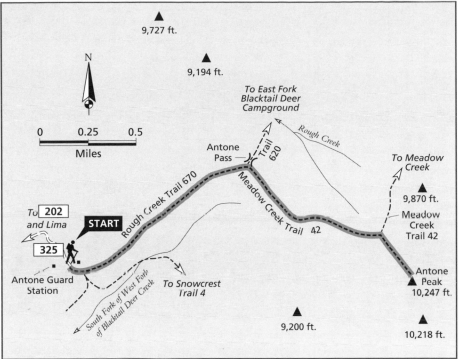

The Hike

Rough Creek Trail 670 starts across the field from the Antone Guard Station parking lot. After leaving the guard station, Rough Creek Trail 670 traverses the right side of the ridge, passing through open sagebrush meadows and limber pine, aspen, and fir forest. The trail is well maintained and popular with horse packers and hunters.

After what feels like a long mile, you reach 8,600-foot Antone Pass. Antone Pass is a grassy open saddle with excellent views north of the Snowcrest Range. Rough Creek Trail 670 continues down the other side toward the East Fork of Blacktail Deer Creek.

At Antone Pass turn right, heading through the grass on the faint Meadow Creek Trail 42. The trail is hard to follow, but look for trail markers and blazes along the left side of the meadows. When the blazes peter out, look uphill and to the left, up the ridge. The trail drops into the bowl below Antone Peak. It's a short but very steep and strenuous climb up this bowl to the 10,247-foot summit of Antone Peak, a Category H ascent. The view here includes the rest of the Snowcrest Range stretching off to the north, the expanse of the Red Rock Valley, and the Centennial Mountains

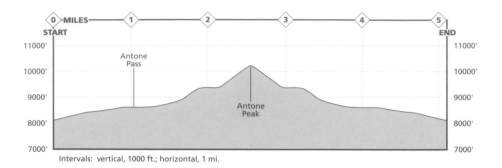

Intervals: vertical, 1000 ft.; horizontal, 1 mi.

on the southern horizon. You also get a good look at Sawtooth Peak to the west, which looks like the teeth of a circular saw blade and could be termed "Sawteeth Peak." (Originally contributed by Herb B. Gloege, rehiked by authors in 1999)

Key Points

0.0   Trailhead

1.0   Antone Pass

2.5   Antone Peak

5.0   Trailhead

62 Helmet and Sphinx

Description: The Sphinx and the Helmet, truly unique geological formations.
Start: 18 miles southeast of Ennis in the Madison Range.
Type of hike: Day hike or overnighter; loop.
Total distance: 11.5 miles (without climbing the Helmet or Sphinx).
Difficulty: Strenuous.

Maps: Lake Cameron and Sphinx Mountain USGS Quads and Southwest Montana Interagency Visitor/Travel Map (East Half) or Lee Metcalf Wilderness Map.
Trail contacts: Madison Ranger District, Beaverhead-Deerlodge National Forest, 5 Forest Service Road, Ennis, MT 59729; (406) 682–4253; www.fs.fed.us/r1/bdnf.

Finding the trailhead: Drive south of Ennis on U.S. Highway 287 for 11.1 miles. Turn left and head east on Bear Creek Road (Forest Road 327) at Cameron. Bear Creek Road heads east on pavement for 3 miles and then turns south on a good gravel road for 1.5 miles until it turns east and goes another mile to the Bear Creek Ranch. Turn south here again and travel less than a mile to a junction; turn left, heading east up Bear Creek to the Bear Creek Ranger Station. It's 8 miles from the highway to Bear Creek Ranger Station, Campground, and Trailhead. The trailhead has ample parking and a toilet.

The Hike

The Madison Range undoubtedly offers some of Montana's finest hiking. Yet only the northern section, the Spanish Peaks, has ever become popular with hikers. The area south of the Spanish Peaks all the way to the Hilgard Basin on the southern tip of the range offers good hiking also. The loop trail between the Sphinx and the Helmet nicely illustrates this fact.

Trail 326 enters the Lee Metcalf Wilderness just beyond the Bear Creek Ranger Station and immediately crosses the Trail Fork of Bear Creek on a bridge. Then it follows the stream for about 2 miles before it joins Trail 357. It crosses the stream three more times, once on a bridge, twice without bridges, but the stream is usually small enough to let you keep your feet dry.

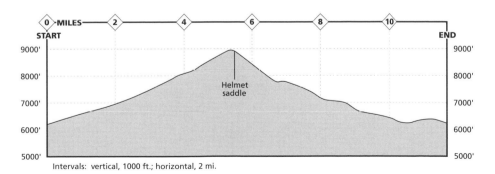

Intervals: vertical, 1000 ft.; horizontal, 2 mi.

On the way to the Helmet saddle.

At the junction turn left (northeast) on Trail 357, which heads uphill toward the saddle between the Helmet and the Sphinx, which is another 3 miles. During this portion of the hike, you'll experience most of the 2,300-foot elevation gain, a Category 1 climb.

From the saddle continue down the north side on Trail 357 into the Middle Fork of Bear Creek. From the saddle down to this junction, the trail drops sharply. From the T junction with Trail 325 at 6.5 miles, where you turn left (west), Trail 325 continues down the drainage 3.5 miles to a bridge across the creek (after five wet crossings!). From the bridge Trail 325 takes you south through mostly open country and directly back to the Bear Creek Ranger Station.

Once you pick up Trail 325, it's about 5 miles out to the road, making this a tough, 11.5-mile hike, not including the mountain climbs. The Middle Fork and a smaller stream on the climb are the only reliable water sources, so plan on carrying water with you.

Helmet and Sphinx

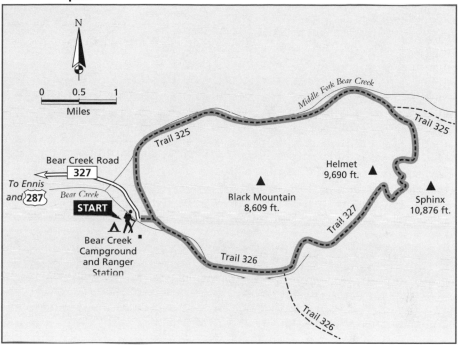

If you're camping, pick one of several good sites along the Middle Fork. You can spend some time after supper trying to spot a member of the area's large moose population.

Options

You can make this an out-and-back hike by retracing your steps back down to Bear Creek.

Side Trips

From the saddle you have two logical side trips—climbs to the summits of the Helmet and the Sphinx, which, understandably, do indeed resemble a helmet and a sphinx. Scaling the Helmet takes less than two hours and the Sphinx slightly more. They're both scrambles, with the Helmet the more technical of the two. The Sphinx has the edge on vistas, with much of the Madison Range visible from the 10,876-foot summit, including the Yellow Mules country to the northeast and Koch Peak, Shedhorn Ridge, No Man Ridge, and the Taylor Peaks to the south. At the summit stay clear of the edge lest you fall over an incredibly steep cliff into the Indian Creek Valley. (Originally contributed by Pat Caffrey, rehiked by authors in 2000)

Key Points

0.0 Trailhead

2.0 Junction with Trail 357; turn left

5.0 Helmet saddle

6.5 Junction with Trail 325; turn left

10.0 Bridge across Middle Fork of Bear Creek

10.5 Junction with North Bear Trail; turn left

11.5 Trailhead

Lewis and Clark
National Forest

63 Gateway Gorge

Description: A long loop in the Rocky Mountain Front and in the northeast corner of the Bob Marshall Wilderness with two fairly easy trips over the Continental Divide.

Start: 35 miles northwest of Choteau.

Type of trip: Extended backpacking trip; loop.

Total distance: 39.5 miles.

Difficulty: Moderate.

Maps: Morningstar Mountain, Swift Reservoir, Fish Lake, Gateway Pass, and Gooseberry Park USGS Quads; Bob Marshall Wilderness Complex Map.

Trail contacts: Rocky Mountain Ranger District, Lewis & Clark National Forest, 1102 Main Avenue NW, Choteau, MT 59422; (406) 466-5341; www.fs.fed.us/r1/lewisclark.

Finding the trailhead: Take U.S. Highway 89 to a rest area on the north edge of Dupuyer (36 miles south of U.S. Highway 2 and 32 miles north of Choteau) and turn left (west) onto Forest Road 146 to Swift Dam. This road runs west for 18 miles to Swift Dam Trailhead—the main trailhead—on your left (south) at the foot of the dam. You can start the hike here or travel 2 miles farther around the north side of the reservoir on a rough road to a secondary trailhead. This road crosses the Blackfeet Reservation and may be closed or restricted, so check for signs near the dam. Also, a permit is required to park on the north side of the trailhead. You can buy one at the general store in Dupuyer. You can make it to the main trailhead in any vehicle, but you need high clearance to access the secondary trailhead on the north side of the reservoir. The following description follows the route from the main trailhead at the foot of the dam. Toilet, campsite, and plenty of parking at the main trailhead. Limited parking available on the secondary trailhead with only undeveloped camping areas.

Recommended itinerary: You can hike longer days on this trip because of the gentle terrain; a well-conditioned hiker could easily do this trek in three nights. Four nights, however, would be less strenuous.

First night: Halfway up the South Fork of Birch Creek

Second night: Big River Meadows

Third night: Meadows just west of Badger Pass or Beaver Lake

Fourth night: Halfway down the North Fork of Birch Creek

The Hike

This trip typifies backpacking in the Bob. It travels through long, gentle, and mostly forested valleys and gradually climbs to low-elevation passes. If you develop a stronger interest in the Bob, you can expect more of the same on most routes. On this route you pass over the Continental Divide twice, but in both cases the climb seems so slight that you hardly break into a sweat.

You can slash 7 miles off the total distance by starting the hike on the north shore of Swift Reservoir, but that is a rough jeep road requiring a high-clearance vehicle, and it crosses through Blackfeet Reservation land. Check carefully at the dam to make sure the road isn't closed.

Gateway Gorge

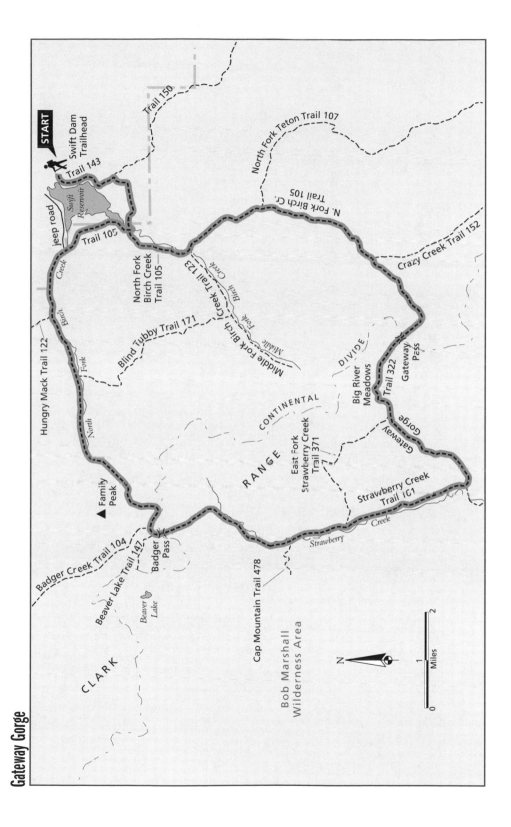

The Bob is horse country, so expect to meet a stock party or two along the route. And expect the trails to be quite distinct because of the high horse traffic—too distinct in many places, where the trail becomes deeply rutted.

The route has adequate water sources, but some can dry up in August. Plan on carrying a full water bottle at all times. You can camp anywhere, but be sure to set up a zero-impact camp. This is grizzly country, so be bear aware and handle food and garbage properly. Anglers can find a few cutthroats in both the South Fork and the North Fork of Birch Creek, but this trip is not known for its fishing.

From the main trailhead you face a short, 200-foot hill to get your heart pumping before dropping down into the South Fork of Birch Creek for the long haul to Gateway Pass. Once you ford the stream (sorry, no bridges on this route), you follow a gradual upgrade all the way to the pass. You'll find five official trail junctions (see "Key points" list) and frequent social trails established by outfitters, but stay on the main trail, North Fork Birch Creek Trail 105, for 14.5 miles to Gateway Pass, the most distinct choice in all cases. At the pass Trail 105 becomes Trail 322.

The trail meanders through sparse forest of lodgepole and Douglas fir with frequent meadows, opening up more and more as you approach the pass. Be alert for campsites. You'll need to find one somewhere along the way, and there isn't an abundance of good choices.

Typically hikers expect a short, steep pull to get over a pass, but not so with Gateway. As you approach the pass, you'll be looking ahead trying to guess where the trail goes. And then, much to your surprise, you'll see a sign on a tree indicating you're standing on the pass. Low-elevation (6,478 feet) Gateway Pass is hidden in a small grove of mixed conifers.

Immediately after the pass, you start out on Trail 322 through Big River Meadows, a logical choice for your second night out. The meadow is gorgeous and so typically Bob, but it should be named Little Brook Meadows because there's no river.

After a pleasant night in Big River Meadows, you drop gradually toward the Gateway Gorge, taking a left (north) turn at 16.6 miles when Trail 371 up the East Fork of Strawberry Creek veers off to the right. When you approach the gorge, the trail climbs up onto the talus slope above the stream to give you a better view. The gorge is impressive but possibly overrated for its scenic beauty.

After the gorge the trail heads into a mature forest and stops there after you turn right (north) onto Trail 161 and begin the gradual upgrade along Strawberry Creek toward Badger Pass. As you approach the pass, the forest opens up into a series of meadows. You can pick one of these meadows for your next campsite or, if you're ambitious, go all the way to the pass at 24.5 miles and take a 1.5-mile spur trail (Beaver Lake Trail 147) over to Beaver Lake for your third night out. This side trip to Beaver Lake adds 3 miles to the total distance of this route.

Badger Pass resembles Gateway Pass, a gentle, forested, no-sweat pass that you hardly notice climbing—and it's very close to the same elevation, too. At the pass and shortly thereafter, stay alert to make sure you get on North Fork of Birch Creek Trail by going right (south or east) at both junctions—with Beaver Lake Trail 147 at 24.7 miles and with Badger Creek Trail 104 at 24.9 miles. You'll know you're on the right trail when you start the only serious climb of this trip out of Badger Creek over a mildly serious, Category 3 hill (about 600 feet in 1.5 miles), into the North Fork of Birch Creek. This climb will get your heart rate up for the first time on the trip.

When you reach the top, take a break and look around. To the north you get a panoramic view into the expansive Badger–Two Medicine area, currently proposed for wilderness status but also proposed for extensive oil and gas development. To the south you get a sweeping view of the North Fork of Birch Creek, the boundary line of the Bob Marshall Wilderness Area. This means all the wild country on the north side of the stream is part of a large undesignated wild land called the Rocky Mountain Front, also proposed for wilderness and energy development.

On the way down the North Fork Trail, stay on campsite alert. Unless you have decided to hike out that day, you'll need to find one about halfway down for your fourth night out. As you watch the stream bottom for a campsite, you'll see the dramatic signs of the major flood that flushed out this area in 1964.

After you drop steeply for about 2 miles from the North Fork/Badger divide (making you happy you didn't do the trip in reverse), the trail settles into a stream grade easy walk until you reach the road leading to the secondary trailhead on the north side of the reservoir. You probably won't see vehicles on this road as you walk along it for a quarter mile because most users park in an open area above tiny Haywood Creek and don't drive on this last half mile of road before it turns into a single-track trail. This section can be confusing, so be alert. You follow the road to the top of a ridge. When you see the road veering off to the left and heading down to Haywood Creek, you go straight on a distinct trail.

Shortly after you leave the jeep road, you drop down and get your feet wet fording the North Fork. Then you climb a short hill over the divide between the North Fork and South Fork, drop down again, and hook up with the trail back to the main trailhead and your vehicle.

Options

You can do this route in reverse, but the climb over the North Fork/Badger divide would make it more difficult. The climbs over the passes would still be no sweat.

Side Trips

You can always find a side trip, but this route doesn't include many logical choices. A short trip over to Beaver Lake is one possibility, and if you like mountaintops, try Family Peak from the top of the North Fork/Badger divide. (Originally contributed by Elaine and Art Sedlack, rehiked by authors in 2002)

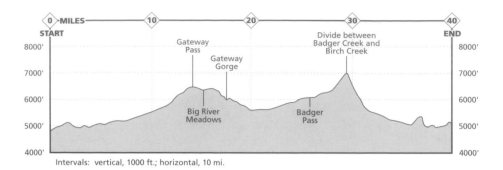

Intervals: vertical, 1000 ft.; horizontal, 10 mi.

Key Points

0.0 Swift Dam Trailhead

1.0 Junction with Trail 150; turn right

2.1 Junction with Trail 150; turn right

3.5 Junction with North Fork Birch Creek Trail 105; turn left

5.0 Junction with Middle Fork Birch Creek Trail 123; turn left

7.5 Junction with North Fork Teton Trail 107; turn right

12.9 Junction with Crazy Creek Trail 152; turn right

14.5 Gateway Pass, Trail 105 becomes Trail 322

15.5 Big River Meadows

16.6 Junction with East Fork Strawberry Creek Trail 371; turn left

17.5 Gateway Gorge

19.5 Junction with Strawberry Creek Trail 161; turn right

20.0 Junction with East Fork Strawberry Creek Trail 371; turn left

21.5 Junction with Cap Mountain Trail 478; turn right

24.5 Badger Pass

24.7 Junction with Beaver Lake Trail 147; turn right

24.9 Junction with Badger Creek Trail 104; turn right

30.5 Junction with Blind Tubby Trail 171; turn left

32.0 Junction with Hungry Mack Trail 122; turn right

34.0 Jeep road (Trail 121 on map) on north side of Swift Reservoir and secondary trailhead

36.0 Junction with South Fork Birch Creek Trail 143; turn left

37.4 Junction with Trail 150; turn left

38.5 Junction with Trail 150; turn left

39.5 Swift Dam Trailhead

64 Our Lake

Description: A very pristine mountain lake with good fishing and mountain goats inhabiting the slopes above the lake.

Start: 29 miles west of Choteau in the Rocky Mountain Front.

Type of hike: Day hike or overnighter; out-and-back.

Total distance: 5-mile round trip.

Difficulty: Moderate.

Maps: Our Lake USGS Quad and Lewis and Clark National Forest Map.

Trail contacts: Rocky Mountain Ranger District, Lewis & Clark National Forest, 1102 Main Avenue NW, Choteau, MT 59422; (406) 466-5341; www.fs.fed.us/r1/lewisclark.

Finding the trailhead: Drive 4.4 miles north of Choteau on U.S. Highway 89 and turn west on Teton River Road 144. Follow this paved road for about 16.5 miles until you see the sign for Far Mountain Ranger Station or South Fork of the Teton River. Here turn left (south) on Forest Road 109. After less than a half mile, you cross the Teton River and turn right (west) at a junction just after the one-lane bridge. Follow this road for 4 miles, turn right at another junction, and follow that road for 6 miles until it ends. You're on FR 109 all the way. Trails 184 to Our Lake and 165 to Headquarter Pass begin where the road ends. The large trailhead is set up for horse trailers and has lots of parking and a toilet.

The Hike

This is a popular hike on a well-maintained trail with outstanding scenery, good fishing, and excellent opportunities to view wildlife.

When I hiked this route in 2001, Our Lake wasn't on the trailhead signs, but that might have been fixed. In any case take Trail 165 toward Headquarters Pass. A half mile up the trail, take the right (north) fork onto Trail 184 to Our Lake, even though it isn't indicated on the sign. There's a big interpretive display about a quarter mile up the trail that tells the story of Our Lake, one of the few alpine lakes on the Rocky Mountain Front. Just below the lake, you pass by a fantastic waterfall

It's only 2.5 miles to Our Lake. The trail climbs 1,500 feet to the lake (Category 2), and the last half mile switchbacks up a steep slope that can be hazardous if tried before the snowbanks disappear. It's best to wait until July or August to try this hike. There is a good source of water at about the 2-mile mark, but the rest of the trail is dry, especially in late August and September.

Bears are common in the area, and you can almost always spot mountain goats on the alpine slopes behind Our Lake. If you're lucky you may also see bighorn sheep near Rocky Mountain, the highest peak in the Bob Marshall Wilderness (9,392 feet). In addition, expect to see marmots and pikas. Asters, daisies, and lupine seem to prevail among the abundant supply of wildflowers along this trail. Skunkflower is common on the alpine slopes above the lake.

Our Lake

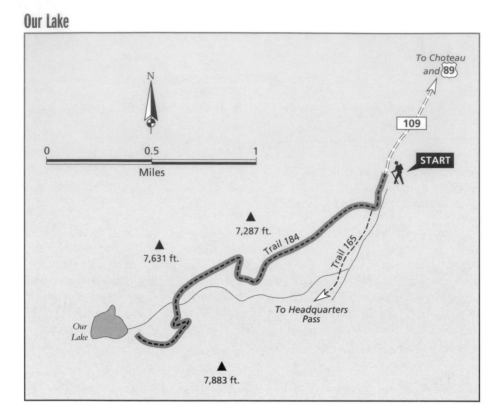

The basin was burned somewhat by the Gates Creek Fire in 1988, but the area around the lake itself was spared entirely. Since access is easy, the lake is heavily used, so the Forest Service recommends camping at least 1,000 feet from the lake to reduce impact.

Even though the fish see lots of lures and flies, the fishing remains good. Ten-inch rainbow trout make up most of the catch. The lake also has cutthroat trout, but they're harder to catch.

Side Trips

For moderately experienced hikers, there's a good side trip to the saddle west of the lake above the basin. From this saddle, you can view the Chinese Wall, the backbone of the Bob Marshall Wilderness. The distance to the saddle is about 0.8 mile. This spectacular mountain country is part of the Teton Peaks Special Management Area and is designated as roadless. (Originally contributed by Dave Orndoff, rehiked by authors in 2001)

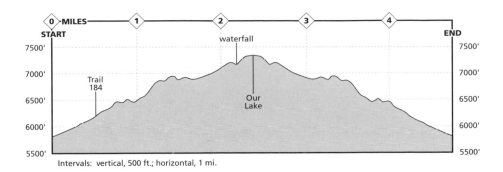

Intervals: vertical, 500 ft.; horizontal, 1 mi.

Key Points

0.0 Trailhead

0.2 Interpretive display

0.5 Junction with Trail 184; turn right

2.2 Waterfall

2.5 Our Lake

5.0 Trailhead

65 Mount Wright

Description: One of the best mountaintop views of the northern Bob Marshall Wilderness Complex.
Start: 30 miles west of Choteau.
Type of hike: Day hike; out-and-back.
Total distance: 6-mile round trip.
Difficulty: Strenuous.

Maps: Wright USGS Quad and Lewis and Clark National Forest Map.
Trail contacts: Rocky Mountain Ranger District, Lewis & Clark National Forest, 1102 Main Avenue NW, Choteau, MT 59422; (406) 466-5341; www.fs.fed.us/r1/lewisclark.

Finding the trailhead: Drive 4.4 miles north of Choteau on U.S. Highway 89 and take paved Teton River Road 144 west into the Rocky Mountain Front for 16.7 miles to the junction with the South Fork of Teton River Road. Go straight on the North Fork of Teton River Road (FR 144) and drive 18 more miles, past the Cave Mountain Campground and turnoff to the Rocky Mountain High Ski Area, to the West Fork Ranger Station. Just before the bridge crossing the Teton River and getting to the campground and ranger station, a small sign on your left points to Mount Wright Trail Trailhead. Extra parking, vehicle camping, and a toilet are available at nearby West Fork Teton Campground. Parking is very limited right at the trailhead.

The Hike

The old lookout is gone, but the trail to the 8,855-foot summit of Mount Wright remains. For those in good physical shape, this is the perfect hike to catch the views that stretch from Glacier National Park to the Scapegoat Wilderness.

At the trailhead the sign says WEST FORK TETON TRAIL 114, not Mount Wright, but this is the right trail. It starts out on a jeep road, but after only about a quarter mile, you reach a trail junction. Turn right (west) here onto Mount Wright Trail 160.

After the junction, you go through a mostly reclaimed (by nature) clear-cut on an old logging road, but this stretch is not unpleasant. The route through the clear-cut is well-marked with cairns and directional signs. After a half mile the trail leaves the clear-cut and enters the uncut forest. From here it switchbacks up the mountain, with the last half of the trip above timberline. The trail goes to a single-track and is easy to follow, except in a few meadows where it fades away and is marked by cairns. Two miles from the trailhead you reach a small pass to the east of the main summit. The trail continues over the pass to a low saddle on the north-south ridge ahead. Once on the ridge it's a short hike to the summit.

The views on the summit are some of the best to be found anywhere in the northern Rockies. Directly north is the knife-edged top of Mount Patrick Gass, named after a lieutenant in the Lewis and Clark expedition. To the east is the thin, steep ridge of Choteau Mountain and the endless expanse of the northern Great Plains. You can pick out Mount Saint Nicholas in Glacier Park, the long limestone

Mount Wright

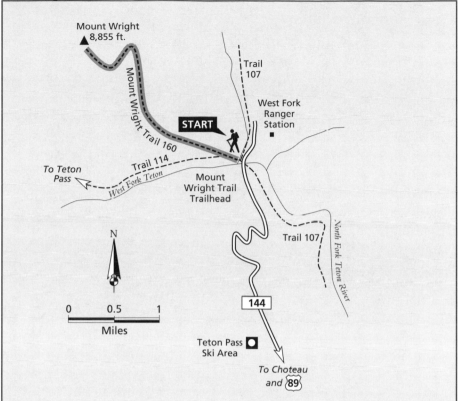

cliffs of the northern Chinese Wall, and the large hulks of Old Baldy and Rocky Mountain Peak to the south. Literally hundreds of other peaks stretch across the horizon on a cloudless day.

While ascending the southeastern slope, watch for mountain goats as the trail breaks out of the sparse tree cover. Also watch the weather closely. You don't want to be up on these windswept slopes in a thunderstorm, a good reason to start early in the morning.

The descent from the summit should take you less than two hours, while the ascent can stretch as long as four or five hours. The 3,500-foot elevation gain (a Category H climb) may deter families with young children, but the trail doesn't require any mountain climbing experience, just strong lungs and legs.

The route is totally waterless, so fill up before you start. Try this one early in the season (June or early July) so that a few snowfields are still around to slake your thirst near the summit. The exposed, south-facing slopes can make for a real scorcher of a trip in August. (Originally contributed by Ed Madej and Rosemary Rowe, rehiked by authors in 2002)

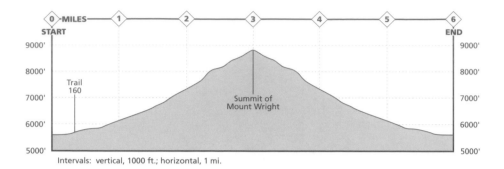

Intervals: vertical, 1000 ft.; horizontal, 1 mi.

Key Points

0.0 Trailhead

0.3 Junction with Trail 160; turn right

0.8 End of clear-cut

3.0 Summit of Mount Wright

6.0 Trailhead

66 Devils Glen

Description: A gorgeous cascade on a super-scenic, untamed river.
Start: 15 miles southwest of Augusta.
Type of hike: Day hike or overnighter; out-and-back.
Total distance: 7-mile round trip.
Difficulty: Easy.

Maps: Steamboat Mountain USGS Quad and Lewis and Clark National Forest Map.
Trail contacts: Rocky Mountain Ranger District, Lewis & Clark National Forest, 1102 Main Avenue NW, Choteau, MT 59422; (406) 466-5341; www.fs.fed.us/r1/lewisclark.

Finding the trailhead: Take the Elk Creek Road 12 miles southwest from Augusta to Bean Lake (or take Forest Road 434 north from Montana Highway 200, 27 miles southwest of Simms). At Bean Lake take Dearborn River Road (Forest Road 577) westward into the mountains until it ends at the trailhead 5.7 miles later, 2 miles past the Diamond X Ranch. The large trailhead has separate areas for hikers and horse people (hikers park on the left; be careful not to park in the area reserved for horse trailers) and a toilet.

The Hike

Floating the lower Dearborn River has become popular, but fewer people take advantage of the nice hike into the river's upper reaches through Devils Glen. This is the perfect family hike with low mileage, very little elevation gain, and a scenic river.

The Forest Service has recently obtained legal access to the Devils Glen Trail at this location. At the request of the private landowners, the Forest Service is advising hikers to stay on the trail until they reach the national forest boundary, which is well-marked, at 1.8 miles. The trail is closed to motor vehicles.

About a mile from the trailhead, Devils Glen Trail 206 crosses the Dearborn River over a newly constructed bridge. Much of the trail has recently been rerouted and reconstructed from the river crossing through Devils Glen. Beyond the bridge the trail stays on the north side of the Dearborn River. After about 3 miles, the trail begins to climb onto a rock pile coming off the southern slopes of Steamboat Mountain where the river has gouged a stunning canyon, called Devils Glen, out of

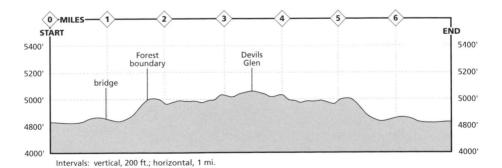

Intervals: vertical, 200 ft.; horizontal, 1 mi.

Devils Glen

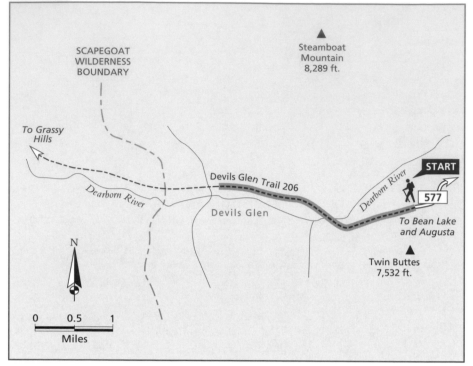

the rock. Devils Glen features a stunning display of wildflowers, including fairy slippers and the mountain lady's slipper. The beautiful moss-covered creek offers a carpet of green with clear water slicing the center.

You'll see a trail veering off to the left, heading down to the canyon. You can take it, enjoy a pleasant break at Devils Glen (or stay overnight), and head back. You can also continue up the river for miles, all scenic and worth the effort. You can camp anywhere along the river at or beyond Devils Glen, but on busy weekends, you might want to ford the stream and camp on the southern side in the trees or continue past Devils Glen for a mile or two more.

This entire area is a recommended addition to the Scapegoat Wilderness. If enough people visit the area and talk to a member of Congress about it, it might become part of the Scapegoat someday.

Side Trips

If you're bored with fishing and appreciating the rushing river, you can bushwhack north up the rocky slopes to the summit of Steamboat Mountain, which offers stunning views of the Rocky Mountain Front and the Great Plains. (Originally contributed by Ed Madej and Rosemary Rowe, rehiked by authors in 2002)

Key Points

0.0 Trailhead
1.0 Bridge over Dearborn River
1.8 National Forest boundary
3.5 Devils Glen
4.0 Scapegoat Wilderness boundary
7.0 Trailhead

THE VIEW FROM HERE: GETTING BALANCED

Who hasn't heard a politician on a stump saying he or she supports wilderness but not everywhere? Instead, they say, we need a "balanced" approach.

Let's get this in perspective. Depending on which set of statistics you use, somewhere between 95 and 99 percent of the continental United States has become nonwilderness. It has roads, mines, subdivisions, clear-cuts, or impoundments. That leaves less than 5 percent—more likely closer to 2 percent—that could possibly become officially designated Wilderness under provisions of the 1964 Wilderness Act.

Then, with little debate over these facts, a politician will nonetheless rush to the podium and suggest compromising that last 2 percent down to, I suppose, 1 percent. Then, ten years later, the next politico gets up and says the same thing, and now it's 0.5 percent. Get the picture? This has been going on for decades and is probably why we're down to the last 2 percent.

Here's a reality check for politicians. Even if every roadless acre in the United States is designated as Wilderness, we wouldn't even be remotely close to any legal or official definition of *balance*, such as "an influence or force tending to produce equilibrium; counterpoise" or "the difference in magnitude between opposing forces or influences."

This middle-ground, "balanced" approach, this need to compromise, is why places like the Crazy Mountains, the East Pioneers, Snowcrest Range, and the Rocky Mountain Front are not protected as Wilderness and as every day goes by become more and more threatened. Anybody who has been to these places knows how clearly they fit into any definition of the term *wilderness.*

So, let's get as balanced as we possibly can and designate these places and all other roadless lands in Montana as Wilderness. Anything so rare is incredibly valuable. We can't afford to sacrifice any more of it at the shrine of compromise.

67 Castle Mountains

Description: A peak high in the little-visited Castle Mountains.
Start: 10 miles east of White Sulphur Springs.
Type of hike: Day hike; out-and-back.
Total distance: 10-mile round trip.
Difficulty: Moderate.
Maps: Fourmile Springs and Manager Park USGS Quads, and Lewis and Clark National Forest Map.
Trail contacts: White Sulphur Springs Ranger District, Lewis & Clark National Forest, 204 West Folsom, Box A, White Sulphur Springs, MT 59645; (406) 547-3361; www.fs.fed.us/r1/lewisclark.

Finding the trailhead: Drive northeast of White Sulphur Springs on U.S. Highway 89 for 3 miles, and then turn right (east) onto U.S. Highway 12 and continue 4 miles. Then turn right (south) onto Fourmile Creek Road (Forest Road 211) to Grasshopper Campground or go 1 mile farther to Richardson Campground. Start from either campground. Grasshopper and Richardson Campgrounds are great places to vehicle camp. Both campgrounds offer quiet settings next to clear mountain streams, lush meadows, and dense forests—plus toilets, ample parking, and water at Grasshopper Campground.

The Hike

Just east of White Sulphur Springs, there is a place where the coyotes scavenge and the elk roam as they have for ages, but not many hikers venture. Here lie the Castle Mountains, a gentle, lodgepole-covered, island mountain range.

The trail leaves from the south end of Grasshopper Campground through a gate, which prevents the cattle that graze on public lands from interfering with campers. The trail follows the East Fork of Grasshopper Creek for less than a mile before turning east and up the slope. Pass through groves of trees and silent meadows. This hike is best early in the morning, when the sun has a chance to shine through beads of dew. At 1 mile the trail opens into Richardson Park, which is a meadow skirted with aspen. At 1.2 miles, the trail intersects Elk Peak Trail 717 from Richardson Campground, where you turn right (south).

After you walk through the trees for a short distance, the trail forks at 1.7 miles. Take the left fork (south), which is still Elk Peak Trail 7170. (Trail 723 goes to the right.) Elk Peak Trail 717 descends quickly, following Richardson Creek into Horse Park at 2.2 miles. Horse Park is a series of beautiful mountain meadows studded with willows that protect the creek. The trail stays on the western side of Richardson Creek across Horse Park and fades away in places. Watch for blazes south across the meadows.

After Horse Park the signs of grazing disappear. Walk softly through the quiet forest and look for wildlife. This isn't bear country, so silence is acceptable. The trail

Castle Mountains

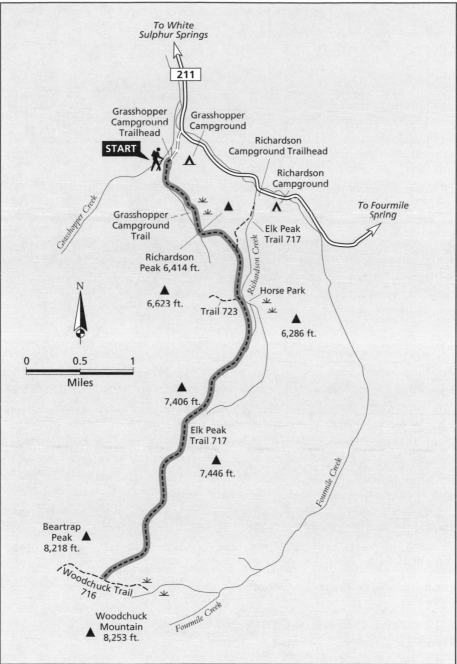

To White
Sulphur Springs

211

Grasshopper
Campground
Trailhead

Grasshopper
Campground

Richardson
Campground Trailhead

START

Richardson
Campground

To Fourmile
Spring

Grasshopper
Campground
Trail

Grasshopper Creek

Elk Peak
Trail 717

Richardson
Peak 6,414 ft.

Richardson Creek

Horse Park

N

6,623 ft.

Trail 723

6,286 ft.

0   0.5   1
Miles

7,406 ft.

Elk Peak
Trail 717

7,446 ft.

Fourmile Creek

Beartrap
Peak
8,218 ft.

Woodchuck Trail
716

Woodchuck
Mountain
8,253 ft.

Fourmile Creek

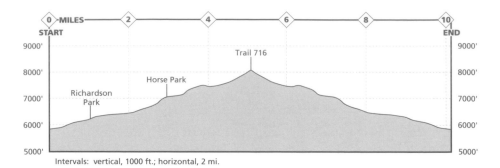

Intervals: vertical, 1000 ft.; horizontal, 2 mi.

climbs steadily, crossing several streams and meadows. The climb lasts between 2 and 3 miles. Bring water. This area dries out fast.

Once the trail flattens out, you are just east of Beartrap Peak. You might not even know it, because the mountain is just a continuation of the slopes above the trail. Curving around the mountain, the trail intersects Woodchuck Trail 716. From here retrace your steps to the trailhead.

This hike is dry in May. It's good physical conditioning for more strenuous summer hikes and a great route for trail runners.

Options

On the way back you can drop down to Richardson Campground and then walk a mile on the road back to your vehicle, which is about the same total distance, but you can see some new country.

You can also start from Richardson Campground, which makes the route a mile shorter but slightly steeper. Cross Richardson Creek on Elk Peak Trail to the west shore, walk through a meadow turning south, and begin ascending the ridge. This half-mile ascent is steep. Be sure to carry plenty of water. At the top of the hill, the trail intersects the Grasshopper Campground Trail.

It's also possible to make a loop using Woodchuck Trail 716. Check your map. (Hiked by the authors in 2003)

Key Points

0.0 Grasshopper Campground Trailhead

1.0 Richardson Park

1.2 Junction with Elk Peak Trail 117; turn right

1.7 Junction with Trail 723; turn left

2.2 Horse Park

5.0 Junction with Woodchuck Trail 716

10.0 Grasshopper Campground Trailhead

68 Sand Point

Description: A large roadless area with major streams and 1,000-foot limestone cliffs.
Start: 100 miles southeast of Great Falls in the Little Belt Mountains.
Type of hike: Extended backpacking trip; loop.
Total distance: 28 miles.
Difficulty: Strenuous.

Maps: Sand Point and Ettien Springs USGS Quads, and Lewis and Clark National Forest Map.
Trail contacts: Judith Ranger District, Lewis and Clark National Forest, 109 Central Avenue, P.O. Box 484, Stanford, MT 59479; (406) 566–2292; www.fs.fed.us/r1/lewisclark.

Finding the trailhead: Take U.S. Highway 12 east from White Sulphur Springs for 20 miles until you reach the small town of Checkerboard. Go 6 miles east of Checkerboard and turn left (north) onto Forest Road 274 to the Whitetall Guard Station. This road is paved for the first 2 miles and then turns to an excellent gravel road. Go past the guard station and stay on FR 274 for 18.4 miles until you intersect FR 487. Turn left (north) here and follow FR 487 for 2.3 miles and then turn left again onto FR 821. Stay on FR 821 for about a half mile until you reach Holiday Camp Trailhead.

The actual trailhead is slightly difficult to find. You can start hiking right from Holiday Camp on a jeep road. When we were there, a sign indicated a road leaving the north end of Holiday Camp was Trail 433, but in a few feet, the road forked with no sign. Start walking on the left-hand fork of the road, or you can also drive this road (if you have a high-clearance vehicle) for 1 mile to the actual trailhead, where there is very limited parking and no facilities, but there is a sign for Trail 433 to Burris Cabin.

The Holiday Camp Trailhead can also be reached via FR 487 from Utica on the north side of the Little Belt Mountains. The trailhead features a large parking area with toilet.

The Hike

Of all the large roadless areas in Montana, the Middle Fork of the Judith River may be the least known to hikers, not because it doesn't offer good hiking, because it does. The 81,000-acre de facto wilderness has great stream fishing, a large wildlife population, and vistas to rival any wild area.

It's uphill from Holiday Camp to the actual trailhead, but from here you lose elevation rapidly for 2 miles from the top of the ridge to the Lost Fork of the Judith

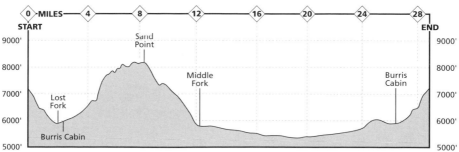

Intervals: vertical, 1000 ft.; horizontal, 4 mi.

Fishing the Lost Fork of the Judith River.

River and to Burris Cabin, an abandoned homestead. Hikers, horses, and motorcycles heavily use this section of trail, which has been reconstructed with the addition of several new switchbacks (and probably about a half mile to the total distance).

If you started late in the day, you might want to camp along the Lost Fork above Burris Cabin. There are plenty of good sites, complete with firewood and a beautiful stream filled with native cutthroat plus a few rainbows and brookies. You can see the aftermath of the Sand Point Fire, which burned more than 11,300 acres in July 1985. You can also see that the beavers have been busy in this area, damming up the still-small river in several places.

At Burris Cabin the trail intersects with Lost Fork Trail 409, which follows the length of the Lost Fork. Turn left (west) and follow Trail 409 up the Lost Fork for about 1.5 miles until you reach Trail 422. Turn right (north) here and start a 4-mile uphill stretch to Sand Point, an 8,211-foot knob on the divide separating the Lost Fork and Middle Fork drainages.

This part of the trip offers an opportunity to study the natural effects of fire on forested plant communities. Close examination will reveal newly established lodgepole

Sand Point

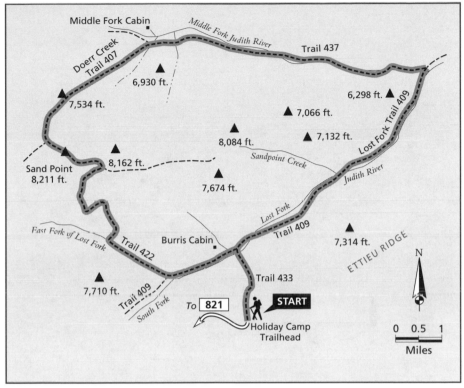

pine seedlings that started from seeds released from storage in thousands of seroti-nous cones. Abundant forage stimulated by fire feeds wildlife, and beaver dams add stability to the riparian system by storing sediment.

After relishing the view from the top of Sand Point for a few minutes, go northwest for about half a mile to a trail junction. Take a right (northeast) here and head downhill on Doerr Creek Trail 407 about 3 miles to the Middle Fork of the Judith River.

You come out onto the bottomland at the Middle Fork Cabin. Don't camp on this private land. Take a right on Trail 437 and head downstream, selecting one of many good campsites along the Middle Fork.

Like the Lost Fork, the Middle Fork offers excellent small stream fishing and scenery, especially towering limestone cliffs. From the Middle Fork Cabin, you actu-ally walk on a lightly traveled jeep road for about 6 miles downstream until you reach the point where the Lost Fork joins the Middle Fork. At the trail junction, take a right (southwest) back onto Lost Fork Trail 409 and follow the Lost Fork about 7 miles upstream to the Burris Cabin, where you must retrace your steps 3 miles uphill to your vehicle at the Holiday Camp Trailhead.

What's left of Burris Cabin in the Lost Fork of the Judith River.

All told, this is about a 28-mile loop trail that introduces you to the drainage of much of the Middle Fork of the Judith River. The Forest Service, in the Lewis and Clark National Forest Plan, has allocated most of the area for semiprimitive recreation. (Originally contributed by Bill Cunningham, partially rehiked by authors in 2003)

Key Points

0.0   Holiday Camp Trailhead

2.0   Burris Cabin and junction with Lost Fork Trail 409; turn left

4.5   Junction with Trail 422; turn right

8.5   Sand Point

9.0   Junction with Doerr Creek Trail 407; turn right

12.0   Middle Fork Cabin and junction with Trail 437; turn right

18.0   Junction with Lost Fork Trail 409; turn right

25.0   Burris Cabin and junction with Trail 433; turn left

28.0   Holiday Camp Trailhead

69 Big Snowies Crest

Description: Flat alpine terrain, an ice cave, and unrestricted views of eastern Montana from the Missouri River to the Beartooth Plateau.
Start: 20 miles south of Lewistown.
Type of hike: Day hike; loop.
Total distance: 12.3 miles, including side trip to ice cave.

Difficulty: Strenuous.
Maps: Crystal Lake, Jump Off Peak, and Half Moon Canyon USGS Quads; and Lewis and Clark National Forest Map.
Trail contacts: Judith Ranger District, Lewis and Clark National Forest, 109 Central Avenue, P.O. Box 484, Stanford, MT 59479; (406) 566–2292; www.fs.fed.us/r1/lewisclark.

Finding the trailhead: Turn south from U.S. Highway 87/Montana Highway 200 onto Crystal Lake Road 275 about 8 miles west of Lewistown (or 5 miles east of Moore). Drive about 22 miles on Crystal Lake Road to Crystal Lake, the last 5.5 miles paved and the rest excellent gravel. There are several junctions, all well signed. The trailhead for Uhlhorn Trail 493 is at the south end of the lake just past the entrance to the campground. It is a large trailhead, with vehicle camping, toilet, and water at Crystal Lake Campground.

The Hike

Anybody who thinks there aren't any great hikes in eastern Montana hasn't hiked this route, now designated as the Crystal Lake Loop National Recreation Trail. The entire trailhead and campground are as clean, well developed, and well signed as any area in this book. It really couldn't be any better than this.

The Big Snowies consist of one massive, broad-based ridge flanked by cirques and streams. Up on the crest, the main ridge runs for 12 miles from east to west and ranges from 8,500 to 8,700 feet in elevation.

From the trailhead go south on Uhlhorn Trail 493. This trail, named after a long-time district ranger and Lewistown community leader, Carl Uhlhorn, climbs more than 2,000 feet in 3 miles to the crest of the Big Snowies. At this point, the hiking becomes a stroll across level prairie-style tundra interspersed with mangled thickets of trees.

At the top Uhlhorn Trail becomes West Peak Trail 490 and Trail 493 goes off to the left on the ridge toward Greathouse Peak. Turn right (east) onto Trail 490, which goes toward the ice cave. You come to a couple more junctions along the way, but all are less distinct than the main trail, so stay to the right on the main route, which is marked by cairns in some cases.

At 4 miles you'll see Devils Chute Cave along the trail on your right. Then a quarter mile later take the half-mile round-trip down and back on Trail 464 to see the ice cave, an incredible sight you'd never expect to see in this environment. Trust me; you'll be surprised. Please be very careful not to despoil it for others who'll follow you. A flashlight is useful but not necessary.

Hiking the Big Snowies Crest, with a lot of prairie in the background.

Once back on the crest trail, turn left (east) and head for Grandview Point. At 5.8 miles, the junction with Dry Pole Creek Trail, West Peak Trail 490 becomes Grand View Trail 403 and goes down a superscenic ridgeline marked by cairns and lined with whitebark pines. You can see forever out into the prairie in all directions.

At Grandview Point you get a great view of Crystal Lake below. From here the trail (called the Jack Milburn Trail) drops sharply down to the campground, going by several junctions. Follow the map and the turns indicated in the "Key points" of this description to stay on the main route.

There's essentially no water on this route, so be sure to carry plenty.

Options

For the extra ambitious who want a very long day (and trail runners), try to make it to Greathouse Peak on Trail 493. Greathouse Peak is the highest point of the range at 8,681 feet. The route to Greathouse Peak holds one surprise after another. The trail crosses large expanses of alpine grasses that give incredible visual harmony to

Big Snowies Crest

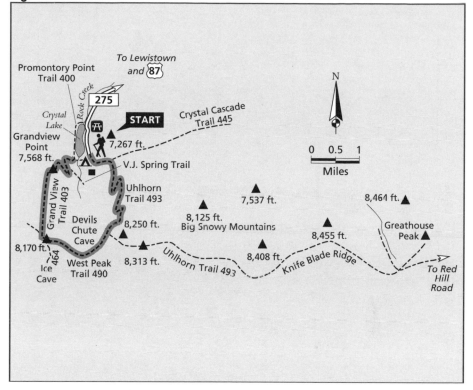

the endless prairies off to either side, 4,000 feet below. Then there is a stretch called Knife Blade Ridge where the mile-wide crest narrows to a few feet and drops off abruptly on either side. In the center of Knife Blade Ridge, the trail dips into a primitive little pass where you'll find a four-way trail junction. Stay on the obvious ridge trail to reach the top of Greathouse Peak. From here retrace your route back to Crystal Lake. (Originally contributed by Pat Caffrey, rehiked by authors in 2003)

Key Points

- **0.0** Trailhead
- **1.3** Junction with Crystal Cascade Trail 445; turn right
- **3.0** Junction with West Peak Trail 490; turn right
- **3.2** Junction with Red Hill Trail; turn right
- **3.7** Junction with East Fork Blake Creek Trail; turn right
- **4.0** Devils Chute Cave
- **4.2** Junction with Trail 464 to ice cave; turn right
- **4.5** Ice cave
- **4.8** Back to Trail 490; turn left

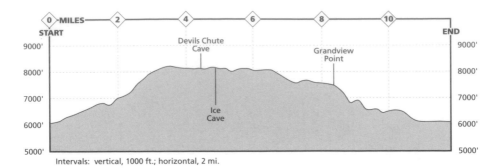

Intervals: vertical, 1000 ft.; horizontal, 2 mi.

5.8 Junction with Dry Pole Creek Trail (becomes Grand View Trail 403); turn right

8.1 Grandview Point

10.4 Junction with spur trail to V.J. Spring; turn left

11.1 Junction with Promontory Point Trail 400; turn right

11.6 Junction with Crystal Lake Loop Trail 404; turn right

12.1 Campground

12.3 Trailhead

Helena National Forest

70 Heart Lake

Description: An easily accessible lake for family fun in the southern tip of the Bob Marshall Wilderness.
Start: 62 miles northwest of Helena, near Lincoln.
Type of hike: Day hike; out-and-back.
Total distance: 8.2-mile round trip.

Difficulty: Moderate.
Maps: Heart Lake, Stonewall, and Silver King USGS Quads and Helena National Forest Map.
Trail contacts: Lincoln Ranger District, Helena National Forest, 7269 Highway 200, Lincoln, MT 59639; (406) 362–4265; www.fs.fed.us/r1/helena.

Finding the trailhead: Turn on Copper Creek Road 330, 5.3 miles east of Lincoln or 4.7 miles west of the junction of U.S. Highway 200 and Montana Highway 279. Drive north on Copper Creek Road for 7.7 miles and turn right onto Forest Road 1882 at a well-signed turn for Indian Meadows Trailhead. After 9.1 miles, you reach Indian Meadows Trailhead. Only the first 3.6 miles are paved, and if you see Snowbank Lake, you missed the turn. The trailhead has a large parking area with separate facilities for hikers and recreational horse packers and outfitters, as well as a toilet.

The Hike

It's 4.1 miles to Heart Lake, 6.7 miles to Webb Lake, and about 9 to Parker Lake. You can take a trail to the right just before Parker Lake to Two Point Lake. Heart Lake is the nicest of the bunch. Webb Lake is small and shallow. Parker Lake is very scenic but also shallow compared to Heart Lake. Two Point is away from the trail and surrounded by forest, more so than the rest of the lakes. It's hard to fly-fish at all of these lakes—no place for the back cast.

Trail 481 gets a lot of horse traffic. The trail is wide and easy to walk in most places, as long as you don't try it in the spring before it dries up or time your trip right after a few days of rain. Fortunately, this well-maintained trail features many bridges over marshy areas.

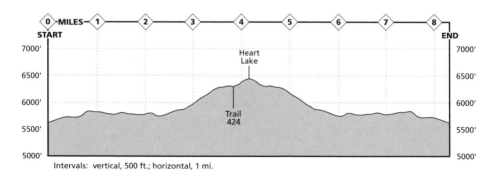

Intervals: vertical, 500 ft.; horizontal, 1 mi.

Heart Lake

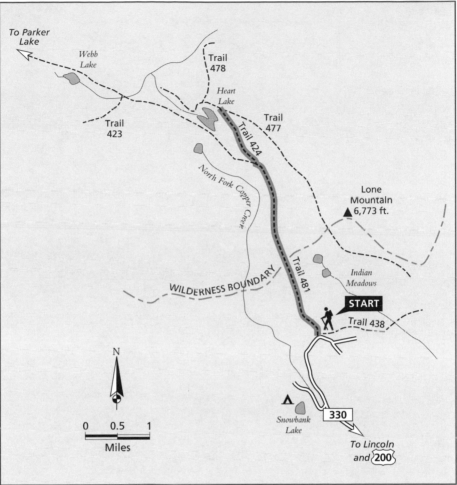

Trail 481 doesn't go directly to Heart Lake. At about the 3.9-mile mark, Trail 424 veers off to the right to the lake. If you haven't planned on Heart Lake as a destination, staying on the main trail will save about half a mile.

Heart Lake and Parker Lake are heavily used, so special regulations are in effect for horse use and camping for both lakes (no horses near the shoreline, no camping on peninsulas in the lakes). Camping restrictions on the peninsulas not only reduce damage from camping but also leave these beautiful areas open to everybody. If somebody camped there, which would be common, they would essentially be keeping everybody else out. In 2002 a forest fire burned sections of Trail 481 between the trailhead and the junction with Trail 424. (Hiked by authors in 1994)

Key Points

0.0 Trailhead

3.9 Junction with Trail 424 to Heart Lake; turn right

4.1 Heart Lake

8.2 Trailhead

71 Bear Prairie

Description: Gates of the Mountains Wilderness and historic points along the Lewis and Clark Expedition.
Location: 20 miles northeast of Helena.
Type of hike: Long day hike or overnighter; shuttle.
Total distance: 14.9 miles.
Difficulty: Strenuous.

Maps: Upper Holter Lake, Candle Mountain, and Hogback USGS Quads; and Helena National Forest Map.
Trail contacts: Helena Ranger District, Helena National Forest, 2001 Popular Street, Helena, MT 59601; (406) 449–5490; www.fs.fed.us/r1/helena.

Finding the trailheads: Drive northeast from Helena on Highway 280 for about 15 miles until you cross the Missouri River via the York Bridge. Then drive for about 4 miles to the tiny community of York. Turn left (north) at the York Bar and follow the well-maintained gravel road until it intersects with another gravel road at the small town of Nelson. Turn right (east) onto Beaver Creek Road and drive for about 5 miles until you see a well-marked trailhead for Refrigerator Canyon. The last 5 miles on Beaver Creek Road can be dangerous because of sharp, blind corners and large trucks. So if you are driving, do not be caught gawking at the scenery. Let the passengers take in the steep-walled Beaver Creek Canyon with its whitish, limestone cliffs and beautiful stream.

This hike is logistically more difficult than most. The 18-mile, point-to-point hike ends at Meriwether Picnic Area on the Missouri River. Leave a vehicle or have somebody pick you up at the Gates of the Mountains Boat Club. Be sure to call ahead for current schedules and prices. For boat tours write to Gates of the Mountains Boat Tours, P.O. Box 478, Helena, MT 59624, or call (406) 458–5241, or check the Web site www.gatesofthemountains.com. Boats run several times daily and stop at Meriwether Picnic Area on the way up and back. When you reach the picnic ground, you will have to wait for the next boat. Be sure to check the schedule before you leave so that you do not miss the last one. Also, bring a few dollars to pay for the ride. To get to the Gates of the Mountains boat dock, take Interstate 15 north from Helena for about 16 miles and turn right at the Gates of the Mountains exit. Follow the paved road 2 miles to the boat dock. There are visitor services (toilet, cafe, and interpretive displays) at Gates of the Mountains boat dock and a picnic area and toilet at Meriwether Day Use Area. You'll find limited parking and no facilities at Refrigerator Canyon Trailhead.

The Hike

The 28,560-acre Gates of the Mountains Wilderness has open parks, deep canyons, and craggy peaks, but no lakes. More than compensating for this void, however, is the area's rich history.

From the Refrigerator Canyon Trailhead Trail 259 gradually climb about a quarter of a mile to Refrigerator Canyon. Even on the hottest summer day, it is cool in this extremely steep, narrow canyon.

Bear Prairie

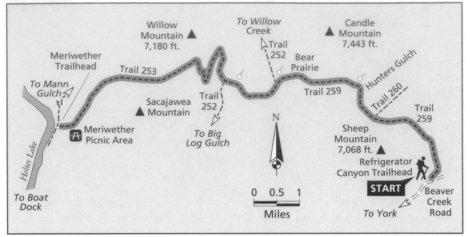

After Refrigerator Canyon the trail gradually switchbacks for about 3 miles up to the junction with Trail 260. Trail 260 continues on to the right toward Willow Creek. Stay left (west) on Trail 259, which leads to Bear Prairie.

About 5 miles later, you reach the wildflower-carpeted Bear Prairie, one of the largest and most gorgeous mountain meadows in the Helena area. Through Bear Prairie the trail is level and well maintained. The only confusing spot occurs just after Kennedy Springs (at 8.7 miles) in a large meadow where the trail swings to the right to the top of a ridge and then starts its descent to Meriwether Day Use Area, where the Lewis and Clark Expedition camped almost two centuries ago. No camping allowed today, however. Just after Kennedy Springs, turn right at the junction with Trail 252. The last 5 miles switchback steeply downhill.

After June this trail is devoid of water with the exception of a short section of Meriwether Creek at the head of the canyon. If you're staying overnight, you'll have to bring enough water for a dry camp. On the plus side, the dry climate holds down the mosquitoes. The snow usually melts early in the year, even as early as late April in dry years. This is one of the few Montana hikes you can safely do in May and early June.

Options

You can do this shuttle in reverse, of course, but the climb up from Meriwether looks significantly harder than coming up from Refrigerator Canyon. (Originally contributed by authors, rehiked in 1994)

Refrigerator Canyon, on the edge of the Gates of the Mountains Wilderness, is usually ▶
12–20 degrees cooler than the surrounding country. Forest Service photo

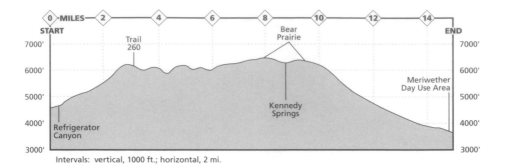

Intervals: vertical, 1000 ft.; horizontal, 2 mi.

Key Points

0.0 Refrigerator Canyon Trailhead

0.3 Refrigerator Canyon

3.5 Junction with Willow Creek Trail 260; turn left

8.3 Bear Prairie

8.4 Junction with Trail 252; turn left

8.5 Junction with Big Log Gulch Trail 254; turn right

8.7 Kennedy Springs

9.0 Trail numbers change from 259 to 253

14.9 Meriwether Day Use Area and boat dock

72 Mann Gulch

Description: A scenic and historical hike in the Gates of the Mountains Wilderness to the site of the second worst forest fire accident in USDA Forest Service history.
Start: North of Helena by Holter Reservoir.
Type of hike: Day hike with boat ride; out-and-back.
Total distance: 8-mile (or 20-mile round trip from Spring Gulch Trailhead).

Difficulty: Strenuous.
Maps: Upper Holter Lake and Beartooth Mountain USGS Quads, and Helena National Forest Map.
Trail contacts: Helena Ranger District, Helena National Forest, 2001 Popular Street, Helena, MT 59601; (406) 449-5490; www.fs.fed.us/r1/helena.

Finding the trailhead: To get to Mann Gulch, the easiest way is to drive 16 miles north of Helena on Interstate 15 and take the Gates of the Mountains exit. Turn right (east) and drive for 2 miles to the Gates of Mountains boat dock. Take the tour boat down the Missouri River to Meriwether Picnic Area. The tours are renowned for wildlife viewing, including bald eagles, osprey, and mountain goats. From the picnic area you can hike 4 miles to see the crosses marking the spots where thirteen firefighters died in the 1949 Mann Gulch Fire.

The tour drops you off at the Meriwether Day Use Area. You can catch a boat back later. The boats usually run at two-hour intervals. It's possible to just see Mann Gulch from the ridge and make the next boat, but don't attempt to visit the crosses and return within two hours. A better approach is to take the early boat at 10:00 A.M. and catch the last boat returning at 5:00 P.M. Be sure to call ahead for current schedules and prices (Gates of the Mountains Boat Tours, P.O. Box 478, Helena, MT 59624; 406-458-5241; www.gatesofthemountains.com).

To reach the hike-in trailhead, drive northeast of Helena on Montana Highway 280 for 19 miles to York. Turn left at the York Bar and drive 8 miles west to Nelson, the Cribbage Capital of the World. Turn left on the gravel road at Nelson and head for the Missouri River. Drive 4 miles and turn right on Forest Road 1812. Follow FR 1812 for another 3 miles to Spring Gulch Trailhead. The last couple of miles are rough but passable with a two-wheel-drive vehicle.

Cafe, toilet, and visitor services are available at Gates of the Mountains boat dock. There are no facilities at the actual trailhead or at the hike-in trailhead in Spring Gulch.

Mann Gulch History

Interest in this area has grown since the release of Norman Maclean's *Young Men and Fire* in 1992. In his book Maclean pieces together a picture of actual events and explains the controversy surrounding the Mann Gulch Fire. This book is considered the most accurate account of what happened at Mann Gulch when thirteen men died in a wildfire in 1949.

The fire was located in the Gates of the Mountains Wilderness just east of the Missouri River near the top of the ridge between Meriwether and Mann Gulches. The general area is steep and jagged and is known as one of the roughest areas east of the Continental Divide.

Hiker on slope where fire occurred in Mann Gulch.

According to the government Report of Board of Review and accounts in Maclean's book, on August 5, 1949, a fire, started by lightning, developed in Mann Gulch. Sixteen smoke jumpers were flown in from Missoula, and fifteen parachuted from their C-47 cargo plane at the northeast end of Mann Gulch. At 3:10 P.M. the fire covered 60 acres. The fifteen smoke jumpers on the ground gathered their cargo, and their foreman, Wagner Dodge, went to meet the Meriwether Canyon recreation and fire prevention guard, Jim Harrison.

Around 5:00 P.M. the crew started up the south side of the gulch toward the fire. Harrison and Dodge met ahead of them. Shortly after, the crew continued climbing toward the fire. Upon reaching them, Dodge ordered Bill Hellman, his second-in-command, to take the crew to the north side of the gulch and "follow contour" toward the river.

At about 5:40 P.M. Dodge gathered his crew, placing Hellman at the rear to keep the line intact while Dodge took the lead toward the river. They continued down the gulch for five minutes before Dodge saw that the fire had crossed the gulch and

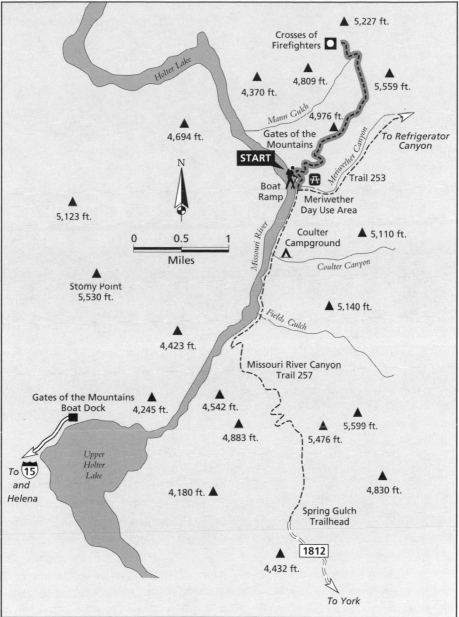

was coming up the ridge toward them. They were less than 200 yards from the fire at 5:45 P.M. They then turned back up the gulch, and the race for the ridge began.

At 5:53 P.M. Dodge ordered the men to drop their heavy equipment. The fire roared closer. Dodge then stopped and did something that was critical for his survival. He lit the dry grass beneath him on fire and yelled desperately for the rest of

Memorial of fallen firefighters in Mann Gulch.

his crew to enter the burned area with him. None listened. Sallee and Rumsey, the lone survivors from the crew, recalled that somebody said, "To hell with that, I'm getting out of here." If the crew had listened to Dodge, more might have survived. This was the first case in Forest Service history that a man had set his own escape fire. Dodge lay down in the burned area with a wet cloth over his mouth while the fire burned around him.

Sallee and Rumsey made it through an opening in the rimrock at the top of the ridge. That opening saved their lives. They stumbled over the other side of the ridge into the safety of a rockslide.

At approximately 5:56 P.M. eleven men died. It was at that exact time that the hands on Jim Harrison's watch stopped. Most of the victims suffocated before the fire charred their bodies. Although Hellman and Joseph Sylvia survived the fire and were carried out through Rescue Gulch on the opposite side of the ridge, they died later in Helena. They were burned beyond recovery.

Granite monuments and crosses mark where the men fell to remind hikers of nature's power. These men died because of a blow up: The fire exploded in size from 30 acres to 2,000 acres in just ten minutes. Just before the fire broke out, the air temperature in Mann Gulch was near one hundred degrees Fahrenheit, the grass had dried to the consistency of hay, and the young ponderosa pine and Douglas fir were dried to the consistency of kindling. Lightning struck, and the whirling winds did the rest.

The Hike

After arriving at Meriwether Picnic Area by boat, walk up the gulch for several hundred yards to the Vista Point turnoff. Turn left (north) for Vista Point. Mann Gulch Trail starts 100 feet before the metal railings that mark Vista Point. Turn right, uphill, and northeast.

A mile of switchbacks now lies between you and Mann Gulch. These trails are well worn and easy to follow, but stay on the designated route instead of cutting the switchbacks. Several points during the climb offer excellent views of the canyon below.

Once you reach the top, the trail fades away, but the view does not. Willow Peak is east up the ridge, and Beartooth Mountain is across the river. Burned and fallen trees lie parallel on the opposite slope. Rockslides and thick grasses cover the steep slope of Mann Gulch. The south side of the gulch has small, densely packed ponderosa pine and Douglas fir like the ones that fed the fire in 1949. Enough wind, enough heat, and enough lightning, and there could easily be another fire.

The Forest Service maintains the thirteen stone crosses marking the spots where the firefighters died. However, you cannot see them from the south ridge. Refer to the map for the location of the crosses. A small talus slope marks the vicinity, but the crosses are not visible until you're within several hundred yards of them. The tall grass hides these monuments well.

To reach the crosses hike off trail up the ridge for 0.3 mile. Descend from the ridge, traversing northeast up the gulch, and angle over to the crosses. The opposite ridge is steep, and the crosses are near the top of the ridge. These men were tough. It's amazing to see how high up the ridge they got before the fire engulfed them.

Return to the picnic area by climbing the south ridge back to the trail, which requires some bushwhacking followed by a steep grade. The minimum reasonable amount of time for seeing the crosses from Meriwether Picnic Area is four hours.

Options

For experienced hikers an alternative to the boat ride is to hike in. Pack plenty of water and food for a long day hike to explore and discover the mystique of Mann Gulch.

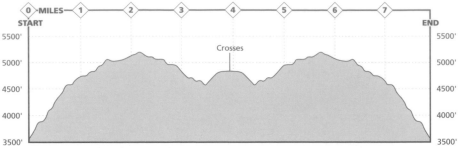

Intervals: vertical, 500 ft.; horizontal, 1 mi.

From Spring Gulch Trailhead on Forest Road 1812, take Missouri River Canyon Trail 257 down to the shoreline of Holter Reservoir and follow it until you reach Coulter Campground and, about a mile later, Meriwether Picnic Area. It's 5 miles to Meriwether Picnic Area from Spring Gulch Trailhead. This part of the trail is seldom used. Several places where trees have fallen, the trail is hard to follow.

About half a mile up from the Spring Gulch Trailhead, the trail disappears into a meadow. There are a couple cairns and a sign at the far end. Head for the saddle north and a little west. In the spring, this meadow is covered with wildflowers. The hardy grasses feed healthy herds of elk and deer. This area is just south of the Beartooth Game Range.

At the top of the ridge, the trail descends in a series of switchbacks for the next 2 miles, a strenuous climb coming out. From meadows along the way, the Gates of the Mountains Wilderness spreads out below. Gray limestone cliffs dominate the landscape. The crowds of people who prefer an interstate to a dirt road seldom experience this part of the hike. On the descent, the trail is easy to follow, although in one section, a game trail continues down the ridge, while the real trail veers left. Watch for blazes. (Hiked by authors in 1995)

Key Points

0.0 Meriwether Day Use Area Trailhead

2.0 Mann Gulch

4.0 Crosses of Firefighters

8.0 Meriwether Day Use Area Trailhead

73 Hanging Valley

Description: A deep, narrow canyon with impressive limestone towers.
Start: 20 miles northeast of Helena.
Type of hike: Day hike; out-and-back.
Total distance: 12-mile round trip.
Difficulty: Moderate.

Maps: Hogback Mountain and Snedaker Basin USGS Quads, and Helena National Forest Map.
Trail contacts: Helena Ranger District, Helena National Forest, 2001 Popular Street, Helena, MT 59601; (406) 449–5490; www.fs.fed.us/r1/helena.

Finding the trailhead: To get to York take Montana Highway 280 northeast of Helena for 15 miles, crossing the Missouri River via the York Bridge. The trailhead starts at Vigilante Campground in the Helena National Forest, 5 miles northeast of York on the old Figure Eight Route (Forest Road 4137). The Figure Eight Route used to go beyond Vigilante Campground until massive floods in May 1981 buried the road under tons of gravel in Trout Creek Canyon. The trailhead is at the far end of the campground loop. Vehicle camping, water, and toilet are available at Vigilante Campground, but there is limited parking for hikers.

The Hike

Hanging Valley is actually a dry tributary of Trout Creek. It enters the canyon from a point high on the southern wall. You'll be able to pick out where you have been

Hiking down Hanging Valley.

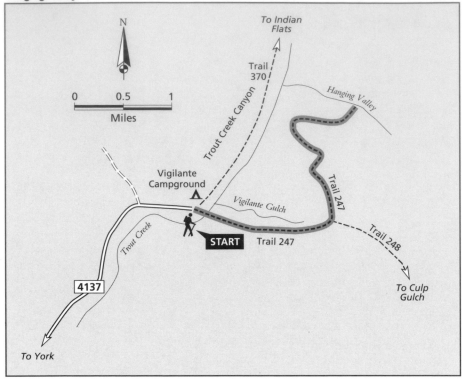

from the bottom of Trout Creek Canyon after you've taken the hike. After exploring this section of the Big Belt Mountains, you'll wonder how part of Utah, complete with narrow canyons and unusual rock formations, ended up in Montana.

Trail 247 starts at the back of the campground and is marked with a National Recreation Trail sign. The path climbs a dry hillside for 3 miles to a low pass between Trout Creek and Magpie Creek. During late May the trail is lined with hundreds of pink fairy slippers and blue clematis just below the pass.

At the pass you reach a junction with Trail 248, which veers off to the right. Turn left to stay on Trail 247 and proceed to the top of the mountain that forms the southern rim of Trout Creek Canyon. The views here are tremendous on a clear day, with the Flint Creek Range appearing from over the Continental Divide to the west and the Spanish Peaks near Bozeman visible some 100 air miles to the south.

The trail is well constructed and practically impossible to lose. Past the summit the trail switchbacks down a heavily wooded slope for about a half mile into Hanging Valley and passes huge Douglas firs that have escaped wildfires. The trail follows the dry watercourse into the canyon.

Looking down into Trout Creek Canyon from Hanging Valley.

Limestone pinnacles 50 feet tall tower over the trail, which soon becomes a route just a few feet wide at the bottom of a narrow canyon. After the trail passes under a small natural bridge, you must descend a 5-foot-high rock step in the trail, adding excitement to the trip. During heavy snow years, the trail at this point may be impassable until mid-June.

The trail dead-ends on the lip of a dry waterfall several hundred feet up a sheer rock face on the southern wall of Trout Creek Canyon, hence the name Hanging Valley. The canyon walls bear a close resemblance to those of Bryce Canyon in Utah. There's a small, fenced platform on the lip of the sheer cliff, which definitely makes this one hike where you know for sure you've reached the end of the trail.

Retrace your steps to Vigilante Campground, where you can briefly hike on Trail 370 up Trout Creek Canyon and try to pick out Hanging Valley, high on the southern rim.

Aside from a few snowfields in the spring, the trail is waterless, so fill your canteens at the campground. Although the 12-mile round trip can be done easily in one day by most well-conditioned hikers, there are a few dry campsites along the trail if you want to make it an overnighter. The trip may prove too steep for younger hikers, but it should not be missed by anyone wanting to see a part of the Southwest right here in Montana. (Originally contributed by Ed Madej and Rosemary Rowe, rehiked by authors in 1995)

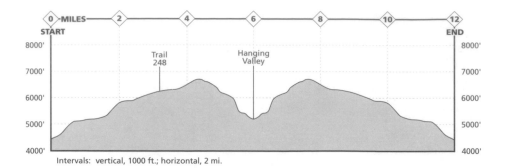

Intervals: vertical, 1000 ft.; horizontal, 2 mi.

Key Points

0.0 Vigilante Campground Trailhead

3.0 Junction with Trail 248; turn left

6.0 Hanging Valley

12.0 Vigilante Campground Trailhead

74 Trout Creek Canyon

Description: A very accessible canyon with a beautiful stream.
Start: 20 miles northeast of Helena.
Type of hike: Day hike; out-and-back.
Total distance: 6-mile round trip.
Difficulty: Easy.

Maps: Hogback Mountain and Snedaker Basin USGS Quads, and Helena National Forest Map.
Trail contacts: Helena Ranger District, Helena National Forest, 2001 Popular Street, Helena, MT 59601; (406) 449-5490; www.fs.fed.us/r1/helena.

Finding the trailhead: To get to York take Montana Highway 280 northeast of Helena for 15 miles, crossing the Missouri River via the York Bridge. The trailhead starts at Vigilante Campground in the Helena National Forest, 5 miles northeast of York on the old Figure Eight Route (Forest Road 4137). The Figure Eight Route used to go beyond Vigilante Campground until massive floods in May 1981 buried the road under tons of gravel in Trout Creek Canyon. The trailhead is at the far end of the campground loop. Vehicle camping, water, and toilet are available at Vigilante Campground, but there is limited parking for hikers.

The Hike

This is a best easy day hike very accessible to all hikers in the Helena area. It's also living proof that we can correct our mistakes, that development can be reversed. This trail used to be a road, and a well-traveled one at that, called the Figure Eight Route, a significant tourist attraction in the Helena area and promoted as such by the Helena National Forest and local chamber of commerce. Then in 1981 a flood washed away the road for the second time, and the Forest Service decided to make it a trail. After you hike through this picturesque canyon, send the agency a thank-you letter.

The first mile of the trail has been made passable for wheelchairs and is very pleasant. Beautiful Trout Creek flows through this limestone-walled canyon even in

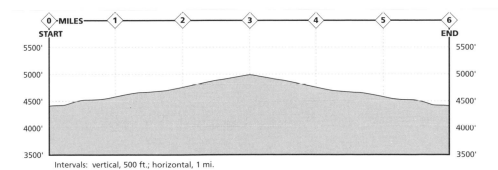

Intervals: vertical, 500 ft.; horizontal, 1 mi.

Trout Creek Canyon

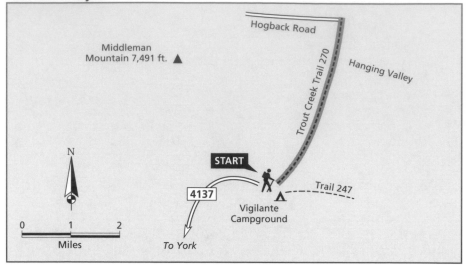

THE VIEW FROM HERE: A HIKER'S BEST FRIEND?

When you hike Montana's trails nowadays, probably about half of the people you meet on the trail have the family dog (or dogs) with them. I have no problem with dogs and have had one most of my life, but I do have a problem with people taking dogs into the backcountry and not keeping them under control.

Fortunately, most dogs are well behaved, and most dog owners are responsible and aware that not everybody loves their dogs as much as they do. Like so many things, however, the few can ruin it for the many. This is why we have restrictions on dogs in many hiking areas.

I'm sorry to say that in recent years I've seen a growing number of problems. I have, in fact, been bitten by dogs twice while out on trails. I've had the stuffing scared out of me by a pack of four dogs charging out of nowhere and looking menacing. I've seen dogs scare little kids to death. I've seen dogs chasing deer. I've lost my lunch to a dog that was quicker than I was (which is not difficult for a dog). I've seen dogs annoy people with incessant crotch sniffing. And I've spent a few sleep-deprived nights in the tent listening to dogs barking in the next campsite.

If you take your dog with you, please be a responsible dog owner and keep your dog under control—and quiet—while enjoying Montana's hiking trails so others can enjoy them as much as you do.

August on a dry year. After the first mile (at a picnic table), the trail narrows (no longer wheelchair accessible), and the stream may stop flowing.

This is a great early-season hike. It's also flush with fall colors in September and October and ideal for small children and elderly hikers any time of the year. It's very gradual uphill, but the grade is so gentle it seems flat. You can hike the entire 3 miles until you see the Hogback Road heading off to the left, or you can turn around whenever you feel like it. (Hiked by authors in 1999)

75 Mount Helena Ridge

Description: A scenic walk along a dry, forested ridge, perhaps the best urban trail in Montana.
Start: 5 miles south of Helena.
Type of hike: Day hike; shuttle.
Total distance: 7.4 miles.
Difficulty: Moderate.

Maps: Helena USGS Quad and Helena National Forest Map.
Trail contacts: Helena Ranger District, Helena National Forest, 2001 Popular Street, Helena, MT 59601; (406) 449–5490; www.fs.fed.us/r1/helena.

Finding the trailheads: Drive south of downtown Helena on Park Avenue until you see the sign for Mount Helena City Park and Reeders Village, a new residential subdivision. Drive up through the subdivision to the dirt parking lot.

To set up the shuttle, drive south on Park Avenue until it forks, just out of town. Take the right fork (Grizzly Gulch) and drive 4.1 miles up the well-maintained dirt road to where another dirt road veers off to the right on an open area on top of a large hill. The upper trailhead (locally called Park City Trailhead after a long-gone ghost town) is a half mile up this road. Look for a small sign marking the direction to the trail and the right turn. After turning right drive a short distance uphill to a parking area. Start here and hike toward Helena. There is limited parking at Park City Trailhead; you'll find a portable toilet and a large parking lot (often full on weekend afternoons) at the Mount Helena City Park Trailhead.

The Hike

This scenic, 7-mile, point-to-point trail has been designated a National Recreation Trail by the Forest Service. Mount Helena is a 620-acre city park with about 20 miles of hiking trails.

From Park City Trailhead follow Trail 373 as it climbs gently up a few long switchbacks along a grassy slope to the northeast. Small clusters of rural ranchettes

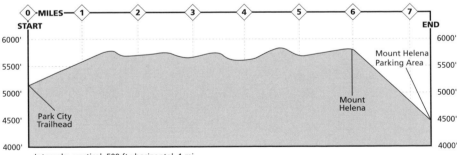

Intervals: vertical, 500 ft.; horizontal, 1 mi

Helena from atop Mount Helena.

dot the valley below. From here to Mount Helena, the trail is well marked. This is probably the most scenic part of the hike, with views of the Mount Helena ridge, Mount Helena, and the Helena Valley. The city of Helena also appears frequently in the distance. You'll see a few retired jeep roads heading off the ride, but you stay right on top. At 5.4 miles you reach the first junction in the Mount Helena trail system with Prairie Trail (stay right) and shortly after Backside Trail (stay left), and then the 1906 Trail (stay right). All three junctions are within a 200-yard stretch of trail. Follow the 1906 Trail about half a mile farther to the top of Mount Helena.

From the summit there are at least three ways to get down, but the most pleasant is to descend to the south on Hogback Trail and turn left on Prospect Shafts Trail, descending gently down to the trail above the new Reeders Village subdivision and your vehicle.

Since this ridgetop trail is totally dry, bring plenty of water. You might also want to give the Forest Service a call and thank them for developing such a fine hiking trail so close to an urban area.

Mount Helena Ridge

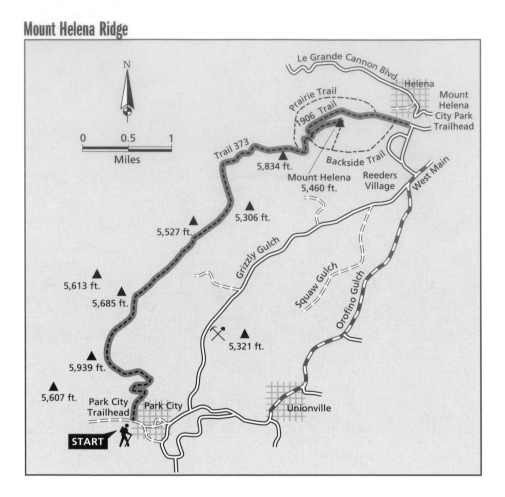

Key Points

0.0 Park City Trailhead

5.0 City park boundary

5.4 Junction with Prairie, Backside, and 1906 trails

5.9 Summit of Mount Helena

7.4 Mount Helena City Park Trailhead

76 Little Blackfoot Meadows

Description: A large, marshy meadow in a subalpine basin along the upper reaches of the Little Blackfoot River.
Start: 20 miles southwest of Helena.
Type of hike: Day hike or overnighter; out-and-back.
Total distance: 11-mile round trip.

Difficulty: Easy.
Maps: Basin USGS Quad and Helena National Forest Map.
Trail contacts: Helena Ranger District, Helena National Forest, 2001 Poplar Street, Helena, MT 59601; (406) 449-5490; www.fs.fed.us/r1/helena.

Finding the trailhead: Turn south off U.S. Highway 12 about 1 mile east of Elliston onto Forest Road 227. After 15 miles of gravel road, you pass Kading Campground on your left. Park just past the campground where the road turns into a jeep track. Park along the road just before the turnaround so that your vehicle does not interfere with horse trailers turning around. There is no parking lot. Vehicle camping and toilets are available in nearby Kading Campground.

The Hike

Little Blackfoot Meadows, a large subalpine basin along the Continental Divide, receives heavy use during hunting season but not much at other times of the year.

Park on the road and continue on foot along the jeep track. At 1.3 miles the jeep track forks, with Kading Grade Trail going off to the right. Take the left fork to stay on the jeep track. Shortly thereafter, the road ends and turns into Trail 329, which heads gradually downhill to the banks of the Little Blackfoot, crossing a new footbridge at 2.5 miles. Rainbow and brook trout frequent the pools along this stretch of stream.

Continuing up the east bank of the stream, the trail passes through some low lying, marshy areas before climbing a dry side hill. Good views of the meadows and the mountain-rimmed basin can be obtained by briefly leaving the trail and climbing uphill into an obvious open area just before the second crossing of the Little

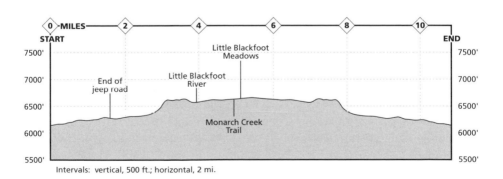

Intervals: vertical, 500 ft.; horizontal, 2 mi.

Little Blackfoot Meadows

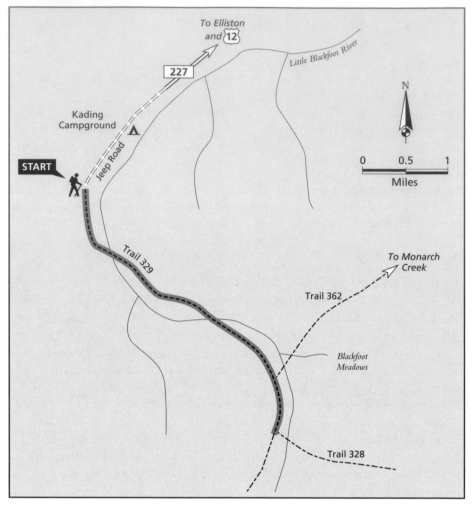

Blackfoot at 4 miles. There is no footbridge at this crossing. Be sure of your abilities before crossing on a log placed across the stream. If you're unsure, wade across the stream. From this crossing it's an easy mile or so to the Little Blackfoot Meadows. On the way, at 5.3 miles, you'll come to a junction with Monarch Creek Trail. Turn right and continue about a quarter mile to the meadows.

The meadows have several nice campsites and make a good base camp for exploring the surrounding roadless country. Trails lead up to the rounded, rocky summits of Cliff Mountain, Electric Peak, Thunderbolt Mountain, and Bison Mountain on the Continental Divide. For those wanting a gentle introduction to hiking or overnight camping, there could be no better place to start than with a trip to Little Blackfoot Meadows. The Forest Service has a proposal to move the trailhead to

Kading Campground—take a moment to support the agency's plan. (Originally contributed by Rosemary Rowe, rehiked by authors in 2001)

Key Points

0.0 Trailhead

1.3 Junction with Kading Grade Trail; turn left

1.5 End of jeep road

2.5 Cross Little Blackfoot River on footbridge

4.0 Ford Little Blackfoot River

5.3 Junction with Monarch Creek Trail; turn right

5.5 Little Blackfoot Meadows

11.0 Trailhead

77 Elkhorn and Crow Peaks

Description: Views of the entire Elkhorn
Mountains area from its two highest peaks.
Start: 15 miles southeast of Helena.
Type of hike: Day hike; out-and-back.
Total distance: 11.5-mile round trip.
Difficulty: Strenuous.

Maps: Elkhorn USGS Quad and Helena
National Forest Map.
Trail contacts: Helena Ranger District, Helena
National Forest, 2001 Popular Street, Helena,
MT 59601; (406) 449–5490; www.fs.fed.us/
r1/helena.

Finding the trailhead: The trail begins at Elkhorn, a historical mining camp and ghost town
on the southern end of the Elkhorn Mountains. From Helena drive 27 miles south on Interstate
15 to Boulder. Take the Boulder exit off the interstate and go 7 miles south of town on Montana
Highway 69; then turn left (east) onto a gravel road. There is a large sign for Elkhorn marking
this turnoff.

The gravel road immediately crosses the Boulder River. Turn right at a junction just after
crossing the river and follow this road for about 13 miles to Elkhorn, bearing left at two junctions
along the way. If you have a two-wheel-drive vehicle, park at the Forest Service picnic area on
the state park site in town. The trail, actually a jeep road, heads north out of town. If you have a
four-wheel-drive vehicle, you can make it another 0.7 mile before needing to park. Park here
even though there might be a sign saying FOUR-WHEEL-DRIVE VEHICLES ONLY. In reality the road to the
Iron Mine is too rough for most vehicles. On the Forest Service map, it is marked as FR 258, but
on some old maps, it's Muscrat Creek Trail 72, and it's definitely more suited to hiking boots
than steel-belted radials. This old road is still open to ATVs.

The Hike

If you are an experienced enough hiker that you are considering cross-country hiking or rock climbing, you might use this hike to break the ice. Half the hike is off-
trail trailless and goes to the summits of the highest peaks in the Helena area.

From Elkhorn hike 2.8 miles along Trail 72 to the Iron Mine, an abandoned
mining camp on the west slope of Elkhorn Peak. Here leave the trail and head

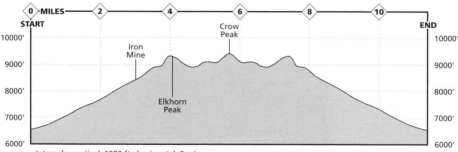

Climbing up Elkhorn Peak.

straight up for about half a mile until you reach the top of the ridge. Follow the ridge north for about another mile to the top of Elkhorn Peak. After leaving Iron Mine Trail 72, it is cross-country hiking and a steep upgrade.

On the ridgetop you are 2,800 feet above Elkhorn. The view is something to behold, especially to the north where you can see the entire Tizer Basin, the glacier-carved heart of the Elkhorn Mountains. To the southeast lies 9,414-foot Crow Peak, which is slightly higher than Elkhorn Peak (9,381 feet).

Pick your way to Crow Peak at 5 miles, or about a mile beyond Elkhorn Peak, along the saddle between the two mountains. Be sure to bear slightly to the north so that you can look down steep cliffs into Hidden Lake and, a little farther on, Glenwood Lake. Both lakes are nestled in steep, glacier-scoured cirques with sheer cliffs on three sides and openings only on the north.

From the Iron Mine to Crow Peak, watch for mountain goats. Remember, if you are close enough for the goats to change their behavior (stop feeding or resting or appear agitated), then you are too close. Also, prepare your heart for the surprise flush of a blue grouse from the weather-beaten whitebark pines between the two peaks.

Unless you spend too much time taking in the vistas, you can easily make it to Crow Peak and back (about 11.5 miles total distance) in one full day. However, this rugged, cross-country hike may be too tough for small children or poorly conditioned hikers.

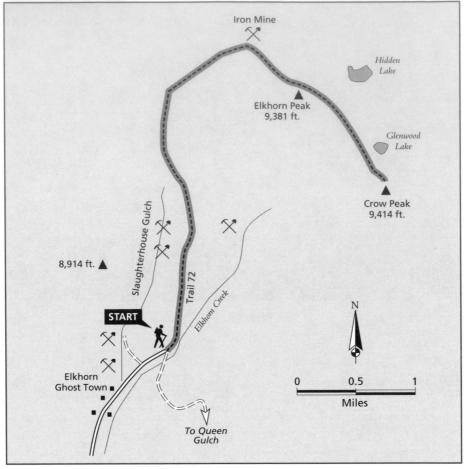

Bring drinking water, as there is only one small stream (about halfway to the Iron Mine), and even that one may dry up by late summer. Snow clings to the area into June and even July in heavy snow years, so plan a late summer or early fall conquest. Mosquitoes can be a problem early in the season at the Iron Mine. (Originally contributed by the authors, rehiked in 1999)

Key Points

0.0   Trailhead

2.8   Iron Mine

4.5   Elkhorn Peak

5.5   Crow Peak

11.0   Trailhead

78 Crow Creek Falls

Description: A stunning waterfall in a place you don't expect it.
Start: 35 miles southeast of Helena in the Elkhorn Mountains.
Type of hike: Day hike; out-and-back.
Total distance: 6-mile round trip.
Difficulty: Easy.

Maps: Crow Creek Falls USGS Quad and Helena National Forest Map.
Trail contacts: Townsend Ranger District, Helena National Forest, 415 South Front, Townsend, MT 59644; (406) 266-3425; www.fs.fed.us/r1/helena.

Finding the trailhead: Drive 11 miles south of Townsend on U.S. Highway 287 and turn right (west) on the paved County Road 285 for 9 miles to Radersburg. Go through Radersburg and onto a good gravel road (Crow Creek Road 424) and drive for 17 miles until you see the sign for Crow Creek Trail 109 on your right. You'll find plenty of parking, plus undeveloped camping at and near the trailhead.

The Hike

This hike was in the first edition of this book, but it was removed after a maverick miner moved into this holding in the Helena National Forest in 1981, dredged below the falls, and denied access to the public. In 2003 the area was acquired by a nonprofit organization, American Land Conservancy, and reopened to the public. So, it seems, since this is such a wonderful hike, it was also time to put it back in *Hiking Montana*.

This is an excellent early-season hike that you can safely take after the Crow Creek opens in mid-May. The trail is in excellent shape all the way, and it's obvious the Forest Service is taking great care to make this route a nice hike. The Forest Service plans more improvements on this trail in 2004–05, which should make this an even better hike. That is, of course, so apropos because the falls is truly remarkable. The force of the water casts up a fine mist that makes the entire area around the falls much more lush than the fairly dry environs all around it.

The hike starts out down Crow Creek Trail 109 with a sharp drop on two or three switchbacks down to Crow Creek. Just before the bridge over the creek, you'll

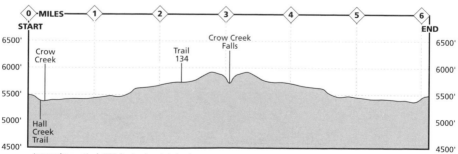

Intervals: vertical, 500 ft.; horizontal, 1 mi.

Crow Creek Falls

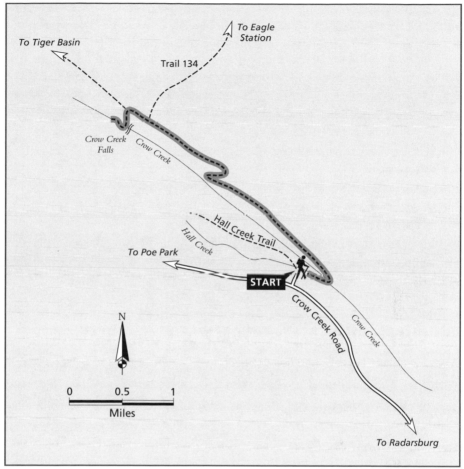

see the junction with the Hall Creek Trail 128. Turn right (east) here to stay on the Crow Creek Trail 109 and cross Hall Creek and then Crow Creek. Then the trail turns back west and closely follows the stream for about 1.5 miles. Two or three sections are mildly hazardous as the trail cuts through steep banks above the stream, enough for the Forest Service to discourage the use of horses on this section of trail but not too dangerous for hikers. If you have small children, though, be sure to watch them closely in these segments.

At about 1.5 miles, the trail climbs up to the bench above the stream onto an old jeep road that the Forest Service is converting to a trail, part of it gone to single-track already. You stay on the bench until you drop sharply down to the falls, going left (west) at the junction with Trail 134 about a half mile before you get there.

◄ *Crow Creek Falls, the jewel of the Elkhorn Mountains.*

Try to do this trip early in the morning, because it can get hot on the east slope of the Elkhorns. On the plus side, mosquitoes usually aren't too bad, but watch out for the horseflies. There is one sort of marginal campsite at the falls, and a few better campsites on the bench above the stream, so you can make this an overnighter. If you camp at the falls, don't expect privacy. Most hikers don't camp, though, because it's hard to get much privacy with people coming down to enjoy an hour or two at the falls. (Originally hiked by the authors and rehiked numerous times)

Key Points

- **0.0** Trailhead
- **0.5** Junction with Hall Creek Trail; turn right
- **0.7** Cross Crow Creek on log bridge
- **1.5** Climb out of stream bottom to old jeep road; turn left
- **2.2** Junction with Trail 134 to Eagle Station; turn left
- **3.0** Crow Creek Falls
- **6.0** Trailhead

THE VIEW FROM HERE: THE LEGACY OF CROW CREEK FALLS

When I was young, I went to Crow Creek Falls many times. I went there with my wife before we started a family. Later I walked into Crow Creek Falls with my babies on my shoulders, and a few years later, I walked with them, ever so slowly. This was a special place for me, my little piece of paradise, a family retreat, a mirage we always reached. It was probably the nicest, most popular short hike in the Helena area.

Then in the late 1980s, one careless man destroyed Crow Creek Falls. He built an illegal road over public land. He drove in earth-moving equipment on that illegal road. He dredged the sparkling pool below Crow Creek Falls. He didn't find gold, so he abandoned the site, leaving behind the most sickening mess you could imagine.

The Forest Service let it happen. The Montana Mining Association let it happen. The politicians let it happen. They all let it happen because they felt they had to, because Crow Creek Falls was private land. It used to be public land, but the ancient, archaic Mining Law of 1872 still allows anybody who fancies himself or herself a miner to claim public land—even an extremely rare, irreplaceable public treasure like Crow Creek Falls. At best this law is an absolute embarrassment to a civilized society, and there is no better testimony to this description than the desecration of Crow Creek Falls.

So, for a long, long time, I didn't go to Crow Creek Falls. It hurt to go there. I even took the hike to Crow Creek Falls out of this book. Then the worm turned, perhaps because we really don't realize how valuable something is until it's gone.

Obviously I wasn't the only person who missed Crow Creek Falls, who took his children there so an appreciation of wild nature could take root in their souls. Lots of people did, and they all missed Crow Creek Falls. It was like a piece of us was taken away, and we found it hard to fill in the void.

Well, it took a long, long time, but sometimes we are strong enough and smart enough to do the right thing, to do what sometimes seems impossible: to go back and correct our mistakes. We finally put the jewel of the Elkhorn Mountains, Crow Creek Falls, back in the public trust. We reclaimed the road. We cleaned up the disgusting mess left behind by one uncaring miner.

The resurrection was carried out by the same players as the destruction—the Forest Service, the mining association, the politicians. They had all made a tragic mistake decades ago by standing idly by and allowing the devastation of this natural wonder, but they all realized the blunder and stepped forward to rectify it.

Now I go back to Crow Creek Falls. I take my grandchildren to Crow Creek Falls. And when I'm there I think about the legacy of Crow Creek Falls, which is: Nothing is a lost cause. We can admit our mistakes and correct them. We've made a lot of environmental mistakes through the years. This little story should give us incentive to correct more of them.

79 Boulder Basin

Description: Three lakes and views of the Missouri River Valley.

Start: 10 miles north of Townsend in the Big Belt Mountains.

Type of hike: Day hike or overnighter; out-and-back.

Total distance: 12-mile round trip.

Difficulty: Moderate.

Maps: Boulder-Baldy USGS Quad and Helena National Forest Map.

Trail contacts: Townsend Ranger District, Helena National Forest, 415 South Front, Townsend, MT 59644; (406) 266-3425; www.fs.fed.us/r1/helena.

Finding the trailhead: Drive 2.5 miles east of Townsend on U.S. Highway 12 to Highway 284 and turn left, heading north for 12 miles to the Duck Creek Road turnoff. Turn right on Duck Creek Road for an additional 12 miles to Forest Road 139-F1 and turn left. Drive 2 miles on FR 139-F1 until you reach the parking lot next to a spring. There's plenty of parking.

The Hike

These high mountain lakes offer scenery, solitude, and the simple joy of a good hike. Head north of the parking lot across a meadow to the trailhead for Big Belt Divide Trail. Turn left at the sign for Boulder Lakes.

The first mile of the hike is a climb and does not allow for much of a warm-up. Trail 118 traverses a field of sagebrush, a remarkable plant that flourishes at 8,000 feet without much water. Since there's no water along the ridgetop, carry plenty.

At the top of the climb, a jeep trail joins the main trail from the right. It looks more like a wide, two-person trail than a road. Hikers can walk side by side. A unique whitebark pine forest covers the highest point of the hike. Then the trail descends slightly along the ridge. At this point the hardest part of the hike is over. The next 4 miles are on relatively flat terrain. To the east you can see the Camas Creek Valley, which has been proposed for wilderness designation. It has not been logged like the slopes along the drive up to the trailhead. To get to the lakes, turn

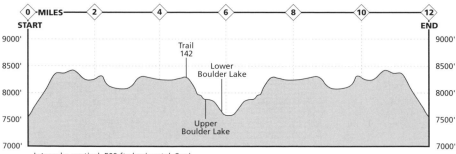

Intervals: vertical, 500 ft.; horizontal, 2 mi.

Boulder Basin

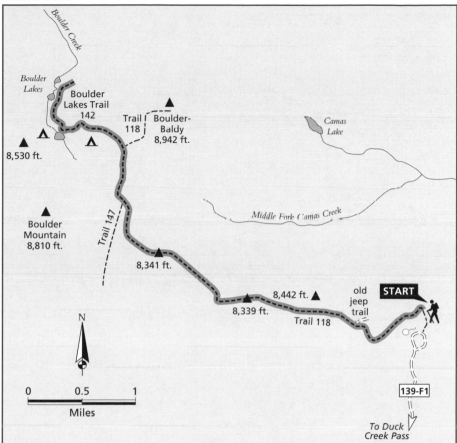

left at the 5-mile point at the intersection with Boulder Lakes Trail 142. (The main trail to the right continues up Boulder-Baldy Mountain.) After turning left the trail descends almost 1,000 feet into the Boulder Basin. The upper lake is below Boulder Mountain to the south at 5.5 miles. It has no fish, but in spring when the snow melts, buttercups cover the southeast shore. The next (lower) lake, at 6 miles, is smaller and full of good-size brook trout.

The hike out is easier than the one in but just as long. It follows the same trail.

Side Trips

For a spectacular view of the Big Belts, turn left at 5 miles back onto Trail 118 up to Boulder-Baldy Mountain. This is a good side trip on the way out. (Hiked by the authors in 1998)

Key Points

0.0 Trailhead

1.0 Jeep trail joins main trail

4.0 Junction with Trail 147; turn right

5.0 Junction with Boulder Lakes Trail 142 to Boulder Lakes; turn left

5.5 Upper Boulder Lake

6.0 Lower Boulder Lake

12.0 Trailhead

80 Edith-Baldy Basin

Description: A high lake-filled basin.
Start: 30 miles southeast of Helena in the Big Belt Mountains.
Type of hike: Day hike or backpacking trip; out-and-back with loop option.
Total Distance: 12-mile round trip for day hike or 25-mile round trip for Edith–Baldy loop.

Difficulty: Moderate; strenuous for loop option.
Maps: Mount Edith and Duck Creek Pass USGS Quads, and Helena National Forest Map.
Trail contacts: Townsend Ranger District, Helena National Forest, 415 South Front, Townsend, MT 59644; (406) 266-3425; www.fs.fed.us/r1/helena.

Finding the trailhead: Drive 2.5 miles east of Townsend on U.S. Highway 12 to Highway 284 and turn left, heading north for 12 miles to the Duck Creek Road turnoff. Turn right on Duck Creek Road for an additional 12 miles to the top of Duck Creek Pass. Turn right into a turnaround just after reaching the summit. The trail begins at the south side of the turnaround. There is limited parking, so don't block the turnaround.

The Hike

Driving along the highway and seeing Mount Edith and Mount Baldy in the distance, you would never guess that a spectacular, lake-filled basin, accessible to all hikers, lies nestled in their northeastern shadow.

From Duck Creek Pass Trailhead, either hike or drive (extreme four-wheel-drive terrain) for the first 3 miles. Trail 151 parallels the jeep trail on the east side for the first 3 miles, climbing steeply. Hikers should bypass the jeep trail. Be sure to bring water because there is none for the first half of the hike.

At 3 miles, stay left on Trail 151 away from the jeep road. Trail 151 has long switchbacks down to the junction at 4.7 miles with Trail 150, which leads to Gypsy Lake. Stay to the right here on Trail 151 and continue until you reach a small, unnamed lake. This is not Hidden Lake. Hike around the southern shore of the small lake until you see the junction at 5.9 miles with Trail 152 to Edith Lake. Stay to the right here and hike about a quarter of a mile to Hidden Lake, which stays hidden until you almost fall into it. Retracing your steps back to the trailhead completes the 12-mile hike.

Options

You can also hike farther to Edith Lake. Once at this lake you can retrace your steps to Duck Creek Pass or take the longer loop option. If you are in good shape and knowledgeable about cross-country hiking, you can make a spectacular loop by continuing past Edith Lake and over Mount Baldy to Duck Creek Pass.

Although Edith and Baldy are rock and talus, the basin is heavily timbered. Some of the lakes in the basin do not have trails to them. You will want to spend at least one night in the basin before heading home.

Fishing Hidden Lake in the Edith-Baldy Basin.

The loop is 20 to 25 miles depending on how many lakes you visit, and about a third of the trip is cross-country. (The shorter hike into Hidden Lake and back is only 12 miles round-trip.)

Although the ridge is devoid of water, the basin has plenty. This area accumulates a surprising amount of snow, so wait until at least late June (or August if you want to escape the mosquitoes).

If you are more ambitious, instead of dropping down into the basin for Hidden Lake, you can head cross-country toward the summit of Mount Baldy directly from Duck Creek Pass. All along this ridge the vistas are incredible, with the Smith River drainage to the east and Canyon Ferry Reservoir to the west. Expect to see mountain goats around the summits of Baldy and Edith. Remember, if your behavior affects the behavior of the goats, you are too close.

After leaving the top of Mount Baldy, you drop rapidly for a quarter of a mile into the saddle between the two peaks, crossing the Trail 152 to Edith Lake. Then gradually work your way over several false summits to the top of Mount Edith, with Upper Baldy Lake on your left most of the way. It is 4 miles between the two summits, but it is 4 miles of very scenic hiking. Although it is cross-country, the terrain is easy to traverse. In addition to mountain goats, this area seems to attract unusually large numbers of golden eagles.

Edith-Baldy Basin

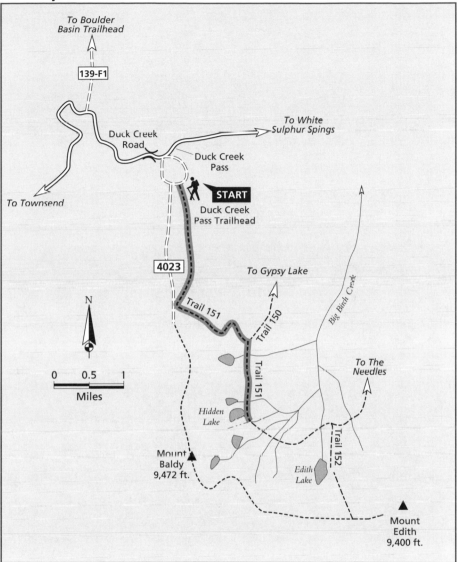

From the top of Mount Edith, you can see a penetrating limestone formation known as the Needles to the north and Edith Lake to the northwest. Follow a series of rock cairns toward this gorgeous, high-altitude lake.

About a mile before Edith Lake, you intersect Trail 152 again. This time, turn right onto this trail (which you crossed on the way to the summit of Edith) and work your way back through the basin to Hidden Lake and then up a series of tough

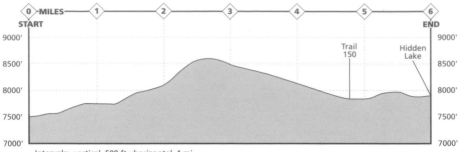

Intervals: vertical, 500 ft.; horizontal, 1 mi.

switchbacks to Duck Creek Pass and your vehicle. After enjoying this area, take a moment to tell the Forest Service you support the agency's proposal to move the trailheads closer to the main road and hence make the roadless area larger. (Originally contributed by authors, rehiked in 1999)

Key Points

0.0 Trailhead

3.0 Junction with jeep road from microwave tower; turn left

4.7 Junction with Gypsy Lake Trail 150; turn right

5.9 Junction with Edith Lake Trail 152; turn right

6.0 Hidden Lake

12.0 Trailhead

Gallatin National Forest

81 Cottonwood Lake

Description: A high alpine lake in the spectacular Crazy Mountains.
Start: 30 miles northeast of Livingston.
Type of hike: Day hike or overnighter; out-and-back.
Total distance: 10-mile round trip.
Difficulty: Strenuous.

Maps: Campfire Lake and Crazy Peak USGS Quads, and Gallatin National Forest Map (east half).
Trail contacts: Livingston Ranger District, Gallatin National Forest, 5242 Highway 89 South, Livingston, MT 59047; (406) 222-1892; www.fs.fed.us/r1/gallatin.

Finding the trailhead: Finding this trailhead can be tricky, so heads up. Take exit 340 off Interstate 90 (6 miles northeast of Livingston) and drive 14 miles north on U.S. Highway 89 to Clyde Park. About half a mile past Clyde Park, turn right onto heavily used Cottonwood Bench Road (Forest Road 198). Follow FR 198 east for 6.4 miles to the junction with Cottonwood Creek Road. Turn left (north) here, and after only half a mile, turn right (east) on Upper Cottonwood Road. Follow this road for 4.6 miles to the junction with the road to the Ibex Guard Station. Turn right (east) and go 3.1 miles to the trailhead. The road continues but has a closed gate and is closed to the public. Please respect private property rights by closing the gate behind you. There is ample parking at the trailhead.

The Hike

From the trailhead the first 2 miles of the hike are on the jeep road and are sublimely uphill along Cottonwood Creek. Since this road is closed to the public, there's no vehicular traffic, which makes it a pleasant walk. The Crazies get lots of snow, so wait until late summer for this trip. Water is everywhere along this route, so you can take the filter and leave the extra water bottles behind.

After 2 miles stay left on Trail 197 where the road turns right to a cluster of private cabins. The checkerboard pattern between private and public land in the Crazy Mountains makes this development possible. This route is open to motorcycles and ATVs, but the steep, rocky trail limits their use.

From the road the trail heads straight up for about a mile. This Category 1 hill is a real calf-stretcher that could use two or three switchbacks. It's also difficult coming down. Make sure you have your toenails clipped or they'll be black in the morning. This steep section is mostly on private land and a great example of what happens over time when people cut switchbacks. This section used to have switchbacks but enough people chose the straight up and down alternative, and this gradually became the main route. The Forest Service is currently working with the private landowners to re-establish the historic switchbacks.

Cottonwood Lake in the Crazy Mountains. ▶

Cottonwood Lake

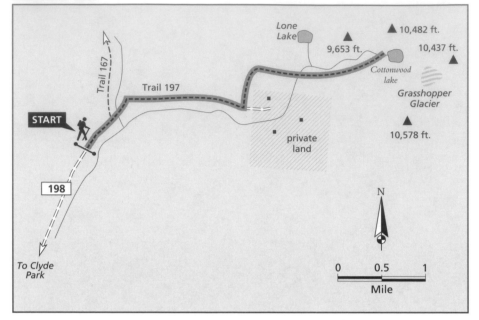

After a mile the upgrade becomes gentler but continues to climb all the way to Cottonwood Lake at 6 miles. Fortunately, the scenery is so spectacular that you might not notice the steady uphill grind. The gorgeous meadows have multihued carpets of wildflowers. The trail slips away in the rocks here and there, but you can always find it again. Other sections of trail are braided, so try to use only the major route (most hardened and usually with trail markers) and let the other routes through this delicate landscape return to their natural condition.

This is one of the more popular destinations in the Crazies. The lower end of the lake has several excellent campsites, but since this is high, fragile country, be careful to have a zero-impact camp. Don't forget your stove, as firewood is scarce and should be used only in an emergency. Please don't build fire rings. The lake has a population of pan-size cutthroat trout, but use them for fun, not for dinner. Regrettably, Cottonwood Lake is currently open to ATVs, but the steep terrain limits their use.

Any visit to the Crazies should make you realize that perhaps more than any place in Montana, this area deserves some type of formal protection or at least some alternative management that resolves the endless land-use conflicts caused by checkerboard ownership and ATV use. This will require some type of land swap, conservation easement, or outright acquisition from willing landowners. To institute any positive change in the Crazies, the Forest Service will need support and help from the people using and enjoying the area. In the meantime, it's important to understand that all trails in the Crazies cross private land—please respect private property rights. If you

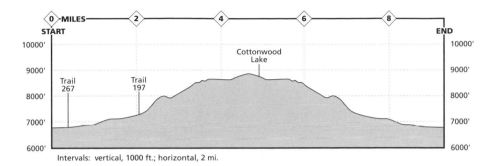

Intervals: vertical, 1000 ft.; horizontal, 2 mi.

don't, even the limited access now available in the Crazies could be lost. (Originally contributed by Bill Cunningham, rehiked by authors in 2003)

Key Points

0.0 Trailhead

0.3 Junction with Trespass Creek Trail 267; turn right (stay on jeep road)

1.8 Closed gate, inholding

2.0 Leave jeep road; turn left onto Trail 197

5.0 Cottonwood Lake

10.0 Trailhead

82 Crazy Mountains Crossing

Description: Rugged mountain scenery along a transmountain range route.
Start: 25 miles north of Big Timber.
Type of hike: Backpacking trip; shuttle.
Total distance: 23.0 miles.
Difficulty: Strenuous.
Maps: Campfire Lake and Crazy Peak USGS Quads, and Gallatin National Forest Map (east half).

Trail contacts: Big Timber Ranger District, Gallatin National Forest (east half), Box 196, Highway 10 East, Big Timber, MT 59011; (406) 932-5155; Livingston Ranger District (west half), Gallatin Mountain Forest, 5242 Highway 89 South, Livingston, MT 59047; (406) 222-1892; www.fs.fed.us/r1/gallatin.

Finding the trailheads: Drive 11.2 miles north of Big Timber on U.S. Highway 191, and then turn left (west) on the well-marked Big Timber Canyon Road. Go 1.9 miles and turn right (west) at a major junction, staying on the Big Timber Canyon Road. Drive 13.3 miles on this road until it ends at the trailhead and Half Moon Campground. The trailhead is on your right just before entering the campground. You pass through a guest ranch a few miles before the end of the road. This is a public road, but there is a gate. Be sure to close it behind you. You'll have ample parking and toilet at this trailhead; water and developed camping are available in the nearby campground.

To leave a vehicle at the end of the hike (Cottonwood Creek Trailhead), take exit 340 off Interstate 90 (6 miles northeast of Livingston) and drive 14 miles north on U.S. Highway 89 to Clyde Park. About half a mile past Clyde Park, turn right onto heavily used Cottonwood Bench Road (Forest Road 198). Follow FR 198 east for 6.4 miles to the junction with the Cottonwood Creek Road. Turn left (north) here and after only half a mile, turn right (east) on Upper Cottonwood Road. Follow this road for 4.6 miles to the junction with the road to the Ibex Guard Station. Turn right (east) and go 3.1 miles to the trailhead. The road continues but has a closed gate and is closed to the public. There's ample parking at this trailhead.

The Hike

The Crazy Mountains stand majestically above the plains near Livingston and Big Timber. Severe glacial scouring has produced the enchanting valleys that contain numerous high-elevation lakes. Beautifully sculptured peaks and serrated ridges radiating from the core of the range rise above 11,000 feet and offer stunning views of the surrounding prairies and distant mountains. This hike description is for two nights out, giving you a glimpse of how pleasant life can be in the heart of mountain goat country, the Crazy Mountains, but don't hesitate to stay longer.

Unfortunately hiking across the Crazy Mountains means dealing with the checkerboard land situation. Much of the Crazies is privately owned, and some of the private landowners do not tolerate trespassers. Be sure to take the Forest Service map and watch carefully to avoid trespassing. The Forest Service has negotiated an easement for "foot and horse travel only" on Trail 119 from the Big Timber Trailhead to Trespass Pass even though some of it goes through privately owned sections.

Upper Twin Lake in the Crazy Mountains.

But this easement does not include off trail travel, so check the map before making any side trips. When you cross the divide above Campfire Lake, you go from the Big Timber Ranger District into the Livingston Ranger District and onto Tresspass Creek Trail 268, which passes through a private section after going over the pass, so please stay on the trail.

Shortly after leaving the Half Moon Campground on Trail 119 Trailhead, drop your pack for a few minutes and check out Big Timber Falls and the cascade above it. You can hear the churning water from the main trail, and you might be surprised at the size of the waterfall.

The first 1.5 miles of this trail is on the remains of a hastily bulldozed jeep road built long ago to accommodate dredge mining for gold on private land near Twin Lakes at the head of Big Timber Canyon. Later the Forest Service closed the road to motor vehicles. Now it's gradually returning to a scenic single-track, but you can still see some scars left by the bulldozer. You can also still see some signs of mining activity above Twin Lakes, but fortunately not too much, because this place is a face of beauty and the mining didn't leave too big of a scar on it.

Crazy Mountains Crossing

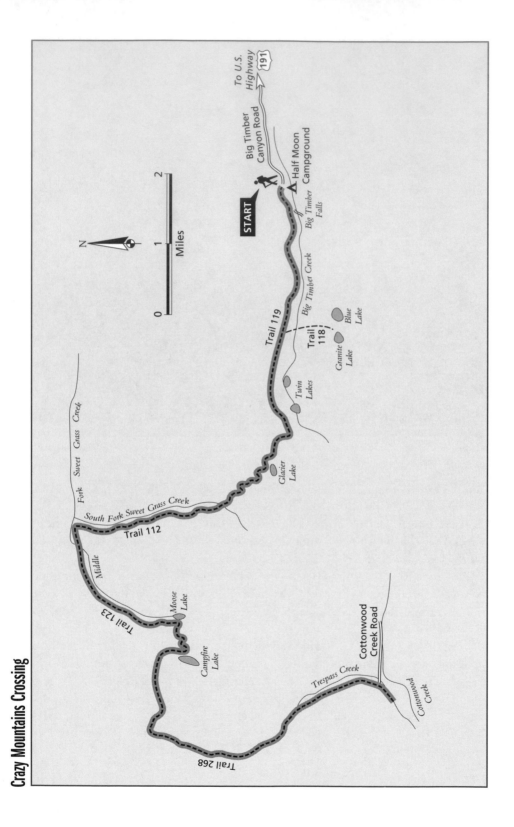

Before you get to Twin Lakes, at the 3-mile mark, turn right (west) at the junction with Trail 118 up to Blue and Granite Lakes. This is, incidentally, a nice side trip if you have the time and energy. On the way to the junction, you pass over Big Timber Creek twice on two large bridges built to handle pack trains. Both bridges have natural swimming holes, which can be quite seductive on a hot, dusty day.

After the Blue Lake junction, the trail skirts the slopes of Granite Peak for another 1.5 miles to Lower Twin Lake, smaller and shallower than its twin a half-mile farther up the trail. This lake basin makes a logical first campsite. You'll find an abundance of good campsites at both lakes and along the stream between the lakes, but check carefully to make sure you're on public land.

From Upper Twin Lake the trail begins a steep, Category 1, mile-long, 2,000-foot ascent to the pass above the lake, which is the divide between Big Timber and Sweet Grass drainages. Switchbacking across this high, open country, you'll be treated to wildflowers and cascading brooks. The stiff climb is more than compensated for by an awesome view from the top of the Big Timber Creek drainage and surrounding ridges.

From the pass you drop down about a mile into the South Fork of Sweet Grass Creek drainage and Glacier Lake. This alpine lake is fed by sheer waterfalls and a long summer snowmelt. Because of the rocky landscape, campsites are hard to find at Glacier Lake (but at least it's on public land!), so instead of staying the night, have lunch, drink some of the chilled water, watch the little icebergs float in the blue-green lake, and then move on.

From Glacier Lake the trail continues to drop sharply for about 1.5 forested miles to the South Fork of Sweet Grass Creek. Sorry, no bridge, and the crossing can be tricky early in the year, so be careful.

About a quarter mile past the creek, you pass through a series of meadows and rockslides where the trail can fade away at times. There are some choice campsites in these meadows, so you can spend the second night here, if you can find one on public land because the boundary runs near this stream. Another option would be about 2 miles farther down the trail where the South Fork and Middle Fork of Sweet Grass Creek merge.

At the junction with the trail coming up Sweet Grass Creek, turn left (west) and head upstream toward Moose and Campfire Lakes. It's 2 forested miles to Moose Lake, and another mile (and a steep one at that) to Campfire Lake. Don't get this large lake confused with small trailside tarns in the basins near the lake. Campfire Lake is a large, irregularly shaped beauty that reflects the surrounding peaks in its waters and has fair fishing for rainbows.

Campfire Lake has good campsites but is very heavily used, so if you stay here, please don't make it any worse—and even make it better by reclaiming fire rings and other damage left by previous campers. Try to resist the temptation to have a campfire even though the lake's name seems to call for it.

Moose Lake might look like a logical alternative to camping at Campfire Lake, but sadly, it's all private land, as is the inlet of Campfire Lake.

From Campfire Lake you face another Category 1, mile-long, 900-foot climb up the divide between Sweet Grass Creek and Trespass Creek. From this 9,500-foot pass, the well-defined Crazy Mountain high country is at eye level. Goat trails cross the rock and snowfields that cling precipitously above the green valleys and shining lakes. On a clear day you can see the Absarokas, Castles, Bridgers, and Spanish Peaks, an inspiring view to say the least. The lakes of the Sweet Grass drainage shine in the morning sun, and to the east the endless expanse of prairie overwhelms visitors unaccustomed to such grand vistas. It's a tough climb to get up here, but suffice it to say, you won't regret it. While up here you can pause to reflect on the amazing fact that the Crazy Mountains are not even being seriously considered for Wilderness designation.

From the divide drop sharply down into the head of the Trespass Creek drainage. The trail winds through talus slopes and lush meadows for about 2 miles before entering the west-side forest where it stays along the east side of Trespass Creek for 5 more miles to a jeep road built to a cluster of second homes in the heart of the Crazies on one of the private sections.

When you reach the road, turn right and walk on the road (closed to the public) for less than a half mile to the Cottonwood Creek Trailhead. Walking on the road might prompt you to make a call or write a letter when you get home about solving the checkerboarding problem and supporting permanent protection for the incredible Crazies.

Options

This shuttle hike can be done in reverse. It's strenuous, with lots of climbing either way.

Side Trips

It's about a mile off the main trail up to Blue Lake, steep and on switchbacks most of the way. You also have to get your feet wet in Big Timber Creek at the bottom of the climb, unless it's late in the year when you might be able to cross on fallen

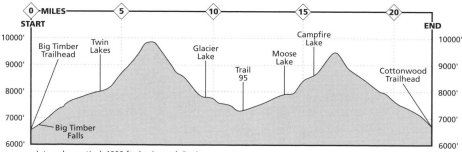

logs. You get a sweeping view of massive Crazy Peak, the highest in the range at 11,112 feet. (Originally contributed by Bruce Chesler, partially rehiked by authors in 2002)

Key Points

0.0   Half Moon Campground Trailhead

0.2   Big Timber Falls

3.0   Junction with Trail 118; turn left

3.8   Lower Twin Lake

4.5   Upper Twin Lake

7.0   Divide between Big Timber and Sweet Grass Creeks

8.0   Glacier Lake

9.5   South Fork of Sweet Grass Creek

11.0   Middle Fork of Sweet Grass Creek and junction with Trail 95; turn left

14.0   Moose Lake

15.5   Campfire Lake

16.5   Divide between Sweet Grass and Trespass Creeks

22.5   Cottonwood Creek jeep road; turn right

23.0   Cottonwood Creek Trailhead

83 Blue Lake

Description: A fairly accessible alpine lake basin below Crazy Peak in the Crazy Mountains.
Start: 25 miles north of Big Timber.
Type of hike: Day hike or overnighter, also suitable for extended base camp; out-and-back.
Total distance: 8-mile round trip.

Difficulty: Moderate.
Maps: Crazy Peak USGS Quad and Gallatin National Forest Map (east half).
Trail contacts: Big Timber Ranger District, Gallatin National Forest, Box 196, Highway 10 East, Big Timber, MT 59011; (406) 932–5155; www.fs.fed.us/r1/gallatin.

Finding the trailhead: Drive 11.2 miles north of Big Timber on U.S. Highway 191 and turn left (west) on the well-marked Big Timber Canyon Road. Go 1.9 miles and turn right (west) at a major junction, staying on Big Timber Canyon Road. Drive 13.3 miles on this road until it ends at the trailhead and Half Moon Campground. The trailhead is on your right just before entering the campground. You pass through a guest ranch a few miles before the end of the road. This is a public road, but there is a gate. Be sure to close it behind you. You'll find ample parking and a toilet at the trailhead. Water and developed camping are available in the nearby campground.

The Hike

Blue Lake and four other beautiful lakes are nestled in a high basin in the shadow of mighty Crazy Peak, the highest point in the Crazy Mountains at 11,214 feet. Climbers use the lakes as base camps for an ascent of this magnificent mountain or to fish in the lakes or just relax for a few days. On weekends this area gets heavy use, but if you go during the week, you might have it to yourself.

From the trailhead Trail 119 climbs steadily but not brutally for about 3 miles. The trail is very distinct, even double wide in places, with some rocky sections.

About a quarter mile up the trail, be sure to take the spur trail to the left to see spectacular Big Timber Falls. The main trail crosses Big Timber Creek, a fairly large stream, twice, but both times on sturdy bridges. Note the great swimming holes at each bridge; you might need them on the way out on a hot, dusty day.

At Trail 118 turn left (south) and climb a fairly steep mile up to the lake basin on right-sized switchbacks most of the way. The trail ends at the short section of stream between Granite and Blue Lakes, which is actually private land as is part of both Blue and Granite Lakes. From here spend a few minutes searching for a good campsite. Be sure to find one on public land and don't pitch your tent next to another camper. New Forest Service regulations prohibit campfires in this lake basin.

The lakes have an abundance of huge whitebark pines, which you don't see often, and a few rainbow trout, which can be a challenge for a fly caster.

Ice stays all summer in the slot canyon above Granite Lake. ▶

Blue Lake

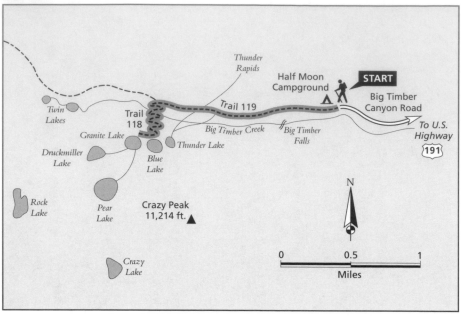

Side Trips

Thunder Lake (smaller than Blue and Granite Lakes but nice) and Thunder Rapids are a short jaunt along the shoreline of Blue Lake on a good social trail.

Pear and Druckmiller Lakes are more challenging, all-day trips, made more difficult by having to find a way around blocks of private land along logical routes.

Crazy Peak is probably the most common side trip, but it's only for fit, experienced peak baggers and those who want to trespass. Crazy Peak, the highest point in the Crazies, is privately owned!

If you have extra time the day you hike, hang your packs at the junction and take the short jaunt up to gorgeous Twin Lakes. (Hiked by authors in 1997 and 2003)

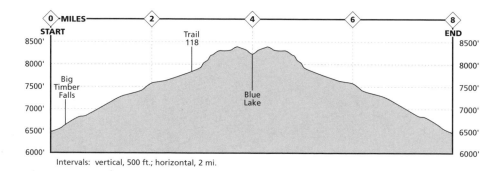

Intervals: vertical, 500 ft.; horizontal, 2 mi.

Key Points

0.0 Trailhead

0.2 Big Timber Falls

3.0 Junction with Trail 118; turn left

4.0 Granite and Blue Lakes

8.0 Trailhead

84 Sacajawea Peak

Description: A hike to the top of the highest peak in the Bridger Range.
Start: 15 miles north of Bozeman.
Type of hike: Day hike; out-and-back.
Total distance: 5-mile round trip.
Difficulty: Strenuous.

Maps: Sacajawea Peak USGS Quad and Gallatin National Forest Map.
Trail contacts: Bozeman Ranger District, Gallatin National Forest, 3710 Fallon Street, Box C, Bozeman, MT 59715; (406) 522–2520; www.fs.fed.us/r1/gallatin.

Finding the trailhead: From Bozeman drive 20 miles up Bridger Canyon Road (Montana Highway 86), past the Bridger Bowl Ski Area. About a mile past Battle Ridge Campground, turn left (west) and take the Fairy Lake Road (FR 74) for 6 miles to the campground and trailhead. This road is passable by vehicle but a difficult route for camper trailers. You'll find ample parking, a toilet, and vehicle camping at Fairy Lake Campground.

The Hike

Hundreds, if not thousands, of Bozeman-area residents have climbed Sacajawea Peak. Here is your chance to find out why. Pack the car with a picnic lunch. Bring water: You won't find any along this route.

Find the trailhead and note the massive furrowed limestone on the east face of Sacajawea Peak just above the lake. The route, Trail 534, is a 2.5-mile, 2,000-foot, Category H climb that goes right to the top of Sacajawea Peak. First you climb to the saddle between Sacajawea Peak and Hardscrabble Peak, where you take the trail to the left (south) and follow its twists and turns up to the top.

When we took this hike in 2002, the Forest Service trail crew was working on the first part of the trail, which was a confusing maze of new trails, old trails, social trails, new switchbacks, and switchback cuts. However, this should all be fixed by the time this book comes out.

When you reach the summit, you'll know why so many people go here. On a clear day you can see half the hiking areas this book describes. On a nice weekend

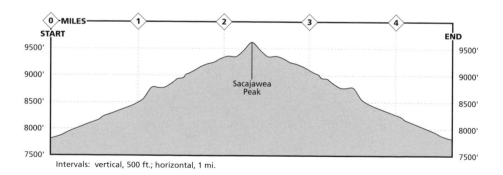

Intervals: vertical, 500 ft.; horizontal, 1 mi.

Sacajawea Peak

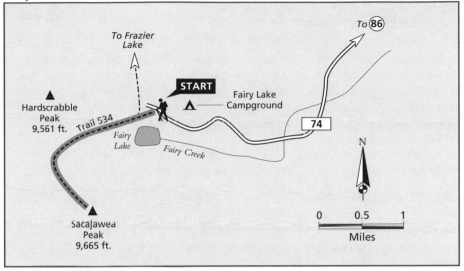

in the summer, you'll most certainly encounter other hikers on the trail and at the summit. This isn't the place for wilderness isolation and introspection but rather a place to meet friends and neighbors who just thought they'd take a couple hours to work up a sweat and remind themselves how really swell Montana is. (Originally contributed by Pat Caffrey, rehiked by authors in 2002)

85 Spanish Peaks

Description: A long circuit through the mid-section of a smaller wilderness area with many high alpine views, lakes, and fishing opportunities.
Start: 20 miles southwest of Bozeman.
Type of hike: Backpacking trip; loop.
Total distance: 23 miles.
Difficulty: Strenuous.

Maps: Hidden Lakes, Gallatin Peak, Garnet Mountain, Beacon Point, Willow Swamp, and Cherry Lake USGS Quads; and Lee Metcalf Wilderness Forest Service Map.
Trail contacts: Bozeman Ranger District, Gallatin National Forest, 3710 Fallon Street, Box C, Bozeman, MT 59715; (406) 522-2520; www.fs.fed.us/r1/gallatin.

Finding the trailhead: From Belgrade drive 7.5 miles south on U.S. Highway 191. Just before entering Gallatin Canyon, take a right (west) up Spanish Creek at a marked turnoff. After 5.2 miles turn left (south) up the South Fork of Spanish Creek. Drive about 4 miles until you reach the trailhead. It has a large parking lot, toilet, campground, and picnic area.

Recommended itinerary: This trip is nicely suited for two nights out but can be extended by making a base camp and exploring the high country for one or two additional days.

First night: Upper Falls Creek Lake or Jerome Lakes
Second night: Big Brother Lake

The Hike

Spanish Peaks is a popular hiking area—and you'll probably see some stock parties, too. This route, however, skirts the most heavily used portions while still providing the same incredible scenery that has made the Spanish Peaks Wilderness nationally famous.

The Spanish Peaks could be called a pocket wilderness. It's isolated on the north edge of the massive Big Sky development. In the 1970s Montana wilderness advocates agreed to give up Jack Creek in exchange for the designation of a segmented Lee Metcalf Wilderness. The South Fork of the Gallatin (now filled with residential and commercial development associated with Big Sky) and Jack Creek form a corridor of civilization between the two sections of the wilderness, the Taylor-Hilgard to the south and the Spanish Peaks to the north.

You should wait until at least early July to try this trip, preferably mid-July. Before going you might want to call the Forest Service for snow conditions. You want the snow line to be below 9,000 feet before taking this trip. Below 8,700 feet would make it easier to find a dry campsite and safely cross a small pass just west of Jerome Rock Lakes.

This is a 23-mile loop hike going up the South Fork of Spanish Creek and coming back to the same trailhead through the headwaters of Camp and Cuff Creeks, using Trails 407, 401, and 409 in a clockwise direction.

A good reason to wait until late July to hike the Spanish Peaks.

From the trailhead begin hiking on South Fork of Spanish Creek Trail 407, which is well maintained (thanks to local backcountry horsemen). All major creek crossings have bridges.

At 3 miles turn left at the junction with Falls Creek Trail 410 to stay on Trail 407. At 5.5 miles Trail 469 turns off to the left and heads to Mirror Lake. Stay right on the South Fork of Spanish Creek Trail 401 to Upper Falls Creek Lake. Shortly after the Mirror Lake junction, at 6 miles, you pass a junction with Trail 411 to Spanish Lakes. Again stay right, heading southwest and uphill on Trail 401.

At 8.5 miles Trail 401 junctions with Trail 412, which heads southeast to Lake Solitude. Lake Solitude is a good side trip, with many campsites, great views, and lots of fish. For now stay right on Trail 401 for Jerome Rock Lakes. You'll pass Upper Falls Creek Lake on your right at 9 miles.

Just before Jerome Rock Lakes, at 9.3 miles, Trail 401 junctions with Falls Creek Trail 410. If you want to cut your trip short, this is a possible shortcut. From here it's about 8 miles back to the trailhead. If you haven't had enough of the spectacular high lakes of the Spanish Peaks, however, stay left, continuing west on Trail 401 for Jerome Rock Lakes at 9.5 miles.

This first day can be strenuous, especially the big hill out of the South Fork of Spanish Creek. The second day is short and easy, though, and the third day is mostly downhill.

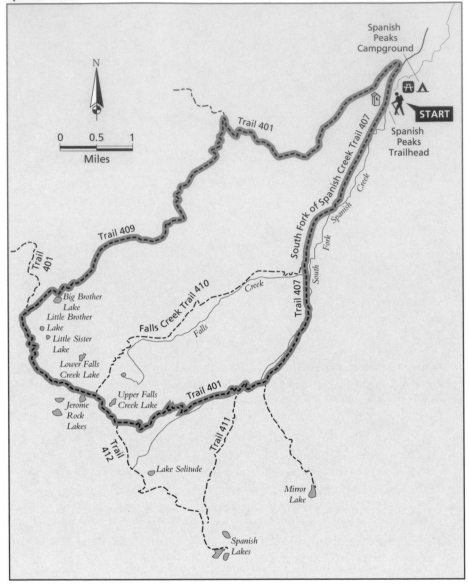

All three Jerome Rock Lakes support smart populations of Yellowstone cutthroat trout. The lower and middle lakes have adequate campsites, but camping is marginal at the upper lake. You can find the middle lakes by following the stream. Resist the temptation to build a campfire in this high-altitude area where wood is sparse and scenic. Jerome Rock Lakes is a good spot to set up a base camp to spend a day or two exploring the Spanish Peaks.

Wildflowers abound in this area, especially glacier lilies and yellow columbine. In fact I saw more glacier lilies and yellow columbine in this area than in more well-known wildflower havens like Glacier Park and the Beartooths.

After enjoying Jerome Rock Lakes, continue northwest on Trail 401 and cross a 9,200-foot pass before Brother and Sister Lakes Basin. In June and early July, there can be some potentially dangerous snowbanks on both sides of the pass. Hike on snowfields in the afternoon, when soft snow allows for better footholds.

After descending from the pass, look for two cairns at 12 miles that mark the junction with Trail 409 and the continuation of Trail 401 to Cherry Lake. Turn right, heading northeast on Trail 409, descending to Big Brother Lake at 12.9 miles. Keep your map out, because this junction is easy to miss.

The trail from Big Brother Lake is a pleasant walk in the woods for about 7 miles. You pass through several open meadows with views.

Upon reaching the junction with another Trail 401 (unconnected to the 401 you previously hiked on), turn right, heading east on Trail 401 through a logged area and open meadows and finally looping around Ted Turner's Flying D Ranch and back to the trailhead. Stay on the trail and avoid trespassing.

Options

You can do this hike in reverse with about the same level of difficulty. You can also cut this hike short by 6 miles by coming down Falls Creek Trail 410.

Side Trips

Lake Solitude (about 2 miles round-trip on Trail 412 and easy) is close to a must-do side trip. For the especially ambitious, try making it over to Spanish Lakes and back for a long, strenuous day hike. (Originally contributed by Art Foran, rehiked by authors in 1998)

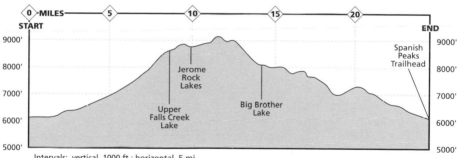

Intervals: vertical, 1000 ft.; horizontal, 5 mi.

Key Points

86 Hilgard Basin

Description: A popular trip into the southern Madison Range into a high-altitude, lake-filled basin.

Start: 15 miles north of West Yellowstone.

Type of hike: Base camp backpacking trip; out-and-back.

Total distance: 19-mile round trip plus side trips from base camp.

Difficulty: Moderate.

Maps: Hilgard Peak and Pika Point USGS Quads and Lee Metcalf Wilderness Map.

Trail contacts: Hebgen Lake Ranger District, Gallatin National Forest, Box 570, West Yellowstone, MT 59758; (406) 646-7369; www.fs.fed.us/r1/gallatin.

Finding the trailhead: Drive south of Ennis on U.S. Highway 287 for 47.5 miles or northwest of West Yellowstone 24.5 miles (14.5 miles to the junction of U.S. Highways 89 and 297) and turn north on Beaver Creek Road (Forest Road 985). Follow Beaver Creek Road for about 4.5 miles until it ends at Potamogeton Park Trailhead. Three trails leave this trailhead; take Sentinel Creek Trail 202 on the north side of the parking area. You'll find plenty of parking, a toilet (with bullet holes in it!), undeveloped camping along Beaver Creek, and the developed Cabin Creek Campground on U.S. Highway 287 just east of the Beaver Creek turnoff.

Recommended itinerary: This could be an overnighter or even a long day hike, but it would be your big loss to head back without spending at least one day exploring, climbing, and fishing in the main basin or the south basin by making this a two- or three-night base camp. Of all the Madison Range's natural wonders, the Hilgard Basin is one of the most beautiful and popular.

The Hike

Three trails leave the Potamogeton Park Trailhead. You want Sentinel Creek Trail 202 on the north edge of the trailhead.

Sentinel Creek Trail 202 crosses Sentinel Creek on a bridge and then climbs gradually all the way to the rim of Hilgard Basin. It really doesn't seem like you're gaining 2,700 feet. The sign at the trailhead says it's 8 miles to the basin, but it's a

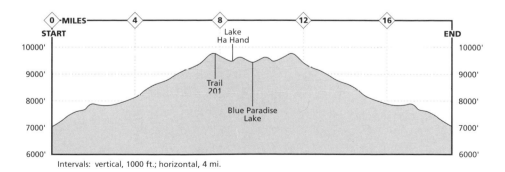

Intervals: vertical, 1000 ft.; horizontal, 4 mi.

long 8 miles, all on a well-worn trail frequently used by stock parties. In recent years several switchbacks have been added, possibly increasing the length by a mile or more. After a few miles periodic feeder streams tumble down to join Sentinel Creek, so you can plan on finding water along most of the trail.

About a mile before Expedition Pass, on a high saddle, the splendor of the Hilgard Basin unfolds before you. Trail 201 turns left (south) into the basin; follow it down. At the saddle you can see Expedition Lake and several others in the foreground and Echo Peak, creating a perfect backdrop. Spend a few minutes taking in the views. Get out the map and start to make the difficult decision on which nearly perfect campsite you would like to try. You have at least a hundred great options.

You can camp anywhere in Hilgard Basin, and there are dozens of wonderful campsites. They aren't officially designated but have become established through heavy use. Make sure you set up a zero-impact camp to preserve the scenic beauty for the next backpacker to follow your steps. Plan on using your backpacking stove, leaving the area's scarce wood supply intact. Recently Hilgard Basin has become increasingly popular, and with greater use, increased regulation usually follows. Camping is not allowed within 200 feet of the trail. Hilgard Basin is among the most fragile of hiking areas, so take every precaution to leave zero impact.

For peak baggers the basin acts as a base for several climbs, with 11,214-foot Echo Peak being the most popular and an easy scramble. Also in the vicinity is 11,316-foot Hilgard Peak, which is the highest and most technical peak in the Madison Range and only for more experienced climbers.

Most of the lakes used to support trout populations, but the harsh winters have frozen out some lakes. The treat here is the thrill of discovery. You never know which lake has the good fishing until you try it.

After your hike (not before it) stop into the Grizzly Bar and Grill about 10 miles north of Quake Lake for a Grizzly Burger, which may be bigger and better than the famed Grizzly Burger of the Grizzly Bar in Roscoe near the East Rosebud Trailhead.

Options

You can make this a shuttle by coming back to Sentinel Creek Trail 201 and going left (east) down into the Finger Lakes Basin and out Moose Creek. This is a long shuttle, however, and the trail here is not nearly as nice as the one on the west side.

Side Trips

Hiking an extra mile into the South Hilgard Basin on Trail 201, where you'll find more jewel-like lakes in the shadow of mighty Hilgard Peak, is the one must-do side trip. A new trail leads past Blue Paradise Lake into the south basin and ends near

Hilgard Basin

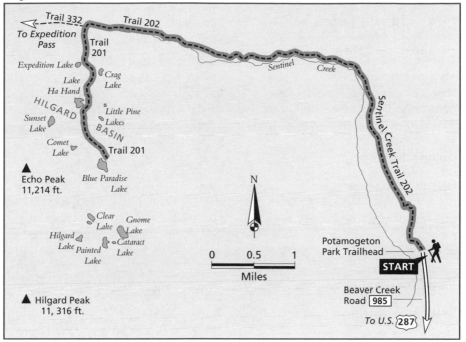

Clear Lake. Also, you can spend an entire day just going from lake to lake in the main basin and testing out the fishing or climbing a peak or two. (Hiked by authors in 1977 and 2001)

Key Points

0.0 Potamogeton Park Trailhead

8.0 Junction with Trail 201; turn left

8.5 Lake Ha Hand

9.5 Blue Paradise Lake

19.0 Potamogeton Park Trailhead

87 Coffin Lakes

Description: A pair of high mountain lakes along the Continental Divide.
Start: 12 miles west of West Yellowstone.
Type of hike: Day hike or backpacking trip; out-and-back.
Total distance: 10-mile round trip.
Difficulty: Moderate.

Maps: Hebgen Dam USGS Quad and Gallatin National Forest Map (west half).
Trail contacts: Hebgen Lake Ranger District, Gallatin National Forest, Box 570, West Yellowstone, MT 59758; (406) 646-7369; www.fs.fed.us/r1/gallatin.

Finding the trailhead: Drive west of West Yellowstone on U.S. Highway 20 for 7 miles and turn north on Forest Road 167 for Cherry and Spring Creek Campgrounds on Hebgen Lake. Drive 11.5 miles (first 1.5 miles paved), and past Spring Creek Campground on your left (west) is Watkins Creek Trailhead. Limited parking, camping, and fishing are available nearby at Hebgen Lake Campgrounds.

The Hike

Contrary to popular belief, the Madison Range does not end with the Taylor-Hilgards but continues south across Quake Lake into the little-visited Lionhead Mountains. Familiar only to a few locals, the Lionheads feature several high mountain lakes surrounded by 10,000-foot peaks.

From the trailhead head west up the creek on Watkins Creek Trail 215 for a little over 3 miles to the junction with Coffin Lakes Trail 209. The first 2 miles go through grassy, sagebrush country, beautiful but also part of a grazing allotment. Don't step in the cow pies.

Turn right onto Coffin Lakes Trail 209, which takes off up Coffin Creek for 2 more miles to Coffin Lakes, all through forested country. At 3.5 miles you reach the junction with Watkins Creek Trail 216, which veers off to the right. Stay on Coffin Lake Trail 209.

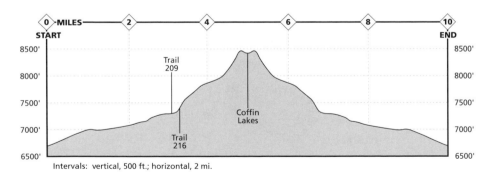

Intervals: vertical, 500 ft.; horizontal, 2 mi.

The first part of the Coffin Lakes Trail goes through a sagebrush flat with the gentle Lionhead Mountains as a backdrop.

The lower lake has two or three good campsites at the lower end. It also has a good population of cutthroat trout, but since the lake has a heavily forested shoreline, it's hard to find a place for a back cast.

Side Trips

Coffin Lakes serve as a good base camp to explore the surrounding area. You can wander over to Upper Coffin Lake and scramble to the flat-topped summit of Coffin Mountain to the north. Here views of the rest of the Madison Range and the vast expanse of Yellowstone Park are stunning. A herd of bighorn sheep also makes its home in the area, and the animals seem to have little fear of hikers.

By climbing out of the lake basin toward the south, you can cross the Continental Divide and gaze down at the many lakes in the headwaters of Targhee Creek in Idaho. One visitor to these lakes reported that he could find absolutely no signs of previous use by hikers, not even the omnipresent fire rings of old hunting camps.

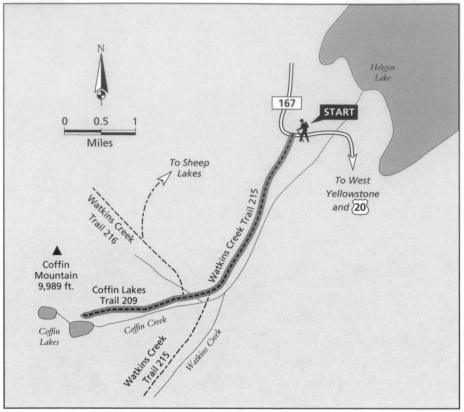

On the way out, you can take a 2-mile one-way jaunt over to Sheep Lakes. (Originally contributed by Ed Madej, rehiked by authors in 2001)

Key Points

0.0 Trailhead

3.0 Junction with Coffin Lakes Trail 209; turn right

3.5 Junction with Watkins Creek Trail 216; turn left

5.0 Coffin Lakes

10.0 Trailhead

88 Hyalite Lake

Description: Cascading waterfalls, eleven of them no less, and the subalpine Hyalite Basin.
Start: 20 miles south of Bozeman.
Type of hike: Day hike or overnighter; out-and-back.
Total distance: 11 miles.
Difficulty: Moderate.

Maps: Fridley Peak USGS Quad and Gallatin National Forest Map (east half).
Trail contacts: Bozeman Ranger District, Gallatin National Forest, 3710 Fallon Street, Box C, Bozeman, MT 59715; (406) 522-2520; www.fs.fed.us/r1/gallatin.

Finding the trailhead: Drive south from Bozeman on Montana Highway 345 for 7 miles before turning left, heading east and then south up Hyalite Canyon Road 62. This junction is marked with Forest Service signs. Drive 12 miles on Hyalite Canyon Road to the Hyalite Reservoir. Then drive around the north side of the reservoir. When the road forks, turn right and go past Window Rock Cabin for 3 more miles to the end of the road. The trailhead has a large parking lot, a toilet, and nearby vehicle campgrounds.

The Hike

While walking 5.5 miles south and 1,800 feet up on the well-maintained Trail 427, you pass eleven waterfalls cascading in a stair-step fashion out of a red-rocked mountain bowl. Although none is a large waterfall, each has its own unique character, as their names suggest: Grotto, Arch, Twin, Silken Skein, Champagne, Chasm, Shower, Devil's Slide, Apex, S'il Vous Plait, and Alpine. Each waterfall lures you onward to see the next cascade. Time on Trail 427 seems to pass quickly, and before you know it, you're climbing out of the timber about 5 miles later into the wide bowl that holds Hyalite Lake.

The Hyalite Lake Trail is justly popular with people in the Bozeman area, but most usage occurs at the lower end by day hikers who come for a short walk to see a couple of the waterfalls. By the time you reach the lake, you may have the surrounding country to yourself. The first 1.2 miles to Grotto Falls is a wheelchair-accessible trail. In some places, such as Grotto Falls, the trail doesn't go directly to the waterfall. Instead, you take short spur trails to see them.

The trail is open to mountain bikers, and regrettably, motorcycles. There aren't many places you can see motorcycles and wheelchairs on the same trail.

The lake has a few good campsites at its lower end, but they are very heavily impacted, so please have a zero-impact camp. No campfires, please.

Don't count on trout for dinner; the lake is too shallow to stay liquid in some winters. Instead, enjoy the spectacular vistas, which include Fridley Peak to the southeast and Hyalite Peak just to the southwest. A large meadow stretches around the lake and expands out to the base of Fridley Peak.

Hyalite Basin in the Gallatin Range. MIKE SAMPLE PHOTO

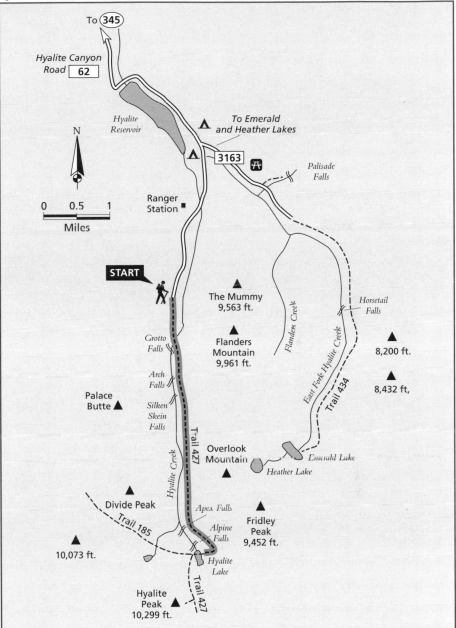

Birds seem to like the basin. On the edges of the timber, Clark's nutcrackers and gray jays flash their black-and-white patterns; Steller's jays catch the eye with their iridescent blue crests. Moreover, hummingbirds hover out in the meadow, attracted by the wildflowers. Especially abundant are paintbrush, lupine, fleabane, and four-o'clock.

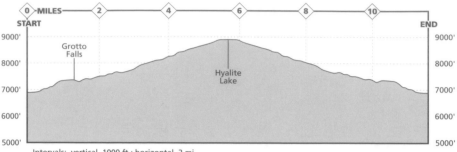

Intervals: vertical, 1000 ft.; horizontal, 2 mi.

In the evening you may hear or see a deer come down for a drink at the lakeshore. Spotting an occasional elk, mountain goat, or black bear is a possibility. Even the mighty grizzly has been sighted in the vicinity, so practice all the principles of bear awareness described at the beginning of this book. Most assuredly, a few marmots will whistle at you as you explore the bowl.

Winter releases its grip on the Hyalite Basin quite late by lowland standards. Snowbanks may not melt off the trail until late June, and winter may return quickly, making late September and October trips a gamble.

While enjoying your stay, try to figure out why such a stunning piece of landscape has not been made part of the wilderness preservation system.

Side Trips

While at Hyalite Lake consider a couple of short but interesting side trips that begin at the outlet of the lake. One is an easy 2-mile walk to the top of Hyalite Peak (10,299 feet) for views down into Horseshoe Basin and out into the Yellowstone River country. The other is a 2-mile hike across a neighboring cirque and up a ridge to the Hyalite/Squaw Creek Divide. Both provide high vantage points from which to enjoy the beautiful Gallatin Range. (Originally contributed by Mike Sample, rehiked by authors in 2002)

Key Points

0.0   Trailhead

1.2   Wheelchair-accessible spur trail to Grotto Falls

5.3   Junction with Trail 185 to Hyalite Divide; turn left

5.4   Junction with Trail 427 toward Hyalite Peak; turn left

5.5   Hyalite Lake

11.0   Trailhead

89 Emerald and Heather Lakes

Description: Two beautiful mountain lakes.
Start: 20 miles south of Bozeman.
Type of hike: Day hike or backpacking trip; out-and-back.
Total distance: 11-mile round trip.
Difficulty: Moderate.

Maps: Fridley Peak USGS Quad and Gallatin National Forest Map (east half).
Trail contacts: Bozeman Ranger District, Gallatin National Forest, 3710 Fallon Street, Box C, Bozeman, MT 59715; (406) 522-2520; www.fs.fed.us/r1/gallatin.

Finding the trailhead: Drive south from Bozeman on Montana Highway 345 for 7 miles before turning left, heading east and then south up Hyalite Canyon Road 62. This junction is marked with Forest Service signs. Drive 10 miles on Hyalite Canyon Road to the Hyalite Reservoir. Then drive around the north side of the reservoir for 2 miles to a fork in the road. Here, turn left onto East Fork Road 3163 and continue east (past the turnout on the left for the short hike to Palisade Falls) for 2.2 miles until the road ends at the trailhead. You'll find ample parking, a picnic area with toilets nearby, and camping in nearby campgrounds.

The Hike

Although somewhat rocky in places, Trail 434 to Emerald Lake is generally well maintained. Over the 5.5-mile, gradual uphill pull, you emerge from the thick forest to gain increasingly expansive views of the rugged cliffs to the east. These cliffs eventually pinch in and meet the mountainous ridge from the west to form the walls of the cirque that holds Emerald and Heather Lakes and a few unnamed tarns.

The trail follows the East Fork of Hyalite Creek most of the way, and drinking water is readily available. Wait until July to try this hike, however, as the area remains clogged with snow through June. This route gets lots of use, and the trail is double wide much of the way. The trail is open to mountain bikes and motorcycles.

At about 2 miles from the trailhead, the East Fork of Hyalite Creek tumbles over Horsetail Falls, a sight well worth seeing. The falls are plainly visible from the trail; the sound of falling water will be a tonic for anyone who has stayed out on the plains too long.

Perhaps the highlight of the trip is the incredible display of wildflowers. Color is everywhere. You will find glacier lily, columbine, lupine, paintbrush, alpine forget-me-not, shooting star, and many more flower species. About a half mile before the lake, you walk through a gorgeous meadow surround by stately whitebark pines where the wildflower display is especially vivid.

Once at Emerald Lake you can easily understand how it was named. It's a real jewel.

You have a wide choice of campsites in the meadows interspersed around the lake with sparse stands of subalpine timber, including lots of stately whitebark pines.

Emerald Basin in the Gallatin Range. MIKE SAMPLE PHOTO

They are all heavily used, however, so leave zero impact. You'll find a pit toilet at the far end of the lake.

A rough trail departs from the west side of Emerald Lake and travels about a half mile and up 250 feet in elevation to Heather Lake. From the trailhead to Heather Lake, Trail 434 climbs a total of about 2,000 feet, yet there are no prohibitively steep pitches.

Heather Lake doesn't have as many potential campsites as does Emerald. The wall of the cirque falls sharply down to the shore of Heather Lake on the west side, while rock shelves and snowbanks protrude on the other shores. Both lakes offer fair fishing for pan-size trout.

Emerald and Heather Lakes

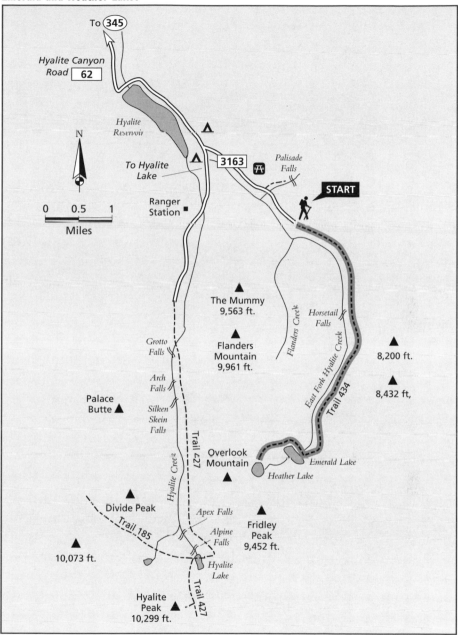

To (345)

Hyalite Canyon
Road [62]

Hyalite
Reservoir

N

To Hyalite
Lake

⚠️

[3163]

🏕️

Palisade
Falls

START

Ranger
Station ■

0   0.5   1

Miles

The Mummy
9,563 ft.

Flanders
Mountain
9,961 ft.

Flanders Creek

Horsetail
Falls

8,200 ft.

Grotto
Falls

Arch
Falls

Palace
Butte ▲

Silken
Skein
Falls

East Fork Hyalite Creek

Trail 434

8,432 ft,

Hyalite Creek

Trail 427

Overlook
Mountain

Emerald Lake

Heather Lake

Divide Peak

Trail 185

Apex Falls

Alpine
Falls

Fridley
Peak
9,452 ft.

10,073 ft.

Hyalite
Lake

Hyalite
Peak
10,299 ft.

Trail 427

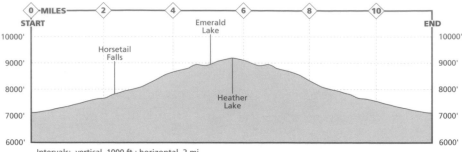

Intervals: vertical, 1000 ft.; horizontal, 2 mi.

These lakes are just north of Yellowstone National Park, but the chance of stumbling into a grizzly bear is remote. Nonetheless, take the standard precautions. The chances of seeing deer, black bears, elk, or mountain goats are good.

Although the trail receives above-average use, most hikers apparently have taken care not to leave signs of their passing. Please pay special attention to wilderness camping manners, however, as this is fragile, beautiful, alpine country. (Originally contributed by Mike Sample, rehiked by authors in 2002)

Key Points

0.0 Trailhead
2.5 Horsetail Falls
4.5 Emerald Lake
5.5 Heather Lake
11.0 Trailhead

90 Pine Creek Lake

Description: A beautiful mountain lake with attractive side trips.
Start: 15 miles southeast of Livingston.
Type of hike: Day hike or overnighter; out-and-back
Total distance: 10-mile round trip.
Difficulty: Moderate.

Maps: Mt. Cowen USGS Quad and Mt. Cowen and Gallatin National Forest Map (east half) or Rocky Mountain Survey Mt. Cowen Area Map.
Trail contacts: Livingston Ranger District, Gallatin National Forest, 5242 Highway 89 South, Livingston, MT 59047; (406) 222-1892; www.fs.fed.us/r1/gallatin.

Finding the trailhead: Drive south from Livingston on U.S. Highway 89 for 5 miles. Then turn left (east) on East River Road (Highway 540) and head south for 9 miles; 0.7 mile past the cabin community of Pine Creek, turn left (east) onto paved Forest Road 202. Go to the end of this road (2.5 miles, paved all the way), where Trail 47 starts at the far end of the campground. For an alternate route from US 89, take the Pine Creek Road between mile markers 43 and 44. The Trailhead features ample parking, a toilet, and a Forest Service vehicle campground at the trailhead.

The Hike

From the trailhead the first mile of Trail 47 is deceptively flat. At the end of the flat stretch, you stand at the foot of beautiful Pine Creek Falls. This is far enough for some hikers who have heard about the next 4 miles. In those 4 miles the trail climbs more than 3,000 feet. For others, however, the allure of a mountain lake held in a glacial cirque is too much to resist. The trail is usually dry, so draw some water at the falls.

Because the trail climbs 1,000 feet per mile, most people take between three and four hours to reach the lake. On the bright side, coming out takes only two hours. Therefore, this could be a day hike.

The lake lies beneath 10,940-foot Black Mountain in an obvious glacial cirque. On the north side of the lake, the bedrock shows pronounced striations where the glacier shoved its rocky load across the granite. At the outlet a broad slab of granite

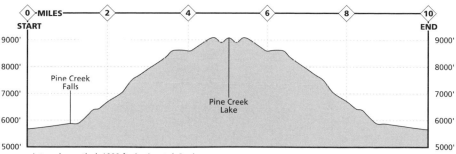

Intervals: vertical, 1000 ft.; horizontal, 2 mi.

Pine Creek Lake

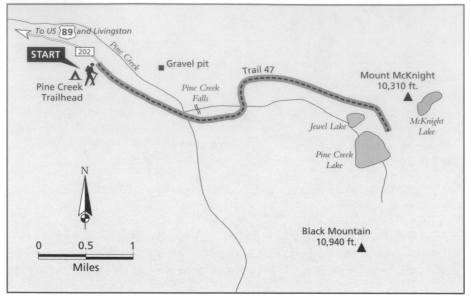

impounds the lake. Overly friendly ground squirrels, marmots, pikas, and a few mountain goats are common around the lake.

The best time to visit Pine Creek Lake is between July 15 and September 30. To attempt it any earlier will mean wading through snowdrifts on the last part of the trail; in October those drifts may reappear quickly. If you prize solitude, wait until after Labor Day. Before school starts, youth camps use the trail heavily.

One of the pleasures of camping at Pine Creek Lake is the possibility of seeing alpenglow on the peaks. As the sun moves lower in the west and begins to set behind the Gallatin Range, the atmosphere deflects a portion of the color in the spectrum, leaving a pronounced reddish hue in the last few moments of sunlight. When the conditions are right and this red light bounces off the polished rock surfaces just north of the outlet, the effect is startling. With only a little poetic license, one could say it looks like the peaks are on fire.

Good campsites are scarce, but you can find one at the lower end of Pine Creek Lake or at the small tarn below the lake. Pine Creek Lake has a nice population of cutthroats, but these fish see lots of flies and lures, so they can be difficult to catch.

Side Trips

If you have extra time, hike around to the east end of the lake and climb the divide to look into Lake McKnight and the Davis Creek drainage. There is no trail into Lake McKnight, and the country is so rough and remote that few hikers ever walk its shores. (Originally contributed by Mike Sample, rehiked by authors in 2001)

Key Points

0.0 Trailhead

0.2 Junction with George Lake Trail; turn left

1.0 Pine Creek Falls

5.0 Pine Creek Lake

10.0 Trailhead

91 Elbow Lake

Description: Mount Cowen, an incredible mass of rock and the highest point in the Absaroka Range, rises beyond Elbow Lake.
Start: 30 miles south of Livingston.
Type of hike: Long day hike or overnighter; out-and-back.
Total distance: 16-mile round trip.
Difficulty: Strenuous.

Maps: Knowles Peak, The Pyramid, and Mt. Cowen USGS Quads; Gallatin National Forest Map (east half); and Forest Service's Absaroka-Beartooth Wilderness Map; or Rocky Mountain Survey Mt. Cowen Area Map.
Trail contacts: Gardiner Ranger Station, Gallatin National Forest, Box 5, Highway 89, Gardiner, MT 59030; (406) 848-7375; www.fs.fed.us/r1/gallatin.

Finding the trailhead: Drive south from Livingston on U.S. Highway 89 for 16 miles and turn left (east) at a well-marked turn onto the Mill Creek Road. You cross the Yellowstone River after 0.8 mile. Continue driving southeast on Mill Creek Road (Forest Road 486), which turns to gravel after 6 miles. You can cut about 2 miles off the route by taking the East River Road south from Livingston and turning left on the well-signed Mill Creek Road. For the East Fork Mill Creek Trailhead, go 9 miles from US 89 and turn left (northeast) on FR 3280, which is well signed, for 1.5 miles to the trailhead, which is located a quarter of a mile before the Snowy Range Ranch. Snowbank Campground, a Forest Service vehicle campground, is on the main Mill Creek Road 1.3 miles past the West Fork Road. There is limited parking, so be careful not to block the road to Snowy Range Ranch.

The Hike

The rugged north Absaroka Range forms the east wall of the Paradise Valley south of Livingston along the Yellowstone River. Of all these formidable peaks, 11,206-foot Mount Cowen is the highest.

As you leave the trailhead on Trail 51, it stays high and skirts around the south side of the Snowy Range Ranch for a little more than a mile before crossing the East Fork Mill Creek on a bridge to the junction with Upper Sage Creek Trail 48, which is not right at the bridge but about a quarter mile down the trail. (No sign when we hiked this in 2001.) Turn left and follow Trail 48 north along Sage Creek. As you cross the bridge at about 4 miles, a major social trail comes in from the Snowy River Ranch. Don't go left here. Instead, go down the trail about 200 yards and take a left at a well-defined junction (no trail sign when I hiked this route).

The trail climbs steeply with no switchbacks and then crosses Sage Creek. After the creek it continues an unrelenting, Category 1 climb (with good switchbacks, i.e., not too long) across an open hillside. You probably will want to carry extra water for this stretch. Otherwise there is plenty of water along the trail even in late August. Check with the Forest Service about snow conditions before trying an early summer trip.

Elbow Lake

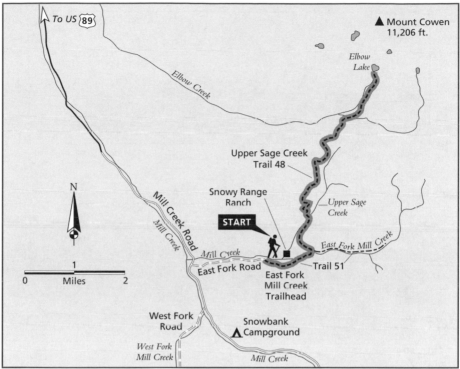

Elbow Lake is 8 miles from the trailhead. You gain almost 3,500 feet of elevation, making this a tough hike even for the extra-fit visitor. The trail is in good shape most of the way. The last 1.5 miles to the lake get rough, muddy, and difficult for horses. If you hike to Elbow Lake in July, expect to see lots of wildflowers, including a sea of balsamroot.

Start early and plan to make the entire hike to the lake in one day, as good campsites are nonexistent along the way. Starting early helps you get through the major climbing before the afternoon sun starts beating you down.

Elbow Lake is very scenic, with a gorgeous waterfall crashing down into the lake. Mount Cowen does lure a fair number of climbers, but don't attempt it unless you know what you're doing. Unlike most of the other peaks in the Absaroka Range, Mount Cowen is a technical climb.

There are no great campsites along the way to the lake, but you can find four or five nice sites at the lake. This lake receives surprisingly heavy use, so the campsites are quite overused; be sure to set up a zero-impact camp. You can catch some pan-size cutthroats in Elbow Lake and in Elbow Creek, but these fish see lots of artificial flies, so you might plan on having beans and rice for dinner instead of trout.

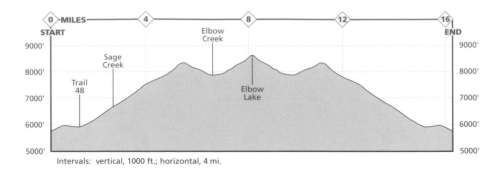

Intervals: vertical, 1000 ft.; horizontal, 4 mi.

Side Trips

Explore the nearby nameless lake to the northeast by following the stream that enters Elbow Lake's eastern side. Incidentally, the unnamed lake has no fish. For spectacular views of Mount Cowen, hike up the little valley on the eastern side of Cowen to the top of the ridge. You may spot some mountain goats. (Originally contributed by Art Foran, rehiked by authors in 2001)

Key Points

0.0 Trailhead

1.2 Junction with Upper Sage Creek Trail 48; turn left

2.7 Sage Creek

4.0 Junction with major social trail; turn right and then left 200 yards later

6.5 Elbow Creek

8.0 Elbow Lake

16.0 Trailhead

92 Passage Falls

Description: A gorgeous waterfall.
Start: 35 miles south of Livingston.
Type of hike: Day hike; out-and-back.
Total distance: 4-mile round trip.
Difficulty: Easy.
Maps: The Pyramid USGS Quad, Forest Service's Absaroka-Beartooth Wilderness Map, or Rocky Mountain Survey Gardiner–Mt. Wallace Map.
Trail contacts: Gardiner Ranger District, Gallatin National Forest, Box 5, Highway 89, Gardiner, MT 59030; (406) 848-7375; www.fs.fed.us/r1/gallatin.

Finding the trailhead: Drive south from Livingston on U.S. Highway 89 for 26 miles and turn left (east) at a well-marked turn onto the Mill Creek Road. You cross the Yellowstone River after 0.8 mile. Continue driving southeast on Mill Creek Road (Forest Road 486), which turns to gravel after 6 miles. You can cut about 2 miles off the route by taking the East River Road south from Livingston and turning left on the well-signed Mill Creek Road. For the Passage Falls Trailhead, continue 4 miles past the West Fork Road or 2.7 miles past Snowbank Campground. It is a large trailhead with a one-way road through it and ample parking, including room for horse trailers.

The Hike

This is a delightful, short hike along Trail 58 to the magnificent Passage Falls on Wallace Creek, a fairly large stream. The falls is most spectacular in the spring but worth the trip anytime. Be sure to stay on Trail 58 to the right at 1.2 miles, where Wallace Creek Trail veers off to the left.

Trail 58 is double wide except for the last 0.2 mile, where you turn left onto a single-track for a small drop down to the waterfall. This last section has a few steep spots, so hang onto the kids. The route follows the stream until the junction with the Wallace Creek Trail. It's quite heavily traveled, so don't plan on being alone. The trail goes right down to the falls for an up close and personal view.

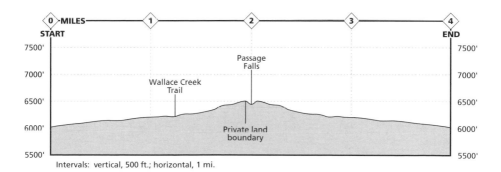

Intervals: vertical, 500 ft.; horizontal, 1 mi.

Passage Falls

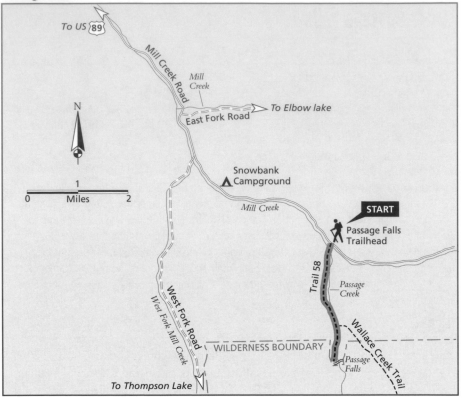

The waterfall is on Gallatin National Forest land but right on the edge of an inholding that's being developed for wilderness cabin sites. Be sure to respect the landowners' rights and stay on the trail.

Unfortunately, this trail is open to motorized vehicles, so you might see a dirt bike or an ATV on the trail. (Hiked by authors in 2001)

Key Points

0.0 Trailhead

1.2 Junction with Wallace Creek Trail; turn right

1.8 Boundary of private property

2.0 Passage Falls

4.0 Trailhead

THE VIEW FROM HERE: ATV ROADS

A trail is a trail. And a road is a road. Trails are places where you hike or bicycle or run or ride your horse. We do nonmotorized things on trails. They're not places where you drive. Places where you drive vehicles with four wheels and an internal combustion engines are roads. We do motorized things on roads.

That seems simple enough, right?

Regrettably, no.

On Forest Service and Bureau of Land Management maps and directional signs, places where ATVs travel are still called trails, or more specifically, "trails with restrictions." To that I say: No kidding!

In this book I've decided to call routes open to motorized vehicles "ATV roads," and I hope land managers will start doing the same. This is more than semantics. It's public relations and customer service and conflict management. Hikers really need to know if a trail has been designated as an ATV route, which means, of course, that it's no longer a trail. Knowing this, hikers can still choose to hike there, just like they can hike along the freeway if they choose. Neither of these places are closed to hiking. But we might choose to hike elsewhere, someplace where ATVs don't go.

ATV roads are not only open to hiking—and in some cases might even be a nice walk—but they are also a place where the chance of social conflict is high, and some hikers might want to avoid that. Anybody can spend the time researching forest travel plans and maps to determine what routes are "trails with restrictions," but calling them roads would make it easier for all of us to know what to expect when we leave for the trailhead—where, incidentally, the directional signs (at the trailhead and along the road to the trailhead) still call these ATV roads "trails." In addition, the numbers used to identify trails and ATV roads are the same, so it's a setup for confusion.

I'm not saying we shouldn't have routes for ATVs. These recreationists have a right to travel on public land. I am saying this simple switch in our vernacular would help greatly reduce social conflict by making it clear to hikers that they're entering an ATV zone instead of letting them be surprised later and, perhaps, have a conflict and then make that phone call the district ranger doesn't like to get.

93 West Boulder Meadows

Description: The scenic, fish-filled West Boulder River flows along the entire route.
Start: 20 miles south of Big Timber.
Type of hike: Day hike or overnighter; out-and-back.
Total distance: 6-mile round trip.
Difficulty: Easy.

Maps: Mount Rae and Mt. Cowen USGS Quads, Forest Service's Absaroka-Beartooth Wilderness Map, or Rocky Mountain Survey Mt. Cowen Area Map.
Trail contacts: Big Timber Ranger District, Gallatin National Forest, Box 196, Highway 10 East, Big Timber, MT 59011; (406) 932-5155; www.fs.fed.us/r1/gallatin.

Finding the trailhead: After driving 16.5 miles south of Big Timber on Boulder River Road, half a mile past McLeod, you cross the West Boulder River. Then half a mile later, 17 miles from Big Timber, turn right (west) on West Boulder Road, which starts out as pavement but quickly turns to gravel. After 7 miles, turn left (south) at a well-signed junction, continuing on West Boulder Road. Don't go straight here—it's private land. (West Boulder Road also goes over private land, but it's a public road.) Go 7 more miles until you see West Boulder Campground on your right. Park at the trailhead, which has an ample parking area left of the vehicle campground with toilet.

The Hike

One of the highlights of this hike is the drive to the trailhead. West Boulder Road winds through a scenic slice of the "real Montana"—wide-open spaces, snowcapped mountains, big valleys with rustic cattle ranches, aspens coloring the transitions between grassland and forest, and, of course, a beautiful stream all the way. We drove to the trailhead at dawn, and it looked like a video game as we tried to dodge all the deer on the road.

You can make this trip any length that suits you. It's 3 miles to West Boulder Meadows and 8 miles to the junction with the Falls Creek Trail. The West Boulder is a great day hike, but it also makes an easy overnighter for beginning backpackers or families.

From the campground hike up a dirt road, through an open gate, for about 100 yards. Then watch for a sign on the left and a trail heading left to the sign. Turn left here. Don't continue on the road, which goes to a private residence. This is all private land, but the landowner has been cooperative. Please show your appreciation by respecting the landowner's private-property rights.

The first part of the trail is very well constructed—raised, drained, graveled, lined with logs, a regular highway. After the bridge over the West Boulder River about a mile down the trail, you enter the Absaroka–Beartooth Wilderness, where it becomes a normal trail.

West Boulder Meadows

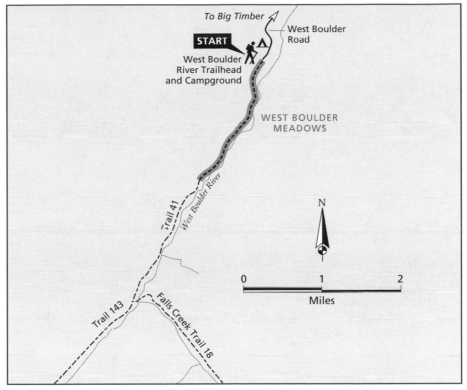

The first mile is flat, but then you climb two switchbacks and get a good view of the river. From here the trail goes through a pleasant, unburned forest, interspersed with gorgeous mountain meadows—and large, too, especially West Boulder Meadows at 3 miles. Several of the meadows have excellent campsites, and the river offers good fishing all the way. After West Boulder Meadows if you decide to go farther, you can see a beautiful waterfall.

This hike provides a reminder that wilderness is multiple-use management with livestock grazing allowed. A local rancher holds a grazing allotment in West Boulder Meadows. You'll see an unsightly steel-post fence at the west end of the meadows, very out of character for the surroundings. If you continue on to Falls Creek, you go through another barbed wire fence at about 5 miles with a gate over the trail. And, of course, expect to see a few cows and cow pies.

The entire trail is in great shape, with a gradual stream-grade incline all the way. Unlike many trails, this one stays by the stream throughout its length. There are many opportunities to set up a zero-impact camp in meadows along the route. In the lower stretches of the river, you can catch cutthroats, rainbows, or browns, but if you proceed upstream and get close to the Falls Creek junction, it's mostly cutts.

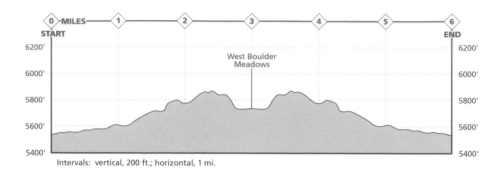

Intervals: vertical, 200 ft.; horizontal, 1 mi.

Options

This trip provides the option of going as far as you choose, instead of targeting a specific destination.

Side Trips

An ambitious and experienced hiker staying two nights and planning a long side trip could try Kaufman Lake, which is partly off-trail hiking, or a long trek up the trail to Mill Creek Pass. (Hiked by authors in 1999)

Key Points

0.0   Trailhead

0.2   Trail turns off private road; turn left

1.0   Bridge over West Boulder River and Absaroka-Beartooth Wilderness boundary

3.0   West Boulder Meadows

6.0   Trailhead

94 Bridge Lake

Description: A remote, uncrowded mountain lake, one of the nicest places in the entire Wilderness Preservation System that nobody goes to.
Start: 50 miles south of Big Timber.
Type of hike: Backpacking trip; out-and-back.
Total distance: 20-mile round trip.
Difficulty: Strenuous.

Maps: The Needles USGS Quad, Forest Service's Absaroka-Beartooth Wilderness Map, or the Rocky Mountain Survey Mt. Cowen Area Map.
Trail contacts: Big Timber Ranger District, Gallatin National Forest, Box 196, Highway 10 East, Big Timber, MT 59011; (406) 932-5155; www.fs.fed.us/r1/gallatin.

Finding the trailhead: On the Boulder River Road south from Big Timber, drive 47 miles to the Bridge Lake Trailhead on your right (west), less than a mile past the Upsidedown Creek Trailhead. There is minimal parking at the trailhead; Hicks Park Campground, a full-service vehicle campground, is right at the trailhead.

The Hike

Only well-conditioned backpackers could make it into Bridge Lake in one day; on the other hand, it's a tad short for two days, so make your choice.

The trail starts out with a serious upgrade for about 2.5 miles. Then it levels out for about 5 miles until you start the last pitch up to the lake. At 2.5 miles you'll see one of the few private cabins still remaining in the wilderness. This cabin is on public land, and the Forest Service has decided to let nature gradually reclaim it instead of destroying it.

After you cross Bridge Creek on a bridge shortly after leaving the trailhead, you stay on the north side of the stream until about 2 miles before the lake. You cross several feeder streams with no bridges. At about 4 miles from the trailhead, the trail leaves the thick forest and winds through a series of scenic meadows before breaking out above timberline.

The trail is in great shape over the entire route. I especially liked the "no non-sense" switchbacks on the first climb and on the last pitch up to the lake. These

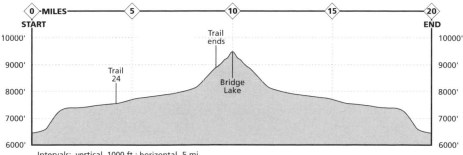

Intervals: vertical, 1000 ft.; horizontal, 5 mi.

Bridge Lake

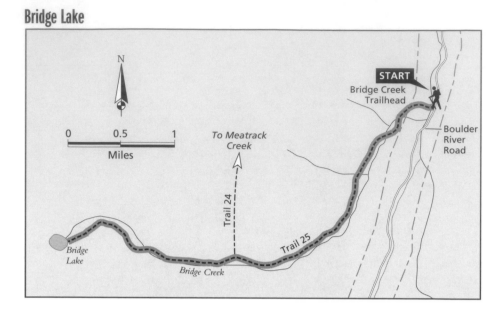

switchbacks are generous curves in the trail as opposed to the near-level switchbacks that double the length of the trail. If the switchbacks on this route were like those on the Upsidedown Creek Trail, it would add 2 or 3 miles to the route.

You might think the map is wrong because the trail doesn't go all the way to the lake, but the map is correct. The trail ends about a mile before the lake, and you go off-trail the rest of the way. This stretch is well above timberline, though, and easy hiking, with the exception of one 50-foot stretch along the creek just before the lake. Stay on the left (south) side of Bridge Creek even though it looks easier on the other side. It isn't. Keep your topo map out so you can see where the lake is.

If you decide to camp at Bridge Lake, look for a good campsite on the bench above the right (north) side of the lake. This search involves a little more climbing, but it's worth it. If you're wasted and can't make that last quarter mile to this campsite, you can camp on the bench just before you get to the lake, but this camping area isn't as nice. Bridge Lake is almost free of signs of past campers, so please practice strict zero-impact principles to keep it that way. And no campfires or fire rings, please.

Bridge Lake has nice-size cutthroat trout, but they can be quite temperamental, so you could go home skunked. Don't plan on them for dinner.

Options

You could camp along Bridge Creek about 6 or 7 miles up the trail and take a day hike to Bridge Lake. Doing so will spare you the pain of lugging your overnight pack up the last off-trail pitch to the lake. It wouldn't be hard to find a good campsite, but it's probably not as nice as staying at the lake. (Hiked by authors in 1999)

Key Points

0.0 Trailhead

0.5 Bridge over Bridge Creek

2.5 Wilderness cabin

4.0 Junction with Trail 24; turn left

9.0 End of trail

10.0 Bridge Lake

20.0 Trailhead

95 Lake Plateau

Description: A popular hiking area with myriad side trip opportunities on a gorgeous, lake-dotted, high-altitude plateau, plus the equally spectacular Columbine Pass.
Start: 50 miles south of Big Timber.
Type of hike: A weeklong backpacking adventure; loop with shuttle or out-and-back options; nicely suited for those who like to base camp.
Total distance: 34.3 miles.
Difficulty: Moderate.

Maps: Mount Douglas, Tumble Mountain, Pinnacle Mountain, and Haystack Peak USGS Quads; Rocky Mountain Survey Mount Douglas–Mount Wood and Cooke City–Cutoff Mountain Maps; and the Forest Service's Absaroka-Beartooth Wilderness Map.
Trail contacts: Big Timber Ranger District, Gallatin National Forest, Box 196, Highway 10 East, Big Timber, MT 59011; (406) 932–5155; www.fs.fed.us/r1/gallatin.

Finding the trailhead: To find the trailhead take County Road 298 (locally referred to as the Boulder River Road) south from Big Timber. The road doesn't take off from either of the two exits off Interstate 90. Instead go into Big Timber and watch for signs for County 298, which heads south and passes over the freeway from the middle of town between the two exits.

It's 48 miles from Big Timber to the Box Canyon Trailhead, so make sure to top off the gas tank. It's 16 miles to the small community of McLeod and another 8 miles until the pavement ends—which means 24 miles of bumpy gravel road are still ahead. There are two major trailheads with parking areas (Upsidedown Creek and Box Canyon) providing access to the Lake Plateau and Slough Creek. Upsidedown Creek is about 1.5 miles before Box Canyon. Both trailheads are well signed. Box Canyon's parking lot can accommodate horse trailers.

A jeep road continues on to the Independence Peak area, where signs of early 1900s mining operations still remain. But almost all of the trails in this region can be accessed without bumping and grinding up this very rough road. At best it is passable only with four-wheel-drive or all-terrain vehicles.

Recommended itinerary: This trip works best if you get an early start from Box Canyon, but since the drive is long, it might be difficult to hit the trail early. If you start later in the day, try East Fork Boulder River for the first night out. This may lengthen the trip by one day—not a bad price to pay for sleeping late. The following recommended itinerary lays out a five-day trip, but you could easily spend more time on Lake Plateau.

First night: Columbine Lake

Second night: Lake Pinchot, Wounded Man Lake, Owl Lake, or other nearby lakes

Third night: Same campsite

Fourth night: Diamond or Horseshoe Lake

Lake Plateau

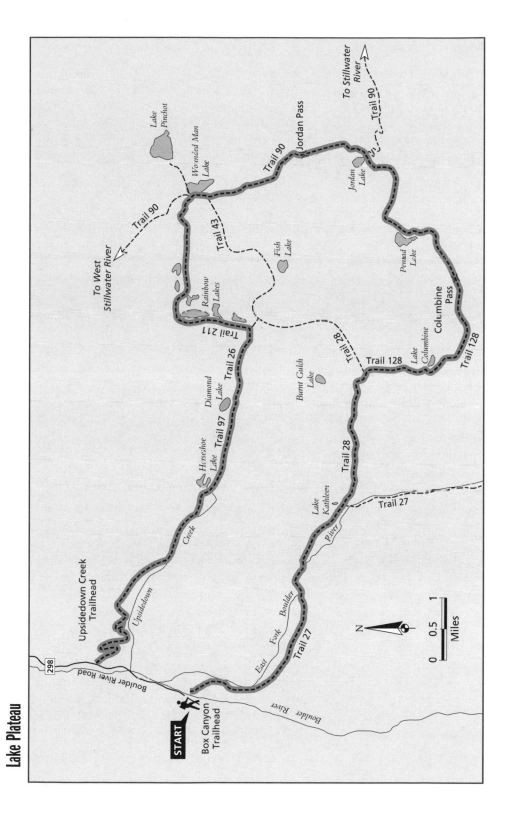

The Hike

Most locals consider the Boulder River the dividing line between the Beartooths to the east and the Absaroka Range to the west. Boulder River Road ends 48 miles south of Big Timber at Box Canyon Campground. In the 1970s there was a proposal to punch the road all the way through to Cooke City, splitting the Absaroka-Beartooth Wilderness into two smaller wild areas. Look at a topo map and the feasibility (or lack) of such a road becomes obvious. After a hard fight by wilderness advocates, the two spectacular mountain ranges were permanently joined into one wilderness, and the controversial road proposal was dropped.

The Boulder River is a popular place. The road is lined with dude ranches and church camps in addition to numerous summer homes. During the early hunting season in September, dozens of horse trailers may be parked at Box Canyon Trailhead.

The Lake Plateau region of the Beartooths is as popular as any spot in the entire wilderness. The Boulder River trailheads (Box Canyon and Upsidedown Creek) attract many backpackers. Few backcountry horsemen use Upsidedown Creek, but many hunters and outfitters use the Box Canyon trailhead to access the Slough Creek Divide area.

The Lake Plateau is a unique and spectacular part of the Beartooths accessed by four major trails. Two of these trailheads (Box Canyon and Upsidedown Creek) originate along the Boulder River. Others leave from the West Stillwater and the main Stillwater. This variety of trails creates a variety of options for hiking into the Lake Plateau, but the route described here is special because there aren't many opportunities like this one to see so much wild country without working out a burdensome shuttle or retracing your steps for half of the trip.

From the Box Canyon Trailhead, Trail 27 climbs gradually through timber and open parks along the East Fork Boulder River for about 3.5 miles before crossing a sturdy bridge. If you started late, you may wish to stay the first night in one of several excellent campsites located just before the bridge.

It would be wise to get up early on the first day, drive to Box Canyon Trailhead, and cover at least the first 3.5 miles to a series of excellent campsites just before the bridge over the East Fork Boulder River. This area can accommodate a large party or several parties, as long as Forest Service limits for group size aren't exceeded.

After crossing the East Fork, the trail follows the river for a half mile before climbing away through heavy timber. Several trout-filled pools beckon along the riverside stretch, so be prepared to fight off temptations to stop and rig up the fly casting gear.

At 5.2 miles you reach the junction with Trail 28. Trail 27 goes straight and eventually ends up in Yellowstone National Park. Turn left here onto Trail 28. In about a quarter mile, watch for tranquil little Lake Kathleen off to the left. This is also a possible first-night campsite.

At 7.9 miles, about 2 miles beyond Lake Kathleen, the trail joins Trail 128 to Columbine Pass. Turn right (east) onto this trail, which climbs a big hill and breaks out of the forest into a subalpine panorama. From the junction it's about 1.5 miles to Lake Columbine. With an early start on the first day, this would also make a good first campsite. If it's your second day out, consider pushing on to Pentad or Jordan Lake for the second night's camp.

From Lake Columbine continue another scenic 2 miles or so up to 9,850-foot Columbine Pass. In a good snow year snowbanks cover the trail on Columbine Pass well into July. The trail fades away twice between Lake Columbine and the pass, so watch the topo map carefully to stay on track. A few well-placed cairns make navigation here easier.

After the Category 2 climb to Columbine Pass at the 11.1-mile point, take a break and enjoy a snack and the vistas, including 10,685-foot Pinnacle Mountain to the south. From here the trail leaves the Boulder River drainage behind and heads into the Stillwater River drainage. Hereafter, the trip leapfrogs from one lake to another for the next 14 miles.

Those who camped at Lake Columbine can make it all the way into the Lake Plateau for the next night's campsite. Otherwise, plan to pitch a tent at Pentad or Jordan Lake. Pentad is more scenic, but Jordan offers better fishing (and suffers more from overuse). There are also several smaller lakes near Pentad—Mouse, Favonius, Sundown, and several unnamed lakes. Many great campsites can be found in the area, and they won't be as crowded as Jordan Lake probably will be. Don't rush to take the first campsite. Look around for a while and you'll find a better one. It might be wise to stop at the south end of Pentad anyway, as the trail is difficult to follow because of all the tangent trails created by backcountry horsemen to various campsites. To untangle the maze check the topo map. Trail 128 skirts the east shore of Pentad Lake heading north.

Jordan Lake, another 2 miles down the trail from Pentad, has limited camping, with one campsite at the foot of the lake. The campsite is, however, large enough to serve a large party or several parties—although it may be too heavily impacted to be used by parties with stock animals.

At Jordan Lake at 14.5 miles, Trail 128 meets Trail 90, coming out of Lake Plateau and dropping east down into the Middle Fork of Wounded Man Creek. Turn left (north) here onto Trail 90, which climbs gradually 1.5 miles over Jordan Pass and drops into the Lake Plateau. This isn't much of a pass, but it's a great spot to take fifteen minutes to marvel at the mountainous horizons in every direction.

If you camped last at Jordan or Pentad Lake, you have lots of options for the next night out or for a base camp. The closest site is at Wounded Man Lake, but this is a busy place. The best campsite is along the North Fork of Wounded Man Creek just southwest of the lake. But consider hiking the short mile northeast from Wounded Man Lake to Lake Pinchot to stay at the crown jewel of the Lake Plateau. The third option is to turn left onto Trail 211 at the junction on the west side of Wounded Man Lake, at 18.7 miles, and stay at Owl Lake or one of the Rainbow Lakes that follow shortly thereafter. These sites offer some of the best base camps in the area because there are innumerable sights to see all within a short walk.

After a night or two on the plateau, follow Trail 211 along the west shore of Rainbow Lakes down to the junction with Trail 26 at the south end of Lower Rainbow Lake. Turn right (west) here, and spend the last night out at Diamond or Horseshoe Lake (sometimes called Upper and Lower Horseshoe Lakes). Horseshoe Lake, at 25.9 miles, is probably better because it has more campsites and leaves the shortest possible distance along Upsidedown Creek the last day—that's still about 8.5 miles to the Upsidedown Creek Trailhead, plus the 1.5 miles some lucky volunteer has to walk or try to catch a ride up to the Box Canyon Trailhead to get the vehicle. Sorry—there are no real campsites anywhere from Horseshoe Lake to the Boulder River Road.

The Lake Plateau has hundreds of terrific campsites, all undesignated. Find one for your base camp, and please make it a zero-impact camp.

Anglers who want to fish the first day of the trip should camp near the East Fork Boulder River or Rainbow Creek, as most of the lakes along this route—including Lake Columbine—are barren. Burnt Gulch Lake is an exception, sporting dinner-size cutthroat trout. Cutthroats dominate the fishery along this route until the Lake Plateau is reached. Cutthroats are fairly easy to catch and are frequently found along rocky shorelines on the downwind sides of lakes. Anglers often fish "past the fish" by casting out into the lake.

Once the Lake Plateau is reached, you'll find a variety of fishing opportunities easily available, and Lake Pinchot would certainly make the desirable list, as would the entire Flood Creek chain of lakes.

Options

If you can arrange transportation for a shuttle, you can hike out the West Stillwater or the main Stillwater. You might need a four-wheel-drive vehicle to get to the West Stillwater Trailhead, depending on the condition of the road. You can also make this an out-and-back trip from either the Box Canyon or the Upsidedown Creek Trailhead.

Side Trips

You could spend weeks exploring the Lake Plateau, and these are only a few of the dozens of great side trips in the area: Lake Pinchot (easy), Flood Creek Lakes (moderate), Asteroid Lake Basin (strenuous), Chalice Peak (strenuous), Lightning Lake (strenuous), Lake Diaphanous (easy), Fish Lake (easy), Barrier Lake (strenuous), Mirror Lake (moderate), Chickadee Lake (strenuous), Squeeze Lake (strenuous), Mount

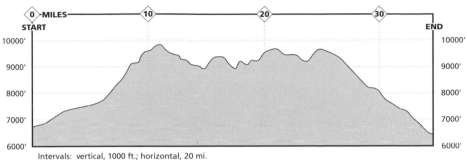

Intervals: vertical, 1000 ft.; horizontal, 20 mi.

Douglas (strenuous), Martes Lake (moderate), Sundown Lake (moderate), Pentad and Favonius Lakes (easy), and Burnt Gulch Lake (strenuous). (Hiked by authors in 1979 and 1996)

Key Points

0.0	Box Canyon Trailhead
3.5	East Fork Boulder River; cross bridge
5.2	Junction with Trail 28; turn left
5.4	Lake Kathleen
7.9	Junction with Trail 128; turn right
9.3	Columbine Lake
11.1	Columbine Pass
12.5	Pentad Lake
14.5	Jordan Lake and junction with Trail 90; turn left
15.9	Jordan Pass
18.7	Wounded Man Lake and junction with Trail 43; turn left
18.9	Junction with Trail 211; turn left after trip to Lake Pinchot
19.5	Lake Pinchot
21.0	Rainbow Lakes
22.5	Junction with Trail 26; turn right
25.9	Horseshoe Lake
34.3	Upsidedown Creek Trailhead

96 Lady of the Lake

Description: A picturesque and accessible forested lake.
Start: 15 miles east of Cooke City.
Type of hike: Day hike or overnighter; out-and-back.
Total distance: 3-mile round trip.
Difficulty: Easy.

Maps: Cooke City USGS Quad, Rocky Mountain Survey Cooke City–Cutoff Mountain Map, and Forest Service's Absaroka-Beartooth Wilderness Map.
Trail contacts: Gardiner Ranger District, Gallatin National Forest, Box 5, Highway 89, Gardiner, MT 59030; (406) 848–7375; www.fs.fed.us/r1/gallatin.

Finding the trailhead: To reach the trailhead from Cooke City, drive east on U.S. Highway 212 for 2 miles to a turnoff to the Goose Lake jeep road, less than a quarter mile before the Colter Campground. Turn left (north) and drive northeast 2 miles on this gravel road and pull into the inconspicuous trailhead on your right. (There were no signs on the highway or at the trailhead the last time I was there.) The gravel road is passable by any vehicle, but it has some nasty water bars that could high-center a low-clearance vehicle, so go very slowly over them. You'll find limited parking and undeveloped camping sites at the trailhead and nearby.

The Hike

Lady of the Lake is an ideal choice for an easy day hike or overnighter with small children. Besides being a short hike, the weather isn't as critical as it is at the higher elevations.

Set off down Trail 31. Unfortunately, you might have to get your feet wet immediately upon starting this trip. The bridge over Fisher Creek washed out years ago, and until late in the year, the stream carries too much water to ford without wading.

After Fisher Creek, the trail goes by a small inholding with a cabin then heads down a well-maintained, forest-lined trail to Lady of the Lake. The Forest Service sign says 1 mile to the lake, but it's probably more like 1.5 miles. The trail breaks out of the trees in the large marshy meadow at the foot of the lake.

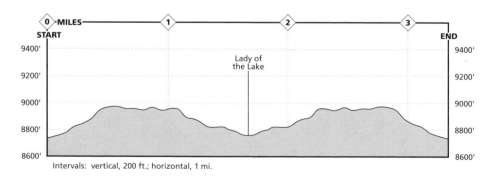

Intervals: vertical, 200 ft.; horizontal, 1 mi.

Lady of the Lake

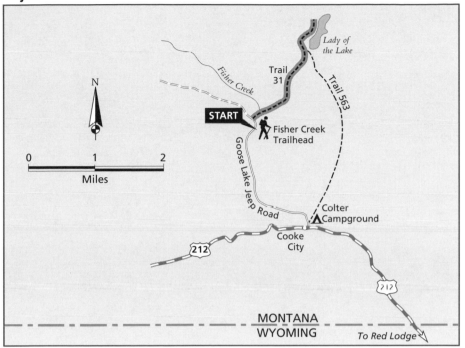

Just before the lake, Trail 563 heads off to the right (south) to Chief Joseph Campground on U.S. Highway 212. Trail 563 also offers fairly easy access to Lady of the Lake, but the route described here is much shorter and faster. Stay to the left on Trail 31 to the lake.

The return trip involves more climbing than the way in, so allow extra time, especially if traveling with small children.

This is a heavily used area, with some major wear and tear along the trail on the west shore of the lake. The Forest Service has prohibited camping at several overused sites to allow rehabilitation. For overnighters, the best campsite is about halfway along the lake on the left just after a cut in a huge log across the trail and through a small meadow. Campfires are allowed but discouraged.

Lady of the Lake is a personal favorite place to take kids for their first wilderness camping experience. The hike is easy, and the brook trout are always willing. For those with some wilderness experience, there are four small lakes nestled in the trees to the southeast. They're a bit tough to find, but they promise solitude. Grayling are stocked in Mosquito Lake when available, while the other lakes are scheduled for stocking with cutthroats. Don't bother to fish Fisher Creek. Acid effluent from mines abandoned before environmental protection laws were in place keeps this stream nearly sterile.

Options

You can reach Lady of the Lake by taking Trail 563 from Colter Campground. You could also use this trail to make this a shuttle trip, which means leaving a vehicle at the Colter Campground. (Hiked by authors in 1981, 1986, and 2001)

97 Aero Lakes

Description: The stark beauty of this high plateau area and a wide diversity of potential side trips.

Start: 15 miles northeast of Cooke City.

Type of hike: Base camp backpacking trip; out-and-back.

Total distance: 11.4-mile round trip, not counting side trips.

Difficulty: Strenuous.

Maps: Cooke City, Fossil Lake, and Granite Peak USGS Quads; Rocky Mountain Survey Cooke City–Cutoff Mountain Map; and Forest Service's Absaroka-Beartooth Wilderness Map.

Trail contacts: Gardiner Ranger District, Gallatin National Forest, Box 5, Highway 89, Gardiner, MT 59030; (406) 848-7375; www.fs.fed.us/r1/gallatin.

Finding the trailhead: To reach the trailhead from Cooke City, drive east on U.S. Highway 212 for 3.2 miles to a turnoff marked with a large Forest Service sign as the Goose Lake Jeep Road, just before the Colter Campground. Turn north off U.S. Highway 212 and drive northeast about 2 miles up this gravel road to a cluster of old buildings. An inconspicuous trailhead on the right shoulder of the road has an old Forest Service sign for Lady of the Lake. The 2 miles of road to the trailhead are passable with any vehicle, but to continue up the road past the trailhead for any reason, a high-clearance vehicle is essential. You'll find limited parking and an undeveloped campground at the trailhead.

Recommended itinerary: You could hike into Aero Lakes and out the same day, but that would be a shame. Instead, plan on a long day hike to get to the lakes and spend the time to find an idyllic campsite. Then, spend two or three days exploring this incredible high country.

The Hike

This trailhead is slightly harder to locate than most others in the Beartooths, but that hasn't lessened its popularity. The area has lots to offer, and it receives heavy use both by locals and by those who travel from afar for a chance to experience this spectacular wild area.

The trailhead lies on the eastern fringe of the section of the Beartooths that has been extensively mined, logged, and roaded. Even in the 2 miles of gravel road to the trailhead, the contrast between this area and the pristine wilderness is clearly evident. To get an early start, camp at the undeveloped campground at the trailhead.

At Aero Lakes you're many miles from the nearest machine. At night neither city lights nor smog blocks the view of the stars. Nearly one million acres of pristine land surrounds you here, more than enough for a lifetime of wandering.

At this altitude, the summer season is very short. Ice may not free the lakes until mid-July. The moist tundra tends to produce a prodigious number of mosquitoes when the wind isn't blowing. Bring lots of bug dope.

The first leg of the trip down Trail 31 takes you to Lady of the Lake, an ideal choice for an easy day hike or overnighter with small children. Unfortunately, they might get their feet wet immediately upon starting this trip. The bridge over Fisher Creek washed out years ago, and until late in the year, the stream carries too much water to ford without wading.

After Fisher Creek the trail goes by a small private inholding with a cabin and then heads down a well-maintained, forest-lined trail to Lady of the Lake. The Forest Service sign says 1 mile to the lake, but it's probably more like 1.5 miles.

The trail breaks out of the trees in the large marshy meadow at the foot of the lake. Just before the lake, Trail 563 heads off to the right (south) to Chief Joseph Campground on US 212. (Trail 563 also offers fairly easy access to Lady of the Lake, but the route described here is much shorter and faster.)

Once at Lady of the Lake follow the trail along the west side of the lake. At the far end of the lake, the trail heads off to the left for about a quarter mile to a meadow on the north side of the lake where two trails depart. The left-hand trail (Trail 31) heads northwest to Long Lake. Take the right-hand trail (Trail 573), which leads almost due north less than a half mile to the confluence of Star and Zimmer Creeks. Ford the stream here and continue north along Zimmer Creek another mile or so until you see Trail 573 switchbacking up the steep right side of the cirque. If you see a major stream coming in from the left, you have gone too far up the drainage.

The scramble up the Trail 573 switchbacks is short but steep and requires good physical conditioning. Locals call it Cardiac Hill, and for good reason. It climbs almost 900 feet in about a mile, close to a Category H on our hill rating chart.

At the top of Cardiac Hill, the trail suddenly emerges from the timber and pauses above Lower Aero Lake. Be sure to notice the dramatic contrast between the treeless plateau here and the timbered country below.

The shoreline around Lower Aero is rocky and punctuated with snowbanks. There are a number of places to camp. They all have great scenery, and the air conditioning is always on. Those planning to stay here for two or three nights should spend some extra time searching for that five-star campsite. Drop the packs and look around for an hour or so. Don't expect to have a campfire on this treeless plateau.

To proceed to Upper Aero Lake, follow the stream that connects the two lakes. Another good camping spot is just below the outlet of the upper lake. It provides a good view of the lake and prominent Mount Villard with its spiny ridges. It also makes a good base camp for fishing both lakes and for exploring east to Rough Lake and then north up the Sky Top Lakes chain.

Although most people visit Rough Lake or Lone Elk Lake on side trips, there's also good camping there. Both are large, deep lakes similar to Aero Lakes. Sky Top Lakes might look inviting on the map, but camping is very limited in this rocky basin.

After a day or two of exploring the high country, retrace your steps down Cardiac Hill to Zimmer Creek—and then, back to civilization.

Aero Lakes

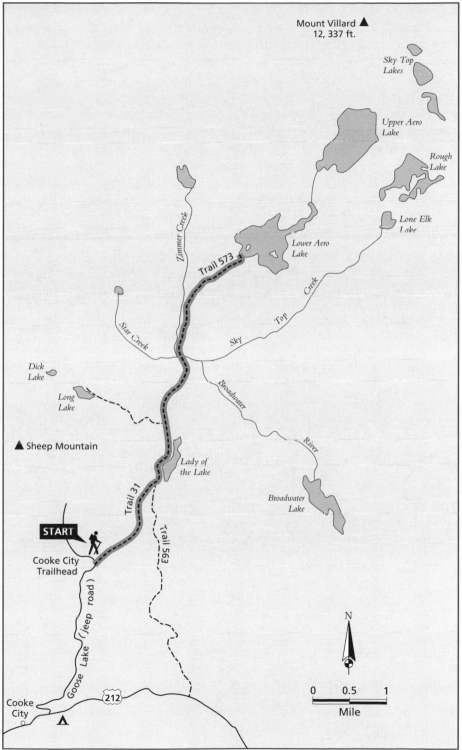

Mount Villard ▲
12, 337 ft.

Sky Top
Lakes

Upper Aero
Lake

Rough
Lake

Lone Elk
Lake

Zimmer Creek

Trail 573

Lower Aero
Lake

Sky Top Creek

Star Creek

Sky

Dick
Lake

Broadwater

Long
Lake

River

▲ Sheep Mountain

Lady of
the Lake

Broadwater
Lake

Trail 31

Trail 563

START

Cooke City
Trailhead

Goose Lake (jeep road)

N

Cooke
City

212

0   0.5   1
Mile

There are no designated campsites in this area, but there are numerous possibilities. Please use zero-impact camping principles to preserve this fragile landscape.

Fishing is generally slow in both Upper and Lower Aero Lakes, but the rewards can be worth it. Lower Aero has brookies that are large, occasionally approaching a pound or more. They are supplemented with cutthroats that have migrated down from Upper Aero and seem to be reproducing. Cutts can be seen trying to spawn between the lakes through most of July. Upper Aero is stocked with cutts, but a change in its current six-year cycle is being discussed. Fishing is tough here as the cutthroats tend to school, and they can be hard to find in a lake of this size.

Sky Top Lakes were once stocked with grayling, and these fish worked down into Rough and Lone Elk Lakes, but all seem to have disappeared, leaving just brook trout in Lone Elk and Rough. The Sky Tops will probably be stocked once again to maintain a fishery in this chain originating on the slopes of Granite Peak.

To the east of Sky Top Creek are a number of lakes, supporting mostly brook trout, although Weasel, Stash, and Surprise Lakes are stocked with cutts. For hearty souls Recruitment Lake holds a few extremely large brookies, but the chances of getting skunked are pretty good. Nevertheless, just one hefty fish from this lake would be the high point of a summer vacation.

Options

This trip could turn into a long (four- or five-day) shuttle for experts only by continuing east from Aero Lakes through the "top of the world" and exiting the Beartooths at the East Rosebud or Clarks Fork trailheads.

You could also make a loop out of your trip by exiting on an off-trail route down Sky Top Creek, but be careful on the steep upper section of the stream where it tumbles off the plateau from Lone Elk Lake. Be forewarned: This route is only for the fit, agile, and adventuresome. It requires carrying your pack cross-country over to Rough Lake (probably named for how hard it is to reach) and then down to Lone Elk Lake. From Lone Elk Lake it's a scramble down a steep route with no trail to a meadow where the stream from Splinter Lake slips into Sky Top Creek. This is a long, slow mile, and it can be hazardous, so be careful and patient. But it's also very

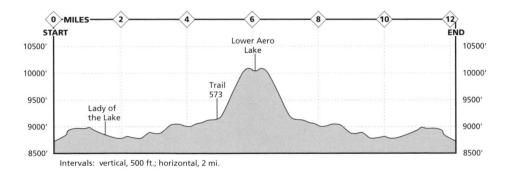

Intervals: vertical, 500 ft.; horizontal, 2 mi.

beautiful, especially the falls where Sky Top Creek leaves Lone Elk Lake. At the meadow there is an unofficial trail along Sky Top Creek all the way to the main trail. Follow cascading Sky Top Creek all the way until near the end, when it veers off to the left to join up with Star Creek to form the Broadwater River. The track comes out into the same meadow (where Star and Zimmer Creeks join) you passed through on the way up Zimmer Creek on Trail 573. From here retrace your steps back to Lady of the Lake and the trailhead.

Side Trips

Possible side trips in this area include treks to Aero Lakes perimeter (moderate), Upper Aero Lake (easy), Leaky Raft Lake (easy), Rough Lake (moderate), Lone Elk Lake (moderate), Sky Top Lakes (strenuous), Zimmer Lake (strenuous), Iceberg Peak/Grasshopper Glacier (strenuous), Mount Villard (strenuous), and Glacier Peak (strenuous). (Originally contributed by Mike Sample, rehiked by authors in 1986 and 2001)

Key Points

0.0 Trailhead

1.5 Lady of the Lake and junction with Trail 563; turn left

2.5 Junction with Trail 31 to Long Lake; turn right

2.8 Stream coming in from Long Lake

3.6 Star Creek

4.8 Start of climb to Aero Lakes on Trail 573

5.7 Base of Lower Aero Lake

11.4 Trailhead

98 Rock Island Lake

Description: An unusually large, sprawling forest-lined lake.
Start: 20 miles northeast of Cooke City.
Type of hike: Day hike or overnighter; out-and-back.
Total distance: 6-mile round trip.
Difficulty: Easy.

Maps: Fossil Lake USGS Quad; Rocky Mountain Survey Cooke City–Cutoff Mountain Map; and Forest Service's Absaroka-Beartooth Wilderness Map.
Trail contacts: Gardiner Ranger District, Gallatin National Forest, Box 5, Highway 89, Gardiner, MT 59030; (406) 848-7375; www.fs.fed.us/r1/gallatin.

Finding the trailhead: Take U.S. Highway 212 east from Cooke City for 3.4 miles or 58.1 miles from Red Lodge and turn north onto Forest Road 306. Drive about a half mile to the large trailhead, which features plenty of parking, a toilet, and a picnic area.

The Hike

Rock Island Lake differs from many high-elevation lakes. Instead of forming a small, concise oval in a cirque, it sprawls through flat and forested terrain, seemingly branching off in every direction. Visitors can spend an entire day just walking around it.

To get to Rock Island Lake, start off on Trail 3 from the Clarks Fork Trailhead. After half a mile the Kersey Lake Jeep Road veers off to the left. Stay on Trail 3. At 1.2 miles you reach the junction with Trail 565, which heads off to the right toward Lake Vernon. Again keep going on Trail 3. You'll pass Kersey Lake on the left at 1.5 miles. At 2.4 miles you come to the junction with Trail 566 to Rock Island Lake. Turn right (east) here for about another half mile to the lake. The trail is well used and well maintained the entire way, with only one hill (near Kersey Lake). The 1988 fires scorched the area around Kersey Lake but missed Rock Island Lake.

Because Rock Island Lake is so easy to reach (3 miles on a near-level trail), it's a perfect choice for a family's first trip into the Absaroka-Beartooth Wilderness. Drinking water is readily available on the trail and at the lake (it must be boiled or filtered), but the mosquitoes can be thick in early summer.

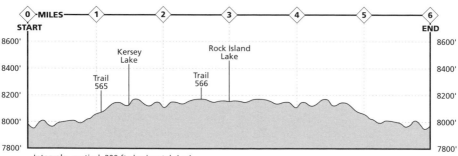

Intervals: vertical, 200 ft.; horizontal, 1 mi.

Rock Island Lake

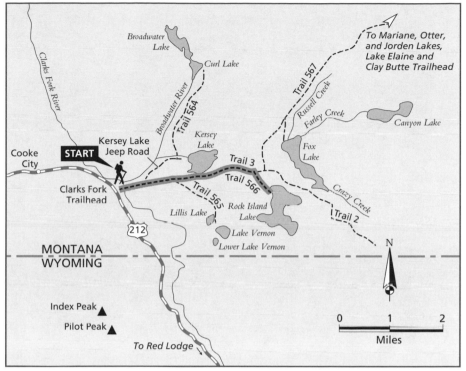

Those planning an overnight stay can camp at one of several places along the west side of the lake. Camping spots are more limited than many other lakes in the Beartooths, however, and you might have to search a while to find an unoccupied spot. Although there might be enough wood for a campfire at the lake, consider using a stove for cooking. The area receives heavy use, and if everyone had a fire, the area would soon show signs of overuse.

This popular lake has a combination of home-grown brookies and cutthroats stocked on a three-year rotation, both of which grow well in this lake. (Hiked by authors in 1985 and 1999)

Key Points

0.0 Trailhead

0.5 Junction with Kersey Lake Jeep Road

1.2 Junction with Trail 565 to Lake Vernon; turn left

1.5 Kersey Lake

2.4 Junction with Trail 566 to Rock Island Lake; turn right

3.0 Rock Island Lake

6.0 Trailhead

Yellowstone National Park

99 Sky Rim

Description: Amazing, ridgeline views from
Sky Rim.
Start: 15 miles north of West Yellowstone on
the north edge of Yellowstone National Park.
Type of hike: Long day hike for extra-fit hikers;
loop (actually a "lollipop").
Total distance: 21.1 miles, plus 0.6 mile for
round-trip side trip to Big Horn Peak.

Difficulty: Strenuous.
Maps: Big Horn Peak USGS Quad and Trails
Illustrated Mammoth Hot Springs Map.
Trail contacts: National Park Service, Yellow-
stone National Park, Park Headquarters, P.O.
Box 168, Yellowstone National Park, WY
82190; (307) 344-7381; www.nps.gov/yell.

Finding the trailhead: Drive north from West Yellowstone or south from Bozeman to the
Daly Creek Trailhead between mileposts 30 and 31 on U.S. Highway 191, 22 miles north of
the US 191/US 89 junction or 0.8 mile south of the park boundary. Black Butte Trailhead is
between mileposts 28 and 29. Stock use is prohibited until July 1. There is ample parking but
no other facilities.

The Hike

For serious hikers who like to "get high" and have lots of panoramic mountain
scenery, the Sky Rim loop trail is probably the best long hike in Yellowstone. It's also
one of the most difficult, but it's ideal for the well-conditioned hiker who likes to
get up early and spend the entire day walking with minimal time devoted to rest
and relaxation. Besides being one of the nicest parts of the park, the far northwest
corner is also the newest, added to the park in 1927.

Be sure to take plenty of water on this hike. The stretch between Upper Daly
Creek all along Sky Rim, up Big Horn Peak, and down to Black Butte Creek is a
very long haul without any reliable water sources. Take more water than you normally would on a long day hike.

Also watch the weather closely. We had a perfect day when we hiked this route,
but it was easy to see that you really don't want to be on Sky Rim in bad weather.
At best, it wouldn't be much fun because you couldn't see the scenery, but more
likely, it would be dangerous because of slippery footing and the specter of
hypothermia. If you get caught in a thunderstorm on Sky Rim, you could become
a lightning rod.

August is the best time to take this hike. You stand a good chance of good
weather, and you avoid hiking the ridgeline with hunters, who tend to take over the
place in early September when the early big game seasons open in Montana.

The first 1.8 miles up Daly Creek along Daly Creek Trail start out in the shadow
of mighty Crown Butte just outside the park to the north. The well-defined trail
winds through expansive open meadows broken here and there by scattered stands
of trees. At 1.8 miles the Black Butte Cutoff Trail veers to the right. Stay left on Daly

Sky Rim

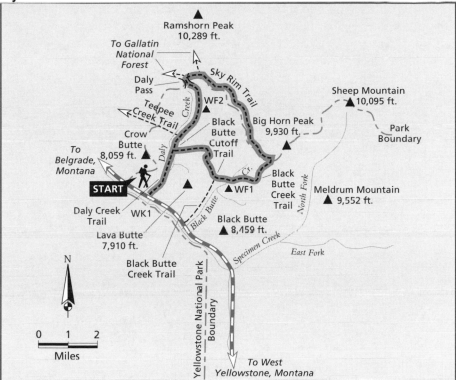

Creek Trail. The Teepee Creek Trail junction comes up on your left at 3.6 miles. Stay to the right on Daly Creek Trail. Also near this junction is backcountry campsite WF2.

The scenery continues through open meadows until about a mile past backcountry campsite WF2, where the trail slips into the trees for the climb up to Daly Pass. The trail is heavily rutted in spots, which makes walking difficult.

When you get to Daly Pass at 4.9 miles, you're actually at a four way junction. The faint trail to the left (not shown on some maps) follows the ridgeline and park boundary, and the trail going straight heads out of the park into the Gallatin National Forest. You go right (east) and continue to climb along the ridgeline.

After the Category 1 climb up to the pass, with only a few short switchbacks near the end, it seems you should be about as high up as you can get, but you aren't even close to the top. The trail follows the ridge for 0.8 mile to the Sky Rim Trail junction. Parts of this trail go along a sharply angled ridgeline, so be careful not to fall off either side. We almost missed this junction because it's natural to keep heading up the ridge, and the trail sign is behind you. At this junction another trail heads north out of the park into the Buffalo Horn region of the Gallatin National Forest.

From the Sky Rim Trail, the view is fantastic. Off to the west loom the Taylor-Hilgards of the Madison Range, with 11,316-foot Hilgard Peak, and, in the foreground, expansive Daly Creek, where you just hiked. Off to the east is the sprawling Tom Minor Basin in the shadow of Canary Bird, Ramshorn, and Twin Peaks, with a majestic backdrop of the Absaroka Range and its highest point, Mount Cowen (11,205 feet).

From here the already strenuous route gets more strenuous. The next leg of your trip, about 5.5 miles along Sky Rim, goes over two more big climbs and is followed by the last pitch up to the Black Butte Creek Trail junction at 11.2 miles, where you turn right, one of the few Category H climbs in the park. In fact, this is the most precipitous section of designated trail in the park, but it's not dangerous.

The scenery stays sensational all the way to Big Horn Peak. The trail gets faint in spots and, about a mile from the next junction, more or less disappears on grassy flanks of Big Horn Peak. You won't get off the designated route as long as you don't drop off the ridgeline.

At the junction take the short, out-and-back side trip to the very top of Big Horn Peak. It's hard to believe the scenery can get any better, but it actually does. This short but nerve-racking (use caution!) side trip is definitely worth the little extra effort. From the true summit of Big Horn Peak, you get a good view of the Gallatin Skyline Trail continuing over to Sheep Mountain to the south.

In addition to the mountain vistas that surround the Sky Rim, you also have a good chance of seeing elk, deer, and moose on the open slopes and along Daly Creek. Also watch for bighorn sheep, commonly seen on Big Horn Peak. In the fall, grizzlies frequent the Gallatin Skyline area to feed on whitebark pine nuts, abundant along this high-elevation trail.

From here it's all downhill as you switchback down Big Horn Peak into Black Butte Creek. The trail is in better shape than the trail up Daly Creek and along Sky Rim, so if you are behind schedule, you can make up some lost time. After about a half mile, you leave the open slopes of Big Horn Peak behind and hike into a lush, unburned forest and through the Gallatin Petrified Forest.

The trail stays in the forest the rest of the way. The trail to WF1 goes off to the left (south) at 15.7 miles, just before the junction with the Black Butte Cutoff Trail at 15.9 miles. Turn right (north), go through a large meadow, and climb over a forested ridge past a patrol cabin at 16.5 miles and back into spacious Daly Creek. At the junction with the Daly Creek Trail at 18 miles, turn left (west) and retrace your steps another 2 miles or so back to the Daly Creek Trailhead.

Options

You could start at Black Butte Trailhead or take the route counterclockwise with the same degree of difficulty. The climbs on the counterclockwise route tend to be longer but more gradual as opposed to the short, steep climbs of the clockwise route.

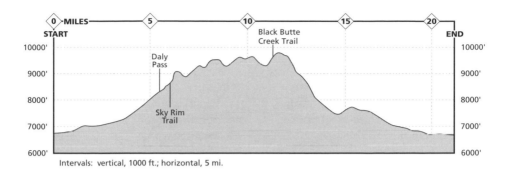

Intervals: vertical, 1000 ft.; horizontal, 5 mi.

If you have two vehicles, you can skip the cutoff trail and shorten your trip by about 2 miles by leaving one vehicle at the Black Butte Trailhead. Because of the location of the campsites, you can't really turn this into an overnighter without making it more difficult; however, you could base camp at WF1 or WF2 and make the long day hike about 2 miles shorter.

Side Trips

You would really miss something if you didn't take the short side trip (0.6 mile round-trip) to the top of Big Horn Peak. You can continue along the Gallatin Skyline Trail to Shelf Lake (6 miles round-trip), but make sure you have enough daylight. You could also camp at Shelf Lake and come out at Specimen Creek, but this would be a Herculean day with an overnight pack to get to Shelf Lake along Sky Rim. (Hiked by authors in 1994)

Key Points

0.0   Daly Creek Trailhead

1.8   Black Butte Cutoff Trail junction; turn left

3.6   Teepee Creek Trail junction, backcountry campsite WF2; turn right

4.9   Daly Pass

5.7   Sky Rim Trail junction; turn right

11.2 Black Butte Creek Trail junction; turn right

15.7 Spur trail to backcountry campsite WF1

15.9 Black Butte Cutoff Trail junction; turn right

16.5 Patrol cabin

18.0 Daly Creek Trail junction; turn left

21.1 Daly Creek Trailhead

100 Black Canyon

Description: An unusual trip along the majestic Yellowstone River nearly the entire route, and since winter gives up this area early, it provides a rare opportunity for early-season backpacking.

Start: Between Tower and Gardiner in Yellowstone National Park.

Type of hike: Backpacking trip; shuttle.

Total distance: 18.5 miles.

Difficulty: Moderate.

Maps: Tower Junction, Blacktail Deer Creek, Ash Mountain, and Gardiner USGS Quads; and Trails Illustrated Mammoth Hot Springs and Tower/Canyon Maps.

Trail contacts: National Park Service, Yellowstone National Park, Park Headquarters, P.O. Box 168, Yellowstone National Park, WY 82190; (307) 344-7381; www.nps.gov/yell.

Finding the trailhead: Drive 14.5 miles east from Mammoth, Wyoming, or 3.5 miles west from Tower, Wyoming, and pull into the Hellroaring Trailhead. The actual trailhead is about a half mile down a service road. To find the west trailhead in Gardiner, Montana, turn on the first road going east on the north side of the Yellowstone River and park by a sign for the Yellowstone River Trail between a private campground and a church. There is ample parking but no facilities. You'll find limited parking and no facilities at the exit point in Gardiner.

Recommended itinerary: There are many ways to enjoy the Black Canyon, but I recommend the following three-day trip.

First night: 1R2 or 1R1
Second night: 1Y2 or 1Y1

Getting a permit: In Yellowstone you must have a permit for all overnight use of the backcountry. If you use the advance reservation system, expect to pay a small fee for this permit. You can still walk into a visitor center without a reservation and get a free backcountry permit, but you take a much greater chance that your chosen campsites will already be reserved.

In 1996 the park installed a new computerized reservation system, which replaced a cumbersome system whereby hikers had to wait in line for permits and often couldn't get their preferred site. With the new system you can usually get the campsites you want—as long as you start planning long in advance.

You should get a Backcountry Trip Planner from the park; it explains the process of getting a permit. Get one by contacting Backcountry Office, P.O. Box 168, Yellowstone National Park, WY 82190; (307) 344–2160 or (307) 344–2163; e-mail: yell_park_info@nps.gov; Web site: www.nps.gov/yell (click on "publications," then "backcountry trip planner").

The reservation system is relatively new, so some specifics might change, but for now, the NPS has established the following policies:

- Reservations are made on a first-come, first-served basis, beginning April 1 each year.

Hiking along the Yellowstone River.

- You can call for help or advice, but phone reservations won't be accepted. Reservations must be submitted by mail or in person.
- Reservation requests must made on the Trip Planning Worksheet that comes with the Backcountry Trip Planner.
- A confirmation notice will be mailed to you. This is not a permit, but you can exchange it for your official permit when you get to the park.
- Get your permit in person at a ranger station not more than forty-eight hours in advance of the first day of your trip, but no later than 10:00 A.M. the first day of your trip. If you miss this deadline, your permit will be released to other backcountry users.
- If the NPS has to close a trail or campsite for resource protection or safety reasons, the Backcountry Office will try to help you plan a comparable trip.
- You can pick up permits at most ranger stations and visitor centers in the park.

The Hike

The Black Canyon of the Yellowstone is one of the classic backpacking trips of the northern Rockies. It seems to offer everything a hiker might want. It's downhill all the way on an excellent trail with a wide choice of 4-star or 5-star campsites. Wildlife is abundant, the fishing is fantastic, and the scenery rivals almost any other hike in the park. The trail closely follows the mighty Yellowstone River most of the way. Unlike most other hikes in this book (except those in Glacier National Park), you must stay in designated campsites, and you must have a backcountry camping permit.

After you get your permit, arranging a shuttle is the next order of business. It's better to start at the east end of the trail because you lose more than 1,000 feet in elevation along the way.

After leaving the Hellroaring Trailhead, you hike through meadows and a few stands of trees down a steep hill to the suspension bridge over the Yellowstone River, staying left (north) at the junction with the trail to Tower just before reaching the bridge. Here's where you pat yourself on the back for your good plan to start at this end of the shuttle hike. If you did it in reverse, you would face this steep hill at the end of your hike when you might not be in the mood for it.

The suspension bridge is one of the highlights of the trip, but don't conjure up images of Indiana Jones movies. This is a very sturdy metal bridge. From here to near Gardiner, you're in the Black Canyon of the Yellowstone.

Shortly after crossing the bridge, you break out into the open terrain around Hellroaring Creek. When you reach the junction at 1.6 miles with the trail up Coyote Creek, stay left (northwest).

When you get to Hellroaring Creek, be alert or you'll get on the wrong trail. Well-defined trails go up both sides of the creek to campsites, and when we hiked this trip, many of the trail signs were missing. There used to be a footbridge across Hellroaring Creek (a large tributary to the Yellowstone), but high spring runoff claimed it years ago. Watch for trail markers on the west side of the creek at about 2 miles so you know where to ford. This ford can be dangerous in June and early July, so if it looks too adventuresome for you, hike about 1 mile north along the creek and cross on a stock bridge and then back down the west side of the creek to the main trail.

After fording Hellroaring Creek you will gradually climb up over a ridge and drop into Little Cottonwood Creek at 4.5 miles and then over another hill into Cottonwood Creek at 6 miles. The section of the trail between Hellroaring and Cottonwood Creek stays high above the river on mostly open hillsides. Then, just after Cottonwood Creek, it drops down to the river's edge.

Also, just before Cottonwood Creek, you cross the border from Wyoming into Montana. If you're an angler, though, it doesn't matter, as long as you have a park fishing license and know the regulations.

Black Canyon

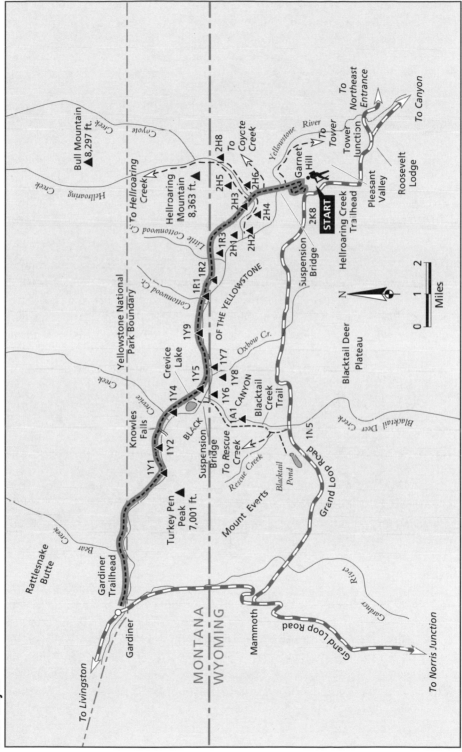

From Cottonwood Creek to the Blacktail Creek Trail junction, the trail stays close to the river, offering up 4 miles of some spectacular scenery and plenty of pleasant resting places. You might notice frequent carcasses and scattered bones along this trail. That's because this is winter range for the park's large ungulates. Each year winter kills some weaker members of the herd, and wolves, bears, and cougars take down a few more.

At the junction with Blacktail Creek Trail off to the left (south) at 10 miles, continue straight (west) along the north side of the river, passing Crevice Lake just after the junction. Then, 1.6 miles later, cross Crevice Creek on a sturdy footbridge. Some older maps show a trail going up Crevice Creek to the park boundary, but this route has been abandoned. Shortly after Crevice Creek, take a short side trip on a spur trail down to see majestic Knowles Falls, a 15-foot drop on the Yellowstone.

From the falls to where the trail ends at Gardiner, the trail continues close to the river, except for one short section at about 12.4 miles, just after backcountry campsite 1Y2, where the trail climbs over a rocky ridge. The river goes through a narrows here, getting white and frothy, so you might feel a bit safer being farther away. Just before Gardiner at 18.5 miles, you can see the confluence of the Gardner and Yellowstone Rivers. (Yes, Gardiner the town and Gardner the river have different spellings for no clearly definable reason. Interestingly, Jim Bridger originally called the river Gardener Creek.)

The trail is in superb condition the entire way with the exception of one short section between Bear Creek and Gardiner. Here the trail is etched out of a steep, clay hillside. If you draw a rainy day, this stretch can be slippery, so be careful.

The Black Canyon of the Yellowstone offers terrific fishing. From Hellroaring Creek to Knowles Falls, it's strictly a cutthroat fishery. Most fish range in the 10- to 14-inch range and are usually suckers for almost any fly or lure. Below Knowles Falls you start to find a few rainbows and hybrids and a few browns, with trout getting up to 17 inches or more, but they are harder to catch. You also find large numbers of whitefish below Knowles Falls. Even though this drier section of the park is suitable for hiking in May and June, the Yellowstone often runs high and murky during the early season, and that limits fishing success.

Options

In addition to the three-day trip described here, this route makes an excellent four-day trip. You could stay the first night at one of the six excellent campsites along Hellroaring Creek, the second at 1R2 or 1R1, and the third at 1Y2 or 1Y1 before hiking out on the fourth day. This itinerary gives you plenty of time for fishing and relaxing. If you have only two days, stay overnight at 1Y9, 1Y7, or 1Y5. You can trim about 4 miles off the trip by leaving Black Canyon at the Blacktail Creek Trail junction.

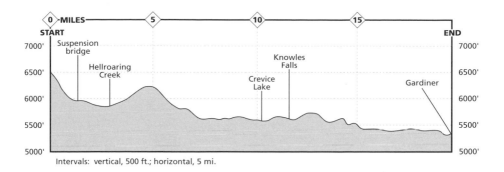

Intervals: vertical, 500 ft.; horizontal, 5 mi.

You could do this shuttle in reverse, but if you did, you'd face a huge climb to the Hellroaring Trailhead at the end of your trip.

Side Trips

If you stay at Hellroaring Creek, you might enjoy a short day hike up the creek toward the park boundary. (Hiked by authors in 1995)

Key Points

0.0 Hellroaring Trailhead

0.9 Junction with trail to Tower; turn left

1.0 Suspension bridge over Yellowstone

1.6 Junction with trail to Coyote Creek and Buffalo Plateau; turn left

1.8 Spur trail going north along the east side of Hellroaring Creek to backcountry campsites 2H6 and 2H8 and to stock bridge; turn left

1.9 Spur trail going south along the east side of Hellroaring Creek to backcountry campsites 2H4 and 2H2; turn right

2.0 Ford of Hellroaring Creek

2.1 Spur trail going south along the west side of Hellroaring Creek to backcountry campsites 2H3 and 2H1; turn right

2.2 Spur trail going north along the west side of Hellroaring Creek to backcountry campsite 2H5, to the stock bridge, and into Gallatin National Forest; turn left

4.5 Little Cottonwood Creek, backcountry campsite 1R3

5.9 Backcountry campsite 1R2

6.0 Cottonwood Creek, backcountry campsite 1R1

8.3 Backcountry campsite 1Y9

9.0 Backcountry campsite 1Y7

9.8 Backcountry campsite 1Y5

10.0 Blacktail Creek Trail junction; trail to backcountry campsites 1Y6 and 1Y8; turn right

10.1 Crevice Lake

10.5 Backcountry campsite 1Y4

11.6 Crevice Creek

11.9 Knowles Falls

12.3 Backcountry campsite 1Y2

13.2 Backcountry campsite 1Y1

18.5 Gardiner

101 Pebble Creek

Description: A mostly downhill hike through the gorgeous meadows along Pebble Creek.
Start: In the northeast corner of Yellowstone National Park.
Type of hike: Day hike or overnighter; shuttle.
Total distance: 12 miles.
Difficulty: Moderate.

Maps: Cutoff Mountain and Abiathar Peak USGS Quads and Trails Illustrated Tower/Canyon Map.
Trail contacts: National Park Service, Yellowstone National Park, Park Headquarters, P.O. Box 168, Yellowstone National Park, WY 82190; (307) 344-7381; www.nps.gov/yell.

Finding the trailhead: Drive 27 miles east of Tower Junction or 1.4 miles west of the Northeast Entrance and turn into a trailhead on the north side of the road. Leave a vehicle or arrange to be picked up at the Pebble Creek Trailhead just east of the turnoff to Pebble Creek Campground, which is 19 miles east of Tower Junction and 9.4 miles west of the Northeast Entrance. Park at an angle in this turnout to leave room for more vehicles. If this small parking area on the highway is full, you can park in the paved lot on your right after you turn north toward Pebble Creek Campground (but please don't take the spots used by horse trailers) or near the information board in the campground, which is possibly the most secure spot because it's near the summer volunteer host who watches the campground. You'll find ample parking at both trailheads. There are no facilities at Warm Creek Trailhead, but there is a full-service campground at Pebble Creek Trailhead.

Getting a permit: Refer to Black Canyon Hike 100.

The Hike

On the map it looks like the Pebble Creek Trail follows the Northwest Entrance Road, but it's actually hidden from view. It goes through spectacular meadows along a totally natural stream, and it's a mostly downhill, 12-mile hike.

The trail starts out in an ominous manner, climbing seriously for about 1.5 miles to the top of a ridge. Once you put out the effort to get over this Category 3 hill, however, it's all downhill for 10.5 miles.

The trail is well defined and maintained the entire way. However, you have to ford Pebble Creek four times—all are safe crossings unless you go during the high runoff period in June or early July.

Once you reach Pebble Creek, follow the stream through wildflower–filled meadows (especially heavy with lupine) for another 2.5 miles to the second ford. This stretch treats the hiker to some of the best mountain scenery in Yellowstone. After this ford you go into a short stretch of burned forest broken by a few meadows. Watch for moose and elk.

After the Bliss Pass Trail junction at 5.5 miles, where you stay left (south), the trail is not quite as scenic. It goes through a mostly unburned forest, again broken

Pebble Creek

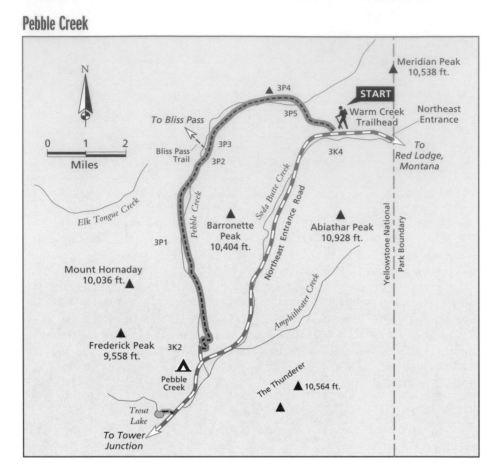

by a few large meadows, all the way back to Pebble Creek Campground. Ford the stream twice more along the way. Within sight of the campground, the trail forks—go right for the campground, left for the trailhead along the highway, depending on where you left your vehicle.

Fishing in Pebble Creek doesn't match up to its famous neighbor, Slough Creek, but it can be excellent in late summer, especially in the lower stretches where the stream gets larger. Don't forget your park fishing permit or the catch-and-release regulations.

Options

Hiking in reverse means 10.5 miles of gradual uphill instead of 10.5 miles of gradual downhill. Beginning backpackers might want to hike into 3P5, stay overnight, and return to the Warm Springs Picnic Area. This route also works well if you can't arrange the shuttle. Serious hikers will consider this 12-mile trip a moderate day hike. (Hiked by authors in 1985 and 1994)

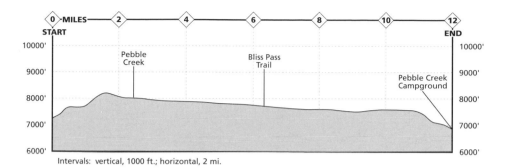

Intervals: vertical, 1000 ft.; horizontal, 2 mi.

Key Points

0.0   Warm Creek Trailhead

1.5   Top of ridge

2.3   First ford

2.5   Backcountry campsite 3P5

3.3   Backcountry campsite 3P4

4.0   Second ford

5.4   Backcountry campsite 3P3

5.5   Junction with Bliss Pass Trail; turn left

6.0   Backcountry campsite 3P2

6.5   Third ford

7.5   Fourth ford

9.0   Backcountry campsite 3P1

11.8   Trail forks (right to campground, left to highway)

12.0   Pebble Creek Campground

Custer
National Forest

102 Island Lake

Description: So much to see and do, all within reach of base camp at Island Lake.
Start: 40 miles southwest of Billings.
Type of hike: Day hike or backpacking trip; out-and-back; nicely suited for a base camp.
Total distance: 12-mile round trip, plus side trips.
Difficulty: Moderate, but with some strenuous (optional) side trips.

Maps: Granite Peak USGS Quad, Rocky Mountain Survey Cooke City–Cutoff Mountain Map, and Forest Service's Absaroka-Beartooth Wilderness Map.
Trail contacts: Beartooth Ranger District, Custer National Forest, HC 49, Box 3420, Red Lodge, MT 59068; (406) 446–2103; www.fs. fed.us/r1/custer.

Finding the trailhead: Drive 15 miles south from Columbus, on Montana Highway 78 through Absarokee. About 2 miles past Absarokee, turn right (west) to Fishtail on County Road 419. Drive through Fishtail and go west and south about 1 mile. Turn left (south) along West Rosebud Road. About 6 miles later, take another left (southeast) at the sign for West Rosebud Lake. It's another 14 miles of bumpy gravel road from this point to the trailhead. In total it's 27 miles from Absarokee and 42 miles from Columbus. The road ends and the trail begins right at the Mystic Dam Power Station. It might not seem clear exactly where the trail begins. After parking your vehicle, walk up the road about 200 yards through the power company compound to the actual trailhead. It has a spacious parking lot with toilet.

The Hike

The West Rosebud Trailhead seems to have one disadvantage—or advantage, depending on your point of view. It's mostly suited for "just passing through." Most trips from this trailhead offer either day hikes or trips that pass through the West Rosebud for other destinations, such as Granite Peak. Island Lake, however, affords a great chance to stay a few days and enjoy the many wonders of the Upper West Rosebud valley. It's especially suited for hikers who like to base camp.

From the trailhead follow West Rosebud Creek along Trail 19. After crossing an overpass and a bridge over the creek, the trail follows a power line for a short way. After leaving this "sign of civilization" behind, the trail switchbacks through open rock fields, offering a great view of the West Rosebud valley, including West Rosebud and Emerald Lakes.

The climb doesn't seem that steep, but by the time the trail reaches the dam at the eastern end of Mystic Lake, it has ascended 1,200 feet in 3 miles, barely a Category 3 climb. Normally, that would be considered a big climb, but for hikers who aren't in a hurry, it really doesn't seem like it.

When the trail finally breaks out over the ridge, it affords a great view of Mystic Dam. Mystic Lake is a natural lake, but the dam increased its size and depth. Now, at more than 200 feet, it is the deepest lake in the Beartooths.

Island Lake

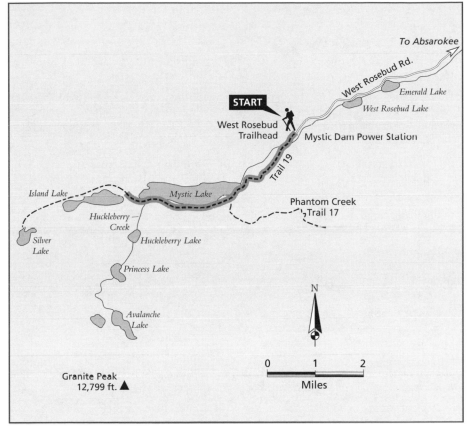

The sandy beach along the east shore of the lake below is perhaps the largest in the Beartooths and a great place for a break if you have the time. This is a huge lake, and a walk along its shore is the best way to appreciate this fact. Some people might think that the presence of the dam detracts from the wildness of the place. But the power company has done as much as possible to keep the intrusion to a minimum, and after all, the dam was here long before the Absaroka–Beartooths was designated as Wilderness.

From the dam walk along the shoreline of Mystic Lake all the way to Island Lake. At 3.5 miles Phantom Creek Trail 17 veers off to the left (east). Keep following Trail 19 as it curves to the right along the lake. The trail is well maintained for 2.5 miles beyond the dam. Then it's another half mile to Island Lake at the 6-mile mark. Just before the end of the lake, at 5.7 miles, the trail crosses Huckleberry Creek, which tumbles down from several lakes in the west shadow of Granite Peak. This is a big stream, but fortunately, the Forest Service has built a sturdy bridge over it.

If you're staying overnight at Island Lake, you must cross West Rosebud Creek to get to the choice campsites on the west side of the stream, and there's no bridge.

In August or September, that won't be a problem. You can cross easily on a logjam at the outlet of Island Lake. Early in the year at high water, however, this crossing could be more difficult. Lots of water comes down West Rosebud Creek. The Forest Service doesn't maintain the trail beyond a point just before crossing West Rosebud Creek or above Island Lake.

Just after crossing West Rosebud Creek, you'll find a huge flat area where many large parties could camp and still not bother each other.

Starting at Island Lake anglers will begin to find an occasional cutthroat trout mixed in with the rainbow population. These cutthroats have migrated down from Weeluma, Nemidji, Nugget, Beckworth, and Frenco Lakes, all pure cutthroat fisheries. Silver Lake sports some nice-size hybrid trout that are hard to catch but worth the effort.

Huckleberry Lake supports a healthy rainbow population, while Avalanche and the Storm Lakes above are stocked with willing cutthroats that grow above average in size and weight.

Options

This route works well as a base camp, but you can also make it an enjoyable day hike.

Side Trips

The trail continues on beyond Island Lake to Silver Lake, which also offers base camp opportunities. The trail to Silver Lake is muddy and brushy, and the campsites aren't as pleasant as those at Island Lake. Instead, consider visiting Silver Lake on a day trip from base camp. Another good possibility is a hike up Huckleberry Creek to Princess Lake and, for the well conditioned, on to Avalanche Lake.

Two more potential side trips include a long trek to Grasshopper Glacier and a climb up to a series of lakes—Nugget, Beckworth, Frenco, Nemidji, and Weeluma— just west of Island Lake. Only those in good shape and savvy in wilderness skills should attempt these side trips. It's possible, of course, to just hang around and

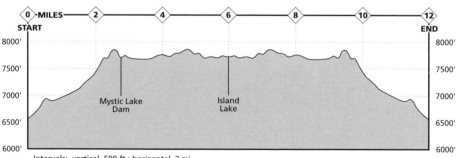

Intervals: vertical, 500 ft.; horizontal, 2 mi.

explore the Island Lake and Mystic Lake country for a day or two and not miss out on anything. (Hiked by authors in 1994)

Key Points

0.0 West Rosebud Trailhead

3.0 Mystic Lake Dam

3.5 Junction with Phantom Creek Trail 17; turn right

5.7 Huckleberry Creek

6.0 Island Lake

12.0 West Rosebud Trailhead

103 Granite Peak

Description: A chance to view or climb 12,799-foot Granite Peak, the highest point in Montana.
Start: 50 miles southwest of Billings.
Type of hike: A long, steep, high-altitude backpack to a traditional launching point for ascents of Granite Peak; strictly for experienced, well-conditioned hikers; out-and-back with shuttle option.
Total distance: 21-mile round trip, plus the climb up Granite Peak.

Difficulty: Very strenuous.
Maps: Granite Peak and Alpine USGS Quads, Rocky Mountain Survey Cooke City–Cutoff Mountain, and Alpine–Mount Maurice Maps, and Forest Service's Absaroka-Beartooth Wilderness Map.
Trail contacts: Beartooth Ranger District, Custer National Forest, HC 49, Box 3420, Red Lodge, MT 59068; (406) 446-2103; www.fs. fed.us/r1/custer.

Finding the trailhead: Drive 15 miles south from Columbus, on Montana Highway 78 through Absarokee. About 2 miles past Absarokee, turn right (west) to Fishtail on County Road 419. Drive through Fishtail and go west and south about 1 mile. Turn left (south) along West Rosebud Road. About 6 miles later, take another left (southeast) at the sign for West Rosebud Lake. It's another 14 miles of bumpy gravel road from this point to the trailhead. In total, it's 27 miles from Absarokee and 42 miles from Columbus. The road ends and the trail begins right at the Mystic Dam Power Station. It might not seem clear exactly where the trail begins. After parking your vehicle, walk up the road about 200 yards through the power company compound to the actual trailhead. It has a spacious parking lot with toilet.

The Hike

The first leg of the Granite Peak adventure is getting up to Mystic Lake, which offers some spectacular scenery with the unusual twist of being able to observe how the Mystic Lake Power Station was built. This is a popular day hike, so don't expect to have this lake (or any part of this hike, in fact) to yourself.

From the trailhead follow Trail 19 along West Rosebud Creek. After crossing an overpass and a bridge over the creek, the trail follows a power line for a short way. After leaving this "sign of civilization" behind, the trail switchbacks through open rock fields, offering a great view of the West Rosebud valley, including West Rosebud and Emerald Lakes.

The climb doesn't seem that steep, but by the time the trail reaches the dam at the eastern end of Mystic Lake, it has ascended 1,200 feet in 3 miles, barely a Category 3 climb. Normally that would be considered a big climb, but for hikers who aren't in a hurry, it really doesn't seem like it.

When the trail finally breaks out over the ridge, it affords a great view of Mystic Dam. Mystic Lake is a natural lake, but the dam increased its size and depth. Now, at more than 200 feet, it is the deepest lake in the Beartooths.

Granite Peak, the highest summit in Montana. MIKE SAMPLE PHOTO

The sandy beach along the east shore of the lake below is perhaps the largest in the Beartooths and a great place for a break if you have the time. This is a huge lake, and a walk along its shore is the best way to appreciate this fact. Some people might think that the presence of the dam detracts from the wildness of the place. But the power company has done as much as possible to keep the intrusion to a minimum, and after all, the dam was here long before the Absaroka-Beartooths was designated as Wilderness.

From the dam, walk along the shoreline for half a mile to the 3.5-mile point and turn left (east) onto Phantom Creek Trail 17. From the lake it's a Category 1 climb to the 10,140-foot saddle, partly on switchbacks. The trail takes you above Mystic Lake and gives you an incredible panoramic view of the Beartooths.

Once at the saddle, turn southwest and follow a series of cairns around the north side of Froze-to-Death Mountain. The destination is an 11,600-foot plateau on the west edge of Tempest Mountain, 1.6 miles north of Granite Peak. You can set up your base camp here.

In past years climbers have built rock shelters (rock walls about 3 feet high) on the west edge of Tempest Mountain to protect themselves from the strong winds that frequently blast the area. The Forest Service may have removed them, however, because the area is designated Wilderness, which prohibits permanent structures.

By the time you reach Tempest Mountain, you have covered more than 10 miles and gained more than 5,000 feet. You have crossed timberline many miles earlier, and now rock, ice, and sky are the predominant elements of the landscape. No plants or grasses can survive the climate and elevation at the plateau, with the exception of a few hardy lichens.

There are some advantages to hiking and camping in such a forbidding place. The wind is so prevalent that few mosquitoes ever attempt takeoffs from ground zero. The bear danger is nil. And, of course, the high altitude grants superb views in all directions.

Along the west edge of the plateau leading up to Tempest, the view of Granite Peak is awesome. Granite buttresses rise almost vertically from Huckleberry Creek Canyon to form a broad wall nearly a half mile wide. The north face is heavily etched with fissures running almost straight up between the buttresses. Granite Glacier clings to the center of the wall. At the top, a series of pinnacles builds from the west side up to the peak.

To those skilled in technical climbing, Granite is an easy ascent in good weather, but for those with little experience, it's challenging, if not dangerous. Probably the best advice is to go with someone who has the experience and proper equipment. Especially important is a good climbing rope for crossing several precipitous spots. The easiest approach is across the ridge that connects Granite to Tempest and then up the east side.

Check with the Forest Service for more information before attempting this climb. The Forest Service has a special brochure for people interested in climbing

Granite Peak

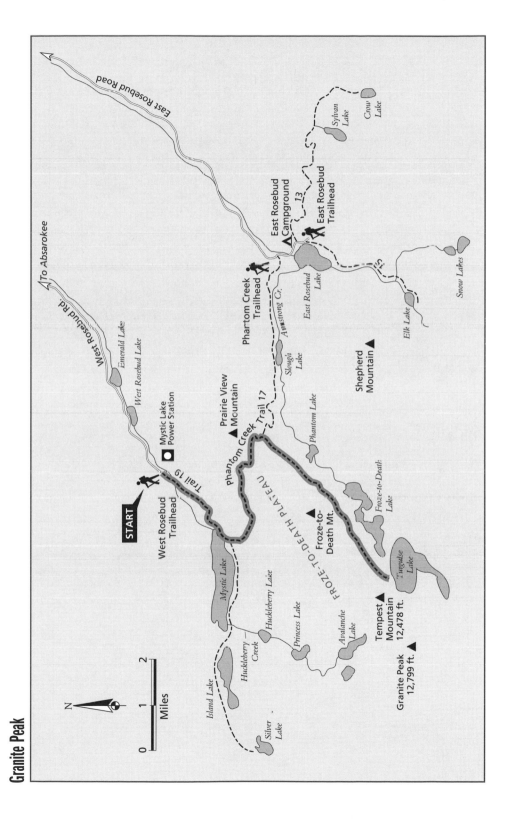

Granite Peak. In recent years not one summer has passed without mishaps and close calls, mostly due to bad judgment. One sobering concern is the extreme difficulty of rescuing an injured person from Granite.

People have tried this hike and climb at almost all times of the year, but August and early September are the most logical choices. Even then, sudden storms with subzero wind chills are a real possibility. Snow can fall anytime. And the thunderstorms around Granite Peak are legendary. Be prepared with warm and windproof clothing and preferably a shelter that will hold together and stay put in strong wind.

Whether or not you climb Granite, take the time to walk up to the top of Tempest. To the north and 2,000 feet below are Turgulse and Froze-to-Death Lakes. On a clear day you can see perhaps 100 miles out onto the Great Plains. And if you move a little east toward Mount Peal, you can look southwest over Granite Peak's shoulder to Mount Villard and Glacier Peak, both over 12,000 feet.

It should be no surprise that there is little wildlife at this altitude. Nearer the saddle, where grass and other hardy alpine plants eke out an existence, mountain goats are commonly seen. An occasional golden eagle soars through this country looking for marmots and pikas. Down closer to the trailheads, a few mule deer and black bears make their summer homes.

Camping on the well-named Froze-to-Death Plateau or Tempest Mountain is for hardy, well-prepared backpackers only. There are plenty of places to camp. The trick is keeping your tent from blowing away. This entire area is way above timberline and gets very heavy use, so please adhere strictly to zero-impact camping ethics.

Options

You can make this a shuttle trip by leaving a vehicle or arranging a pickup at the Phantom Creek Trailhead at East Rosebud Lake (accessible from East Rosebud Road). Of the two trailheads used for this hike (West Rosebud and East Rosebud), the West Rosebud is more popular, mainly because it's slightly shorter and cuts 400 feet of elevation gain off the approach to Granite Peak. Either trailhead leads to the same place—the saddle between Prairie View Mountain and Froze-to-Death

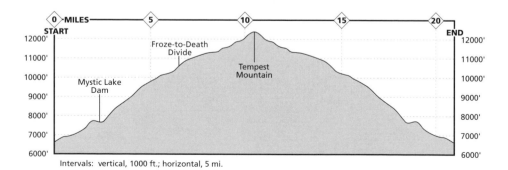

Intervals: vertical, 1000 ft.; horizontal, 5 mi.

Mountain. And whether coming from the east or west, the trails are for rugged individuals. Just reaching the saddle where the two trails meet is a climb of 3,500 feet from Mystic Lake or 3,900 from East Rosebud Lake.

Those who come in from the East Rosebud Trailhead may wish to take an alternate way back. From the east edge of the plateau to the west-northwest of Turgulse Lake, it's possible to descend into the bowl that holds Turgulse and hike past Froze-to-Death Lake and Phantom Lake. Then cross the hill back to rejoin the trail above Slough Lake. There is no trail for most of this route, but it's an interesting way out for the fit and adventurous. And high adventure is what this trip is all about in the first place. If you have arranged a shuttle or pickup, you can go out the East Rosebud instead of retracing your steps back to the West Rosebud.

Side Trips

Even if you elect to retrace your steps back to the West Rosebud, you might want to dip over to Turgulse and Froze-to-Death Lakes. (Originally contributed by Mike Sample, rehiked by authors in 1992)

Key Points

0.0   West Rosebud Trailhead

3.0   Mystic Lake Dam

3.5   Junction with Phantom Creek Trail 17; turn left

6.4   Froze-to-Death Divide; turn right

10.5 Tempest Mountain

21.0 West Rosebud Trailhead

104 Sylvan Lake

Description: One of the few easily accessible golden trout lakes in the Beartooths.
Start: 35 miles southwest of Billings.
Type of hike: A long, hard day hike or overnighter; out-and-back.
Total distance: 10-mile round trip.
Difficulty: Moderate.

Maps: Sylvan Peak USGS Quad, Rocky Mountain Survey Alpine–Mount Maurice Map, and the Forest Service's Absaroka-Beartooth Wilderness Map.
Trail contacts: Beartooth Ranger District, Custer National Forest, HC 49, Box 3420, Red Lodge, MT 59068; (406) 446–2103; www.fs.fed.us/r1/custer.

Finding the trailhead: From Interstate 90 at Columbus drive south 29 miles on Montana Highway 78 to Roscoe. Drive through this small ranching community, being careful not to stop at the Grizzly Bar—until the return trip, of course, when you'll be really ready for the famous Grizzly Burger. At the north end of Roscoe, the road turns to gravel and goes about 14.5 miles to the East Rosebud Trailhead. About 7 miles from Roscoe, the road crosses East Rosebud Creek and forks. Take a sharp right and continue south along the creek. The road is mostly gravel, except for a 4-mile paved section near the end. As the road swings by Alpine and around the east side of East Rosebud Lake, turn left into East Rosebud Campground to reach the trailhead for Trail 13 to Sylvan Lake and the far end of the campground. There is limited parking directly at this trailhead, but ample parking at the East Rosebud Trailhead and a full-service campground at that trailhead.

The Hike

The true beauty of Sylvan Lake lies beneath the surface. There swim the gorgeous, multicolored golden trout in abundance. Biologists call the Sylvan Lake golden trout population one of the purest in the Beartooths, and they use the lake as a source of fish to plant in other lakes. However, even for the nonangler, this lake is worth the uphill trek.

Start up Trail 13 right from the East Rosebud Campground and gradually switchback up the steep slopes of the East Rosebud Plateau. It's 5 miles and almost completely uphill, but, of course, the return trip is all downhill back to the trailhead. The trail is heavily used and well maintained. It's also expertly designed so the climb doesn't seem so steep. The top of the ridge offers a fantastic view ("I climbed that!") of the East Rosebud Drainage, including East Rosebud Lake about 2,400 feet straight down.

On the ridge the trail markers fade into a series of cairns for a few hundred yards, so be alert to stay on the trail. Also, don't miss the junction at 4.6 miles where the spur trail heads up to Sylvan Lake and Trail 13 continues on to Crow Lake. The junction is well marked, but inattentive hikers could end up at the wrong lake.

Sylvan Lake

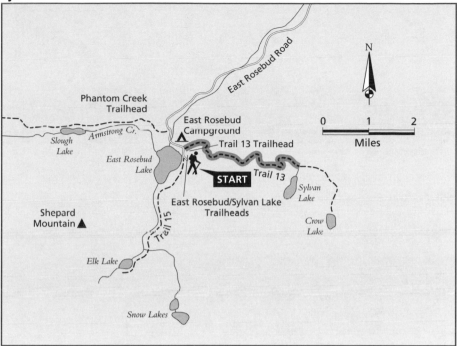

Even though it's 10 miles total, Sylvan Lake is more suited for day trips. There is one campsite on a small plateau to the right just before the trail breaks over the last ridge into the lake basin. Camp here, however, and people will be walking by the front door of your tent. There are no good campsites right at the lake. Sylvan Lake is at timberline, so please refrain from building a campfire.

Anglers seriously intending on pursuing the golden trout of Sylvan Lake might want to spend the night. Goldens are shy and more easily caught in the morning and evening, precluding a day hike. The golden trout of Sylvan Lake reproduce readily, and the Sylvan Lake population is healthy. Anglers who make the trek to Crow Lake will find that the brook trout there are larger than average and are much easier to catch than the goldens at Sylvan.

Side Trips

An overnight stay at Sylvan Lake does allow time for the short side trip over to Crow Lake, which probably surpasses Sylvan Lake for beauty, at least above the surface. Below the surface, the brook trout are not nearly as beautiful as the golden trout of Sylvan Lake. (Hiked by authors in 1994)

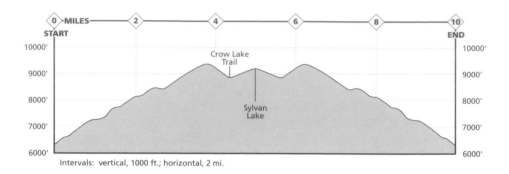

Intervals: vertical, 1000 ft.; horizontal, 2 mi.

Key Points

0.0   Sylvan Lake Trailhead

4.1   Top of ridge

4.6   Junction with trail to Crow Lake; turn right

5.0   Sylvan Lake

10.0   Sylvan Lake Trailhead

105 Silver Run Plateau

Description: An extraordinarily scenic high plateau with a challenging trail to follow.
Start: 10 miles southwest of Red Lodge.
Type of hike: Long day hike for experienced hikers; shuttle.
Total distance: 17 miles.
Difficulty: Strenuous.

Maps: Black Pyramid Mountain and Bare Mountain USGS Quads, Rocky Mountain Survey Alpine-Mount Maurice Map, and the Forest Service's Absaroka-Beartooth Wilderness Map.
Trail contacts: Beartooth Ranger District, Custer National Forest, HC 49, Box 3420, Red Lodge, MT 59068; (406) 446-2103; www.fs.fed.us/r1/custer.

Finding the trailhead: From Red Lodge, drive 11.1 miles on West Fork Road (Forest Road 71) and turn left (south) into the Timberline Lake Trailhead parking lot. You'll find a moderately large trailhead area with toilet but too small for horse trailers.

The turnoff to Silver Run Trail 64 (near the end of this hike) is marked on the south side of the West Fork Road, about 2 miles past the turnoff to Palisades Campground. The spur road to this trailhead can be traversed by any vehicle, but a high-clearance vehicle is better.

The Hike

This is unconditionally one of the most remarkable and unusual trails in the Beartooths. It doesn't feature an endless string of lakes as do most trails here, but most hikers will be too busy enjoying the trip to notice. Only the midsection of this trail is actually within the Absaroka-Beartooth Wilderness, but the entire trip seems exceptionally wild.

Weather is always important in the Beartooths, but it's especially critical on this trail. Double-check the weather report before leaving home. Good weather is essential for this trip. And be sure to take an extra water bottle, as water is scarce, especially in late summer. Another big issue on this trail is transportation. Arrange to be picked up or leave a vehicle (or bicycle) at the end of the trail to get back to the vehicle at the Timberline Lake Trailhead.

From the Timberline Lake Trailhead, hikers share the first 3 miles on Trail 12 with everyone going to Timberline Lake. At the junction with Beartrack Trail 8, however, go left onto that trail, cross Timberline Creek, and head another mile along the east side of the creek to Silver Run Basin.

Since the tiny lakes in the Silver Run Basin aren't much of a fishery, the area doesn't get much use. However, the scenery equals any high-altitude basin in the Beartooths. Backpackers will probably want to spend their night out in the luxurious accommodations found in Silver Run Basin. It's definitely a room with a view.

The trail is easy to follow up to the basin, but in the basin, it becomes difficult to find in places. As the trail leaves the basin and starts switchbacking up a steep slope

Silver Run Plateau

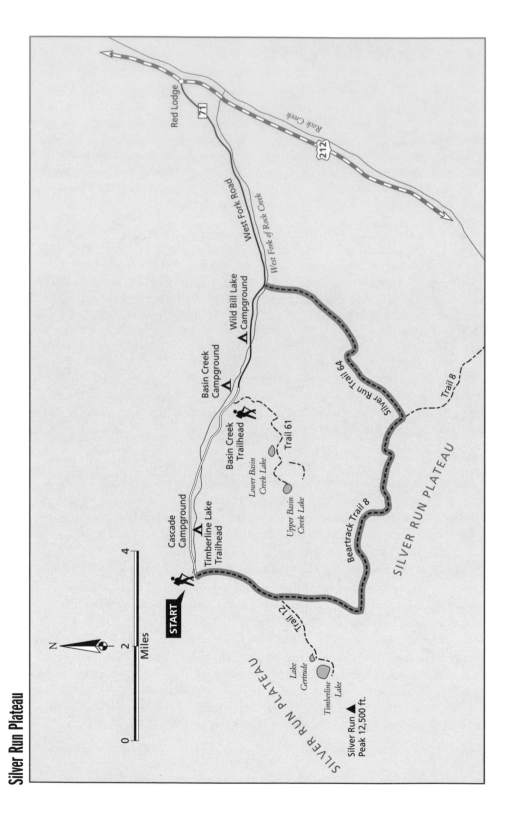

to the plateau, it becomes clearly visible again. If you lose the trail in the basin, look ahead to see where it climbs up to the plateau.

Immediately after the last switchback on the edge of the plateau, at about 5.1 miles, the trail disappears, and from this point on, a long string of cairns marks the way. Other trails in the Beartooths have short stretches of cairns, but in this case the cairns last for about 7 miles. Fortunately, the cairns are well placed, large, and easy to see.

The Silver Run Plateau is all above 10,000 feet and affords a fresh perspective of the Beartooths. It's nearly trackless, treeless, bugless, waterless, and peopleless, but none of these shortages detracts from its raw beauty. For example, take a minute to look over your shoulder to the west for a view of 12,500-foot Silver Run Peak. Or look down at your feet to see the rare Arctic gentian. This is one of the few places in the Beartooths where this lovely, pale green flower is found in abundance.

Traveling from cairn to cairn, do a good deed and help keep the cairns maintained. If a cairn has collapsed, take the time to rebuild it. When approaching a cairn, look for a rock or two that looks like it needs a new home, carry it the last few feet, and then use it to build up the cairn.

After following cairns for about 6 miles, watch for the junction with Silver Run Trail 64 at the 11-mile point. Beartrack Trail 8 continues straight into the Lake Fork of Rock Creek. You turn left (north) onto Silver Run Trail 64 and head down Silver Run Creek into the West Fork of Rock Creek.

After this junction, there's only another half mile or so of the long journey on Silver Run Plateau. Before dropping off the edge of the plateau onto a normal, forested trail, glance backward for a last look at the plateau.

The trail drops rapidly into Silver Run Creek, so steeply that doing this trip in reverse would seem foolish. Stay on this trail for 3.5 miles until it turns into the gravel road where you left a vehicle or bicycle or are being picked up.

On the way down from the plateau, take note of stock driveway signs nailed on trees. This plateau was once heavily grazed by sheep. Since then, the grazing allotment has been closed, mainly because of potential damage to this fragile environment.

This route isn't well suited for backpacking, but if you prefer to stay overnight, you can camp almost anywhere in the Silver Run Basin. The basin is not centrally located on the route, and you can also camp on the plateau, but the only water would be small, snowmelt rivulets, which you can't rely on, so bring enough water for a dry camp. Wherever you camp, follow strict zero-impact practices to keep this area as pristine as it presently is. No campfires or fire rings, please.

Options

Doing this shuttle in reverse would be more difficult.

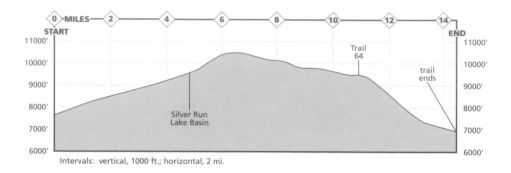

Intervals: vertical, 1000 ft.; horizontal, 2 mi.

Side Trips

On the way up, you could take a side trip to see Timberline Lake. (Hiked by author in 1995)

Key Points

0.0 Timberline Lake Trailhead

3.0 Junction with Beartrack Trail 8; turn left

4.4 Silver Run Lake Basin

5.1 Trail turns to string of cairns

11.0 Junction with Silver Run Trail 64; turn left

14.5 End of Trail 64 turns into gravel road

17.0 West Fork Road (FR 71)

106 Glacier Lake

Description: A rugged, alpine environment accessible with a short (but steep) hike.
Start: 15 miles south of Red Lodge.
Type of hike: Day hike or overnighter; out-and-back.
Total distance: 4-mile round trip, plus side trips.
Difficulty: Moderately strenuous but short.

Maps: Silver Run Peak USGS Quad; Rocky Mountain Survey Alpine-Mount Maurice and Wyoming Beartooths Maps, and Forest Service's Absaroka-Beartooth Wilderness Map.
Trail contacts: Beartooth Ranger District, Custer National Forest, HC 49, Box 3420, Red Lodge, MT 59068; (406) 446-2103; www.fs.fed.us/r1/custer.

Finding the trailhead: Drive south from Red Lodge on U.S. Highway 212 for 10.9 miles. Watch for a well-marked turnoff on the right (west) to three Forest Service campgrounds. Stay on this paved road for 0.9 mile until you cross a bridge near the entrance to Limberpine Campground. Immediately after the bridge, the pavement ends and you reach a fork in the road. For Glacier Lake turn left (southwest). You really want a high-clearance vehicle to get to this trailhead, but you can get there slowly with any vehicle. Snow usually blocks this gravel road until at least early July. Once on the road to the Glacier Lake parking area, there's no chance of making a wrong turn because there are no other forks or spur roads. The road crosses the state line and dips down into Wyoming for the start of your hike, but most of the trail lies in Montana. It's a long, slow, bumpy 7.6 miles to the trailhead. The small parking area there is frequently full, so be careful not to take more than one space. There's a toilet at the trailhead, along with a National Weather Service precipitation gauge. Plenty of undeveloped camping areas and one developed campground are scattered along this road, as well as plenty of vehicle camping at the start of the road to Glacier Lake.

The Hike

Although this route could be done as an overnighter, the Glacier Lake area seems nicely suited to a long day of exploring, fishing, photographing, and simply enjoying high-elevation majestic vistas. It's easily accessible by a 2-mile trail. The Forest Service has restricted stock use on this trail due to hazardous conditions for horses.

The trail to Glacier Lake is short but very steep. The trailhead is at 8,680 feet and the lake is at 9,702 feet, but the route actually climbs more than the difference (1,022 feet) in the 2 miles to Glacier Lake. That's because there's a ridge in the middle that's about 800 feet higher than the lake, making the first part of the trail a Category 1 climb.

Start on Trail 3. After climbing for about a half mile, the trail crosses Moon Creek on a bridge. After Moon Creek, the trail gets even steeper—and the higher it goes, the better the scenery. Shortly after Moon Creek, a faint, unofficial trail veers off to the north to Moon Lake and Shelf Lake. Turn left (west) and stay on what is obviously the main trail. For most of the way, the trail is rough and rock-studded, but it remains easy to follow and without hazards.

Glacier Lake

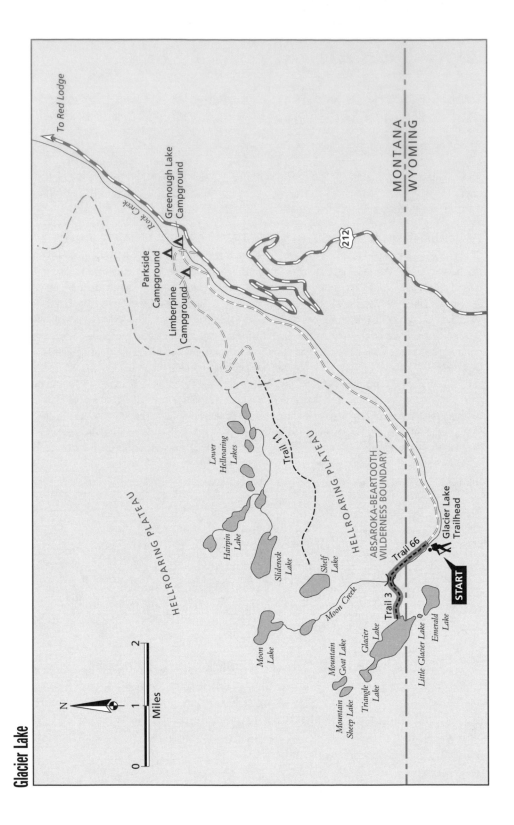

Once atop the ridge, cross some rock shelves on the way down to massive Glacier Lake. Even though the lake sits at 9,702 feet (above timberline), some large trees stand along the shoreline.

The trail reaches the lake at a small dam built long ago to increase the depth of Glacier Lake. A faint trail heads off to the right and goes about halfway around the lake. After a large point jutting out into the lake, the trail degenerates into a series of boulder fields and talus slopes. Watch for the amazing numbers of pikas that inhabit the area.

Bearing right along the north shore of the lake affords views of Triangle Lake and access to Mountain Sheep Lake and Mountain Goat Lake at the head of the basin. Bearing left and across the dam around the south shore of the lake leads directly to Little Glacier Lake, a small jewel just barely separated from Glacier Lake. Continuing south on this trail over a small ridge treats wanderers to the sight of lovely Emerald Lake.

If you're fishing be sure to keep track of which state you're in, and make sure you have the right license. The state line goes right through Glacier Lake. Little Glacier and Emerald Lakes are in Wyoming

Because of topography, Glacier Lake tends to become remarkably windy during midday, so try to arrive early to catch the scenery before the winds start ripping through this valley. Emerald Lake is not quite as windy.

All of the potential campsites along the north shore of Glacier Lake are cramped and marginal at best and probably too close to the lake. For those planning to stay overnight, there are several quality campsites on the north side of Emerald Lake. The south side of the lake is spectacularly steep. This is high alpine country, so please resist the temptation to have a campfire.

The ice-cold, swift-running water and high canyon walls make Rock Creek extremely attractive to look at, but these conditions also make life hard for fish. Rock Creek is home to small populations of cutthroat and brook trout. Fish concentrate in the slower water, so look for good holding places out of the current. The main fork of Rock Creek winds in and out of Wyoming and Montana, so anglers need to know which state they're in and have the appropriate license.

Glacier Lake supports cutthroat and brook trout, both of which grow to above-average size. The fish tend to school, with cutthroats working rocky shorelines, so anglers should work the shoreline as well. When water levels are high, water flows between Glacier and Little Glacier Lakes, so the fishery is the same in both. But the fish are easier to find in Little Glacier. Emerald Lake supports both cutts and brookies as well, though slightly smaller than those in Glacier. Cutts are stocked in Mountain Goat Lake and work their way down to Mountain Sheep Lake. Count on more fish in the upper lake and larger ones in the lower. Shelf Lake harbors hefty brookies, while Moon grows above-average cutts.

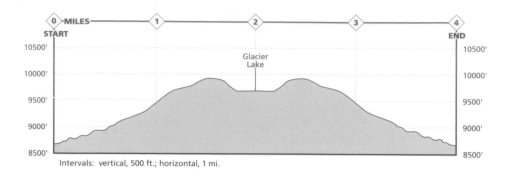

Intervals: vertical, 500 ft.; horizontal, 1 mi.

Side Trips

Mountain Goat and Mountain Sheep Lakes can be reached with a reasonable effort, but Moon and Shelf Lakes are strenuous side trips. (Hiked by authors in 1995)

Key Points

0.0 Trailhead

0.5 Cross Moon Creek on bridge
        Junction with faint trail to Moon Lake; turn left

2.0 Glacier Lake

4.0 Trailhead

107 Martin Lake Basin

Description: Multitudes of scenic, trout-filled lakes and a high-altitude waterfall.
Start: 30 miles east of Cooke City.
Type of hike: An excellent base camp trip with many opportunities for side trips; out-and-back.
Total distance: 13-mile round trip.
Difficulty: Moderate.

Maps: Muddy Creek, Beartooth Butte, Castle Mountain, and Silver Run Peak USGS Quads; Rocky Mountain Survey Wyoming Beartooths and Alpine–Mount Maurice Maps; and Forest Service's Absaroka-Beartooth Wilderness Map.
Trail contacts: Beartooth Ranger District, Custer National Forest, HC 49, Box 3420, Red Lodge, MT 59068; (406) 446-2103; www.fs.fed.us/r1/custer.

Finding the trailhead: The well-marked Clay Butte Road 142 turns north off the Beartooth Highway 21.2 miles east of Cooke City or 40.3 miles west of Red Lodge. Any passenger car can make it up the moderately steep, well-maintained gravel road to Clay Butte Lookout, but it's not recommended for vehicles pulling trailers. The road to the trailhead turns off to the left 2 miles from the Beartooth Highway. There is a small parking area (way too small for its popularity).

The Hike

For those who like to spend one moderately hard day getting into a beautiful base camp and then spend several days doing scenic day trips, this is an ideal choice.

Trail 614 starts out downhill but then goes uphill after about a mile at the junction with Trail 568 to Upper Granite Lake. Turn right and stay on Trail 614. For the first 2.5 miles, the trail travels through an enormous, high–altitude meadow carpeted with wildflowers. At one point, the trail fades away into a string of cairns, so watch carefully for the next trail marker.

About a quarter mile before Native Lake, at the 2.9-mile point, Trail 614 meets Trail 619 coming from Beartooth Lake. Turn left (west) onto Trail 619. Native Lake is the beginning of a long string of lakes. It's tempting to look for campsites along the way, but the best is yet to come at Martin Lake. Be prepared for short, steep climbs just before and after Mule Lake at 4.2 miles and a long, strenuous climb into the Martin Lake Basin that starts just after Thiel Lake at 4.7 miles. Be careful not to miss Thiel Lake. It's off to the left (south) at the bottom of the hill after Mule Lake, just after the trail breaks out into a lush meadow. You reach Martin Lake at 6.5 miles.

Martin Lake Basin is one of the most fascinating places in the Beartooths. Four major lakes (Martin, Wright, Spogen, and Whitcomb) are linked by a trout-filled stream, and there's a spectacular, high–altitude waterfall between Wright and Spogen Lakes. The waterfall seems larger and more majestic here at 9,600 feet.

As is plain from the topo map, this is lake country. Dozens of lakes lie within a day's trek from this basin. Even avid explorers could spend a week here and not see the same lake twice. Don't forget to spend one of those days simply hiking around

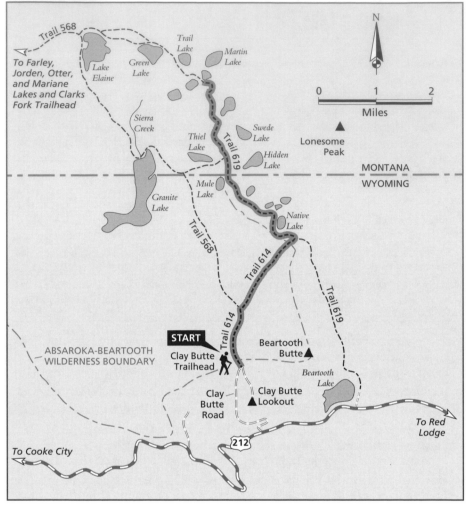

the four lakes in the basin to fully appreciate a place that would put most national parks to shame.

You can camp almost anywhere in the basin, but the most convenient sites are around Wright and Martin Lakes. This is like a five-star hotel: Every room has a view. You could call it nature's penthouse. Firewood, however, is in short supply and essential to the extraordinary charm of this basin, so resist the temptation to have a campfire.

Most of the lakes in this area were stocked with brook trout, and the chain of lakes in Martin Lake Basin is named after the men who hauled in the brook trout. The brookies here are average for the Beartooths, with Whitcomb Lake having slightly larger fish.

For variety, Trail Lake (appropriately named) has cutthroats that are stocked but also reproduce. Head upstream from Martin Lake to reach the cutthroat hotbed found in the Cloverleaf Lakes. On the way in or out, a side trip to Swede and Hidden Lakes is worthwhile for the cutthroats found there. Goldens were once found in Hidden Lake, and a few may still remain.

Options

Another reason Martin Lake is a better base camp than most is that hikers don't have to retrace the exact same route on the way out. On the return trip, from the bottom of the big hill to Thiel Lake, leave Trail 619 and follow a well-used trail that traverses the east side of Thiel Lake. This isn't an official Forest Service trail and doesn't show on the topo or national forest maps, but it's well maintained and well-signed at the south end. In less than 1 mile, it intersects with Trail 568, which goes to Upper Granite Lake. Turn left (south) at this junction and follow this well-used trail back to the trailhead. This route still means retracing your steps the last uphill mile to the trailhead from the junction of Trails 568 and 614, but most of the trip will be new country.

You can also make a loop out of this hike by going west out of the basin, down to Green Lake over to Lake Elaine and then down to Granite Lake and back up the trailhead. This is a rough trip, though, especially the off-trail section north of Green Lake.

Side Trips

From Martin Lake, hikers have a large number of choices for day trips. Here are just a few possibilities: Box Lakes (easy), Surprise Lake (easy), Mule Lake (easy), Thiel Lake (easy), Hidden Lake (moderate), Swede Lake (moderate), Cloverleaf Lakes (strenuous), Kidney Lake (easy), Marmot Lake (moderate), Trail Lake (easy), Green Lake (moderate), Sierra Creek (moderate), and around Martin Basin (moderate). (Hiked by authors in 1987 and 1995)

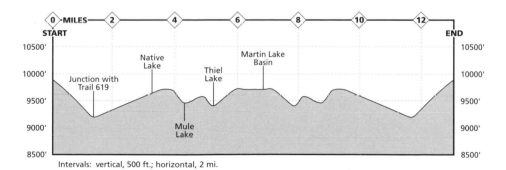

Key Points

0.0   Clay Butte Trailhead

1.2   Junction with Trail 568 to Upper Granite Lake; turn right

2.9   Junction with Trail 619 from Beartooth Lake Trailhead; turn left

3.1   Native Lake

4.2   Mule Lake

4.7   Thiel Lake

6.5   Martin Lake Basin

13.0   Clay Butte Trailhead

108 Sundance Pass

Description: Spectacular mountain scenery, especially the view from Sundance Pass.
Start: 15 miles south of Red Lodge.
Type of hike: Backpacking trip; shuttle.
Total distance: 21 miles, not counting side trips.
Difficulty: Strenuous.
Maps: Black Pyramid Mountain, Silver Run Peak, and Sylvan Peak USGS Quads; Rocky Mountain Survey Alpine–Mount Maurice Map; and the Forest Service's Absaroka–Beartooth Wilderness Map.
Trail contacts: Beartooth Ranger District, Custer National Forest, HC 49, Box 3420, Red Lodge, MT 59068; (406) 446-2103; www.fs.fed.us/r1/custer.

Finding the trailhead: From Red Lodge drive southwest for about 10 miles on U.S. Highway 212. Turn west at the well-marked road up the Lake Fork of Rock Creek. A short, paved road leads to a turnaround and the starting trailhead. Leave a vehicle or arrange for a pickup at the ending trailhead parking lot at the end of the West Fork of Rock Creek Road. To find this trailhead take West Fork of Rock Creek Road (Forest Road 71), which leaves U.S. Highway 212 on the south edge of Red Lodge. To find the West Fork trailhead, drive 2.7 miles to where the road forks. Take the left fork and drive another 11.3 miles until the road ends at the trailhead. Large parking lot, toilet, and several developed campgrounds are nearby.

The Hike

This well-maintained and heavily used trail is not only one of the most scenic in the Beartooths, but it's only a short drive from the Billings area. You can make this hike a three-day trip, staying one night in the Lake Fork of Rock Creek and another in the West Fork of Rock Creek. Although nicely suited to a three-day/two-night trip, the route also offers many scenic side trips. Plan an extra day or two in the backcountry for exploring them.

This trail offers absolutely spectacular scenery. From Sundance Pass, for example, vistas include 12,000-foot mountains, such as 12,548-foot Whitetail Peak, and the Beartooth Plateau, a huge mass of contiguous land above 10,000 feet. Hikers are also treated to views of glaciers and obvious results of glaciation, exposed Precambrian rock, and waterfalls. And watch for mountain goats, deer, golden eagles, and gyrfalcons. Goats are frequently seen from First and Second Rock Lakes.

This is a fairly difficult, 21-mile shuttle trip that starts at the Lake Fork of Rock Creek and ends on the West Fork of Rock Creek just south of Red Lodge. Arrange to be picked up at the trailhead at the end of the West Fork of Rock Creek Road (Forest Road 71) or leave a vehicle there. An alternative is to have another party start at the other end of the trail, meet you up on Sundance Pass, and trade keys.

Plan to do this trip no earlier in the year than July 15. Sundance Pass usually isn't snow-free until then. This delay also avoids the peak season for mosquitoes and no-see-ums, which can be quite bad in this area, especially on the West Fork side.

Keyser Brown Lake from the Sundance Pass Trail. FOREST SERVICE PHOTO

The main route passes by three lakes—Keyser Brown, September Morn, and Sundance—but several others can be reached with short side trips. One of these is Lost Lake, which is a quarter-mile climb from the main trail. This is a very heavily used lake, and it shows it. There are campsites here, but consider staying somewhere else that hasn't been trampled so much. The trail to Lost Lake leaves the main trail on the left, 5 miles from the trailhead or about 200 yards before the bridge over the Lake Fork of Rock Creek.

Another lake-bound trail departs from the main trail at 5.2 miles immediately before the same bridge. The unofficial trail to Black Canyon Lake scrambles uphill to the left also. Black Canyon Lake lies just below Grasshopper Glacier. The undeveloped trail to Black Canyon Lake is a rough but short hike of about 1.5 miles. Part of the route traverses rock talus with no trail, and there is a steep climb near the lake. The hike to Black Canyon is probably too tough for small children or poorly conditioned hikers. There is almost no place to camp at this high, rugged lake, and it's usually very windy at Black Canyon during midday.

The main trail continues west along the Lake Fork another mile or so to Keyser Brown Lake, about 6.5 miles from the trailhead. To do this trip in three days and two nights, plan to start early and spend the first night at Keyser Brown. Although the wood supply is ample enough around Keyser Brown, this is one of the most heavily used campsites in the Beartooths. Please consider doing without a campfire here.

Keyser Brown Lake is about a quarter-mile to the left (southwest), so watch carefully for the side trail. It is an official trail, and it's signed. The lake itself comes into view from the main trail, but if you can see it, you've missed the junction and need to backtrack about 200 yards to the trail to the lake. An angler's trail leads south from the far end of Keyser Brown to First and Second Rock Lakes. This side trip involves some difficult boulder hopping.

For another campsite option, continue 2 miles up the main trail to September Morn Lake. The campsite selection is much more limited here than at Keyser Brown, but it is closer to Sundance Pass.

Get a good night's sleep and a hearty breakfast before starting the second day. From Keyser Brown it's a 1,660-foot, Category 2 climb to the top of Sundance Pass at the 11.3-mile mark. The scenery is so incredible, however, that hikers might not notice how much work it is getting to the top. To the north and east stretch the twin lobes of the Silver Run Plateau, rising to their apex at 12,500-foot Silver Run Peak. Directly south of the pass, 11,647-foot Mount Lockhart partially shields the pyramid of 12,548-foot Whitetail Peak.

Coming down from Sundance Pass into the West Fork won't take long. A series of switchbacks drops about 1,000 feet in 1 mile or so to a bridge over the headwaters of the West Fork. Remember to carry extra water on this stretch—it is scarce on the pass.

Although there are campsites in a meadow about a quarter mile down the trail from the Sundance Bridge, Quinnebaugh Meadows at 16 miles is probably the best choice for the second night out. It offers plenty of excellent campsites, and there's enough downed wood for a campfire. It's a long 9.5 miles from Keyser Brown to Quinnebaugh Meadows, but there aren't many good campsites between September Morn Lake and Quinnebaugh Meadows. Camping at the meadows leaves an easy 5 miles for the last day out. It might also allow enough time for a side trip up to Lake Mary or Dude Lake. Dude Lake is 1 mile west via a rough, steep trail from Quinnebaugh Meadows. And there's a steep but good trail from Quinnebaugh Meadows to Lake Mary at 15.9 miles. Some people use the saddle to the north of Lake Mary as a cross-country route to Crow, Sylvan, and East Rosebud Lakes.

Sundance Pass

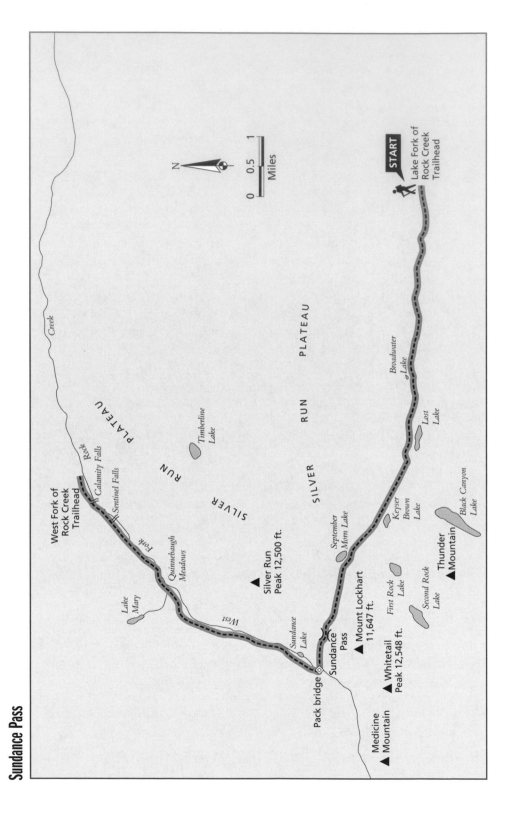

Creek

Rock

Calamity Falls
Sentinel Falls

Fork

PLATEAU

RUN

SILVER

Timberline
Lake

West Fork of
Rock Creek
Trailhead

West

Lake
Mary

Quinnebaugh
Meadows

Sundance
Lake

Silver Run
Peak 12,500 ft.

▲ Medicine
Mountain

Pack bridge

Sundance
Pass

▲ Mount Lockhart
11,647 ft.

▲ Whitetail
Peak 12,548 ft.

First Rock
Lake

Second Rock
Lake

September
Morn Lake

SILVER   RUN   PLATEAU

Keyser
Brown
Lake

Thunder
▲ Mountain

Black Canyon
Lake

Broadwater
Lake

Lost
Lake

START

Lake Fork of
Rock Creek
Trailhead

N

0   0.5   1
Miles

The final day of hiking follows the trail along the north bank of the West Fork all the way to the trailhead. Sentinel and Calamity Falls both offer good places to drop the pack and relax.

Both the Lake Fork and the West Fork are probably used as heavily as any wild area in Montana. Consequently, the Forest Service has rangers out enforcing several protective regulations. These special regulations are listed at a sign on the trailhead. Be sure to read them carefully and then, of course, obey them. They are necessary to protect these fragile environs.

The lakes found along the Lake Fork provide some of the easiest fishing in the Beartooths. Anglers will find plenty of hungry brookies in September Morn, Keyser Brown, and First and Second Rock Lakes. Overnight campers can count on these lakes to supply dinner. Keyser Brown and Second Rock Lakes also support healthy cutthroat fisheries. For those with something other than brook trout on their mind, Lost Lake supports a few cutthroat trout of surprising size. Grayling also have been planted in Lost Lake, and they grow large as well.

The scramble up to Black Canyon Lake rewards anglers with plenty of cutthroats near the glacial moraine that blocks the outlet. While this lake once grew exceptionally large fish, a probable change in food organisms, caused by the fish themselves, now keeps them in the slightly above-average range.

From the crest of Sundance Pass, look to the lakes in the high basin across the West Fork to the northwest. Ship Lake is the largest of these. There are plenty of fish in these waters for hikers who don't mind an off-trail trek up the other side of the valley after coming down Sundance Pass.

Options

This trip can be done from either trailhead with no noticeable difference. Climbing Sundance Pass is a lung-buster from either side.

Side Trips

This hike offers an abundant variety of side trips, including: Lost Lake (easy), Black Canyon Lake (strenuous), Rock Lakes (moderate), Whitetail Peak (strenuous),

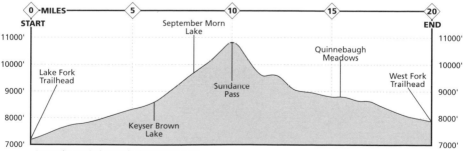

Intervals: vertical, 1000 ft.; horizontal, 5 mi.

Sundance Mountain (strenuous), Sundance Lake (easy), Marker Lake (strenuous), Ship Lake Basin (strenuous), Kookoo Lake (strenuous), Shadow Lake (easy), Dude Lake (strenuous), Lake Mary (moderate), and Crow Lake (strenuous). (Originally contributed by Mike Sample, rehiked by authors in 1994)

Key Points

0.0 Lake Fork of Rock Creek Trailhead

3.5 Broadwater Lake

5.0 Spur trail to Lost Lake

5.2 Spur trail to Black Canyon Lake

6.5 Turn to Keyser Brown Lake

8.5 September Morn Lake

11.3 Sundance Pass

13.0 West Fork of Rock Creek

13.5 Sundance Lake

15.9 Junction with trail to Lake Mary; turn right

16.0 Quinnebaugh Meadows

21.0 West Fork of Rock Creek Trailhead

BLM Areas

109 Humbug Spires

Description: Granite spires in a unique primitive area.
Start: 26 miles south of Butte in the Humbug Spires recommended wilderness.
Type of hike: Day hike or overnighter; out-and-back.
Total distance: 9-mile round trip.

Difficulty: Easy.
Maps: Butte South and Melrose USGS Quads and BLM Public Land States Map 33.
Trail contacts: Dillon Resource Area, Bureau of Land Management, Ibey Building, P.O. Box 1048, Dillon, MT 59725; (406) 683-2337.

Finding the trailhead: After driving south of Butte on Interstate 15 for 26 miles, take Moose Creek exit 99 and head east on Moose Creek Road (Forest Road 0101) for 3.4 miles to the Bureau of Land Management parking lot. The trailhead also has a toilet and interpretive information.

The Hike

Of all the roadless country in Montana, the 11,174-acre Humbug Spires area must rank among the most intriguing. Besides the granite protrusions for which it was named, the area has a lovely stream with small cutthroat trout and a forest of primeval Douglas fir somehow overlooked by early timber cutters.

After leaving the parking area, cross a footbridge to the west side of Moose Creek. In the first 1.3 miles, you pass by numerous ancient trees, possibly 200 years old or older.

At about the 1.5-mile mark, the trail forks. Take the right fork and continue up the east side of the stream, skirting a section of private land. Be sure to respect the landowner's desire to close his land to the public.

Stay on this trail for about a third of a mile, until it begins to fade. At this point you'll have good views of the Humbug Spires in all their majesty. Game trails proliferate here, so, accompanied by topographic map and compass, you can plot your own route into the Humbug Spires.

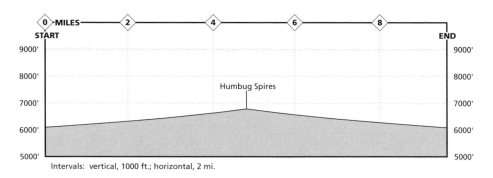

Intervals: vertical, 1000 ft.; horizontal, 2 mi.

Humbug Spires.

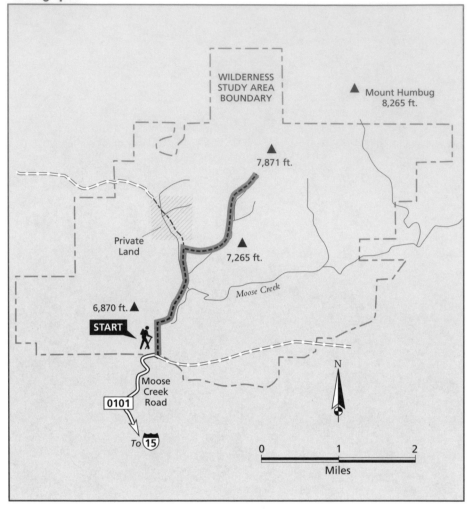

If you camp, plan to spend the first half of your second day wandering around among the spires. You will come home exclaiming about the beauty and uniqueness of the Humbug Spires. (Originally contributed by Herb B. George, rehiked by authors in 1998)

Key Points

0.0 Trailhead

1.5 Trail forks; turn right

1.8 Main trail fades; continue on game trail

4.5 Humburg Spires

9.0 Trailhead

110 Bear Trap Canyon

Description: Primitive flair and nationally famous trout fishing, and a good chance of seeing a rattlesnake.
Start: 30 miles west of Bozeman along the Madison River.
Type of hike: Day hike or overnighter; out-and-back.

Total distance: Up to 18-mile round trip.
Difficulty: Easy.
Maps: Norris and Bear Trap Creek USGS Quads and the BLM 44-Ennis.
Trail contacts: Dillon Resource Area, Bureau of Land Management, Ibey Building, P.O. Box 1048, Dillon, MT 59725; (406) 683–2337.

Finding the trailhead: Drive west from Bozeman on Montana Highway 84 for 30 miles (or drive 8.4 miles northeast of Norris). Immediately before (east side) you cross the Madison River, watch for an unpaved road turning south and a sign for the Bear Trap Recreation Area. Drive 3.2 miles up this unpaved road to the trailhead. You'll find a large parking area with toilet and undeveloped camping along the river before reaching the trailhead.

The Hike

If you're an angler, you've undoubtedly heard of the Madison River, one of the most highly acclaimed fly-fishing streams in the United States. However, you probably have not heard of a special hiking trail developed by the Bureau of Land Management (BLM) along the Madison River in rugged Bear Trap Canyon. If you fancy large trout, this is a 9-mile slice of heaven, but this is for fly casters who are willing to walk. Motorized vehicles, mountain bikes, and horses aren't allowed on this trail.

Bear Trap Canyon Trail winds along the river for 9 miles, gaining a mere 500 feet in elevation. In the past you could leave a vehicle at Old Madison Powerhouse at the end of the hike. For safety reasons, however, this access has been closed, making this an 18-mile round trip if you want to hike all of the way. You can hike as little or as much as you like, however, tailoring your own adventure.

The trail starts out as a double wide walkway and gradually becomes a single-track as the canyon narrows. It gets brushier and rockier as you get closer to the powerhouse and the end of the trail.

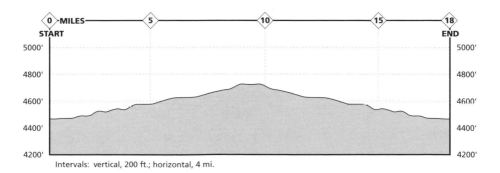

Intervals: vertical, 200 ft.; horizontal, 4 mi.

Walking along the famous Madison River in Bear Trap Canyon.

Since the trail follows the river, there's plenty of water to filter. Bring plenty of insect repellent, as the mosquitoes can be bad, especially in early summer. Many hikers (especially families) choose to stay overnight to take advantage of the early morning and late evening fishing. There are several campsites, but bring your backpacking stove, as firewood is scarce along the narrow canyon. Also, bring a garbage bag, not only for your trash but also to carry out junk left by others. The trail and campsites receive heavy use. There's a three-night limit on backpacking.

Since the canyon remains free of snow most of the year, you can take the hike anytime between April and November. The heaviest use occurs when the fishing is good, especially during the famed salmon fly hatch in mid-June to early July.

The trail wanders through a spectacular canyon with sheer rock cliffs and abundant wildlife. There are lots of rattlesnakes in the area, so be alert and don't forget your snakebite kit.

Bear Trap Canyon

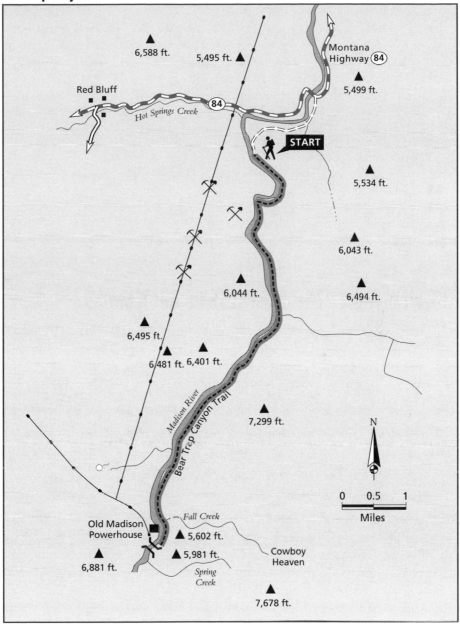

Red Bluff

Hot Springs Creek

84

6,588 ft.

5,495 ft.

Montana
Highway 84

5,499 ft.

START

5,534 ft.

6,043 ft.

6,044 ft.

6,494 ft.

6,495 ft.

6,481 ft. 6,401 ft.

Madison River

Bear Trap Canyon Trail

7,299 ft.

N

0   0.5   1
Miles

Fall Creek

Old Madison
Powerhouse

5,602 ft.

5,981 ft.

6,881 ft.

*Spring
Creek*

Cowboy
Heaven

7,678 ft.

In 1981 Bear Trap became one of the first BLM areas in the state to be recommended for Wilderness designation. Two years later the area became the first BLM-managed Wilderness area and is a unit of the Lee Metcalf Wilderness in the Madison Range. Bear Trap Canyon is connected to the Spanish Peaks by a strip of roadless Forest Service land called Cowboy Heaven. The elevation rises from 4,500 feet along the Madison River to over 10,500 feet in the Spanish Peaks, which presents an unparalleled opportunity to preserve the variety of life zones found in Montana. (Originally contributed by Mike Comola, rehiked by authors in 2001)

Key Points

0.0	Trailhead
3.5	Bear Trap Creek
9.0	Powerhouse
18.0	Trailhead

THE VIEW FROM HERE: THE VALUE OF GUIDEBOOKS

Some people don't like hiking guidebooks. They believe guidebooks bring more people into the wilderness, more people cause more environmental damage, and the wildness we all seek gradually evaporates. I used to believe that, too. Here's why I changed my mind.

When I wrote and published my first guidebook—this book, in fact—which was originally called *The Hiker's Guide to Montana* (1979), some of my hiking buddies disapproved, and I spent a lot of time up in the mountains thinking about the value of guidebooks. Since then, I've published more than a hundred hiking guides (and have written eleven myself), and I'm proud of it. I also hope these books have significantly increased wilderness use.

Some experienced hikers think anybody can buy a topographic map and compass and find his or her way through the wilderness. But the fact is most people want a guide. Sometimes inexperienced hikers prefer a person to show them the way and help them build confidence, but most of the time, they can get by with a trail guide like this one.

All Falcon guidebooks (and most published by other publishers) encourage back country users to respect wilderness and support the protection of wild country. Sometimes, this message is direct editorializing, but more often it's subliminal. By helping people enjoy wilderness, the guidebook publisher sets up a format where the message naturally creeps into the soul. It's a rare person who leaves the wilderness without a firmly planted passion for wild country—and an interest in voting for more of it.

In classes on backpacking taught for the Yellowstone Institute, I've taken hundreds of people into the wilderness. Many of them had a backpack on for the first time. When we started our hike, some of them weren't convinced we needed more wilderness, but they all were convinced that we did when they arrived back at the trailhead. Many, many times, I've seen it happen without saying a single word about wilderness preservation efforts.

It doesn't take preaching. Instead, we just need to get people out into the wilderness where the essence of wildness sort of sneaks up on them and takes root, and before you know it, the ranks of those who support wilderness has grown. I'd go as far to say that in today's political world, it's difficult to get people to support more wilderness if they haven't experienced it for themselves. I recently returned from a long backpacking trip in the Arctic National Wildlife Refuge in Alaska, which is on the menu of the oil industry. I have no doubt that if people could experience what I did on that trip, they would fervently oppose drilling in the refuge.

But what about overcrowding? Yes, it is a problem in many places and probably will be in many wilderness areas. But the answer to overcrowded, overused wilderness is not limiting use of wilderness and restrictive regulations. The answer is more wilderness. And even if we must endure more restrictions, so be it. At least we—and our children and grandchildren—will always have a wild place to enjoy, even if they can't go there every weekend. The landscape can recover from overcrowding, but if we build roads and houses there, it's gone forever.

That's why we need wilderness guidebooks, and that's why I continued to write and publish them. I believe such guidebooks have done as much to build support for wilderness as pro-wilderness organizations have ever done through political and public relations efforts.

And if that isn't enough, here's another reason. All FalconGuides (and most guidebooks from other publishers) include sections on zero-impact ethics. Such guidebooks provide the ideal medium for communicating this vital information.

In thirty-five years of hiking, I've seen dramatic changes in how hikers care for wilderness. I've seen it go from appalling to exceptional. Through the years, I've carried tons of foil and litter out of the wilderness, and I've probably destroyed more fire rings than almost anybody on earth. But nowadays, I can enjoy a weeklong trip without finding a gum wrapper or tissue. Today, almost everybody walks softly in the wilderness. And I believe the information contained in guidebooks has been partly responsible for this positive change.

Having said all that, I hope many thousands of people use this book to enjoy a fun-filled hiking vacation—and then of course, vote for wilderness protection and encourage others to do the same.

Appendix A: For More Information

Kootenai National Forest
Supervisor's Office
Kootenai National Forest
1101 Highway 2 West
Libby, MT 59923
(406) 293–6211
e-mail: aobst@fs.fed.us

Cabinet Ranger District
Kootenai National Forest
2693 Highway 200
Trout Creek, MT 59874
(406) 827–3533

Fortine Ranger District
Kootenai National Forest
P.O. Box 116
Fortine, MT 59918
(406) 882–4451

Libby Ranger District
Kootenai National Forest
12557 Highway 37 North
Libby, MT 59923
(406) 293–7773

Rexford Ranger District
Kootenai National Forest
1299 Highway 93 North
Eureka, MT 59917
(406) 296–2536

Three Rivers Ranger District
Kootenai National Forest
1437 North Highway 2
Troy, MT 59935
(406) 295–4693

Lolo National Forest
Supervisor's Office
Lolo National Forest

Fort Missoula Building 24
Missoula, MT 59804
(406) 329–3750
e-mail: r1_lolo_www@fs.fed.us

Missoula Ranger District
Lolo National Forest
Fort Missoula Building 24-A
Missoula, MT 59804
(406) 329–3750

Ninemile Ranger District
Lolo National Forest
20325 Remount Road
Huson, MT 59846
(406) 626–5201

Plains/Thompson Falls Ranger District
Lolo National Forest
408 Clayton
P.O. Box 429
Plains, MT 59859
(406) 826–3821

Seeley Lake Ranger District
Lolo National Forest
18 Mile Marker, Highway 83 North
HC 31 Box 3200
Seeley Lake, MT 59868
(406) 677–2233

Superior Ranger District
Lolo National Forest
209 West Riverside
P.O. Box 460
Superior, MT 59872
(406) 822–4233

Bitterroot National Forest
Supervisor's Office
Bitterroot National Forest

1801 North First
Hamilton, MT 59840-3114
(406) 363–7100

Darby Ranger Station
Bitterroot National Forest
712 North Main
Darby, MT 59829
(406) 821–3913

Stevensville Ranger Station
Bitterroot National Forest
88 Main
Stevensville, MT 59870
(406) 777 5461

Sula Ranger Station
Bitterroot National Forest
7338 Highway 93 South
Sula, MT 59871
(406) 821–3201

West Fork Ranger Station
Bitterroot National Forest
6735 West Fork Road
Darby, MT 59829
(406) 821–3269

Beaverhead-Deerlodge National Forest

Forest Supervisor's Office
Beaverhead-Deerlodge National Forest
420 Barrett Street
Dillon, MT 59725-3572
(406) 683–3900
e-mail: jdegolia@fs.fed.us

Dillon Ranger District
Beaverhead-Deerlodge National Forest
420 Barrett Street
Dillon, MT 59725-3572
(406) 683–3900

Wise River Ranger District
Beaverhead-Deerlodge National Forest
P.O. Box 100
Wise River, MT 59762
(406) 832–3178

Wisdom Ranger District
Beaverhead-Deerlodge National Forest
P.O. Box 238
Wisdom, MT 59761
(406) 689–3243

Pintler Ranger District (Deer Lodge office)
Beaverhead-Deerlodge National Forest
1 Hollenback Road
Deer Lodge, MT 59722
(406) 846–1770

Pintler Ranger District (Phillipsburg office)
Beaverhead-Deerlodge National Forest
88 10-A Business Loop
Philipsburg, MT 59858
(406) 859–3211

Butte Ranger District
Beaverhead-Deerlodge National Forest
1820 Meadowlark
Butte, MT 59701
(406) 494–2147

Jefferson Ranger District
Beaverhead-Deerlodge National Forest
3 Whitetail Road
Whitehall, MT 59759
(406) 287–3223

Madison Ranger Station
Beaverhead-Deerlodge National Forest
5 Forest Service Road
Ennis, MT 59729
(406) 682–4253

Flathead National Forest

Forest Supervisor's Office
Flathead National Forest
1935 3rd Avenue East
Kalispell, MT 59901
(406) 758–5200

Hungry Horse and Glacier View
Ranger Districts
Flathead National Forest
P.O. Box 190340
8975 Highway 2 East
Hungry Horse, MT 59919
(406) 387–3800

Tally Lake Ranger District
Flathead National Forest
1335 Highway 93 West
Whitefish, MT 59937
(406) 863–5400

Swan Lake Ranger District
Flathead National Forest
200 Ranger Station Road
Bigfork, MT 59911
(406) 837–7500

Spotted Bear Ranger District
Flathead National Forest
P.O. Box 190310
Hungry Horse, MT 59919
(406) 758–5376

Lewis and Clark National Forest

Forest Supervisor's Office
Lewis and Clark National Forest
1101 Fifteenth Street North
Great Falls, MT 59403
(406) 791–7700

Rocky Mountain Ranger District
Lewis and Clark National Forest
1102 Main Avenue Northwest
P.O. Box 340

Choteau, MT 59422
(406) 466–5341

Judith Ranger District
Lewis and Clark National Forest
109 Central Avenue
P.O. Box 484
Stanford, MT 59479
(406) 566–2292

White Sulphur Springs Ranger District
Lewis and Clark National Forest
204 West Folsom, Box A
White Sulphur Springs, MT 59645
(406) 547–3361

Helena National Forest

Forest Supervisor's Office
Helena National Forest
2880 Skyway Drive
Helena, MT 59601
(406) 449–5201
e-mail: r1_helena_webmaster@fs.fed.us

Helena Ranger District
Helena National Forest
2001 Poplar Street
Helena, MT 59601
(406) 449–5490

Lincoln Ranger District
Helena National Forest
7269 Highway 200
Lincoln, MT 59639
(406) 362–4265

Townsend Ranger District
Helena National Forest
415 South Front
Townsend, MT 59644
(406) 266–3425

Gallatin National Forest

Forest Supervisor's Office
Gallatin National Forest
10E Babcock
P.O. Box 130
Bozeman, MT 59771
(406) 587–6701
e-mail: mailroom_r1_gallatin@fs.fed.us

Bozeman Ranger District
Gallatin National Forest
3710 Fallon Street, Suite C
Bozeman, MT 59718
(406) 522–2520

Big Timber Ranger District
Gallatin National Forest
225 Big Timber Loop Road
P.O. Box 1130
Big Timber, MT 59011-1130
(406) 932–5155

Livingston Ranger District
Gallatin National Forest
5242 Highway 89 South
Livingston, MT 59047
(406) 222–1892

Gardiner Ranger District
Gallatin National Forest
P.O. Box 5
Gardiner, MT 59030
(406) 848–7375

Hebgen Lake Ranger District
Gallatin National Forest
P.O. Box 520
West Yellowstone, MT 59758
(406) 823–6961

Custer National Forest

Forest Supervisor's Office
Custer National Forest
1310 Main Street
Billings, MT 59105
(406) 657–6200
e-mail: dlcook@fs.fed.us

Beartooth Ranger District
Custer National Forest
HC 49, Box 3420
Red Lodge, MT 59068
(406) 446–2103
e-mail: jstraw@fs.fed.us

Glacier National Park

National Park Service
Park Headquarters
West Glacier, MT 59935
(406) 888–7800
www.nps.gov/glac

Yellowstone National Park

National Park Service
Park Headquarters
P.O. Box 168
Yellowstone National Park, WY 82190
(307) 344–7381
www.nps.gov/ycll

Dillon Resource Area

Bureau of Land Management
Ibey Building
P.O. Box 1048
Dillon, MT 59725
(406) 683–2337

Appendix B: Checklists

Day Hiking Essentials

For day hiking wear baggy shorts, trail-running shoes or boots, synthetic socks, T-shirt, and your favorite hiking hat. You can go as light as just an extra shell, water, snacks, and survival kit, but it helps to carry other comfort and safety items. Bill also carries binoculars, a camera, film, and fishing gear. Russ often adds fishing gear and field guides.

Individual Items	Weight (oz.)
• One-liter water bottle (full of water)	36
• Day pack	48
• Extra clothing: rain pants, rain jacket, wool gloves, stocking cap, wool or synthetic sweater (may vary with climate)	86
• Survival kit	20.5
• Map (a copy for each person)	3.5
• Money, credit card, driver's license	2
• Sunglasses (in hard case)	3
Weight of individual items	199 oz.

Group Items (for three hikers)	Weight (oz.)
• Water filter (carry backup iodine, too)	19
• Plastic trowel, toilet paper	10
• Bug repellent in sealed plastic bag	2
• Keys (attached to inside of pack)	3
• Snacks	20
• Sunscreen	2
• Headlamp (with fresh batteries)	8.5
• First-aid kit (from "The Backpacking Essentials")	27.3
• Weight of group items	91.8 oz. (30.6 oz./person)
Weight of day hiking items (per hiker)	229.6 oz. (14.3 lbs.)

The Backpacking Essentials

The following list represents a basic checklist for a three-day, two-night backpacking trip for three people. If you go by yourself, you will need to shave off a few pounds, most likely with a lighter tent and less cookware.

The checklist starts with items that all parties should carry, then adds in their percentage of the group's weight if the group items are divided equally. Food is not listed as a group item, because each person would carry the same amount of food with or without a group. The list includes articles of clothing you wear on the first day and hence have to carry the rest of the trip.

Individual Items	Weight (oz.)
• One-liter water bottle (full of water)	36
• Lightweight backpack (internal frame, doubles as partial emergency sleeping shell)	72
• Synthetic sleeping bag (20 degree Fahrenheit rating, in a garbage bag and stuffed into a stuff sack)	61
• Pack fly or poncho (to cover pack while hiking and while breaking camp; can also be used as a ground cloth)	12
• Foam sleeping pad	9
• Heavy-duty garbage bags or trash compactor bags	6

Clothing:

• Baggy hiking shorts	6
• Hiking hat (with brim)	3
• Knit hat (wool or synthetic)	4
• Trail hiking shoes	48
• Polypropylene long underwear (tops and bottoms)	12
• Underwear (at least two sets)	12
• Rain pants	22
• Waterproof or rubberized rain jacket	36
• Wool or synthetic gloves	2
• Wool or synthetic socks (1 pair)	8
• Wool sweater (or synthetic insulated jacket)	22
• Cotton socks (2 pair)	12
• Survival kit	20.5
• Candle	1
• Cigarette lighters (2, in waterproof wrapper)	2
• Compass with signal mirror	2
• Emergency fire starter in film case	1.5
• Emergency food bars (2)	5
• Iodine tablets (backup)	1.5
• Matches (with strike strip in waterproof container)	1.2
• Plastic whistle	0.8
• Space blanket	2
• Pocket knife	3.5

Top of Pack:

• Bug repellent in sealed bag	2
• Duct tape (partial roll on pencil)	1
• Extra batteries (4 AA)	4
• Extra bulbs in film case	2
• Headlamp (with fresh batteries)	8.5
• Keys (attached to inside of pack)	3
• Map (each member of group should have a copy)	3.5

- Money, credit card, driver's license 2
- Sunglasses (in breakproof case) 3
- Sunscreen 2
- Plastic trowel and toilet paper and any needed feminine
- hygiene products 10
- Waterproof journal and pencil 4
- Toothbrush and toothpaste 4

Food (per person—85 oz. total)
- Drink Bag: 6 tea bags, 3 apple cider packets, 6 soup packets, 5 lemon-flavor packets 10
- Snacks/Breakfast: 6 breakfast bars, 2 cups trail mix, bag of almonds, 3 boxes raisins 37
- Meal Bag 1: Baguette and 12 oz. sharp cheddar cheese 23
- Meal Bag 2: Noodles and sauce or rice and sauce dinners 12
- Insulated plastic cup with lid 3
- Plastic spoon and fork 1.5

Weight of individual items .... 539 oz. (33.7 lbs.)

Group Items	Weight (oz.)

- Camp stove (with cigarette lighter) 24
- Fuel bottle (full of gas, 32 oz., may vary with fuel efficiency of stove) 29
- Pans (2 pans, lids, handles) 21
- Pepper spray (in bear country) 16
- 50 feet of cord 4
- Tent (three-person) 91
- Water filter (carry backup iodine in personal survival kit) 19
- Permit (if required) 0.1

First-aid Kit:
- Ace bandage 2.5
- Adhesive bandages (Band-Aids) 1.5
- Adhesive tape (1 roll) 3
- Antibiotic ointment packets (or small tube of Neosporin) 0.5
- Cravat (triangular bandage) 1.8
- Gauze pads (four, 4 x 4 inches each) 1.6
- Gauze rollers 2
- Medications (laxative, antidiarrheal, allergy, aspirin, 2 ibuprofen) 2
- Nonadhesive bandage (for burns) 0.5
- Nylon bag 4
- Rubber/vinyl gloves (2 pair) 1.4
- Safety pins 0.5

- Scissors 3
- Tweezers (forceps) 0.5
- Wound closure strips 0.5
- Moleskin or Molefoam pieces 2

Weight of group items   231.4 (77.1 oz. per person)

Weight per person   616.1 oz. (38.5 lbs.)

Note: If you have any special conditions or allergies (such as to bee stings), you should consult with your physician before taking a backpacking trip. If you are allergic to bee stings, carry an anaphylaxis emergency kit. If you are diabetic, be sure to include necessary insulin and glucose paste for emergencies. If you are traveling in snake country, be sure to carry a snakebite kit. For more information on wilderness first-aid kits, see *Wilderness First Aid* by Gilbert Preston, M.D. (Falcon, 1997).

Post-Trip Checklist

After you get back to the trailhead and change clothes, stop at a pizza place, and grab a cold beverage, don't forget your post trip duties. It is in your best interest to do a little post-trip maintenance, especially if your trip has been a dirty one. Probably the most important thing you can do to preserve your gear is to make sure it is clean and dry before storing it.

- Call or notify those you left word with of your itinerary. This way they know you got back safely and won't call for a massive search. An unwanted search for someone who is not lost is costly and embarrassing.
- For your safety and the safety of other wilderness travelers, you should report all trail dangers to the local ranger district.
- Clean all gear and repair any items damaged during the trip, so you're ready for the next trip.
- Take your sleeping bag out of the stuff sack and put it loosely in a storage bag.
- Dry out your tent, fly, and rain gear before storing.
- Dump your garbage, but don't fill trailhead garbage cans. Drive it in; drive it out.
- Replenish survival and first-aid items used unexpectedly, so you don't forget them on the next trip.

Appendix C: Wilderness Preservation Organizations

Montana Wilderness Association

Since 1958 the Montana Wilderness Association (MWA) has worked to protect the state's vast and renowned wild country. The cornerstone of MWA's work is community organizing. With six affiliate chapters around the state and offices in Great Falls, Bozeman, Billings, Helena, and Kalispell, MWA motivates people to act... and win! Members receive informative seasonal newsletters as well as timely alerts on current wildland issues. With community events, field trips, and the popular Wilderness Walks program (many of the walks visit areas covered in this book), MWA's educational work keeps its members active and informed.

Montana Wilderness Association
P.O. Box 635
Helena, MT 59624
(406) 443–7350
e-mail: mwa@wildmontana.org
Web site: www.wildmontana.org

The Wilderness Society

Today Americans enjoy some 104 million acres of protected wilderness, due in part to the efforts of the Wilderness Society. The Wilderness Society is a nonprofit membership organization devoted to preserving wilderness and wildlife; protecting America's prime forests, parks, rivers, deserts, and shorelines; and fostering an American land ethic. To join in defending America's national forests, national parks, and wilderness as a member of the Wilderness Society, contact:

The Wilderness Society
1615 M Street NW
Washington, DC 20036
(800) 843–9453
e-mail: member@tws.org
Web site: www.wilderness.org

About the Authors

Bill Schneider

Bill Schneider has spent thirty-five years hiking trails all across America. During college in the mid-1960s, he worked on a trail crew in Glacier National Park and became a hiking addict. He spent the 1970s publishing the *Montana Outdoors* magazine for the Montana Department of Fish, Wildlife and Parks—and covering as many miles of trails as possible on weekends and holidays. In 1979 Bill and Mike Sample founded Falcon Publishing and released two guidebooks their first year. One of them was this book. Since then, he has written seventeen books and many magazine articles on wildlife, outdoor recreation, and environmental issues. Bill has also taught classes on bicycling, backpacking, zero-impact camping, and hiking in bear country for the Yellowstone Institute, a nonprofit educational organization in Yellowstone National Park. In 2000 Bill retired from his position as president of Falcon Publishing, which has grown into the premier publisher of outdoor recreation guidebooks with more than 700 titles in print. He now lives in Helena, Montana, with his wife, Marnie, and works as a publishing consultant and freelance writer.

The author and the Old Man of the Mountains at Grandview Point in the Big Snowies. Like so many others, this aged whitebark pine has weathered the worst and still hangs on. (Author on the right.) MARNIE SCNEIDER PHOTO

About the Authors

Russ Schneider

As Bill's son, Russ has benefited from many hiking trips over the years and now carries most of the weight when they backpack together. He was six years old in the original cover photo of *Hiking Montana*. From 1993 to 2002 Russ worked as a backpacking, rafting, and fishing guide with Glacier Wilderness Guides in West Glacier, Montana. This book is Bill and Russ's second project together. The first was a book called *Backpacking Tips*. Russ is also the author of *Fishing Glacier National Park* and *Hiking the Columbia River Gorge*. He lives in Whitefish, Montana, with his wife, Kim, and son, Casey.

Russ and Kim Schneider in Glacier National Park. LISA LUNDGREN PHOTO

Books by Bill Schneider

Learn more about Bill Schneider's books at www.billschneider.net.

Best Hikes on the Continental Divide, 1988
The Tree Giants, 1988
Bear Aware, A Quick Reference Bear Country Survival Guide, 2004
Hiking Carlsbad Caverns & Guadalupe Mountains National Parks, 1996
Best Easy Day Hikes Yellowstone, 2003
Exploring Canyonlands & Arches National Parks, 1997
Hiking Yellowstone National Park, 2003
Best Easy Day Hikes Grand Teton, 1999
Hiking Grand Teton National Park, 1999
Best Backpacking Vacations Northern Rockies, 2002
Best Easy Day Hikes Absaroka-Beartooth Wilderness, 2003
Hiking the Absaroka-Beartooth Wilderness, 2003
Where the Grizzly Walks, 2003

Books by Russ Schneider

Learn more about Russ Schneider's books at www.russschneider.com.

Hiking the Columbia River Gorge, 2004
Fishing Glacier National Park, 2001

Books by Russ and Bill Schneider

Backpacking Tips, coauthors, 1998

What's So Special about Unspoiled, Natural Places?

Beauty   Solitude   Wildness   Freedom   Quiet   Adventure
Serenity   Inspiration   Wonder   Excitement
Relaxation   Challenge

There's a lot to love about our treasured public lands, and the reasons are different for each of us. Whatever your reasons are, the national **Leave No Trace** education program will help you discover special outdoor places, enjoy them, and preserve them—today and for those who follow. By practicing and passing along these simple principles, you can help protect the special places you love from being loved to death.

The Principles of Leave No Trace

- Plan ahead and prepare
- Travel and camp on durable surfaces
- Dispose of waste properly
- Leave what you find
- Minimize campfire impacts
- Respect wildlife
- Be considerate of other visitors

Leave No Trace is a national nonprofit organization dedicated to teaching responsible outdoor recreation skills and ethics to everyone who enjoys spending time outdoors.

To learn more or to become a member, please visit us at www.LNT.org or call (800) 332-4100.

Leave No Trace, P.O. Box 997, Boulder, CO 80306